Urban Design in the
Real Estate Development Process

*To Joe and Pat Tiesdell (Steve's parents); to Sylvia Adams,
and in memory of Richard Adams (David's parents)*

Urban Design in the Real Estate Development Process

Edited by

Steve Tiesdell

Senior Lecturer in Public Policy
Department of Urban Studies, University of Glasgow

David Adams

Ian Mactaggart Chair of Property and Urban Studies
University of Glasgow

WILEY-BLACKWELL

A John Wiley & Sons, Ltd., Publication

This edition first published 2011 © 2011 Blackwell Publishing Ltd.

Blackwell Publishing was acquired by John Wiley & Sons in February 2007. Blackwell's publishing program has been merged with Wiley's global Scientific, Technical and Medical business to form Wiley-Blackwell.

Registered Office
John Wiley & Sons, Ltd, The Atrium, Southern Gate, Chichester, West Sussex, PO19 8SQ, UK

Editorial Offices
9600 Garsington Road, Oxford, OX4 2DQ, UK
The Atrium, Southern Gate, Chichester, West Sussex, PO19 8SQ, UK
2121 State Avenue, Ames, Iowa 50014-8300, USA

For details of our global editorial offices, for customer services and for information about how to apply for permission to reuse the copyright material in this book please see our website at www.wiley.com/wiley-blackwell.

The right of the author to be identified as the author of this work has been asserted in accordance with the UK Copyright, Designs and Patents Act 1988.

Library of Congress Cataloging-in-Publication Data

Urban design in the real estate development process / edited by Steve Tiesdell, David Adams.
    p. cm.
  Includes bibliographical references and index.
  ISBN 978-1-4051-9219-4 (hardcover : alk. paper)
1. City planning. 2. Real estate development. I. Tiesdell, Steven. II. Adams, David, 1954–
  HT165.5.U723 2011
  307.1′16–dc22

                                    2010047411

A catalogue record for this book is available from the British Library.

This book is published in the following electronic formats: ePDF [9781444341157]; Wiley Online Library [9781444341188]; ePub [9781444341164]; Mobi [9781444341171]

Set in 10/13pt TrumpMediaeval by SPi Publisher Services, Pondicherry, India
Printed and bound in Malaysia by Vivar Printing Sdn Bhd

1 2011

The Royal Institution of Chartered Surveyors is the mark of property professionalism worldwide, promoting best practice, regulation and consumer protection for business and the community. It is the home of property related knowledge and is an impartial advisor to governments and global organisations. It is committed to the promotion of research in support of the efficient and effective operation of land and property markets worldwide.

Real Estate Issues

Series Managing Editors

Stephen Brown	Head of Research, Royal Institution of Chartered Surveyors
John Henneberry	Department of Town & Regional Planning, University of Sheffield
K.W. Chau	Chair Professor, Department of Real Estate and Construction, The University of Hong Kong
Elaine Worzala	Professor, Director of the Accelerated MSRE, Edward St. John Department of Real Estate, Johns Hopkins University

Real Estate Issues is an international book series presenting the latest thinking into how real estate markets operate. The books have a strong theoretical basis – providing the underpinning for the development of new ideas.

The books are inclusive in nature, drawing both upon established techniques for real estate market analysis and on those from other academic disciplines as appropriate. The series embraces a comparative approach, allowing theory and practice to be put forward and tested for their applicability and relevance to the understanding of new situations. It does not seek to impose solutions, but rather provides a more effective means by which solutions can be found. It will not make any presumptions as to the importance of real estate markets but will uncover and present, through the clarity of the thinking, the real significance of the operation of real estate markets.

Books in the series

Greenfields, Brownfields & Housing Development
Adams & Watkins
9780632063871

Planning, Public Policy & Property Markets
Adams, Watkins & White
9781405124300

Housing & Welfare in Southern Europe
Allen, Barlow, Léal, Maloutas & Padovani
9781405103077

Markets & Institutions in Real Estate & Construction
Ball
9781405110990

Building Cycles: Growth & Instability
Barras
9781405130011

Neighbourhood Renewal & Housing Markets: Community Engagement in the US and UK
Beider
9781405134101

Mortgage Markets Worldwide
Ben-Shahar, Leung & Ong
9781405132107

The Cost of Land Use Decisions: Applying Transaction Cost Economics to Planning & Development
Buitelaar
9781405151238

Urban Regeneration & Social Sustainability: Best Practice from European Cities
Colantonio & Dixon
9781405194198

Urban Regeneration in Europe
Couch, Fraser & Percy
9780632058419

Urban Sprawl in Europe: Landscapes, Land-Use Change & Policy
Couch, Leontidou & Petschel-Held
9781405139175

Real Estate & the New Economy: The Impact of Information and Communications Technology
Dixon, McAllister, Marston & Snow
9781405117784

Economics & Land Use Planning
Evans
9781405118613

Economics, Real Estate & the Supply of Land
Evans
9781405118620

Management of Privatised Housing: International Policies & Practice
Gruis, Tsenkova & Nieboer
9781405181884

Development & Developers: Perspectives on Property
Guy & Henneberry
9780632058426

The Right to Buy: Analysis & Evaluation of a Housing Policy
Jones & Murie
9781405131971

Housing Markets & Planning Policy
Jones & Watkins
9781405175203

Mass Appraisal Methods: An International Perspective for Property Valuers
Kauko & d'Amato
9781405180979

Economics of the Mortgage Market: Perspectives on Household Decision Making
Leece
9781405114615

Towers of Capital: Office Markets & International Financial Services
Lizieri
9781405156721

Making Housing More Affordable: The Role of Intermediate Tenures
Monk & Whitehead
9781405147149

Global Trends in Real Estate Finance
Newell & Sieracki
9781405151283

Housing Economics & Public Policy
O'Sullivan & Gibb
9780632064618

International Real Estate: An Institutional Approach
Seabrooke, Kent & How
9781405103084

British Housebuilders: History & Analysis
Wellings
9781405149181

Transforming Private Landlords
Crook & Kemp
9781405184151

Urban Design in the Real Estate Development Process
Tiesdell & Adams
9781405192194

Real Estate Finance in the New Economic World: Development of Deregulation and Internationalisation
Tiwari & White
9781405158718

Office Markets & Public Policy
Dunse, Jones & White
9781405199766

Contents

Preface

We are not creatures of circumstance, we are the creators of circumstance.

Benjamin Disraeli (1827)
(*Vivian Grey* – volume II, book VI, chapter 7)

Given the development of urban design over the past 50 years and especially the past two decades, there is, at least to some degree, significant consensus about the qualities of 'good' urban design and of 'better' places. Good places are, for example, those where people want to live, work, rest, play and invest. A number of urban design policy documents also set out general qualities of good urban design – though what these mean for any specific time and place needs to be negotiated and agreed at the local level by key stakeholders and key interest groups. The contemporary challenge for policy and practice, however, is to ensure the delivery of better places. Thus, while the *Urban Design Compendium* (Llewelyn-Davies 2000) concentrated on what was considered good urban design in a UK context, some seven years later a second volume (Roger Evans Associates 2007) focused on delivering quality places.

Bringing together urban design, real estate development and the tools approach in public policy, this book explores the relationship between state and market with respect to design and development processes and outcomes. The overarching research question is:

- How successful are particular public policy instruments in framing (and reframing) the relationship between designers and developers to the advantage of urban design (place) quality?

Subsidiary questions are:

- What public policy instruments are available to facilitate better quality urban development and better places?
- How do particular policy instruments impact on the decision environments or opportunity space of developers and designers?
- In what other ways do particular policy instruments impact on design quality?
- Are some types of policy instruments more effective than others in facilitating higher quality development and better places?

The central research inquiry thus concerns the impact of urban design policy instruments on developers', and thence on designers', decision-making and, in particular, their impact on those factors – reward, risk, uncertainty, time, etc – that would make them more likely, or less likely, to provide higher quality development and to contribute to producing better places. The underlying proposition is that better quality urban design comes about when private developers decide, or are either motivated or compelled, to produce it as an integral part of their business strategies. This raises the important issue of how public policy instruments can be deployed to encourage/compel this shift.

The research questions posed in this book do not have simple and straightforward answers, and up to now relevant research has neither been consolidated nor discussed in terms of a policy instruments framework. In that context, this book seeks to advance the policy agenda in the hope that a clear focus on connecting high quality urban design to the practicalities of the real estate development process will reinforce momentum towards the creation of better places.

Steve Tiesdell and David Adams
University of Glasgow

Acknowledgements

As editors, we would like to thank all our fellow contributors to the book for their wholehearted participation in this venture, and for their patience, good humour and constructive responses to our numerous requests and editorial recommendations.

We would particularly wish to acknowledge the encouragement given to us by Madeleine Metcalfe and Cat Oakley at Wiley-Blackwell both in developing the concept for the book and in helping us with all the practicalities of seeing it through to completion. We would also grateful to Maggie Reid at the University of Glasgow for her thorough and conscientious work in compiling the index.

We wish to thank Building Design for permission to reproduce textual material in Chapter 9 and the Carnyx Group for permission to do likewise in Chapter 12. Throughout the book, UK Parliamentary material is reproduced with the permission of the Controller of HMSO on behalf of Parliament. All other permissions to reproduce photographs, diagrams and other illustrative material are acknowledged where the relevant illustrations appear in the text.

Steve Tiesdell and David Adams

Contributors

David Adams holds the Ian Mactaggart Chair of Property and Urban Studies at the University of Glasgow. His main research interests are in state–market relations in land and property, with a particular interest in land, planning and regeneration policy. He has researched and published widely in these fields, most notably as author of *Urban Planning and the Development Process* (1994), co-author of *Land for Industrial Development* (1994) and *Greenfields, Brownfields and Housing Development* (2002) and as co-editor of *Planning, Public Policy and Property Markets* (2005).

Eran Ben-Joseph is the chair of the PhD programme in urban planning at the Massachusetts Institute of Technology. His research and teaching areas include urban and physical design, design standards and regulations, sustainable site planning technologies and urban retrofitting. He has published numerous articles, monographs and book chapters and authored or co-authored *Streets and the Shaping of Towns and Cities* (2003), *Regulating Place* (2004), *The Code of the City* (2005) and *re:New Town* (2010)

Matthew Carmona is Professor of Planning & Urban Design and Head of the Bartlett School of Planning, UCL. His research has focused on the policy context for delivering better quality built environments. His background is as an architect and a planner, and he has published widely in the areas of urban design, design policy and guidance, housing design and development, measuring quality and performance in planning, and on the management of public space.

Andrew Clarke is an associate director with Taylor Young Ltd. He is an urban designer and town planner and has been with the practice for ten years. In this time he has worked on, and led, projects producing many design guides for sites and areas, design frameworks and strategies and masterplanning projects. Andrew has experience in urban design training and research and is at the forefront of the urban design agenda. He is committed to delivering practical and deliverable design solutions which are contextually based and provide creative responses to client briefs and aspirations.

Christina Crawford is an architect and urban designer currently pursuing a PhD in architectural history and theory at Harvard University. She worked for several years at Utile, Inc., a planning and architecture firm based in Boston, and teaches architectural history and theory at Northeastern

University. Her professional work includes designs for discrete architectural projects, masterplans for local municipalities and open space design for a waterfront city in Dubai, UAE. Christina received her undergraduate degree in Architecture and East European Studies from Yale University and a Masters in Architecture from the Harvard Graduate School of Design.

Nicholas Falk, the founder director of URBED (Urban and Economic Development), is an economist, urbanist and strategic planner, with over 30 years' experience of helping towns and cities plan and deliver urban regeneration and sustainable growth. Co-author of a range of publications, including *Sustainable Urban Neighbourhood: Building the 21st century home* with David Rudlin, he has undertaken pioneering research into lessons to be drawn from European experience in planning new communities. He is a Visiting Professor at the University of the West of England.

Gary Hack is Professor of Urban Design and Dean Emeritus in the School of Design, University of Pennsylvania. He practices urban design and is author (with others) of *Local Planning* (2009), *Urban Design in the Global Perspective* (2006), *Global City Regions* (2000) and *Site Planning* (1984), as well as many chapters and articles.

Tony Hall is a Professor within the Urban Research Program at Griffith University, Brisbane, Australia, where he is carrying out research on sustainable urban form. Until 2004, he was Professor of Town Planning at Anglia Ruskin University, Chelmsford, and had notable publications in the field of design guidance. He was also an elected member of Chelmsford Borough Council and successfully led its planning policy at the political level for seven years leading to the award to the Council by the UK Government of Beacon Status for the Quality of the Built Environment in 2003.

John Henneberry is Professor of Property Development Studies in the University of Sheffield, Department of Town and Regional Planning. His interests focus on the structure and behaviour of the property market and its relation to the wider economy and polity. He has researched and published widely in this field. John is a member of the editorial boards of the Journal of Property Research, the Journal of European Real Estate Research and Town Planning Review. He is an Editor of Regional Studies with responsibility for land, property, planning and regional development. John was recently appointed an Academician of the Social Sciences.

Eckart Lange is Professor and Head of the Department of Landscape at the University of Sheffield. His research focuses on how landscape and environmental planning can influence anthropogenic landscape change, and how landscape visualisation and modelling can be used to explore human reaction to these changes. He holds a PhD and Habilitation from ETH Zurich, a Master in Design Studies from Harvard University and a Dipl.-Ing. in Landscape Planning from TU Berlin. He is a member of the scientific committee of the European Environment Agency, as the scientific advisor in the area of Spatial Planning and Management of Natural Resources.

Tim Love is the founding principal of Utile, an architecture and urban design firm located in Boston. He is also a tenured associate professor at the Northeastern University School of Architecture where he teaches housing, urban design and architectural theory. In the spring of 2009, Tim coordinated and taught the required urban design studio at Yale University; and from 1997 until 2003, he gave weekly lectures on design tactics to first-year students at the Harvard Graduate School of Design. Tim is also a frequent contributor to the *Harvard Design Magazine* and a Contributing Editor of *Places/Design Observer*. He writes about urban design and market-driven building types, among other issues, for both publications.

Nicholas J. Marantz is a PhD student in MIT's Department of Urban Studies & Planning. He holds a JD from Harvard Law School and a Master in Urban Planning from the Harvard Graduate School of Design. He is an MIT Presidential Fellow and a National Science Foundation Graduate Research Fellow. His research analyses the regulation of the built environment and, more generally, the political economy of local decision-making.

Sarah Moore is a researcher on the Urban River Corridors and Sustainable Living Agendas (URSULA) project at the University of Sheffield. Funded by EPSRC, URSULA is a four-year, interdisciplinary project with the working hypothesis that there are significant social, economic and environmental gains to be made with innovative, integrated interventions within river corridors. Originally a biologist, Sarah now undertakes research in two main areas of urban regeneration: the impact of design – in terms of building function and development layout – on the financial viability of development schemes, and storm water disconnection to improve water quality, quantity and amenity values of urban areas.

Ed Morgan is a computer scientist with special interest in landscape visualisation. He is a part-time researcher on the EPSRC-funded Urban River Corridors and Sustainable Living Agendas (URSULA) project at the University of Sheffield, exploring the use of real-time 3D visualisation software to produce virtual models of future design scenarios in various riverside areas of Sheffield. This involves utilisation of various software (including Simmetry 3d), which he has developed and continues to develop commercially.

Sarah Payne is a Research Associate in the Centre for Urban Policy Studies at the University of Manchester. Her PhD, undertaken at the University of Glasgow, assessed the impact of the brownfield development policy agenda on the structure and workings of the UK speculative housebuilding industry. After her doctoral studies, Sarah completed two years' work in the private sector as a land buyer for a major housing developer. Her current research interests include brownfield development, the residential development process and the UK speculative housebuilding industry.

John Punter is Professor of Urban Design in the School of City and Regional Planning at Cardiff University, and previously taught at Strathclyde, Reading and York (Toronto) universities. He is a chartered town planner and a member of the Urban Design Group. His books include *Design Control in Bristol* (1990), *The Design Dimension of Planning* (1997), *Design Guidelines in American Cities* (1999), *The Vancouver Achievement* (2003) *Capital Cardiff 1975–2020* (2006) and *Urban Design and the British Urban Renaissance* (2009). He is a Director of the Design Commission for Wales and was Founder-Chair, now Co-Chair, of its Design Review Panel.

Lynne B. Sagalyn is Earle W. Kazis and Benjamin Schore Professor of Real Estate and Director of the Paul Milstein Center for Real Estate in the Columbia Business School. She is the author of *Times Square Roulette* (2001), *Cases in Real Estate Finance and Investment Strategy* (1999), and co-author of *Downtown Inc.* (1989) as well as several other books and many chapters and articles.

Paul Syms is a chartered planning and development surveyor, who has spent most of the last 35 years working as a consultant, advising on the redevelopment and reuse of brownfield land. Between 2004 and 2008 he was a director at English Partnerships, responsible for the National Brownfield Strategy for England. He is now an Honorary Professor at the University of Manchester and Chair of the RICS Education Trust, the surveying profession's leading research grant awarding body. His publications include *Contaminated Land: The practice and economics of redevelopment* (1997), *Previously Developed Land: Industrial activities and contamination* (2004) and *Land, Development & Design* (2010, second edition).

Steve Tiesdell is Senior Lecturer in Public Policy at the Department of Urban Studies, University of Glasgow. He is an architect and town planner, with research interests in urban design, urban regeneration, public policy and state–market relations in land and property development. He is author (with others) of *Public Places – Urban Spaces: The Dimensions of Urban Design* (2010) and editor (with Matthew Carmona) of the *Urban Design Reader* (2006), as well as many chapters and articles.

Steven Tolson is a chartered surveyor specialising in property valuation and development work for the public and private sectors. His postgraduate urban design studies developed a niche interest in the value and facilitation of good place-making. His work on masterplans includes such projects as Crown Street, PARC URC, Glasgow's Homes for the Future and The Drum, Bo'ness. He is currently a Director of Ogilvie Group Developments, engaged in property regeneration. Steven lectures in urban design and development at a number of Scottish Universities and is a member of RICS Scotland Planning and Development Board, and chairs the RICS Scotland Regeneration Forum.

Ning Zhao obtained her first degree in Urban Planning in Zhejiang University in 2006. As one of the top two undergraduate students in the department, she was recommended directly as a PhD student of architecture at the university without further examination. In 2008, she was awarded a state scholarship to study in the University of Sheffield as a visiting researcher on the URSULA project, where she has worked with John Henneberry on physical-financial modelling. Ning's research focuses on urban redevelopment and financial analysis of physical development. Four of her papers have been published in Chinese core periodicals.

1

Real Estate Development, Urban Design and the Tools Approach to Public Policy

Steve Tiesdell and David Adams

Introduction

Urban design and place-making involves two key challenges – the first involves *recognising* what makes 'good' urban design and what constitutes 'better' places. The second involves *delivering* good urban design and creating better places on the ground. The first challenge involves, *inter alia*, developing and reflecting on normative theory about what constitutes a 'good' place. The second challenge typically requires close engagement with the real estate development process. This book deliberately focuses on the role and significance of design in the real estate development process, on the decision-making of key development actors and on the relationship between developers and designers. Its overarching object is to explore how higher quality development and better places can be achieved in practice through public policy (i.e. by state actions). It does not, however, interrogate the meaning of *higher quality* development, or of *better* places, which have both been addressed at length elsewhere. Instead, for the purpose of analysis, we intend to set aside these issues and focus clearly on delivery. We therefore make the assumption that, in any particular circumstance, 'higher quality' and 'better' can be defined and agreed and, in turn, made the object of public policy and design processes.[1] If we know – or think we know – what better places are, it then becomes essential to understand how best to achieve them.

Urban Design in the Real Estate Development Process, First Edition. Edited by Steve Tiesdell and David Adams.

Urban design can be considered a process of enabling better places for people than would otherwise be created – this is becoming more commonly referred to as 'place-making'. In this study, the primary concern is with urban design as public policy (Barnett 1974; 1982), reflecting its increasing prominence as a policy area in the UK and in many other countries. Although, in the narrowest sense, public policy on urban design might be equated to a planning or zoning system, we see it as a much wider activity, encompassing a fuller spectrum of state activities.

Urban design can be understood as a direct design and as an indirect design activity. George (1997) termed these design activities first-order and second-order design. In first-order design, the urban designer is a direct designer or 'author' of the built environment or a component of it – that is, the designer of a building, a public space, a floorscape, street furniture, an urban event or festival etc – in other words, a relatively discrete 'project' of some sort.[2] In second-order design, urban designers design the decision environments within which other development actors – developers, funders, sundry designers, surveyors etc – necessarily operate.[3] Decision environments are typically designed by means of plans, strategies, frameworks etc, but also by deployment and modulation of incentives and disincentives, such as financial subsidies, discounted land or infrastructure provision. Generally (though not exclusively) undertaken by the public sector, second-order design is similar to planning and to governance.

Second-order urban design occurs before the design of the development proposal/project, and is both proactive and place-shaping. It shapes the design and development processes by creating a frame for acts of first-order design. By setting design constraints and potentials, second-order design can thus give public policymakers significant influence on first-order design.[4]

As a second-order design activity, urban design can be considered similar to much contemporary governmental practice in which, as (Salamon 2002: 15) suggests, public managers must devise incentive systems that obtain cooperation from actors over whom they have only limited control. Those who see governments as hierarchies believe that power flows downwards and outwards from the top or centre, and consider that policy decisions can be implemented through 'command-and-control'. Increasingly, however, this is an outdated view of the relationship between policy and implementation. Instead, the contemporary focus is on the processes of governance, with network metaphors frequently employed to describe and explain the institutional structure and operation of governance systems. Seen as systems of interacting networks of state and non-state actors, power is diffuse, with all actors having some resources with which to bargain in pursuit of their own ends.

The concept of governance means that state actors must operate in new ways: rather than command-and-control, their primary operating mechanism becomes bargaining and negotiation: 'Instead of issuing orders, public managers must learn how to create incentives for the outcomes they desire from actors *over whom they have only imperfect control.*' (Salamon 2002: 15, emphasis added). Arguing that network governance shifts the emphasis in policy delivery from (direct) management to (indirect) enablement, Salamon (2002: 16–17) highlights three enablement skills:

(1) *Activation skills* – those required to activate the networks of state and non-state actors in order to address public problems.
(2) *Orchestration skills* – analogous to those required of a symphony conductor in getting a group of skilled musicians to perform a given work in harmony and on cue so that the result is a piece of music rather than a cacophony.
(3) *Modulation skills* – those required to manipulate rewards and penalties to elicit cooperative behaviour from interdependent actors.

This is highly significant for urban designers working in or for the public sector, because it closely resembles the task they face and, in turn, the skills they need.

Providing the context for the book, this chapter is in four main parts. The first explores the real estate development process. The second discusses opportunity space theory. The third introduces the tools approach in public policy, discusses urban design policy instruments and presents a new typology. The fourth part discusses developers' decision environments, and then outlines the structure of the book.

Real estate development

The real estate development process is a production process that creates the built environment. Acting as a form of intervention, public policy is a means of managing – 'steering' – real estate development, in pursuit of *policy-shaped*, rather than merely *market-led*, outcomes. To operate effectively, such policies and policymakers must have knowledge of the real estate development process, the calculus of risk and reward that drives it, the interests of and constraints upon key development actors – developers, designers, landowners, investors etc – and, as explained later, the likely impact of policy instruments on key actors' decision environments.

Real estate development is highly cyclical and volatile. The old adage of 'location, location, location' oversimplifies the factors that make a successful development: both the design quality of the product and the timing of delivery are now recognised as being equally important to development success as the right location (Adams & Tiesdell 2010). In recent years, the neat separation between public and private-sector development has also begun to break down: very few development projects occur entirely within the private sector, unmediated by any form of public regulation and intervention, and development is increasingly a process of co-production between public and private sectors.

State–market relations in real estate can be approached from various disciplinary perspectives. At a simple level, it is possible to identify the various tasks or events involved in the process of development and to pinpoint those occasions when state and market interact (Barrett *et al.* 1978). At a more advanced level, an agency-based form of analysis recognises the way in which important roles within the development process – landowner, developer, designer, financier and regulator etc – are played out by a range of people and organisations, sometimes separately and sometimes in combination. Such forms of analysis also begin to highlight the power relations involved in development, and to explain how these actors come together in complex networks to constitute and reconstitute the structural context within which development takes place (Doak & Karadimitriou 2007).

As previous reviews of models of the development process have shown (Gore & Nicholson 1991; Healey 1991), state–market relations in real estate are not the exclusive possession of economics, but have been addressed across the social sciences, showing that the real estate development process is not simply an economic process but is also highly social (Guy & Henneberry 2000; 2002a). As Michael Ball's 'structures of building provision model' emphasises, development is a function of social relations specific to time and place involving a variety of key actors – landowners, investors, financiers, developers, builders, various professionals, politicians, consumers etc (Ball 1986; 1998). At the same time, the state – both local and national – is an important actor both in its own right and as a regulator of other actors. Ball stresses how these relations must be seen in terms of both their specific linkages – functional, historical, political, social and cultural – and their engagement with the broader structural elements of the political economy.

Actors become involved in development to the extent that it contributes to achieving their basic objectives. Table 1.1 examines the motives of the main actors in the development process in terms of five considerations – timescale, financial strategy, functionality, external appearance and relation to context. The nature of development means that these objectives are bundled, with each actor internally trading-off between objectives. The objectives are also traded-off *between* actors. The latter cannot be taken as an unproblematic process – actors have different strengths and powers, 'quality' may be interpreted differently and achieving 'better' design may not be an objective shared by all participants. Examination of Table 1.1, for example, indicates a mismatch between supply and demand sides. Supply-side actors typically have short-term, financial and economic motives and tend to see the development as a financial commodity. Demand-side actors typically have long-term and 'design' objectives and tend to see the development as an environment to be used.

Table 1.1 Motivation of development actors.

	Factors of motivation				
	Cost			Design issues	
Development roles	Timescale	Financial strategy	Functionality	External appearance	Relation to context
Supply-side actors – those who 'produce' the development or contribute to its production					
Landowner	**Transient**	**Profit maximisation**	**No**	**No**	**No**
Developers	**Transient**	**Profit maximisation**	**Yes** But only as a means to financial end	**Yes** But only as a means to financial end	**Yes** To extent that there are positive or negative externalities
Funders (short-term development finance)	**Transient**	**Profit maximisation**	**No**	**No**	**No**
Builder	**Transient**	**Profit maximisation**	**No**	**Yes**	**No**
Adviser I e.g. Managing Agent	**Enduring**	**Profit maximisation/ seeking**	**Yes**	**Yes** But primarily as a means to financial end	**No**
Adviser II e.g. Designer	**Transient**	**Profit maximisation/ seeking**	**Yes**	**Yes** But indirectly, to the extent that external appearance reflects on them and their future business	**No**
Demand-side actors – those who 'consume' the development					
Investors (long-term investment funding)	**Enduring**	**Profit maximisation**	**Yes** But primarily as a means to financial end	**Yes** But primarily as a means to financial end	**Yes** To extent that there are benefits to making positive connections
Occupiers	**Enduring**	**Cost minimisation**	**Yes**	**Yes** But only to the extent that external appearance symbolises/represents them and their business	**Yes** To the extent that there are benefits to making positive connections

(continued)

Table 1.1 (cont'd).

| Development roles | Factors of motivation | | | | |
| | Cost | | Design issues | | |
	Timescale	Financial strategy	Functionality	External appearance	Relation to context
Adjacent landowners	**Enduring**	**Protect property values**	**No**	**Yes** To the extent that new development has positive or negative externalities	**Yes** To the extent that new development has positive or negative externalities
Community (local)	**Enduring**	**Neutral**	**Yes** To the extent that buildings are used by general public	**Yes** To the extent that it defines and forms part of public realm	**Yes**
Regulatory actors – those who 'regulate' the development					
Public sector	**Enduring**	**Neutral** (in principle)	**Yes**	**Yes** To the extent that it forms part of a greater whole	**Yes** To the extent that it forms part of a greater whole

Source: Adapted from Carmona *et al.* 2003: 221; Tiesdell & Adams 2004.

The conflicting objectives of producer and consumer sides can lead to producer–consumer gaps. When traded-off between roles effectively played by a single actor (i.e. where a single actor is both 'developer *and* funder', or 'funder, investor *and* occupier'), conflict over objectives is internalised, producing the most satisfactory outcome subject to budget constraints. When different actors' objectives and motivations have to be reconciled externally (i.e. through market transactions), there is scope for significant mismatch or gaps between supply and demand. Development quality frequently falls through these producer–consumer gaps. Such gaps can be closed or narrowed in any of three main ways:

(1) Through regulation[5] – developers *'have-to'* provide better quality development.
(2) Through remunerative means – developers calculate that it is *'worth-it'* (financially beneficial) to provide better-quality development.
(3) Through normative preferences – developers *'want-to'* provide better quality development.

It is important to note that the first of these is coercive and the other two voluntary.

Closing producer–consumer gaps is a necessary but not sufficient condition of 'good' design. Responding to investors' and occupiers' needs, developers can exclude the general public's needs. Segregated housing estates, gated communities and inward-focused developments, for example, provide what purchasers and occupiers purportedly want, but may contribute little to the wider public environment. The broader challenge is thus to encourage or compel developers to look across site boundaries, at their development's impact on the wider context and, more generally, to contribute to making better places. Public intervention through judicious deployment of policy instruments *might* be a means of compelling or encouraging this.

Opportunity space theory

Drawing on Giddens' structuration theory, Bentley (1999) argues that all development actors operate by rules and command 'resources' – finance, expertise, ideas, interpersonal skills etc – which other actors want and need. As Bentley argues, various webs of rules create 'opportunity space' – or scope for autonomous action – within which actors necessarily operate. The rules are internal (i.e. those actors place on themselves) and external (i.e. those placed upon them). For private developers, the external rules relate to budget constraints, appropriate rewards, the amount of risk to be incurred and the need to make a saleable product. Such rules are not arbitrary, cannot simply be ignored and are enforced through sanctions, such as bankruptcy. All development actors thus act within constraints – their opportunity space is not limitless but bounded.

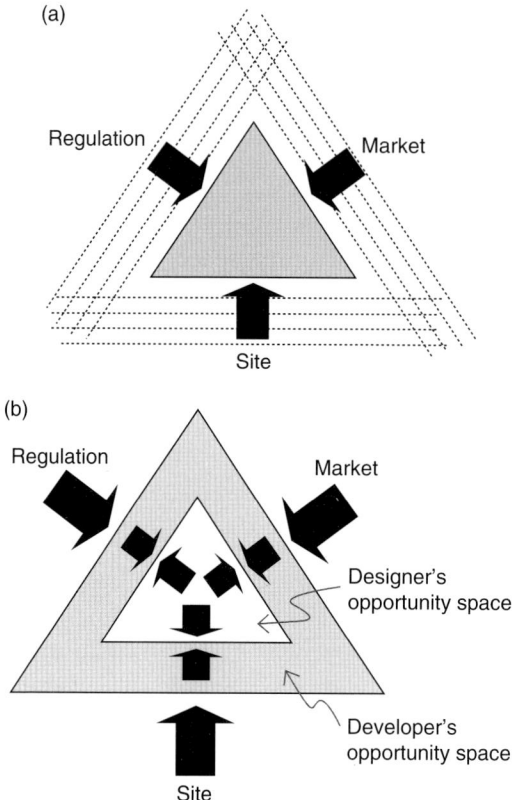

Figure 1.1   (a) Developer's opportunity space; (b) Developer's and designer's opportunity space.
The developer's opportunity space (room for manoeuvre) is constrained by three forces or contexts:

(1)   *Site context* – the more problematic, difficult or constrained the site the smaller the developer's opportunity space.
(2)   *Regulatory context* – the more demanding the regulatory context the smaller the developer's opportunity space.
(3)   *Market context* – the more demanding or competitive the market context the smaller the developer's opportunity space.

A larger opportunity space gives the developer more autonomy to carry out development in his/her own direct interests – a situation of producer sovereignty. If external forces eradicate the opportunity space, then development is not feasible or viable at that particular time. The designer's opportunity space is contained *within* the developer's opportunity space and is constrained by the same forces constraining the developer's opportunity space, by how the developer filters those forces and by the other development actors' agency. *Source:* Adapted from Tiesdell & Adams 2004.

This is conceptualised in Figure 1.1a. Here, the developer's opportunity space is substantially determined by three major external forces or contexts – the development site and its immediate context; the market context (e.g. the need to create a saleable product); and the regulatory context (e.g. the need for compliant development). The boundaries of the opportunity space are best conceived as fuzzy rather than hard-edged and ultimately depend on the respective negotiating abilities of the development actors and on the social dynamics between them. Furthermore, while relatively fixed at any particular time, they are dynamic and open to transformation as policy and markets change. Hence, alongside opportunity space, we can identify changing 'windows of opportunity'.

Within the developer's opportunity space, other development actors – surveyors, designers, landscape designers, engineers etc – negotiate and compete for space. For current purposes, the critical relationship is that between the developer and the designer. This is conceptualised in Figure 1.1b. Here, the designer's opportunity space is contained *within* the developer's opportunity space and is constrained or determined by the same external forces, by how the developer *filters* those forces, and by other development actors.

The designer's opportunity space will grow in size (relative to the developer's opportunity space) where the developer needs the designer's skills to create viable or more profitable development. For developers, the key issue is the freedom they are *willing* to give and the freedom they *must* give to designers. Factors that make the design task more difficult – those requiring more design expertise such as a more difficult or demanding site (including the challenge of putting a required quantum of floorspace on a site within a preset budget), more exacting public regulatory expectations or requirements, a greater need to respond to user or investor needs etc – mean that the developer must yield opportunity space to the designer because in such circumstances the developer needs a skilled designer to unlock development potential. Thus for example, the designer's opportunity space is generally larger on more-constrained brownfield sites than on less-constrained greenfield sites (Tiesdell & Adams 2004). The larger the designer's opportunity space, the greater the scope for the designer to influence or determine development design. But this is only potential for better design, since a larger opportunity space for design does not necessarily result in better design since designers may (mis-)use it to impose their own 'heroic' view. Interpretations of better design will also vary.[6]

By negotiating with developers, designers try to enlarge their own opportunity space – both to create the opportunity for better design and, less nobly, to further their own self-interest. The negotiations are continuous, often subconscious and implicit. The development site, the developer's brief (or programme) and the available budget (based on anticipated end values and available capital) set the initial agenda and broad parameters for design. These provide the starting point for discussion and negotiation about design. In some situations, designers may be permitted freedom to interpret the developer's brief – and, indeed, may have been involved in drawing it up. This is, in effect, a crucial part of exploring the design problem. In others, the opportunity space for design may be severely constrained, with designers expected merely to provide 'packaging' or 'styling', perhaps because all the fundamental design decisions have already been taken according to a preset formula. This happens, for example, with 'standard' real estate products (see Leinberger 2005; 2008) since the designer's task consists of merely arranging standard units.

An advantage in negotiation lies in knowing the limits of the other actors' opportunity space. Bentley (1999: 39) thus argues that the more designers understand other actors' opportunity space (e.g. their financial feasibility calculations), the more effectively they can target their own resources. Designers may thus be able to operate more effectively (at least, in terms of achieving their own objectives) by knowing how far developers can be pushed. Bentley then identifies three specific types of power that designers could deploy in negotiating with developers:

(1) *Knowledge and expertise* is a product of their learning, professional experience and, more generally, detailed and extensive awareness of precedents and technological possibilities. Here, the designer has expertise and knowledge that the client-developer wants and requires in order to undertake a successful development.
(2) By making proposals for physical designs, designers have the *power of initiating* and then developing design proposals.
(3) A designer's reputation constitutes a form of *reputation capital*. A designer will be hired in part because this reputation is valuable to the developer. In theory, a designer can exploit this capital by (say) threatening to resign. However, this 'works' only to the extent that the developer wants a building or project designed by that particular designer and is prepared to forestall their resignation. It is debatable how many designers have sufficient reputation capital to deploy in negotiation, so the real power may derive from the developer's reluctance to incur the costs and inconvenience of appointing a new designer.

To explore the developer–designer relation further, Bentley (1999: 30–39) suggests four metaphors to characterise the designer–developer relation:

(1) *Heroic-Form-Giver* – This metaphor suggests that development form is generated primarily through the creative efforts of designers. Bentley dismisses this as a 'powerful myth' that vastly overstates the role of designers. This is 'the Fountainhead' scenario (Rand 1993), where the designer is the creative genius to which other players look in an unquestioning way for the correct design solution.
(2) *Master-and-Servant* – This metaphor suggests that development form is determined by powerplays, where decisions are dictated by those with most power (reflecting McGlynn's (1993) 'Powergram'), whereby those with most power (the masters) can issue orders to those with less (the servants). In practice, this results in developers making the fundamental decisions which designers then package. This view understates the autonomy of designers, which derives from their expertise and knowledge, and that of

other built environment professionals, which developers need. In practice, power is diffused among development actors.

(3) *Market Signals* – This metaphor suggests that resource-poor actors such as designers are acutely conscious of who pays their salaries, and so produce what they think the market wants, even if they personally disagree with the product. In short, the designer makes a passive response to the market, rather than a creative response to the context or to his/her design philosophies.

(4) *The Battlefield* – which Bentley argues is the most common scenario. This metaphor recognises that as the different development actors bring different professional expertise to the table, the resulting development is shaped by how these actors negotiate with each other to achieve their objectives.

For Bentley, the first metaphor is illusory, while the second and third understate or ignore the practicalities of controlling the development team and the inherent uncertainties of the development process. As principal-agent theory suggests, where complex knowledge is needed, detailed control of experts requires equally well-qualified controllers. The transaction costs of such controls and supervision are frequently prohibitive, making autonomy and discretion for professionals unavoidable. This will not be checked merely by professionals knowing 'on which side their bread is buttered'. Bentley also highlights how problems can arise when members of the development or design team have incentives to emphasise their own contributions and operate according to their own value-systems, while ignoring those of others. For example, architects may stress only the 'art' dimension, surveyors only the 'financial' dimension. This may be difficult for the developer to control, especially since designers and other professionals might use their discretion to act against the developer's real interests. Bentley argues that this makes a battlefield metaphor more appropriate rather than a 'friendly-and-bustling' marketplace. Indeed, he suggests that actors variously negotiate, plot and scheme with, and against, each other to achieve the built form they themselves want, making the character, personality and interpersonal skills of the various actors crucially important.

Against this background, we now consider how public policy can influence the relationship between developers and designers.

The tools approach to public policy

The 'tools approach' in public policy focuses on the range of instruments, mechanisms, tools and actions that policymakers can deploy in response to particular problems and challenges. It thus concentrates on the *means* rather than the ends of government and of policy. In the literature, the terms 'tools' and 'instruments' are used interchangeably – in this book, we will generally use the term instrument (though we shall still refer to the 'tools approach').[7] Instruments should be distinguished from 'policies': in this context, Elmore (1987: 175) draws an analogy with chemistry where compounds (policies) are made up of elements (instruments).

Within this field, a key task has been to identify and categorise available policy instruments. There are two main reasons for classifying policy instruments. The first is to provide a frame for empirical research on the impact of policy actions – that is, to discover what works, where, how and why? The second is to create a resource or heuristic for policy design, since knowledge of a fuller repertoire of possible policy actions reduces problems of path dependency and 'tunnel vision' (i.e. reliance on familiar tools regardless of whether they are successful). Urban designers unaware of the full range of tools available, will tend to use those readily available or those with which they are already familiar. The limitations of such approaches are nicely encapsulated in Mark Twain's epigram: 'If your only tool is a hammer, all your problems are nails.'

Vedung (2007: 22) suggests two paired approaches to classifying policy instruments. The first approach contrasts maximalist with minimalist methods. Simply listing all possible policy instruments with little attempt to arrange them into groups, the maximalist method is of limited interest. Of more value is the minimalist method, which involves creating a small number (i.e. analytic parsimony) of fundamental and generic types under which all specific kinds of policy instrument can be categorised (i.e. comprehensive coverage). This method usually involves building a typology (i.e. a conceptual or top-down grouping) or taxonomy (i.e. an empirical or bottom-up grouping) (see Smith 2002).

The second approach compares choice and resource methods (see Howlett 1991). Later in this chapter we offer a variation on the resource method. Choice methods involve classifying tools according to the basic choices open to governments. Taking the amount of coercion as an example, the choice may range from complete freedom from government intervention to total government coercion. In urban design terms, this is a choice between the state 'designing' everything and the state allowing a 'free-for-all'. Choice approaches are not, however, classifications of policy instruments per se, so for the purpose of this book, the most useful classifications are resource methods. A brief review of one well-known resource classification illustrates existing work in this field.

In his 1983 book, *The Tools of Government* – republished in 2007, co-authored with Helen Margetts and retitled, *The Tools of Government in the Digital Era* (Hood & Margetts 2007) – Christopher Hood began with a cybernetically based categorisation of policy instruments, and then identified four basic social resources ('detectors') normally available to government for 'gathering information' from its citizens and for modifying their behaviour ('effectors'):

(1) *Nodality* – the capacity of government to operate as a node in information networks.

(2) *Authority* – the government's legal power and other sources of legitimacy (i.e. power officially to demand, forbid, guarantee, adjudicate etc).
(3) *Treasure* – the possession of stocks of money, assets or other 'fungible' resources (i.e. the capacity to be freely exchanged).
(4) *Organisation* – the government's capacity for direct action, for instance, through armies, police or bureaucracy, including the creation of, and change to, the built environment (Hood & Margetts 2007: 5–6).

In a subsequent paper, Hood (2008: 129–130) identified three limitations of his own work:

(1) It deliberately analysed government instruments in an institution-free and technology-free way, treating government as a 'single undifferentiated actor'.[8]
(2) It looked only at the point at which 'government' (in all its various institutional forms) came into touch with citizens at large – in other words, the state was effectively a black box.
(3) It was restricted to only two of the standard analytic components of any control system, detectors and effectors, and had not considered a third element, the 'director' (i.e. the means for setting a standards or target).

These issues are of interest but, for the present, they form the background, rather than the foreground, to our enquiry. Instead, this book is primarily concerned with how urban design objectives are formulated, how appropriate instruments within the state apparatus are selected to achieve those objectives, and how those instruments impact on developers' decision-making.[9]

Classifications and typologies of policy instruments exist within the planning literature (see, for example, Lichfield & Darin-Drabkin 1980; Healey *et al.* 1988; Vigar *et al.* 2000). Typically derived from a welfare economics tradition, these have tended to concentrate on market failure and on state interventions (i.e. the 'state' part of the state–market dialectic), with less attention given to the impact of each policy instrument on development actors' decision environments.

Classifications are much scarcer within the urban design literature. At MIT, however, John De Monchaux and Mark Schuster developed their urban design 'toolkit' over a number of years – though only a single published exposition exists (De Monchaux & Schuster 1997) (see Table 1.2).

Contending that there are only five fundamental instrument-types, De Monchaux & Schuster offered a prize to any student who could suggest a sixth. They never awarded the prize, as they considered most suggestions either subdivisions of one or other instrument or attempts to emphasise a particular instrument. However, De Monchaux & Schuster concede that 'do nothing' could be considered a sixth instrument.

Table 1.2   De Monchaux & Schuster's classification of urban design tools.

Tool type	Operation
Ownership & operation	The State implements policy through direct provision, in the sense that the State will do 'X'.
Regulation[†]	The State regulates the actions of other actors, particularly those private individuals or institutional entities, in the sense that you must (or must not) do 'X'.
Incentives & disincentives	The State provides incentives or disincentives designed to bring the actions of other actors into line with a desired policy, in the sense that if you do 'X', the State will do 'Y'.
Establishment, allocation & enforcement of property rights	The State can establish, allocate and enforce the property rights of individual parties, in the sense that you have a right to do 'X', and the State will enforce that right.
Information	The State collects and distributes information intended to influence the actions of others, in the sense that you should do 'X' (i.e. a command or exhortation) or you need to know 'Y' in order to do 'X' (i.e. advice or guidance).

Source: Adapted from De Monchaux & Schuster 1997.
[†]Economists commonly use regulation to refer to all forms of government intervention. In the public policy literature it is used in a narrower and more specific sense to refer to instances where governments seek to compel an action or to constrain the range or nature of the actions available.

Although most classifications of policy instruments concentrate on the government resource deployed, we seek here to shift the focus from the resource to its impact on the decision-making behaviour of key development actors – in other words, how they operate as second-order design actions and thus how they affect the decision environments of key development actors. Thus, treating decision environments and opportunity space as interchangeable, certain public policy actions may enlarge the developer's opportunity space. Financial subsidies and grants, for example, may ease the market context; a less constraining regulatory context may encourage development; while infrastructure improvements on or near the development site may ease the site context.

The shift in focus from the governmental resource deployed to the impact on decision-making of target actors is akin to Elmore's notion of 'backward mapping'. In contrast to 'forward mapping' (which starts with government actions), Elmore (1987) suggests 'backward mapping', which starts at the policy problem on the ground, considers the actors closest to that problem and then asks what policy instruments are available to shape, compel, constrain or incite etc their behaviour, choices and actions. Backward mapping also suggests that those intending to deploy policy instruments need to identify – and then target – certain key actors, usually as classes or groups rather than as individuals.[10] Private developers and designers are most commonly the key actors at which urban design policy actions are directed, but landowners, investors, politicians, planners, highway engineers, the general public and other specific groups may also be the target of policy. The focus here is primarily on developers and their designers.

The present authors (see Adams *et al.* 2003 & 2005; Tiesdell & Allmendinger 2005) have previously characterised policy instruments into four types, according to how they affect development actors' decision environments:

(1) Those intended to *shape* behaviours – these set the context for market decisions and transactions, and so shape the decision environment.
(2) Those intended to *regulate* behaviours – these control and regulate market actions and regulations, and so define the parameters of the decision environment.
(3) Those intended to *stimulate* behaviours – these lubricate market actions and transactions, and so restructure the contours of the decision environment.
(4) Those intended to develop the *capacity* of development actors/organisations – these enhance the ability of actors to operate more effectively within a particular opportunity space (see Table 1.3).

Two qualifications should be noted. First, policy instruments operate neither in isolation, nor within a vacuum. Rather new initiatives are frequently introduced within an already crowded policy context, which may create undesirable secondary effects and unintended outcomes, with consequential difficulties in terms of accurately identifying and distinguishing the cause-and-effect of any particular policy instrument. Second, policy instruments are generally deployed and operate in bundles or packages. The tools approach thus also provides a means of unbundling complex packages of policy instruments – or in Elmore's words, identifying 'elements' within 'compounds'. Masterplans, for example, are frequently part of a broader 'place procurement strategy', which bundles shaping, regulating, stimulating and capacity building instruments. Bearing these qualifications in mind, we now turn to exploring each of these four main types of policy instruments in more detail, with particular emphasis on their design relevance.

Information is rarely communicated in a wholly neutral fashion. Instead, seduction, manipulation, falsehood and spin are deployed to present selective information in the form of argument or persuasion. There are also a series of what are commonly referred to as 'framing effects' (Lakoff 2006; Tversky & Kahneman 1981). 'Framing' explains how decisions can be influenced by the manner in which information is presented (the 'frame') (Pryce & Levin 2008).

Shaping instruments

The first set of policy instruments are those that shape the decision environment of individual development actors by setting the broad context for market decisions and transactions. Shaping instruments are articulated at a general level to achieve desired policy goals. While such instruments are subsequently

Table 1.3   State actions/urban design policy instruments.

Instrument types	Common subtypes
Shaping instruments shape behaviour by providing the general rules-of-the-game, that is, shaping the general context for decision-making	• **Market structuring** – actions establishing the overarching context within which market actions and transactions occur. Examples include legal frameworks, property rights and national taxation systems. • **Investment provision** – actions involving macro-level (non-site-specific) public investment in the provision of public and collective goods, through *either* direct (e.g. by a public agency) *or* indirect provision (e.g. by providing funding to third parties). • **Generating information or promoting coordination** – actions providing information to inform decision-making (e.g. listed building registers) and/or to increase the coordination of otherwise independent actions. Examples include plans, policy statements, guidance, advice, etc, produced by governmental agencies/authorities (and others), which, *inter alia*, provide coordinating information, information about the government or other authority's intentions, and information about regulatory policies.
Regulatory instruments affect decisions by restricting the set of choices available	• **Regulatory instruments** – actions compelling, eradicating and/or managing aspects of an activity. Examples include the more general controls over development (e.g. planning systems and development controls, highway consents, historic preservation) and more specific controls over the design of that development (e.g. design policies/design review procedures). • **Enforcement procedures** – actions ensuring that a regulatory action is undertaken. • **Regulatory procedures** – actions relating to the fact of, and procedures for, regulation, which add uncertainty and other costs. Examples include various methods of deregulation/streamlining, such as fast-tracking applications from registered architects, and simplified planning zones/enterprise zones.
Stimulus instruments make some actions more (or less) attractive to, and rewarding for, particular development actors	• **Direct state actions** – actions at the site- or area-specific level, usually intended to overcome particular obstacles to development. Examples include the provision of public infrastructure (e.g. access roads, public spaces), environmental improvements and land assembly/subdivision. • **Price-adjusting instruments** – actions adjusting the price to the actor of an activity. Examples include imposition of site-specific taxes, tax credits/incentives/breaks, subsidies/grants. • **Risk-adjusting instruments** – actions adjusting the risk to the actor associated with an activity. Examples include creating a more predictable investment environment through, for example, demonstration projects, policy stability, investment actions, and active place-management. • **Capital-raising instruments** – actions facilitating the availability of development finance or, alternatively, enabling selected developers to access sources of finance previously or otherwise inaccessible to them and/or to access it on more favourable terms.

Table 1.3 (*cont'd*).

Instrument types	Common subtypes
Capacity-building instruments facilitate the operation of the other policy instruments	• **Developing human capital** – actions involving developing skills and abilities of development actors, both as individuals and as organisations, to deploy the other instruments more effectively. Examples include on-the-job training, CPD, expert seminars, job swaps and secondments, exposure to good or innovative practices, field visits, role models, 'inspirational others' (e.g. design champions within organisations). • **Enhancing institutional and organisational networks and capacity** – actions involving establishing formal and informal arenas or organisations for exchanging information and knowledge and for building or extending actor networks and relationship webs. Examples include Architecture Centres, local urban design/design review panels etc. • **Reframing cultural mindsets/cultural change** – actions seeking to challenge mindsets and encourage 'mindshifts'. Examples include instruments that facilitate and encourage blue-sky thinking, thinking-outside-the-box and creativity (e.g. through ideas competitions). In addition to producing and generating ideas, they may also enhance the receptivity of decision-makers to new ideas, by challenging and perhaps changing their worldview (e.g. seeing a new tram line as place-shaping infrastructure rather than merely as transport). • **Enlarging the stock of ideas and concepts** – actions that create an 'ideas bank' of exemplars of successful places and practices that encourage development actors to broaden their appreciation of what may be possible in the particular circumstances they face.

Source: Adapted from Adams *et al.* 2003 and 2005; Tiesdell & Allmendinger 2005.

interpreted for particular cases by individual actors, they are primarily intended to set 'the rules of the game', rather than to provide case-specific direction. As Table 1.3 shows, there are three common types of market shaping instrument, which operate respectively through market structuring, investment provision and by generating information or promoting coordination. We now consider each of these in turn, with particular interest in their design aspects.

Market structuring

Real estate development takes place in a context that is shaped, and indeed guaranteed, by the state. At its most basic, development involves reorganisation of property rights. Without the effective rule of law, enforced where necessary in the courts, there would be little point in private capital investing in real estate. Recognition in law of particular forms of property right, such as long leasehold tenure, may well have design implications in terms of what is built and how it is subsequently maintained. Edinburgh's New

Town and London's Mayfair, with their sophisticated landlord–tenant relationships, are good examples of how the outward appearance of what was then a pioneer form of development could not have taken place without the system of property rights guaranteed by the state. The same principle applies today to gated communities – what makes the 'gate' effective is not its physical strength, but the rights of those residing behind the gate to resort to law to protect their own privacy. These examples of 'market structuring' are illustrative of how the legal and political framework of the state provides an overall context for real estate development, and its design component.

Investment provision

Public infrastructure investment offers a good example of how the provision of collective goods by the state, such as the construction of new transport infrastructure, can make land and property more 'ripe' for development. Two critical issues arise here, one financial and the other concerned with design, which ultimately are closely linked. Financially, mechanisms are required to ensure that those private interests who benefit, or who are likely to benefit, from public infrastructure investment, at least repay the costs of that investment and thus make the effort involved in its creation worthwhile to the state. This same principle applies to privately funded infrastructure – no investor is likely to become involved in such provision unless there is a clear financial return. In design terms, infrastructure provision, if well-planned, is centrally concerned with achieving better quality development by joining up what might otherwise be disconnected, either in time or space. This is a design process, creating added development value that, in the right circumstances, has the potential to be reinvested in a better designed product. Too often, however, the state succumbs to the temptation to appraise its own investment projects in very narrow terms, with the result that the potential added value of sustainable design is not well realised.

Generating information or promoting coordination

The production of plans is the most familiar means by which the state seeks to shape market behaviour through generating information or promoting coordination. Plans have potential to achieve this in three main ways:

(1) By specifying regulatory polices, for example, on permitted and prohibited land uses, development densities and development forms.
(2) By indicating government intentions in relation, for example, to future infrastructure provision.
(3) By specifying what is intended to happen on any particular parcel, and on neighbouring parcels, plans help set value, protect against negative externalities and thus reduce market uncertainty.

Development actors are likely to take more notice of plans that they consider more authoritative. Authoritativeness is, however, socially constructed. According to Alexander (2001: 65), it depends of the plan-maker's reputation for commitment and reliability, and on whether the planning system is rigid or flexible. The information conveyed in plans may be considered less reliable by development actors in more flexible and discretionary systems like the UK, than in more rigid systems like the Netherlands.

It is important to distinguish between three main types of plans:

(1) *Development plans* (in their true sense of the term, and not as misused in UK legislation) set out a series of actions (such as investments in public infrastructure) to be taken or led by the state, to achieve an intended spatial pattern by a particular time. Representing an authoritative commitment, the plan shapes market-initiated development, because location decisions take account of, and anticipate, public investment.

(2) *Regulatory plans* establish the basis for development regulation, usually by the state (or sometimes by third parties). They set out what is expected of individual developments, and involve an element of compulsion to ensure regulatory standards are achieved.

(3) *Indicative plans* provide 'guidance', which is essentially advisory, making compliance voluntary. Where such plans run counter to market trends, they may prove hard to implement, unless supported by long-term stakeholder interests.

Design policies can appear in (true) development plans, but generally take the form of regulatory or indicative plans. Plot ratios, for example, have been widely used in regulatory plans in the UK to specify the total floor-space likely to be allowed on development sites in particular parts of British cities, most notably in city centres. Design guides, which encourage developers to achieve higher design standards, fall into the category of indicative plans. Whether design briefs and other forms of supplementary design guidance operate as regulatory or indicative plans often depends on the particular political circumstances of the locality, and the extent to which higher design aspirations are backed by a broader support coalition. In practice, to be effective, design policies, as with all plans, may need to be supported by other (regulatory, stimulus or capacity building) instruments.

Regulatory instruments

Market regulation seeks to regulate or control market actions and transactions. Whereas plans affect decisions by providing information (and thereby shaping the context for decision-making), regulations affect decisions by restricting the set of choices available and so place limits on an actor's opportunity space.

The extent to which design matters are considered a legitimate focus of development regulation may vary according to the three factors: (1) the perceived definition that regulators hold of design (which may range from architectural aesthetics right through to place-making), (2) the political philosophy then in the ascendancy (and specifically, the extent of market intervention considered appropriate) and (3) the health of the real estate market, both spatially and cyclically. Put simply, where design is conceived in narrow terms by regulators, where market actors are regarded as the best judge of what is appropriate in design terms, and where conditions in the local real estate market are known to be weak, there may be a strong temptation not to lose 'welcome' development 'simply on design terms', especially if it provides jobs.

In Table 1.3, we distinguish between regulatory instruments, enforcement procedures and regulatory procedures. In real estate development, regulatory instruments generally operate by the state taking certain rights in land and by making subsequent exercise of those rights subject to express permission. The 1947 nationalisation of development rights in land in the UK is an obvious example, where the grant of planning consent releases certain development rights. Under a zoning system, the detail of the zoning ordinance constrains development rights within the zone. In many countries, regulatory instruments are associated with land transfer or subdivision, especially when all, or substantial areas of, land are held by the state. Regulatory instruments may also be created voluntarily under force of contract, for example, by conditions attached to private land transfers.

Design regulatory instruments

In terms of their impact on the resulting urban form, a useful distinction can be made between 'positive' and 'negative' design regulatory instruments. Positive design regulatory instruments are those that establish a predictable urban form. A prime example would be a 'build-to line', which requires all development to be built up to a defined street edge. Mandatory on each side of a street, the regulation ensures a desired three-dimensional profile for the street. Negative design regulatory instruments are those that do not establish a predictable urban form. Here a prime example would be a 'build-behind' line, which merely ensures that no development occurs in front of a defined line (see Figure 1.2). Build-to lines are a feature of many New Urbanist form-based codes. Both build-to and build-behind lines feature in the German *Bebauungsplan (B-Plan)* system (see Stille 2007). Here, the key mechanisms to control urban form include maximum building heights and site coverage. The latter operate through the *Baufenster*, which sets out the area within

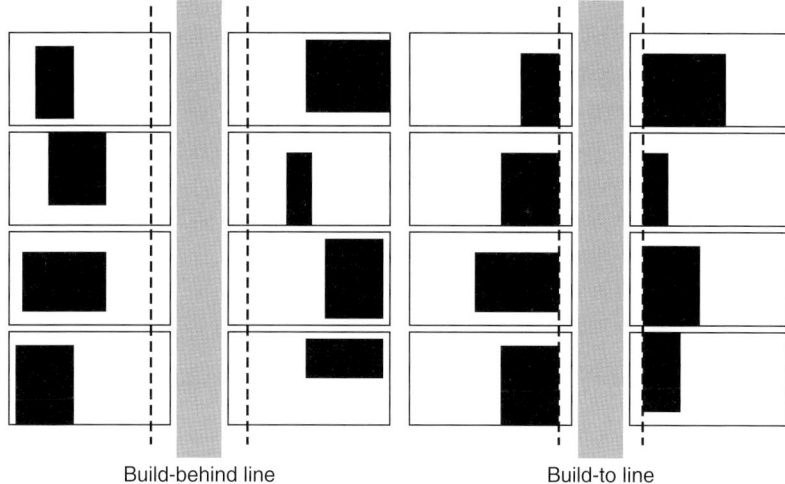

Build-behind line   Build-to line

Figure 1.2   A 'build behind line' is a negative design regulatory instrument, which produces a whole that is no greater than the sum of the parts (in this case, eight buildings and a road). In contrast, a 'build to line' is a positive design regulatory instrument, which creates synergy by producing a whole that exceeds than the sum of the parts (in this case, eight buildings *plus* a street). *Source:* Courtesy of Steve Tiesdell.

which any development has to be located by combining two different boundary conditions: the *Baulinie* (or line on which any building has to be located – i.e. a build-to line) and the *Baugrenze* (or line identifying the maximum footprint that the building may occupy – i.e. a build-behind line).

Enforcement procedures

To ensure compliance, regulatory instruments need to be underpinned by effective and credible enforcement procedures. If enforcement is erratic or inconsistent, market actors may gamble on regulation not being enforced. Certain advantage might accrue to developers who successfully evade regulation – they could, for example, develop larger buildings than permitted by regulation. For regulation to be effective there must be credible prospect of its enforcement.

Regulatory procedures

Since regulation procedures, which determine how regulatory instruments are operated in practice, may themselves speed up or slow down regulatory decisions, market actors may exert pressure for some form of deregulation to streamline the decision-making process. Public choice economists are quick to highlight the costs and inefficiencies of regulation, which are often direct and borne by identifiable actors such as developers, but much less quick to highlight the benefits, which are more diffuse and difficult to measure, but reaped by the community-at-large. Regulatory processes can also be captured by the vested interests that they are intended to control, as Marantz & Ben-Joseph show powerfully in Chapter 6 in relation to zoning in the USA. Regulation is a blunt instrument that bears on all actors within its jurisdiction, regardless of their individual attitudes towards design. For reasons of equity and fairness, regulation tends to operate a 'one-size-fits-all' system, but to do so it often has to regulate at the lowest common denominator, without offering any incentives to do better. If, as a result, actors merely conform to minimal regulatory requirements, regulation can act as a barrier to change and innovation. However, regulators may often wish to exercise some from of principled discrimination – they may prefer, for example, to impose strict rules on the place-breakers, while giving flexibility to the place-makers. Reflecting Douglas Bader's well-quoted remark that 'Rules are for the obedience of fools and the guidance of good men', what may be needed are regulatory systems with some degree of discretion or discrimination.

Although problematic in practice, this suggests the need for 'earned autonomy' for developers who have proved themselves to be place-makers rather than place-breakers. 'Earned autonomy' is a concept associated with local government modernisation in the UK, and refers to those authorities deemed to be performing well, which are then subject to less scrutiny and given greater freedom and flexibility to decide issues as they see fit (see Lowndes 2002: 140). In practice, local planning authorities may unofficially operate some form of positive regulatory discrimination in favour of developers whom they think they can trust. In this context, Duany and Talen (2002a, 2002b) advocate designing regulatory systems and instruments to make 'the good' easy and 'bad' difficult by requiring individual approval only for developments that contravened what they consider to be good design rules.

Regulatory control of real estate development, including that of its design component, has been subject to more fundamental critique. Drawing on Ben-Joseph & Szold (2005), Schuster (2005: 333), for example, lists some standard critiques of regulation:

> ... regulation is inefficient, ignoring important market signals as to what is desired by individuals in society in its pursuit of a broader loosely specified 'public interest'; moreover regulation visits the cost of serving that broader public interest on the few who are regulated – the few pay for the benefit to the many.

Brain (2005: 230) highlights what he terms the 'substantive irrationalities of a technically rational regulatory' structure. One of these irrationalities is a focus on perfecting the parts in isolation regardless of their impact on the whole, rather than on achieving the best combination of those parts. According to Brain (2005: 231) 'The various unintended consequences of our well-engineered road system, from arterial to interstate, provide a long list of examples of highly rationalised, specialised expertise that often creates as many problems in cities as it solves.' This technical failure may be compounded by the tendency of some local politicians, when discharging a regulatory function, to concentrate on the minutiae of design matters to the neglect of the overall picture. Many planning practitioners can recount stories of planning committees that have felt confident enough to comment on matters of taste (colour schemes, window details, balcony details etc) associated with developments of several hundred houses but remain wholly silent about the place-making or place-breaking implications of such developments.

This raises issues of confidence and competence. 'Tick box' approaches and itemised checklists of so-called 'aspects of good design', which neglect the totality of the design product, exacerbate the problem by reducing design thinking to formula thinking (Landry, 2000). What really matters in design is less the individual design components and more their combination into the greater whole. As one commentator said of Sophia Loren, '*Her feet are too big. Her nose is too long. Her teeth are uneven. She has the neck, as one of her rivals has put it, of a 'Neapolitan giraffe.' ... Her hands are huge. Her forehead is low. Her mouth is too large. And mamma mia, she is absolutely gorgeous*' (*Time Magazine*, 6 April 1962).

At its worst, design regulation can degenerate into design-by-committee, producing the design equivalent of a camel, rather than a racehorse. Defining characteristics of design-by-committee are 'needless complexity, internal inconsistency, logical flaws, banality, and the lack of a unifying vision' (Wikipedia 2010). Poor choices may be made to appease the egos of individual committee members or because some representatives are particularly forceful and others more retiring. The original motivation, specifications and technical criteria take a backseat. Compromise, rather than synthesis, triumphs. The problems resulting from design-by-committee highlight the need for a design leader (or, more simply, a meta-designer) who understands both the value of the parts and also the need to combine them into a greater whole, and thus is concerned about the totality of what is being created. This is where independent design review, as part of any regulatory process, may be able to offer a reflective and holistic view of development proposals and guide regulators, whether elected or professional, towards focusing on key design elements that determine how the scheme comes together as a whole.

In the end, however, the force of design regulation often lies in its coercive power to 'say No'. It can be argued that there would have been almost no design improvements in the UK in recent decades had there not been the background threat of refusal backed up by likely dismissal of an appeal. Indeed, the threat of veto, rather than the actual exercise of veto, may be all that is required to persuade developers to turn to skilled designers and submit schemes of higher design quality. In essence, the certain 'stick' of regulation may be more effective (at least in the short term) in making developers produce better places, than the uncertain 'carrot' of enhanced commercial benefit, to which we now turn.

Stimulus instruments

Regulation derives its power from its capacity to restrict the choices available to market actors. It can be regarded as a negative instrument in the sense that it may serve to direct demand away from specified locations, but cannot generally attract demand (and development) to a location. In certain circumstances, to achieve policy intentions, it may need to be supported by more positive stimulus instruments that seek to facilitate markets working better. Such instruments 'lubricate' the market by, for example, having a direct impact on financial appraisals. While regulatory instruments are about compulsion (the actor has no choice and 'has to' comply), stimulus instruments are about incentives and disincentives (they are essentially voluntary, and work by making the actor 'want to' take the incentive or incur the disincentive). Stimulus actions thus increase the likelihood of some desired event happening by making some actions more (and sometimes less) attractive to, and rewarding for, particular development actors. In short, they change the pattern of incentives within the decision environment.

We can distinguish between development and design stimulus instruments. Development stimulus instruments typically encourage development to happen in a particular location, to happen sooner, to be of higher quality or for there to be more of it. Such policy instruments impact directly on the developer and would increase their reward, reduce their risk etc. As Table 1.3 shows, four main types of development stimulus instruments can be identified, namely direct state actions, price-adjusting instruments, risk-adjusting instruments and capital-raising instruments. Examples of each are given by Syms and Clarke in Chapter 7.

Design stimulus instruments specifically encourage the creation of 'better places'. Such instruments typically impact on developers in such a way as to encourage them to yield opportunity space to designers. Increasing regulation of development can become a (de facto) design stimulus because, at some point, incremental adjustment to the increasing regulatory requirements is no longer adequate or cost effective. To 'get through' the regulation (i.e. to achieve timely regulatory consents), the developer elects to employ designers (i.e. has to yield opportunity space to a designer), which can well result in a more financially attractive development, as well as a better designed one that satisfies all the requirements of the various regulatory bodies.

Development and design stimulus instruments can operate in isolation, but are most likely to produce a high quality development where they reinforce each other. More commonly, development stimulus instruments can be changed into development + design stimulus instruments by adding 'design strings' to the basic development stimulus instruments (i.e. on a quid pro quo basis). For example, a land developer may undertake site preparation (i.e. land consolidation and land remediation), infrastructure provision and then subdivide the land into serviced sites. Assuming that there is (sufficient) demand for the serviced sites (and thus also a degree of competition between potential parcel developers), then, as a component of the price of access to those serviced sites/land parcels, the land developer may also require the parcel developers to achieve certain threshold levels of design quality. The justification for this on the part of the land developer would be twofold. First, it gives parcel developers confidence that the value of their development will not be wiped out by poorer quality development on adjacent or nearby parcels (i.e. it ensures community value). Second, the land developer can benefit from any uplift in the value of the remaining land parcels due to the quality of the initial development (i.e. the quality of the initial development enhances the site's desirability and thus enhances its value).

Capacity-building instruments

Market-shaping, market regulation and market stimulus instruments are only as good as the people involved. This highlights the importance of personal attributes such as: the enthusiasm and the ability of key actors to create ideas and visions that inspire others; the ability to promote, sell, manipulate, persuade and seduce others; the determination to make tough choices; and the willingness to take risks.

Appearing in many forms and difficult to define precisely, capacity-building actions include building 'trust' – often encompassed by the term 'social capital' – among the range of development actors. Such actions seek to enhance the abilities and capacity (e.g. skills, knowledge, networks, rules of operation, working practices etc) of actors and institutions in various ways. They can be viewed as a form of investment in the development of human, social and institutional capital that carries the expectation of future returns, which, as with all investment decisions, is uncertain, intangible and immeasurable (Elmore 1987: 178). In developing effective capacity building measures, public agencies often demonstrate insight into market and governance processes.

Capacity building enables development actors to operate more effectively within their opportunity space, while influencing the opportunity space of other development actors to their own advantage. While capacity-building actions could be regarded simply as further forms of market-shaping or market-stimulating instruments, they are better seen as means of facilitating the operation of these other policy instruments. The effect of future regulation and stimulus actions, for example, may depend on an institutional and human capacity that does not presently exist – hence, appropriate capacity-building is a condition of future success (Elmore 1987: 178).

As Table 1.3 shows, we can identify four important forms of capacity building that may help deliver higher quality development and better places. These are: developing human capital; enhancing institutional and organisational networks and capacity; reframing cultural mindsets/cultural change; and enlarging the stock of ideas and concepts. We will now deal with each in turn.

Developing human capital

The first type of capacity-building action involves developing the skills and abilities of key actors. Policy actions may include the provision of education and training programmes, continuing professional development (CPD) events, expert seminars, job swaps (e.g. between public and private sectors) and exposure to good or innovative practice and aspirational examples. The interactive nature of such techniques may be directed at facilitating the communication of tacit knowledge – that is, wisdom, insight and intuition – through networking. Developing skills-type actions may result in the ability to handle and process information better. Skill development includes not just enhanced intrinsic capability but also the ability to identify opportunities, execute complex tasks more quickly (i.e. within a particular window-of-opportunity) to persuade, cajole, seduce, manipulate and entice and to generate new, original or novel ideas.

Leadership is often instrumental in delivering design quality. To provide design leadership, many local authorities, public bodies and some private companies have sought to build capacity by employing design champions. As Chapter 10, explains, these design champions are charged with changing the thinking of both public (politicians, planners etc) and private sector (developers, designers etc) actors with regard to design.

Enhancing institutional and organisational networks and capacity

A second type of capacity-building action involves building or extending formal and informal networks. The key idea is that actor behaviour is often influenced by the behaviour of others. Some models of interacting actors assume that the links between actors are random – that is, each actor has an equal probability of being 'connected' to any other actor. People, however, spontaneously form social and business networks, and are embedded in various ways within social webs and clusters. The networks created are inevitably selective and partial (i.e. actors tend to link to other like-minded actors), such that any assumption of randomness cannot be sustained. Referring to this as 'embeddedness', Granovetter (1985: 490) explains how the concept highlights...

> ... the role of concrete personal relations and structures (or "networks") of such relations in generating trust and discouraging malfeasance. The widespread preference for transacting with individuals of known reputation implies that few are actually content to rely on either generalised morality or institutional arrangements to guard against trouble.

Capacity-building policy actions may seek to foster the development and sustainability of actor-networks and, thereby, to develop social capital – that is, '... the productive resources mobilised by interpersonal networks of co-operation and coordination for mutual benefit.' (Amin 2003: 124). A distinction is commonly made between 'bonding' and 'bridging' forms of social capital. As Putnam (2000: 22–23) explains, bonding capital exists in networks that are, by choice or necessity, inward-looking and tends to reinforce exclusive identities and homogeneous groups. By contrast, bridging capital exists in networks that are outward-looking and encompasses people across diverse social cleavages.

Reframing cultural mindsets/cultural change

Cultural mindsets – 'frames', perspectives or 'world views' – establish how 'things' are perceived, interpreted and appraised. Taking many different forms, cultural mindsets emerge, develop and are sustained in different ways. Reframing cultural mindsets and, more generally, generating new ideas is an important third type of capacity-building action.

Relevant cultural mindsets include those of the established professions (i.e. 'professional cultures'), those developed and sustained within particular firms and organisations (i.e. 'house views') and those developed and held by key individuals. A product of education, expertise and socialisation, professional cultures provide a predisposition to frame situations and problems in particular ways: '... to analyse them according to specific categories, to synthesise them into specific structures, and to represent them in specific verbal, graphic, or numerical ways.' (Fischler 1995: 21). As Harvey (1989: 2) has observed, each profession has a cultural worldview – viewing the same street scene, architects may appreciate architectural design, visual rhythms and historical references, while real estate developers see buildings in terms of rents per square foot, planning or zoning regulations, setbacks and height limitations. Similarly, firms and other organisations develop 'house views' relating to how they see the world, how they make that world and, in essence, how they interact with it.

An important means of editing and processing information, cultural mindsets may inhibit the seeing of the world in a more holistic, or even simply a different, fashion. New information or ideas, for example, may not be fully evaluated or appreciated fully. Cultural mindsets may also establish an often questioned 'conventional wisdom', which, *inter alia*, inhibits the development and exploitation of new ideas. New ideas will ultimately be tested in the marketplace, but because of entrenched culture mindsets, they may never get to the market to be tested. Such cultural mindsets affect the reception given to proposals for new production and development types. 'Loft living' was an emergent market in the 1980s and early 1990s, but the prevailing conventional wisdom was that people did not want to live in former industrial units with bare brickwork and exposed wooden floorboards and pipework.

Because policy delivery is reliant on negotiating with and persuading third parties, reframing cultural mindsets becomes an essential component of effective policy delivery. Landry (2000: 52), for example, discusses 'mindshifts' – the process of changing mindsets:

> A mindshift is the process whereby the way one thinks of one's position, function and core ideas is dramatically re-assessed and changed. At its best it is based on the capacity to be open-minded enough to allow this change to occur.

Landry (2000: 12) describes how 'linearity' and 'box-like thinking' characterised his discussions with property developers, planners and accountants. Challenging – and perhaps altering – established or conventional cultural perspectives involves creativity and encouraging actors to think outside the box. By viewing the same 'objective' criteria differently, those outside the mainstream often bring different cultural perspectives to bear, challenging how the underlying 'reality' is perceived, interpreted and appraised. This may be a crucial factor in stimulating development. Studies of institutional investment in regeneration areas (Adair *et al.* 1998; 1999; 2003; Guy *et al.* 2002a), for example, show how attitudes to risk, to the period of time over which return is expected and to design affect investment decisions. It is also notable how some highly successful investment and development firms, such as Urban Splash in Manchester, UK, have succeeded by bringing a different house view to bear (see Guy *et al.* 2002a).

Enlarging the stock of ideas and concepts

A further mode of capacity building involves enlarging the stock of ideas and concepts in circulation. Bringing successful design studies, design strategies and masterplans to the attention of the development actors might increase their awareness of and receptivity to those ideas and concepts, and in turn, encourage them to commission their own specialist design work. Charles Landry (2000: 165), for example, highlights how design thinking '… gives decision makers an ideas bank with which to work and out of which innovations can emerge.' This recognises the power of the artefacts of design-thinking (i.e. drawings and concepts diagrams etc), and of design language to frame and embody ideas in ways that encourage various city audiences to see (and understand) their city in new, perhaps better and more revealing ways.

Developers' decision environments

So how do urban design actions affect developers' and investors' perceptions of the factors that make them more (or less) likely to develop or invest and more (or less) likely to provide higher quality development? A start can be made by identifying issues that are most salient in developers' decision-making and which may, in turn, be amenable and susceptible to influence by urban design policy instruments. Table 1.4 lists these important factors in all developers' decision environments. Actors will vary in their trade-offs between the factors – attitudes towards risk, for example, will vary, although considerations of risk feature in every developer's decision-making.

As well as the likely developer reaction to policy instruments, a related question is which is the best, most appropriate, or most effective instrument for the task. This highlights the importance of policy design. The appropriate instrument (or bundle of instruments), for example, is likely to be highly situational, dependent on time and place and the particular characteristics of the actors involved. This suggests the need for targeted policy approaches, but also the possibility of highly idiosyncratic reactions to policy instruments. The heterogeneity of real estate as a market commodity should not be underestimated – every development site is different and so is every developer – though, equally, we might seek to simplify the task by theorising and identifying common patterns of behaviours and by grouping developers with similar behaviours. While developers have differing operating characteristics – or, more formally, differing business strategies with respect to rates of return, project scale, areas of operation, attitudes to risk, attitudes to design etc – they can still be grouped in terms of their behaviour

Table 1.4   Key factors in developers' decision making.

Developer's concern	Impact
Information	Does the policy instrument make more information available to the actor for decision-making?
Coordination	Does the policy instrument enable the actor to benefit from joining up his/her actions with those of other actors?
Reward	Does the policy instrument increase the magnitude of the actor's reward?
Risk	Does the policy instrument reduce the actor's risk?
Time	Does the policy instrument increase the probability of the actor undertaking the action sooner (or later)?
Timing	Does the policy instrument give the actor greater control over the timing of a particular action?
Decision-making capacity	Does the policy instrument enhance the actor's decision-making capacity (and hence the quality of decision made)?
Range of possible actions	Does the policy instrument expand (or reduce) the range of actions available to the actor?
Competitive advantage	Does the policy instrument give the actor an advantage over his/her competitors?
Skilled designer	Does the policy instrument make it more (or less) likely that a skilled designer will be employed?

Source: Authors' own analysis.

and operating strategies or, more specifically, in terms of how they respond to the particular public policy instruments that shape the decision environment.

Given that some developers seem to 'care' more about design than others, then, in terms of their attitudes and practices, we can hypothesise a spectrum from more design-aware 'place entrepreneurs' to less design-aware 'non-place entrepreneurs'. Place entrepreneurs might be seen as actively working within the grain of the local place, seeing design as a positive strategy of adding value, and basing their appraisals on a view of the area changing in the future. Such developers are typically local, relatively small-scale, and independent. Non-place entrepreneurs, by contrast, typically ignore, undervalue or actively work against the grain of the place. They are generally risk averse, and base their appraisal on what happened in the past and on the area not changing significantly in the future.

As outlined in the preface, the research inquiry at the heart of this book concerns the impact of urban design policy instruments on developers' – and thence on designers' – decision-making and, in particular, their impact on those factors – reward, risk, uncertainty, time etc – that would make them more likely, or less likely, to provide higher quality development and to contribute to producing better places. The overarching research question is: *How successful are particular public policy instruments in framing (and reframing) the relationship between designers and developers to the advantage of urban design (place) quality?* This leads on to four subsidiary research questions, namely:

(1) *What public policy instruments are available to facilitate better quality urban development and better places?*
(2) *How do particular policy instruments impact on the decision environments or opportunity space of developers and designers?*
(3) *In what other ways do particular policy instruments impact on design quality?*
(4) *Are some types of policy instruments more effective than others in facilitating higher quality development and better places?*

There are no simple and straightforward answers to these questions. As yet, the relevant research has neither been consolidated, nor discussed explicitly in terms of a policy instruments framework. This is both this book's general purpose and the specific purpose of the chapters that follow. These move through informally, and with much overlap, from a focus on market shaping to regulation, stimulus and capacity-building.

In Chapter 2, Nicholas Falk considers the importance of masterplanning and infrastructure provision to shaping the context for high quality design in new communities in Europe, while in Chapter 3, Matthew Carmona argues that design codes have significant potential to shape developers' behaviour, by reconciling their need for certainty and flexibility. In Chapter 4, Tony Hall provides a fascinating case study of Chelmsford to show how developer behaviour and attitudes towards urban design can be transformed through clear policy direction combined with firm regulation. In Chapter 5, Tim Love and Christina Crawford argue that intelligent parcelisation can be used to craft the character of successful new urban districts, and demonstrate how this has been achieved by looking at examples from Europe, North America and the Middle East. Chapter 6, by Nicholas J. Marantz & Eran Ben-Joseph, provides a more critical take on design regulation, with its historical account of how powerful real estate interests in the USA have managed over decades to capture successive regulatory initiatives and turn them to their own advantage. As this suggests, it is important not to regard the real estate industry as a passive recipient of policy instruments but to recognise instead the often close involvement of powerful interests in policy formulation.

Chapter 7 by Paul Syms and Andrew Clark moves the debate on to consider the use of stimulus instruments in encouraging good design in the redevelopment of brownfield sites. Drawing on several British examples, they offer a broad interpretation of design stimulus instruments, which they compare and contrast with development stimulus instruments. This is followed, in Chapter 8, by a critique of development competitions by

Steven Tolson, who draws out lessons from his own practical experience to highlight the circumstances under which such competitions may and may not lead to higher-quality design.

Chapter 9 by John Punter considers whether design review represents an effective means of raising design quality, emphasising the importance of early comment before designs and accompanying financial appraisals become too fixed.

Chapter 10 by David Adams and Sarah Payne explores how UK speculative housebuilders have responded to the design challenge of brownfield development, and draws an important distinction between the different approach of three types of company, who they term pioneers, pragmatists and sceptics. Chapter 11 by John Henneberry, Eckart Lange, Sarah Moore, Ed Morgan and Ning Zhao investigates whether a suitable physical-financial model can be developed to enable developers to assess more clearly the benefits of design investment. In Chapter 12, Steve Tiesdell draws on recent evidence from Edinburgh to consider how far the appointment of design champions can foster a place-making culture and capacity. In Chapter 13, Gary Hack and Lynne B Sagalyn provide an extensive cross-cutting review of how urban design can add value to development projects and how this value can be part captured for public benefit.

In the final chapter, we reflect on these various connections between urban design and real estate development and consider what they have to say about the comparative effectiveness of the four main types of policy instrument in helping to achieve higher quality development and better places.

Notes

1. This is the production function of public policy-making.
2. The reduction and conflation of urban design to or with project design is characteristic of an architectural or 'Big Architecture' approach to urban design (see Cuthbert 2010).
3. In their book, *Nudge*, Thaler & Sunstein (2008: 2) use the term 'choice architect', who '... *has the responsibility for organising the context in which people make decisions.'* They illustrate the principle by analogy with a building designer: '*As good architects know seemingly arbitrary decisions, such as where to locate bathrooms, will have subtle influences on how people who use the building interact. Every trip to the bathroom creates an opportunity to run into colleagues (for better or for worse). A good building is not merely attractive; it also "works".'* (2008: 2)
4. Urban design's legitimacy as a professional activity is different from, and thus separate from, architecture. This is challenged by some architects, who regard urban design as a component of architecture that should be practised only by architects. Nonetheless, much urban design and place-making is about governance and requires a distinctly different set of skills from those typically held by the architectural profession.
5. While economists often use regulation to denote all and any form of government intervention in market processes, public policy writers generally adopt a narrower and more specific understanding of regulation, as reflected in this chapter.

6. In the conclusion chapter (14) we consider the notion of 'designer failure'.
7. In some cases, policy actions or mechanisms will be used. Given that surgeons use instruments, while mechanics use tools, the former suggests greater precision and begs the question whether dependent on the precision and impact of their instruments urban design policymakers might be considered surgeons or mechanics.
8. Hood (2008: 129–130) justifies this as '...an application of the classic (and arguably still valid) Marshallian principles that analysis can only progress if we do not allow too many elements to vary at once.'
9. We return to these issues in the concluding chapter.
10. This also means that a policy instrument might be of a different type depending on whom it acts on. Labelling of food packages, for example, is a combination of 'regulation' and 'information'. For the manufacturer, it is a regulation – an obligation to include information on the packaging about the food; for the consumer, it is information about the food contained within the package (Vedung 2007: 37).

2

Masterplanning and Infrastructure in New Communities in Europe

Nicholas Falk

Introduction

Fifty years ago, Britain looked to the USA for inspiration, and European cities were outclassed by their American counterparts. Over the past few decades, the situation has been transformed. Rather than New York or Chicago, the Urban Task Force (1999) pointed to places such as Barcelona and Rotterdam as models for how British cities might achieve an 'urban renaissance'. Its report was one of the first to draw attention to the importance of three-dimensional masterplanning.

While the UK used the dividend from offshore oil to fund imports and to fuel private consumption, other European countries invested in infrastructure on a much larger scale, from urban trams to wind farms and local energy generation systems. At the same time, as comparative studies such as the *State of European Cities* (European Commission 2007: 41) report bring out, their cities have thrived: 'If all available variables are being given equal weight, then it becomes clear that many of Europe's high performers are located in Denmark, Sweden, Finland, the Netherlands and the western parts of Germany.' Outside southern England, English cities have not done as well as their surrounding regions.

Of course British cities have had to cope with a legacy of industrial decline, and a weak economy. But urban decay can be reversed. The amazing

Urban Design in the Real Estate Development Process, First Edition. Edited by Steve Tiesdell and David Adams.

renaissance of cities destroyed by war-time bombing, such as Hamburg and Rotterdam, show that the key to sustainable growth is joining up development and infrastructure. A short trip by Eurostar from London St Pancras to the Continent will confirm this important message:

- *Lille*, and the neighbouring towns of Roubaix and Tourcoign, used to be seen as one of the worst cities in France. Thanks to the efforts of its mayor, and his ability to persuade over 80 communes to back a surcharge on the payroll tax, this former industrial city positioned itself on the European high speed rail network, built a new driverless metro costing some £700 million and upgraded its trams, making the whole conurbation highly connected (see Cadell *et al.* (2008) for detailed case studies of Kop van Zuid in Rotterdam and Roubaix in the Lille conurbation). As is common in France, a *société mixte* – a 50:50 partnership between the city and the private sector – was set up to develop the mixed use scheme on the old barracks around the new railway station. Lille also pioneered the system of *Contrats de Ville*, between the city and central government, to provide the long-term security needed to restructure the city's economy, and enable disadvantaged areas like Roubaix to share the benefits. While opinion is divided on the quality of Rem Koolhaas's masterplan for Eurolille, there is little doubt that the city as a whole has undergone a renaissance.
- Carry on to the *Randstad*, where the cities of Rotterdam and Amsterdam are now on the European high speed network. The Randstad is similar in extent to Greater London, but more polycentric. As well as the new metro stations and high speed station in Rotterdam, there is a new light rail system connecting all the main conurbations. A short trip by metro, tram or river taxi to the former dockland peninsula of Kop van Zuid, with its masterplan by Norman Foster and others, shows that what was formerly a poor relation of Amsterdam has become a creative centre in its own right.
- One could also travel on to Karlsruhe (with its extensive tram train network) and visit *Freiburg* in Southern Germany – known as the solar capital of Europe as there are solar panels everywhere (see Figure 2.1). Though Freiburg benefits from publicly owned utilities, it was the city council that led the way by insisting on higher standards of renewable energy on all land owned by the council, with combined heat and power commonplace. Thousands of 'green collar' jobs have followed.

What is not so obvious to the visitor is how northern European cities have managed to overcome all the obstacles that plague doing anything similar in the UK, from articulate opposition to building anywhere (NIMBY and BANANA), to endless arguments over funding, even when routes have long been agreed. There is also little understanding of the interrelationships

Figure 2.1   Solar panels in Vauban help make Freiburg the solar capital of Germany. Reproduced by permission of Nicholas Falk.

between physical infrastructure, and the wider goals of improving our quality of life and tackling the issues that shape political change, or how individual cities have overcome the loss of traditional industries. There is no agreement on – even awareness of – the link between higher levels of connectivity and success in economic or social terms.

The focus of this book is on delivery. In this chapter, I review what might be learnt from Continental approaches to masterplans and infrastructure provision. I summarise some common challenges before drawing lessons from case studies of innovative urban extensions. Dutch experience, with new settlements in the Randstad, shows how masterplans and infrastructure provision can be joined up. Finally I draw out lessons for the UK. The findings are drawn from both study tours and published sources, starting with research for the Joseph Rowntree Foundation (Cadell *et al.* 2008). Our work on The *Cambridgeshire Quality Charter for Growth* (Cambridgeshire Horizons 2008) was inspired by study tours to both Amersfoort in the Netherlands and Freiburg in southern Germany. In a project with PRP and Design for Homes we visited and compared ten possible models for 'eco-towns' in Germany, the Netherlands, Sweden and the Republic of Ireland to establish what they had in common (see PRP *et al.* 2009). Some of the findings have been published by the Smith Institute and the Housing Forum (Falk 2009; Housing Forum 2009). Evidence for how the Dutch system works is also drawn from successive editions of *Built Environment*, and discussions with its editor, Sir Peter Hall[1] and Han Lorzing at the Netherlands Institute for Spatial Research, to whom I owe special thanks.

Differences between the UK and Europe

In *Sustainable Urban Neighbourhoods* (Rudlin & Falk 2009), David Rudlin and I explain how Britain and North America chose to pursue very different sets of values from the social-market countries of northern Europe in misguided attempts to contain the city, and draw firm boundaries between town and country. If you get the foundations right with a shared vision, quality growth will follow. Unfortunately masterplans have been taken over by architects who assume that if you can visualise everything, you have solved the main problems of development. Design guides or codes are then seen as ways of regulating how things are built. Yet inevitably circumstances change, and plans need to be flexible. So a masterplan should not be seen as a blueprint (after all a new community is not a machine), but as a trellis, which will help guide the community's growth.

British planning is rightly criticised as being over-concerned with the end state, and not with how to get there. As Carmona *et al.* (2010) have noted, masterplans are often criticised as overly rigid and inflexible, and for suggesting or proposing a greater degree of control than is actually desirable, necessary or possible. Garreau (1991: 453, from Brand 1994: 78), for example, defines masterplanning as

> … that attribute of a development in which so many rigid controls are put in place, to defeat every imaginable future problem, that any possibility of life, spontaneity, or flexible response to unanticipated events is eliminated.

Garreau is, however, referring to a particular type of masterplan – 'blueprint masterplans', which are associated with 'big architecture' projects. A less rigid form is the 'development framework'. The key difference is that while blueprint masterplans specify a single intended outcome, framework masterplans generally set out broad urban design and place-making aspirations and principles. They allow scope for interpretation and development within the framework's parameters – the final outcome is also typically multi-authored as in the Cambridgeshire Quality Charter and the Hulme Design Guide. What is needed is a menu from which good choices can be made, not a cookbook for each site.

Regulatory and indicative plans are not enough when the market is weak, and when the development may take several decades to complete. Advance infrastructure is needed with serviced plots so that smaller builders can

undertake development on the place-promoter's terms. Advance infrastructure incentivises developers to (a) take part and (b) take part now. In the UK,
there are often numerous masterplans produced for the same site and yet little
happens on the ground (over 70 masterplans have been produced for the Royal
Docks in London for example). Masterplanning is often an exercise in architecture on a grand scale, wasting resources rather than mobilising them.

In contrast, in the examples in continental Europe that we have examined,
there is a *single* masterplan *and* it gets implemented. The masterplan also
positively shapes the context within which developers act, while the incentive of infrastructure means that 'design strings' can be attached. In other
words, infrastructure *is* fundamental to place-shaping and to putting urbanist
principles into practice. The term infrastructure, incidentally, needs to
embrace not just the hard physical infrastructure of roads and utilities, but
also the soft or social infrastructure of schools, shops and meeting places
that can make or break new communities. Exemplary schemes such as in
Freiburg or Stockholm also benefit from their connectivity to high quality
infrastructure, such as municipal tram systems or district heating schemes.

Challenges for sustainable development

Despite the common belief that Britain is uniquely built-up and vulnerable
to all the problems of traffic congestion, a simple air flight or, better still,
satellite view of Europe by night reveals that the London agglomeration is
dwarfed by the extent of the conurbations across the Channel. Though
London likes to think of itself as a 'world city' competing only with places
such as New York and Tokyo, in practice the whole of the greater South-East
is a 'polycentric conurbation' that has to compete for both key workers and
investment with a number of other agglomerations in terms of the quality
of life it offers its residents. The closest rivals are the Randstad and the Paris
region, with which Britain shares a close history, and also the Rhine Ruhr
area. In southern Europe there is also a major agglomeration in northern
Italy centred on Milan, with links being improved both along the
Mediterranean and also through to Switzerland.

It is these agglomerations that attract what, in his novel the *Bonfire of the
Vanities*, Tom Wolfe described as the 'masters of the universe'. It is where
national politicians and media figures tend to congregate, and consequently
where some of the most important strategic decisions are taken – whether
to go to war, build a rapid transit line, or put the resources into stadia or galleries instead. Over the course of a generation, neighbourhoods go up and
down in popularity, as the gentrification of places like London's Islington
illustrate. But in general in the UK, those with choice and families leave the
inner city areas for the leafy suburbs. The major challenge is consequently

how to create new residential areas that can compete with the appeals of living in established areas close to the country and a good school for the children.

The forces of polarisation

Residential populations are somewhat arbitrary. What matters is the functional urban area or travel-to-work area which is determined by commuting times (and in places that are highly rated, such as Amsterdam and Zurich, on average this is half an hour each way). Where travel times are cut, and services improved, there is a tendency for those who can afford to do so to live even further away. Hence different kinds of urban life are evolving, which overlap but do not connect, and which have very different carbon footprints. Not only are people far from equal, but they practise quite different lifestyles, as the multi-coloured maps produced by commercial research organisations such as Experian Mosaic clearly reveal. What looks like a constellation or galaxies of stars turn out to be made up of different kinds of places, with a great deal of 'dark matter' in between.

Thus, highly accessible areas surrounding both London St Pancras and Brussels Midi International stations attract populations from all over the world. A combination of lack of language and other skills can result in local residents lacking paid work and facing the highest competition for the jobs that can be done with least qualifications, such as working in bars serving coffee. Customers too will have come from all over the world, and may be making the most of the new infrastructure. Such places attract the 'rising stars', but also those on their way down. The value they add to the stream of human capital flowing through them is the product of social infrastructure (such as educational and health institutions) and a city's capacity to help people make good connections.

Need for holistic masterplans

Physical masterplans usually have little to do with how well people get on with each other, or with the quality of area management and the maintenance of the public realm. However, they should be a mechanism for coordinating public services, and securing co-investment, not just a means of regulating private developers. In a global economy, and one where competitive advantage comes from the ability to deploy knowledge to good effect, basic levels of infrastructure and connectivity – energy, water and waste removal – are no longer enough. Companies choose to locate where they can be in easiest range of key customers and skilled labour as the growing commercial areas around Heathrow and Amsterdam Schipol airports illustrate.

In turn clusters of activity create their own dynamics, through spin-offs and the products of the collaboration that comes from 'agglomeration economies', whether these be a good choice of restaurants or readily accessible broadband communications, both of which enrich social capital. The easy access offered through better infrastructure can work both ways. Hence investments in major new infrastructure projects need to be combined with social measures if they are to pay off in the full sense. Planning for development and for infrastructure need to go hand in hand.

The relationship between infrastructure and urbanity is complex and crucial. At its roots are the streets themselves. A great city will inevitably have a few great streets – its boulevards and arcades. But it will also have many more less obviously 'special places' where people can express themselves. The dynamics of property development mean that the very places that are special today may become commonplace tomorrow, as the pioneers move on. It is this process of discovery, colonisation and coproduction or gentrification, which enables great cities to reinvent themselves again and again as writers like Jane Jacobs have vividly pointed out in, for example, *The Economy of Cities*.

Because infrastructure tends be long-lived, the networks of sewers and water pipes, metro lines and bus routes, and gas and electric distribution systems form a 'nervous system' that enables the conurbation as a whole to function and deal with huge numbers of people coming and going all the time. This 'spaghetti of tubes' lies at the root of the 'wealth of nations'. The number and quality of nodes, just as in a brain, support urban intelligence, as evidenced by London having many times the nodes of an equivalent-sized area in Luton. The maintenance and upgrading of these nodes should be central to efforts to improve our quality of life, and deal with the long-term effects of climate change and resource depletion, as they are in mainland Europe. Indeed, they were what gave rise to the formation of local authorities in the first place. In Britain, however, unlike the rest of Europe, local authorities have ended up with planning responsibilities, but without the means of delivering either the basic infrastructure or conditions required to attract quality investment.

The common challenges that these agglomerations have to address include congestion and stress caused by people trying to reach other places at the same time, and the consequent impact on carbon emissions and air pollution. Competition for limited space causes prices to rise, particularly if there is no agreed way of improving supply. House price inflation widens inequalities, which in turn weakens the sense of community, and may contribute to social malaise (Wilkinson & Pickett 2010). The solutions include not just urban renewal and regeneration (where in the 1970s British cities were making some major advances), but also urban extensions and new settlements (where, since the era of the New Towns, the UK has lagged far behind Continental practice).

The infrastructure deficit

Changing infrastructure is now much more difficult than a century ago. When Hampstead Garden Suburb was originally developed, the houses required little more than connections to municipal gas and water systems. Development was viable because it was grafted on to the extension of the Northern Underground Line out to Golders Green. An entrepreneurial American raised the finance to build a major new railway line from the expected proceeds from selling season tickets, and a multitude of small builders created small blocks of houses within an overall masterplan. There was little choice for those getting to work from the new suburbs other than using the Tube to reach the City – a location next to Hampstead Heath was thus inherently desirable as a place to live. As a result of a ready supply of infrastructure, the development of areas such as Metroland on the north-west of London helped produce the greatest period of housebuilding that Britain has enjoyed, with some four million homes built largely in the 1930s.

The situation today is very different. Most people living outside the centre of London no longer use public transport to get to work. Many will drive out of London altogether, making use of the M25 for part of their journey, and will also drive to the shops or to take their children to school. Their lives are closer to what the American writer Joel Garreau (1991) calls 'Edge City'. The town centres that formed the hubs of suburban life – and helped make London what the Danish writer Rasmussen (1937) called the 'Unique City' – which, for the most part now look run down, worn out and very ordinary. There is no longer the cheap land available on which to build, with a green belt acting as a further barrier to getting on the housing ladder.

Today's residents not only want high accessibility by car, they also demand a much more sophisticated energy system, and use much more energy to heat and run their homes. Instead of simple monopolies to supply the energy, there is now competition though regulated private companies. Given the much greater uncertainties over both demand and supply, and a very much more complex planning system, it is not surprising that housebuilding levels have dropped far below the levels achieved in the inter-war period on the back of extensions to the capital's public transport system. Less obvious (apart from holes in the capital's main streets) is the strain being placed on all the utilities, due to low levels of investment in modernising the infrastructure. Privatisation may have opened up sources of capital for replacing corroded Victorian water pipes, but it has not solved the problems of replacing worn-out transport, waste and energy systems.

Even projects as seemingly vital as Thameslink, and its east–west equivalent Crossrail, have taken decades in planning, and, when built, will still have nothing like the capacity of the RER system in Paris, or the complex of different routes and transport modes that connect the different parts of the Randstad. Meanwhile the rest of the system suffers from continual breakdowns and closures for planned maintenance, and is relatively expensive to use. Where once British cities were the envy of the world for their complex infrastructure, such as the ubiquitous arches that carried the railways into the centre, much of the capital now looks like a poor relation that has seen better times.

Joined-up planning

The connections between infrastructure, masterplanning and quality places are thus profound. A city sustains itself by offering a high quality of cultural life, from restaurants to galleries, and by attracting a significant part of its working (and student) population to its centres in the evening as well as the day. Such a social life is crucial to persuading those with most talent to stay or relocate. But it needs to be combined with the ability to get quickly and safely to residential areas, including the kind of suburban areas where many families prefer to live. The prices paid for private housing (and the resultant land values) reflect the combination of inherent amenity (such as views of water or open space) and the social and physical capital that a location has accumulated over many decades. For a city to grow sustainably, house prices have to reflect the replacement costs of the infrastructure while being affordable to those entering the housing market for the first time.

   Values can be created through inspired planning, as isolated examples like Milton Keynes – with its adage 'start with a park' – illustrate. Milton Keynes, however, is inherently car-based. The original masterplan was largely disregarded, but this did not matter because the Development Corporation owned the land and could sell off serviced plots to volume house-builders. Public transport is poor because a high quality public transport system depends on having a dense enough population living close by. Sheffield's tram system has suffered from low usage because it was built on the cheap along old railway lines through areas with low population densities. Similarly a high quality energy system, such as combined heat and power or district heating, depends on building not only at relatively high densities (over 50 to the hectare), but relatively rapidly in order to amortise the initial investment. It also requires an assured heat load. Where areas have been redeveloped in British cities at high densities over the past couple of decades, they have usually been former industrial areas, such as London Docklands, in areas cut off from good public transport and amenities. Rather than being joined up at a neighbourhood or sub-regional level, planning, development and infrastructure have been kept in isolated silos, and quality has suffered as a consequence.

European success stories

Though all European agglomerations complain of similar problems of congestion and air pollution, their new urban areas are generally built to much higher standards of quality, with a more balanced population as a result, and they also use less energy. What holds British cities back is that they are trying to compete as places to live and work using ideas, technologies and management systems that are increasingly out of date and wasteful, and without the long-term control that comes from owning the land. They also have the legacy of a worn-out Victorian infrastructure to contend with, which escaped the wholesale destruction suffered by many Dutch and German cities. Whereas the prevailing European model has been the compact city and spatial planning, the British model has been one of urban sprawl, based on leaving the crucial decisions to the market.

Comparative political studies have highlighted the contrast between the Anglo-American liberal model and the northern European social-market or 'Rhenish' model. This is not just about appointing elected mayors or raising funds locally (though both can help), because even quite centralised public finance systems can be made to work, as in the Netherlands. Rather it boils down to a concern for public or communal capital, and a sense of civic pride.[2] Places with apparently similar levels of wealth, expressed as GVA per capita or economic activity levels, such as Freiburg and Cambridge, offer quite different qualities of life. The difference or 'infra-structure deficit' is readily experienced by travelling around a city as a first-time visitor.

Infrastructure contrasts

The deficit can be seen by comparing British cities that have sought to improve their situation with their continental equivalents. Thus Leeds and Bradford, whose development was largely based on the woollen textile trade, can properly be compared with Lille and Roubaix in north-west France. Both conurbations have suffered from the snobbery against provincial cities and from the need to find new economic roles to support large populations. Both were progressive cities – Leeds, for example, boasted for many years of its position on the motorway network and as the first city to complete its ring-road. Leeds is also one of the few British cities that find it relatively easy to attract institutional investment in property. It was committed to a vision of going up a league, but also of narrowing the differences between different areas.

Lille not only benefited from attracting a station on the high speed rail network, but went further and built a high quality metro and tram system to connect its centre with its suburbs. This was because Lille was better able to put the funding together, in part because it happened to have a mayor who became Prime Minister of France, but also because it could raise a proportion of the funds locally. In Leeds the professional classes have to leave home very early to avoid the long crawl into the centre and to beat the rush to find a parking spot. Though, just as in London, there are suburban railway lines, they suffer from neglected stations on routes that stretch too far out to run frequent services. Councils depend largely on putting together successful bids to government, as all the business income goes to government, and, unlike in France, there are no local sales or payroll taxes. This is a game where private developers hold all the cards.

Though Leeds Station has been modernised, and does boast some electrified suburban lines, the centre itself has neither a metro nor a tram system, and much is dominated by cars. This is not for lack of planning: some £50 million was spent on planning the Leeds Supertram, which, as in Lille, would have linked up a much poorer area at Seacroft (a large peripheral council estate) with the city centre. The land had been acquired and everything designed, when the Labour Government, which had encouraged the City to be ambitious, decided that trams were not the way forward. Instead of going for systems that could divert wealthier people from their cars, the view was taken that public transport was basically for the poor and that buses offered a more cost-effective solution. In turn the plans that had been made for developing land alongside the tram were invalidated. As those running the city had little faith in public transport (nor much interest in learning from Europe), perhaps its demise was inevitable.

It is not just Lille that has made a breakthrough from its previous subservience to Paris, but so have all the French provincial cities. As a result their economies have grown much faster than that of the capital, in marked contrast to the UK. The results are visible and are symbolised by the advanced tram systems that have given new life to older cities such as Bordeaux, or that form the spine of the growing technological centre of Montpellier (see Box 2.1). In turn, rebuilding city infrastructure has provided good business for French (and other European companies). The UK now has to depend on foreign locomotive and rolling stock manufacturers, and once-enterprising British companies, such as the one that built the Strasbourg tram, have been bankrupted by lack of sustained orders.

Civic leadership and local financing mechanisms have combined to enable cities that once seemed to have no future to go up a league. Where there has been huge public investment in infrastructure, such as the high speed train or nuclear power stations in France, there also seems to be a culture that takes pride in modern engineering rather than in money making. Marketing campaigns are used to express the benefits of nuclear power, such as the significant contribution to jobs, and affordable, if not cheap, energy.

Box 2.1 Montpellier reborn

Like Cambridge, Montpellier is an ancient university town. It is also the fastest-growing provincial town in France. Unlike Cambridge, however, in 2000 it opened its first 15 km tramway after three years of construction, and two more lines have been built since. The decision to build a tram was taken in 1995 because there was no space for new bus lines, while bus lanes were often parked on. A tram also creates a sense of *joie de vivre*. The idea of the tram-way is to double the modal share of public transport from 17 per cent. There are 75,000 people living within 5 minutes of its 28 stops, and the tram also serves the hospital, university, exhibition centre and railway station, which all act as traffic generators, and this ensures that major attractions are linked.

   The project's success is attributed to the city's mayor, George Frêche, who is also chair of the local transport undertaking. He managed to change atti-tudes to the tram. He also led the conversion of the old vineyards and barracks into business parks through a vision that made the most of the city's location in the sunny south. The university has also been relocated to the city's north with a tram stop in front of the main entrance. The 41 communes that make up the district have a population of 228,000, and Montpellier has grown from being the 25th to the 8th city in France in 20 years, thanks to its position as a centre for high-tech businesses. The total cost was 2288 million French francs (approximately £700 million), of which grants accounted for just over half (the district raised FrF650 million, with the state government providing 28 per cent of the total. The rest came in the form of loans from a consortium of nine banks. The operating franchisee was also the project manager. Many other provincial cities in France, such as Bordeaux, have also invested in tramways, inspired in part by Montpellier's example.

Promotion has gone beyond advertising and PR to include tours of nuclear plants taken up by six million people. Generous compensation has been used to overcome opposition. Public–private partnerships through *sociétés mixte* led by local authorities help dispel some of the ideological opposition that plagues major projects in the UK. Specialised banks such as the Banque de Caisses and the Bank Nederlandse Gemeenten provide municipalities with low-cost long-term loans for infrastructure so that they do not depend on bidding to government.

   Because most infrastructure lies beneath the surface, it is inherently easier and less expensive to install new forms in new developments around the edges of a city than to redevelop older areas, provided they can piggy-back off existing infrastructure. Location rather than density shapes the economics of development. This gives rapidly growing cities an advantage, particularly if they can acquire the land at its existing agricultural value, as the New Towns were able to do. As a generalisation, based on cost calculations for the growth

of Cambridgeshire, the cost of building a new home divides three ways more
or less equally between land, infrastructure and the house itself.

Whereas continental cities see their role as providing serviced sites for
development, housebuilders in the UK compete for sites, and have to fund
the infrastructure through Section 106 agreements. As a result they bid up
land prices, and build smaller and worse-equipped homes than on the continent. They naturally resist adding to the building costs by making new
homes carbon-free, pointing out that customers will not value the improvements. Even before the fall-out from the 'credit crunch', first-time buyers
were no longer entering the market. Once higher deposits were required, the
whole house of cards that is the British home-building industry came tum-
bling down. In turn, the masterplans and their complex and expensive
Section 106 agreements rapidly became redundant.

Comparisons between similar developments in Hammarby-Sjostad in
Stockholm and Greenwich Peninsula in London (which was masterplanned
by Ralph Erskine, an Englishman who lived and worked in Sweden) showed
that the Swedes are building at some five times the rate, and this seems to
apply more widely (see Falk 2008). As a result, though there is generally
higher investment in advanced infrastructure up front, this is amortised far
faster, and the profit rates can be reduced because the risks are much less
(see Cadell *et al.* 2008). The failure to build effective long-term partnerships
between the public and private sectors could be blamed on an adversarial
and legalistic culture, and on a professional middle class that thrives on
disputes, with much greater status and rewards for accountants and lawyers
than for engineers or planners. It also stems from relying on large private
developers to take the initiative, and overcome all the obstacles, rather than
having the confidence to sell plots of land off to a multiplicity of housebuilders within clear planning frameworks but flexible development briefs.

The best examples of masterplanning for sustainable development can
be seen in the influential urban extensions of Rieselfeld and Vauban in
Freiburg (see Box 2.2). The circumstances in this historic university town
are surprisingly similar to those in Cambridge, with the difference being
that the centre of Freiburg had to be completely rebuilt after Allied bombing.
By providing quality public transport from the start, and making it more
expensive and difficult to park a private car, Freiburg has succeeded in
shifting people away from their car towards public transport and cycling.
Indeed for Germany as a whole, while car ownership levels are higher than
in the UK, car usage is less, and people seem to take pleasure in well-run
public systems that support communal life.

Though what has happened in Freiburg is in many ways exceptional, and
owes much to the leadership of both the city's director of development,
Wulf Daseking, and its Green Party mayor, similar schemes can be seen
in many other cities. Though the general pattern is one of municipal

Box 2.2 Freiburg reinvented

The historic German city of Freiburg has gone for several planned extensions to cope with demands for more space. There are some 215,000 inhabitants, and the population is youthful and growing fast. The two settlement extensions of Rieselfeld and Vauban of 12,000 and 5000 residents respectively, have won many awards, and tackle some basic issues that apply equally to British cities, such as attracting families to live at high enough densities so that they do not depend on the private car, and can secure the benefits of combined heat and power.

The apartments have been made attractive through a number of features. First, they are set in a natural landscape, which creates the sense of living in the country. Access to allotments is easy. Each block looks different and this is encouraged by the high proportion being developed by cooperatives, in which the occupiers invest 'sweat equity'. In Vauban, inspired perhaps by the 'whacky' conversions of the old barracks, the residents take great pride in the semi-communal gardens.

The pattern of splitting blocks into maisonettes with separate entrances and large balconies overcomes many of the disadvantages of flat living. But it is probably the appeal of children growing up with ideal play conditions that attracts so many young parents to these new developments (though possibly storing up problems for later when they become teenagers). While the blocks tend to be similar in height and footprint, each block looks individual because of the rich variety of materials and colours used. In Vauban, the policy of keeping cars in peripheral car parks also helps to make the development quieter and safer. The use of crossroads without priority helps to keep traffic speeds down without any need of humps.

The developments are controlled through relatively simple B-Plans that specify all the basic rules, such as plot ratios and provision for public space. The sites are then sold off to a profusion of relatively small builders, often working through cooperative groups, which helps cut costs as well as secure pre-sales, thus reducing the development risks.

leadership, as in Kronsberg in Hannover, there are also examples of public–private partnership, such as the new settlement of Kirchsteigfeld in the suburbs of Potsdam to the East of Berlin. What they have in common is the greater availability of local finance, which in turn enables a much wider range of builders and tenures. Cooperative housing is much more commonplace, which again helps speed up the process of building a new community, as it takes away many of the risks. Competitions are used to appoint developers on the basis of quality rather than price. Instead, the price of land is determined as a proportion of the expected sales value at around 25–30 per cent, a principle which seems to apply in a number of northern European countries.

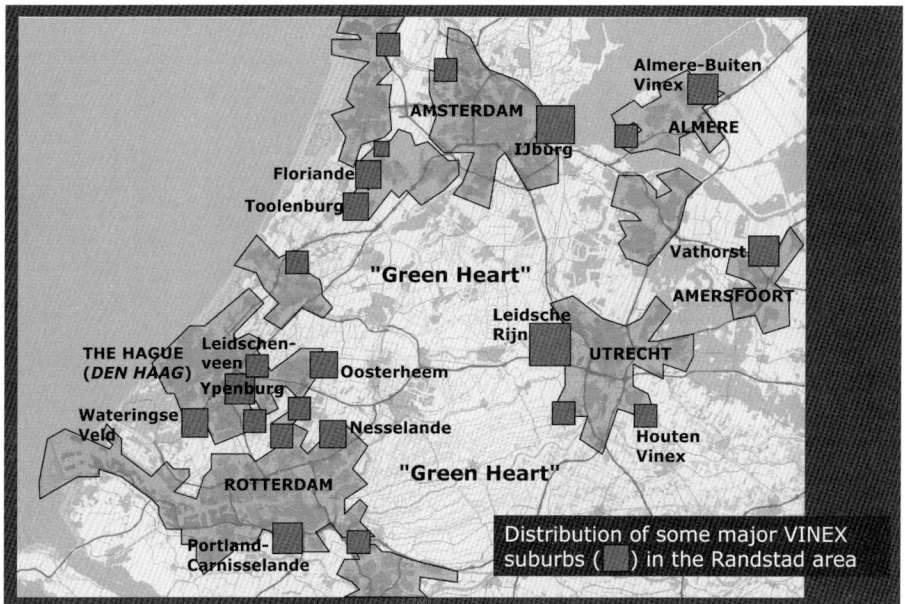

Figure 2.2   The VINEX programme involves extensions to major towns and cities in the Randstad. Reproduced by permission of Han Lorzing.

Joined-up planning in the Randstad

The clearest, and in many ways most replicable, model for combining planning, development and infrastructure comes from the Netherlands, and the way the different towns and cities of the Randstad have worked together for the common good over many decades. The Randstad or 'rim city' is a ring of 15 towns and cities around a 'Green Heart' (see Figure 2.2) that has been at the heart of much of European thinking, from contracts between the government and the cities, to the Spatial Development Perspective, and also the idea of mixed or balanced neighbourhoods. The original masterplan for the Randstad, which dates back to 1956/8, was to develop along the main traffic arteries, with compensating green wedges and buffer zones. High quality public transport connects the cities to the High Speed European Network and reinforces suburban transit systems with a new light rail route. Possibly because much of the land itself was created from the sea, the Dutch have a long tradition of municipal enterprise and leadership – the so-called 'polder mentality'. Some 80 per cent of building land was supplied by the municipalities who had acquired and serviced it. It is this factor, rather than the profusion of plans, that Barry Needham (1989) contends is at the heart of what makes the Netherlands feel so orderly and well-planned.

The Netherlands has been leading the way for a number of decades. As far back as the 1970s, as Andreas Faludi (1989) points out, there was a programme for building 'growth centres' of 6000 dwellings each. Between 1979 and 1984 Structure Schemes were drawn up for all aspects of infrastructure, from traffic and transport and electricity supply through to outdoor recreation and waterways. Planning, however, was not a political hot potato, as in the UK, but rather part of a way of life that set out to use national resources in ways that promote a better quality of life for the ordinary citizen. Architecture centres in all the main Dutch cities are part of a complex set of processes aimed at enabling ordinary citizens to appreciate and get involved in the way their cities are developed. However, reliance is not placed on prescriptive physical plans or standards, but rather on a more fruitful dialogue between the different stakeholders.

With similar objectives to the UK's *Sustainable Communities Plan* (ODPM 2003), which set out to build 3 million new homes, VINEX – the fourth Dutch Ten Year Housing Programme (1996–2005) – deserves much more attention in the UK than it has yet received (see Lorzing 2006). House price inflation in the Netherlands has been restrained by continuously building new homes, much on land which has had to be won from the sea through super dikes or 'polders'. The housing stock has been increased by almost 8 per cent in ten years through the VINEX plan, which produced some 90 sustainable urban extensions – 23 in the Randstad alone. Over half the 455,000 new homes have been built in new suburbs on the edge of existing towns and cities. The secret lies in the way that different agencies work together. The sustainable urban extension of Vathorst in Amersfoort, near Utrecht, provides a good example of how the process works (see Box 2.3 and Figure 2.3).

As with the Sustainable Communities Plan and the English Growth Points, local authorities were invited to submit bids for inclusion in the VINEX programme. Though there has been criticism from Dutch architects, English visitors generally like the results, and indeed they have proved very popular. Though government assisted with seed capital to help in decontaminating land and providing access, the schemes have had to be self-funding. VINEX sought to create places that were relatively compact (over 30 dwellings/ha), well-connected by public transport to jobs and services, and with at least 30 per cent of the housing being affordable.

While the objectives behind the two national plans were similar, the process for implementation was very different. In VINEX, local authorities played the leading role in both commissioning masterplans and providing infrastructure. There is focus on 'branding' different neighbourhoods with distinct identities as Han Lorzing (2006) has shown. Walking and cycling are favoured, with home zones almost everywhere. Settlements are much greener than UK housing estates, with, for example, the retention

---

Box 2.3   Vathorst, Amersfoort – a sustainable urban extension

In 1998, the municipality and the government drew up an agreement on the size of the extension, the contribution they would make to reclaiming contaminated land and how the settlement would be connected to the two motorways it adjoined. Vathorst, consists of some 11,000 homes plus shopping facilities, business and community facilities, and is almost half completed. The Vathorst Development Company (OBV) was set up as a 50:50 joint venture between the local authority and a consortium of private landowners and developers. The private sector included those who had bought land in the area but also those whom the city wanted to be involved as a result of their track record.

The company drew up the masterplan and then installed the basic infrastructure before selling sites on to its partners. The borrowings are repaid out of the proceeds from land sales. Each shareholder/developer carries out the detailed architectural work for the area it has been allocated. The company then provides the services and infrastructure. When these are ready, the site is sold to the developer to construct within an agreed and binding programme.

Over the three-year period prior to building starting in 2001, a number of exercises took place to determine the shape of the project. Theme groups were set up to develop certain ideas, such as how people might live in the 21st century, which identified changes such as more people living and working from home.

The company formally commissioned the masterplan with the city's planner working alongside a notable Dutch urban designer. All the partners were involved in the process. Amersfoort consists of four separate districts in very different styles. For example, one contains a modern version of canal-side housing, with 60 per cent of the homes having views of water, while another is designed to feel like living in the country.

Eight different builders and some 50 different architects were involved with no architect designing more than 80 units to ensure choice and variety. The social element, which covers both subsidised renting and housing for sale, is allocated through the municipality, but provided through associations. The focus is very much on social sustainability. Ensuring a balance of housing at a neighbourhood level (originally 300 now 500 units to reflect four different price ranges plus social housing) helps create cohesive communities.

---

of water run-off on site in open canals and streams that add to the attractions of living in a new neighbourhood.

There are also important cultural differences, as the Netherlands is much less class-conscious and a more equal society than the UK. According to the OECD they have the happiest children and the UK some of the unhappiest; they also do better on many other measures of wellbeing and equality (Wilkinson & Pickett 2010). As in the other 'social market' countries of

Figure 2.3 New canals in Vathorst deal with water run-off and add to the attractions of living there. Reproduced by permission of Nicholas Falk.

northern Europe such as Sweden, people are less individualistic and more considerate, partly due to conscious efforts to secure integration and 'social etiquette'.[3] It is common to live in rented housing in cities, and indeed 30 per cent of the population are eligible to live in social housing, which gives housing associations a strong role. Thus, into the 1980s, home ownership in the largest Dutch cities accounted for a mere 20–30 per cent of homes, compared with 60–70 per cent in the post-1995 suburbs. There has also been a substantial devolution of powers and responsibilities to local authorities over the past four decades, and a tradition of using regional planning to link transport investment and development.

Conclusion: lessons for the UK

The most powerful objections to building more housing in the South-East and around some other conurbations are that the supporting infrastructure is over stretched, and that we cannot afford to fix it. The reforms of the planning system have also done little to overcome the doubts. As well as the perennial problem of congestion and stretched schools, climate change and declining reserves of gas and oil mean that we now face crises of even greater dimensions. Cities have to compete for investment in a global market, and offer a comparable quality of life. Rebuilding our power supplies could add 25–60 per cent to energy bills according to Ofgem (the official UK regulator of gas and electricity prices). A similar dilemma applies to transport.

Though drawn from cities with very different institutional structures and national cultures, the examples in this chapter have a number of ingredients in common. I call these the ABC of leadership, and the principles are universal.[4]

(1) They start with the *ambition* to create quality places, and do not simply react to unwanted developers' schemes. Their ambition is founded on a realistic assessment of what is possible, often forged through visits to comparable places. The process is led by intelligent local authorities, not driven by government targets.
(2) They act as *brokers* and pursue a balance of objectives and schemes. Hence they secure benefits for their existing communities, not just those wealthy enough to afford a new home or office. Planning for infrastructure and development go hand in hand, and new developments aim to change attitudes and behaviour.
(3) Finally, they go for *continuity*, with many of the same officers and councillors being involved over several decades. Regeneration takes a generation and cannot therefore be secured through a succession of consultants, however talented, or through continual reorganisation.

Through positive planning at the sub-regional level, for example in designating well-located growth points following sustainability appraisals, good government saves resources and reduces risks. By taking a long enough time span of some 20 years, projects benefit from the uplift in land values following the upgrading of infrastructure, and improvements to the public realm. By planning holistically (which means giving equal weight to economic, social and environmental considerations) projects not only change an area's image, but also attract new sources of wealth creation.

The long-term approach needed for 'green recovery' means getting away from the 'lottery' of bidding to national government, the 'silos' of departmental policies and the roundabout of ministers and council Leaders. It means working up schemes that are resilient enough to withstand shocks, for example by focusing on natural 'growth points' and avoiding the principle of 'worst first' through local authorities working in partnership with private developers. Almost coincidentally, 15–20 years is exactly the time horizon needed by long-term investors such as pension funds and insurance companies. It is also the time needed for children to reach maturity and for saplings to grow into trees.

Rather than trying to patch up a leaky vessel, we should use the financial crisis to innovate. We must use strategic planning as we did in war time to focus enough resources on a few fronts where we have a hope of winning, rather than spreading our limited capital and expertise too thinly to make any difference. Local authorities need to be freed up so that resources can be joined up at local level, and funds raised for long-term investment, for example through infrastructure bonds. Even if investment managers sometimes act like 'irrational herds', government should encourage some of the banks (particularly those that are in public control) to follow the Dutch or French models. Investors, such as pension funds, would benefit from rental growth extending beyond the usual business cycles, and from funding infrastructure without relying on government grants or suppliers.

This 'natural' way of building – 'balanced incremental development' – holds the key to securing 'smarter growth'. By investing in the right locations, starting where it is easiest, and then reinvesting the surplus, just as a good farmer or gardener would do, much stronger, more resilient and better quality growth can be achieved that will meet the demands of the 21st century, whatever they may be. It will create the diversity that leads to healthier places and people. It will also provide a model that could inspire people in other places because it can be readily replicated.

Notes

1. The contents of this excellent magazine can be sampled on www.rudi.net/bookshelf. The special edition *Towards Sustainable Suburbs* (Falk 2006) includes an excellent account of the highly successful Dutch VINEX housing programme by Han Lorzing (2006), whose research shows how to build new suburbs that can rival established places.
2. These are lessons that have emerged from a series of study tours followed up by Leadership Masterclasses in Cambridge, and expressed in the Quality Charter for Growth, which identified a series of features that successful places have in common, including collaboration between all the stakeholders.
3. More information on Dutch cities can be gained from the reports of TEN Group study tours (see www.urbaned.com), and also from the case studies in Cadell *et al.* (2009).
4. These lessons are drawn from masterclasses on developments in Amersfoort, Freiburg and Harlow organised for Cambridgeshire Horizons.

3

Design Coding: Mediating the Tyrannies of Practice[1]

Matthew Carmona

Introduction

In England until the mid 1990s, design quality was either given lip service to, or actively excluded from, the political agenda, resulting in open inter-professional conflict, substandard design outcomes, and the resort, in the public sector, to crude development standards as a substitute for design. In this chapter, it is argued that at the root of these problems were three tyrannies of practice that actively undermined positive engagement in design. More recently, driven by local and national growth agendas, public administrations have increasingly sought policy instruments to once again engage in the delivery of design quality, one of these being design coding.

   This chapter uses the example of design codes to explore the process-based tyrannies and the potential of such tools to overcome them. It is in four main parts. It starts by presenting three tyrannies through the literature, concluding, in the process, that the typical large-scale development project is hampered by its journey from inception to realisation taking place within a context of professional conflict and compromise. The second part discusses the role of design coding, exploring how site-specific coding differs from generic development standards. Drawing on an empirical research study, the third part explores the use and potential of design codes and their value in helping to mediate the tyrannies of practice. A final part draws out conclusions from the work.

Urban Design in the Real Estate Development Process, First Edition. Edited by Steve Tiesdell and David Adams.
© 2011 Blackwell Publishing Ltd. Published 2011 by Blackwell Publishing Ltd.

The three tyrannies

As discussed in the opening chapter, the built environment is a collective endeavour, influenced by a diversity of stakeholders, each with a role to play in shaping what we see and experience as the architecture, urban form, public space and infrastructure that constitute the urban environment. In her 'Powergram', McGlynn (1993) argues that developers have the real power to shape the built environment though their ability to fund development. The state has power over some aspects of design through its regulatory powers (particularly through the planning processes), while designers have wide-ranging responsibility but little real power. Instead, they gain their influence through their unique professional skill (to design) and via their professional/technical knowledge. The community has almost no power, or only indirectly through the right to complain to those with regulatory authority, whom (usually) they elect.

Taking these ideas further, Bentley (1999) postulates four potential relationships between the designer and the developer: *Heroic Form-Giver*, *Master-and-Servant*, *Market Signals* and *The Battlefield* (see Chapter 1). Bentley argues that the latter is the most common scenario and reflects the fact that different actors bring different professional expertise to the table, while the resulting development is shaped by how these actors negotiate with each other to achieve their objectives.

Individual development episodes are likely to adopt different relationships or even different combinations of the relationships, depending on the relative power positions of stakeholders in each case. Moreover, the field is much more complex with, as discussed above, many competing stakeholder influences determining the final form of the built environment; the battlefield is in fact multi-actor, multi-objective and multi-dimensional. Nevertheless, Bentley's metaphors, the idea of conflicting and varied power relationships, and the notion of multiple stakeholder aspirations, can each be understood in terms of the modes of praxis from which they emerge.

These can be considered in terms of three distinct traditions – creative, market-driven and regulatory – each with a major impact on the built environment as eventually experienced. At their worst, each can be characterised as a particular form of professional 'tyranny', with the potential to impact negatively on the design quality of development proposals. The word tyranny is favoured here because it epitomises a single-minded pursuit of narrow ends in a manner that undermines, or oppresses, the aspirations of others. Though actual practice is not typically situated at such extremes, there is value in exploring these positions which are extensively discussed in the literature and which, it is contended, to greater or lesser degrees underpin all practice.

The creative tyranny

The first tyranny results from the fetishing of design where the image, rather than the inherent value – economic, social or environmental – is of paramount concern, and where the freedom to pursue the creative process is valued above all else. Such agendas are most closely associated with the architectural profession, often under a guise of rejecting what is sometimes seen as a further tyranny, that of 'context'.

Perpetuated by the dominant model of architectural education, and by the continuing impact of Modernism (Walters 2007: 96), many designers see all forms of regulation as limiting their freedom for self expression: 'It is time to challenge the tawdry and compromised architecture. ... Instead we must seek a new sensibility ... one that refuses to bow to preservation, regulation and mediation.' (Mantownhuman 2008: 3). In this mode of praxis, the aspiration is for '... discovery, experimentation, innovation.'

Lang (2005: 384–385) questions the importance of creativity. For him, the design professions place great esteem on what they see as 'creative' designers, those individuals or companies able to challenge the status quo by producing schemes that depart from the norm in response to a perceived problem in the name of art, or simply to further their careers: 'Those observers who regard urban design as a fine art would argue for little or no outside interference into what an individual designer/artist does. The population simply has to live with the consequences in the name of Art.' Analysing 50 international urban design projects of the past 50 years, he argues that this 'art defence' has often been used to justify design decisions that have later proved detrimental to the enjoyment of the city. To him, this is simply antisocial – a conclusion also reached through a body of Joseph Rowntree Foundation-funded research in the UK which found that in focusing on the aesthetic qualities of public spaces, designers often ignored more fundamental factors about how those spaces would actually be used as social places (Worpole & Knox 2007: 13).

The market tyranny

The second tyranny reflects the argument that the market knows best, and what sells counts. In the UK, this argument has most frequently and most vociferously been made in relation to the speculative housing market, where housebuilders have long campaigned for a free hand to use their standard housing designs and layouts on the basis that they know their market (Carmona 2001: 105–109). Design quality here is ...

> ... perceived by developers as a complex mix of factors which include dominant economic aspects of supply and demand revolving around costs

and sales potential – buildability, standardisation, market assessment, customer feedback – within which the visual or spatial quality is a secondary set of values (Heriot-Watt University 2007: 2).

In this market, architects have often been cut out altogether from the development process, while because producers are primarily concerned with their profitability and have typically (pre-credit crunch) built in a speculative market where demand exceeds supply, they have been willing and able to produce the lowest quality development that will sell and gain the necessary permissions without too much delay. As Rowley (1998: 172) has argued, they build 'appropriate' rather than 'sustainable' quality.

Lang (2005: 381) asks 'Who leads?', concluding that in capitalist countries, private corporations are the drivers of urban development; while Wellings' (2006) instructive analysis of the British housebuilding industry reveals that within these corporations it has been personal ambition, stock market position and market share that has driven their agendas. Thus issues such as design quality or sustainability are simply part of the context that needs to be negotiated: (1) when it is in the interest of the corporation to do so, for example if it returns higher profits (Carmona *et al.* 2001); (2) when relevant permissions (in the UK critically planning permission, highways adoption and building regulations) are dependent on it (Heriot-Watt University 2007: 3); or (3) when the particular site context requires it (for example complex brownfield sites – Tiesdell & Adams 2004: 25).

The regulatory tyranny

For some, the regulatory tyranny can be analysed (and challenged) in terms of the political economy it represents – that is, as an attempt to correct market failure. Van Doren (2005: 45; 64), for example, argues that regulation is inherently costly and inefficient, but difficult to change because of political support for it from 'bootleggers' (special interests who gain economically from the existence of regulation) and 'baptists' (those who do not like the behaviour of others and want government to restrict it). He cites the work of regulatory economists who have generally come out against regulation, arguing that in most cases no market failure existed in the first place. So, while admitting that design regulation has not been subject to such analysis, he concludes that it will inevitably create barriers to change and innovation.

Encapsulating these positions and, in the process, distorting the workings of a 'natural' market might be the reactionary local politician proclaiming 'we know what we like and we like what we know', or the unbending municipal technocrat determined that 'rules is rules'. The tyranny also reflects McGlynn's (1993) concern that the state only has real power through the right to say 'no' to development proposals via the series of overlapping regulatory regimes – planning, building control, conservation, highways adoption, environmental protection, etc. However, the state's power to make positive proposals is typically limited by the private sector's control of access to resources – both financial (to deliver development) and skills (to design it).

Regulatory processes themselves reflect one of two major types, either they are based on fixed legal frameworks with unquestioning administrative decision-making, or they are discretionary, where a distinction is drawn between law and policy, the latter enacted through 'guiding' plans, skilled professional interpretation in the light of local circumstances, and political decision-making (Reade 1987: 11). Typically most regulatory regimes represent a mix of the two. In the UK, for example, planning, conservation and environmental protection are discretionary (although a shortage of key skills among the professionals charged with their interpretation can lead authorities back in the direction of adopting fixed standards – Carmona 2001: 225–227). Building control and highways adoption, by contrast, are fixed technical processes, not open to interpretation or appeal.

Both forms of decision-making (reflecting the local politician/council technocrat positions above) contribute to the tyranny: the first because of its perceived arbitrary, inconsistent and subjective nature; the second because of its lack of flexibility or inability to consider non-standard approaches (Booth in Cullingworth 1999: 43). Moreover, the diversity of regulatory process and systems, and their often disjointed, uncoordinated and even contradictory nature, adds to a perception that '… a marathon of red tape needs to be run' (Imrie & Street 2006: 7).

A zone of conflict and compromise

The tyrannies represent extremes, perhaps even caricatures, but arguably they also reflect realities that practitioners from whichever side of the tyranny trinity are repeatedly faced with during the development process. They result from profoundly different motivations, respectively: peer approval, profit and a narrowly defined view of public interest; and very different modes of working and associated professional knowledge fields, respectively: design, management/finance and social/technical expertise. Long driving practice and debate both in the UK (Carmona 1998) and the USA (Ellis 2002: 262), the result has often perpetuated profound and ingrained stakeholder conflict within the development process (see Carmona *et al.* 2003) and led to substandard development solutions based on conflict, compromise and delay (CABE 2007a).

At the heart of each is also a different and overriding imperative, respectively to achieve an innovative design solution (within given constraints of site, budget, brief, etc), to make a good return on investment (in order to sustain a viable business), and to satisfy a broad range of public policy objectives.

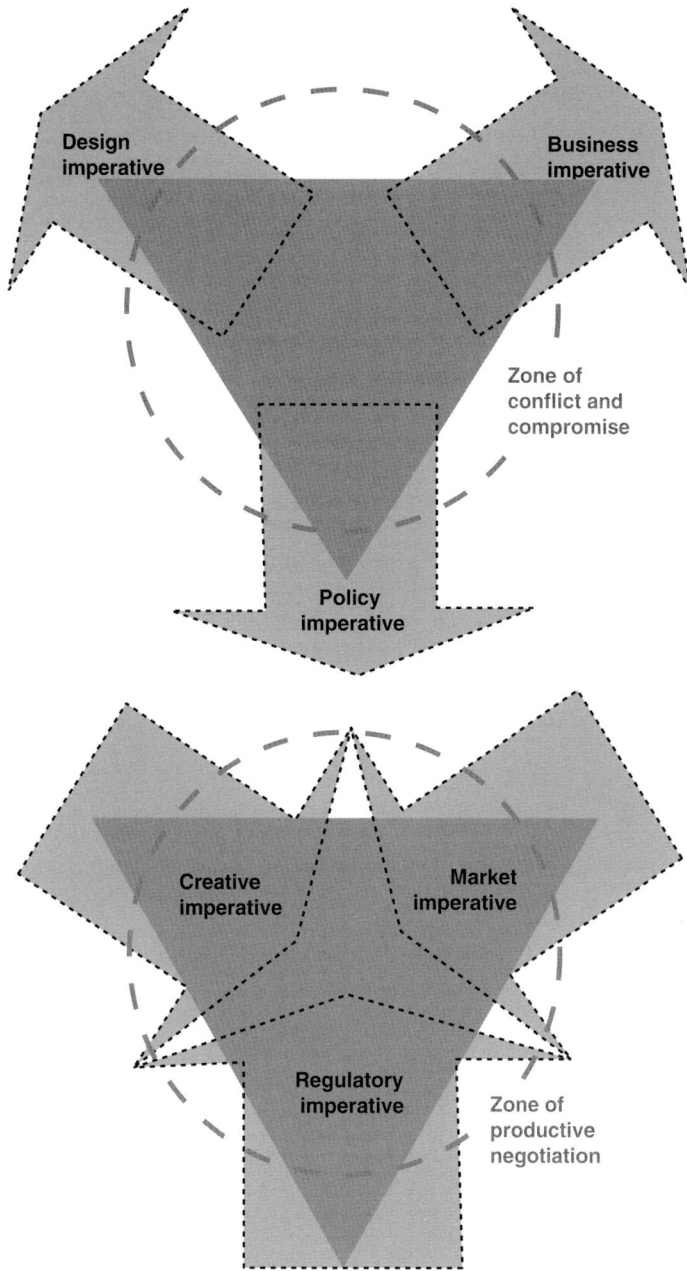

Figure 3.1   Zones of conflict and compromise and of productive negotiation.

As these are often in opposition to each other, the result will be a three-way tug of war, with the central ground stretched thinly within what can be characterised as a zone of conflict and compromise (see Figure 3.1).

From development standards to design codes

This caricature has long typified development processes in the UK (Bateman 1995) and in the USA (Duany *et al.* 2000: 109; 180), particularly in the residential sector. Thus while attention and resources have tended to be focused on urban centres, rather than in predominantly residential areas (Colomb 2007), it is in the latter areas where the standard of design is open to greatest criticism (when judged by the satisfaction of new residents with their neighbourhoods – CABE 2007b), and to greatest challenge (when judged by the complaints of existing communities faced with the prospect of new development in their backyard – Savage 2001). The need to deliver large new housing allocations while avoiding the revolt of suburban and rural England, led the UK Government to review the potential of design coding to deliver better design and a smoother regulatory process.

In February 2003, the Government launched its Sustainable Communities Plan for England, setting out its long-term ambition to create sustainable communities in urban and rural areas to meet the increasing demand for new homes, particularly in the South-East (ODPM 2003). An implicit assumption in this and other related policy documents was that to achieve the government's challenging targets for housing, new delivery mechanisms were needed. Following the launch of the Sustainable Communities Plan, there was growing media debate about the potential use of design codes as a mechanism to deliver the large-scale housing development envisaged by the plan, spurred on by high-profile visits made by the then Deputy Prime Minister – John Prescott – to codes-based New Urbanist schemes in the USA, most notably Seaside in Florida.

Coding of one form or another is nothing new. Different forms of regulation of the built environment have occurred throughout recorded history (Gardiner 2004: 28; Southworth & Ben-Joseph 1996; Rowland & Howe 1999; Carmona *et al.* 2006). Many of the development standards currently used to guide the design of buildings and the urban environment can be described as coding, of sorts, controlling almost every aspect of the built environment:

- National building regulations are a set of codes that dictate the internal and (to some degree) external design of buildings.
- Highway standards (national and local) control a good part of the public realm through their impact on road and footpath design and layout (often disastrously).
- Planning standards (national and local) dictate density levels, space between buildings, parking requirements, open space requirements, and so forth.
- 'Secured by Design' criteria determine lines of sight, permeability, access points, etc.

- Emergency service access guidelines dictate distances between buildings and points of access.
- Health and safety standards are increasingly pervasive across the built environment.

Ben-Joseph (2005b) traces the evolution of the 'hidden codes' that dictate much of the form and function of urban space around the world. He argues that the original purpose and value of these regulations are often forgotten as bureaucracies implement the standards with little regard to their actual rationale, and even less to their knock-on effects. Furthermore, most of these are limited in their scope, and technical in their aspirations, and are neither generated from a physical vision of the intended place nor have any understanding of a particular site or context (DCLG 2006a: 11).

Instead, these forms of development standards are about achieving minimum requirements across the board (regardless of site context) and in many cases the slavish adherence to such standards has led to the creation of bland and unattractive places (HBF & RIBA 1990; Cullen 1961: 133–137). Arguably this represents a classic case of regulatory (rather than market) failure. Indeed Ben-Joseph (2005b: xxi) has observed that today we excel at making development standards but frequently fail to make good places. In doing so he makes a cogent argument for the existence of the regulatory tyranny.

A site-specific tool

To what extent can the use of design codes as a policy instrument overcome or mediate between the conflicting tyrannies? The evidence on the ground suggests that coding in the form of generic (i.e. non-site-specific) development standards is unlikely to assist the delivery of better places. Moreover, faced with a perceived increase in regulation of different types, architects (Imrie & Street 2006) and developers (Heriot-Watt University 2007: 3) have become increasingly concerned about the impact this has on their room to manoeuvre – their 'opportunity space' (see Chapter 1) – or their space to deliver, respectively, creative and profitable solutions. The key question, therefore, is what is a good code and whether such a tool can be used to deliver public interest objectives such as more housing and better places, while still allowing for creative architectural design and enhanced economic value (the preoccupations of the other two components in the tyranny trinity)?

As used in England, the term 'design code' refers to a distinct form of detailed design guidance that stipulates the three-dimensional components of a particular development without establishing the overall design vision or outcomes (see CABE 2004a, reported in full in Carmona *et al.* 2006). Design codes were seen as providing clarity over what constitutes acceptable design quality for a particular site or area, thereby (in principle at least) achieving a level of certainty for developers and the local community, and, within an appropriate planning framework, helping to improve the speed of delivery (ODPM 2005: 5). Used in this way, and unlike generic development standards, they provide a positive statement about the desired qualities of a particular place.

As such, design codes are site-specific tools, typically building upon the design vision contained in a masterplan, development framework or other site- or area-based vision. The codes themselves focus on urban design principles aimed at delivering better-quality places, for example the requirements for streets, blocks, massing and so forth, but may also cover landscape, architectural and building performance issues such as those aiming to increase energy efficiency. They encompass what in New Urbanist parlance has come to be known as form-based codes (Burdette 2004).

A national pilot programme

For Ministers in England, design codes seemed to hold the promise of a new and different approach, and in 2005 they funded a national pilot programme to fully test the potential of design coding. A research programme, led by the present author, evaluated 19 case studies of three types:

(1) Seven 'pilot' projects at the start of the design/development process where design codes were to be produced as an integral part of evolving development projects. The development of these codes was monitored from their early stages.
(2) A retrospective evaluation of eight 'advanced' coded projects, where codes had already been prepared and used independently of the pilot programme. In these case studies, development had already been delivered on the ground using design codes.
(3) Four 'non-code' projects that used other forms of detailed design guidance. These examples were chosen as comparisons, and were also advanced in the sense that they had all been used on site to deliver projects in various stages of completion.

The case studies reflected a geographical spread, a range of different development and physical contexts, as well as variety in size, ownership and stakeholder engagement. The monitoring and evaluation process was structured using a common method for all of the case studies, with case studies analysed in terms of their approach to each stage of a hypothetical coding process from code inception to build out (see Figure 3.2). (See DCLG 2006b for a detailed discussion of methodology, case studies and findings.)

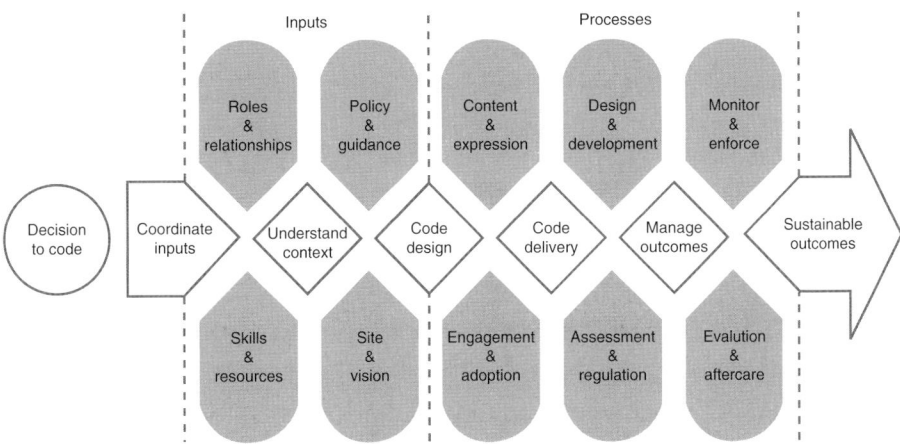

Figure 3.2   A hypothetical coding process.

Initial stakeholder reactions – the critiques

The announcement of the national pilot programme brought immediate and negative reaction in the professional press, particularly in specialist architectural trade journals. The reaction was further stoked by the Deputy Prime Minister's visit to Seaside – the film set for the 1998 film the Truman Show in which an insurance salesman discovers his entire life is actually a TV show. The nightmarish vision – at least in some commentators' minds – was of waves of Truman-Show-like dystopia inexorably spreading across England.

Alongside the more predictable headlines, a range of reoccurring critiques appeared across the press, arguing that design codes posed a significant danger on a number of counts. These directly attacked what the writers saw as an attempt to extend the tyranny of regulation through the introduction of design coding. In making the arguments, however, they directly reflected creative and market tyranny perspectives.

One set of critiques focused on design outcomes, suggesting that design codes would:

- suffocate the creativity of designers by reducing their scope to innovate;
- deliver only traditional design solutions through an in-built presumption against contemporary design;
- promote formulaic design solutions through the delivery of 'tick-box architecture' and 'standards-based urbanism'.

Focused more on process-related issues with an economic impact on the development process, a second set of critiques opined that design codes would:

- lead to excessively bureaucratic decision-making with less discretion and more paperwork and delay;

- result in a cost-cutting culture through the cutting out of designers from the development process;
- result in very restrictive and prescriptive planning through which the freedom of the market would be curtailed.

Clearly based on the in-built presumptions and professional mind-sets (tyrannies) discussed above, positions were taken early, and certainly before any empirical evidence from the pilot process was forthcoming.

Over the course of the two years of research that followed, the same arguments continued to be made, including from the Urban Task Force of Richard Rogers. Repeating the assertion that a side effect of coding would be a reduction in professional design input, it argued: 'Design quality is threatened by an excessive reliance on design codes rather than design professionals' (Urban Task Force 2005: 7).

The research findings

The research delivered a substantial evidence-base on which judgements about the potential of design codes (see DCLG 2006b for detailed findings) could be made. It showed that as a particularly robust form of design guidance, design codes can play a major role in delivering better places, and this should be the major motivation for opting to use them. They do this by 'fixing' and delivering the 'must have' urban elements that form the common and unifying urban framework for schemes. They provide synergy and integration, by ensuring that the parts amount to a larger whole. This was a particularly strong finding among the 'advanced' case studies, where the built results on the ground provided tangible evidence of outcomes exceeding market norms.

They also have a significant role to play in delivering a more certain development process and – when well managed – provide the focus around which teams of professional stakeholders can coordinate their activities, in the process delivering a more integrated and consensus-driven development process. In one 'advanced' case study, for example, the line-up of key stakeholders included 19 key groups including everything from the landowner to marketing and cost consultants. To achieve this, however, design codes require a significant up-front investment in time and resources from all parties, although the evidence suggested that for commercial interests this was compensated by the enhanced economic value that better design and a stronger sense of place could deliver (again, a finding common to all the 'advanced' case studies).

Interestingly the use of design codes made no discernable difference to the duration of the formal planning process (a key objective of Government

was to streamline planning). However, as pay-back for the up-front investment, a streamlined process of applying for and obtaining detailed 'reserved
matters' consents for successive development phases was apparent, following the granting of an initial outline permission for the development
as a whole.

The research therefore concluded that – in appropriate circumstances –
design codes were valuable tools to deliver a range of more sustainable processes and built-development outcomes. They are, however, just one
possibility among a range of detailed design guidance options, and it is
important to understand where they should and should not be used. They
are, for example, not normally of value for small sites, or where only one
developer and design team is involved, and are of most value when sites pos-
sess one or more of the following characteristics:

- large sites (or multiple smaller related sites) that will be built out over a
  long period of time;
- sites in multiple ownership;
- sites likely to be developed by different developers and/or design teams.

This reflects the key benefit of design codes (confirmed by the research) –
namely their ability to coordinate the outputs of multiple teams and development phases across large sites to realise a coherent design vision.

Delivering new development entails a series of linked but often disparate
processes. Design codes have a potential role to play in each, but more than
that, they can provide an integrating focus through which to bring together
the various processes and those involved in them. They do this because
their preparation necessitates engaging all creative, market and regulatory
parties early in these linked processes, with the resulting detailed discussions helping to resolve issues that otherwise typically cause tensions later
in the development and undermine the quality of the built outcome:

- *Design processes* – design codes set the detailed urban design parameters
  of projects across the different scales of design intervention, from street
  and block sizes and layouts to landscape and architectural concerns, to
  help achieve a coordinated vision of place.
- *Development processes* – design codes provide a means through which
  stakeholders can explore and negotiate detailed design options, and allow
  these concerns to feed into costing models and development options from
  an early stage.
- *Planning processes* – design codes provide a ready means to consider,
  establish and adopt design parameters in a more objective manner, and
  then to regulate and monitor design solutions through the development
  control process.

- *Adoption processes* – design codes allow adoption considerations (e.g. public-sector adoption of highways, open space and drainage) to be coordinated at an early stage with design, development and planning matters, providing explicit standards for rigorous enforcement where necessary.

The research, however, also showed that design codes do not sit in isolation and are not a panacea for delivering better quality development. What is needed are good design codes and rigorous coding processes in which the role of coding within the wider design, development and planning processes is fully considered (see DCLG 2006a for a detailed discussion). Moreover, if the commitment to their production and use is lacking among any key stakeholders, codes can become a divisive force and a waste of resources. A number of prerequisites are thus necessary for successful coding:

(1) A coding team needs to be in place with the requisite design skills and leadership to drive the coding process forward.
(2) Stakeholders need to be prepared to make an up-front investment in time and resources.
(3) A commitment to design quality is needed both across the team and between public and private stakeholders.
(4) The code should deliver on the basis of a strong site-based vision (typically a masterplan).

Rebutting the critiques

Returning to the critiques outlined above, the research demonstrated that design codes are not without problems – logistics-, resource-, skills- and time-based. As with other forms of detailed design guidance, if design codes are themselves poorly designed, or inappropriately used, they will be as much part of the problem as the solution. Despite this, evidence from across the pilot programme, supported by that from a range of international experiences (Australia, Germany, the Netherlands, the USA – see Carmona & Dann 2007) suggested that the arguments against codes are based on a range of common misconceptions.

Taking the group of critiques that broadly reflect a creative tyranny perspective – (1) to (3) above – far from stifling the creativity of designers, design codes were shown to have the potential to increase creative input into the development process. Whereas much volume housebuilding in the UK has occurred without the input of architects and urban designers (Adam 1997), design codes (and the masterplans to which they relate) cannot be prepared without these skills. Moreover, while some of the design codes examined strongly favoured traditional architectural design, others demonstrated that coding is equally suited to delivering innovative contemporary housing design.

The research showed that design codes encourage delivery of a stronger and more unified sense of place, including architectural variety within a theme, and – critically – require that developers depart from standard house types and local municipalities from crude local development standards. They do this by encouraging stakeholders to think together about each development in its entirety as a specific place, then fixing this through the codes, rather than as a series of separate and discordant parts.

This integration of activity extends to the second set of critiques – (4) to (6) above – which broadly reflect a market tyranny perspective. The research revealed that rather than adding to and complicating the bureaucratic burden, when used correctly, codes can clarify regulatory processes and reduce the uncertainty faced by developers. In part, this is because codes also reduce the discretion available to regulators by establishing and tying down the critical design components of schemes well in advance of detailed planning applications being received. In turn, this considerable investment up front in the design process ensures that far from representing cost-cutting devices, design codes cannot be prepared without a significant injection of design time, skills and resources early in the process alongside the positive engagement of key stakeholders. As such they add to, rather than reduce, the overall design input into schemes, but also require additional resources to fund this (consultants' one-off fees ranged from £25K to £100K).

In fact, design codes require the exercise of advanced design skills throughout the process of their preparation and use. Unlike other processes of development, coding distributes the creative input across three distinct phases of design – establishing the spatial design vision (typically a masterplan), coding that vision, and designing each parcel as they come forward against the code (see Figure 3.3).

The quality of the final development is therefore dependent upon the quality of the site-based spatial vision (and the skills of the masterplanner), the quality of the code itself (and the skills of the code designer) and the quality of the parcel or scheme design (and the skills of the scheme designer). This compares favourably with other design intensive approaches such as development based solely on a detailed masterplan where the design work is split between two phases of design (see CABE 2004b). It also marks a major advance on what has been the dominant model for large-scale residential development in the UK, where the basic design parameters are established to gain outline planning permission after which a specialist layout designer prepares detailed 'reserved matters' schemes based on standard units and technical development standards (POS *et al.* 1998).

The codes were not uniformly prescriptive, restricting in the process the designer's and/or the developer's room for manoeuvre (a major concern of both creative and market critics). The case studies suggested that local circumstances and the vision of those responsible for each code's design

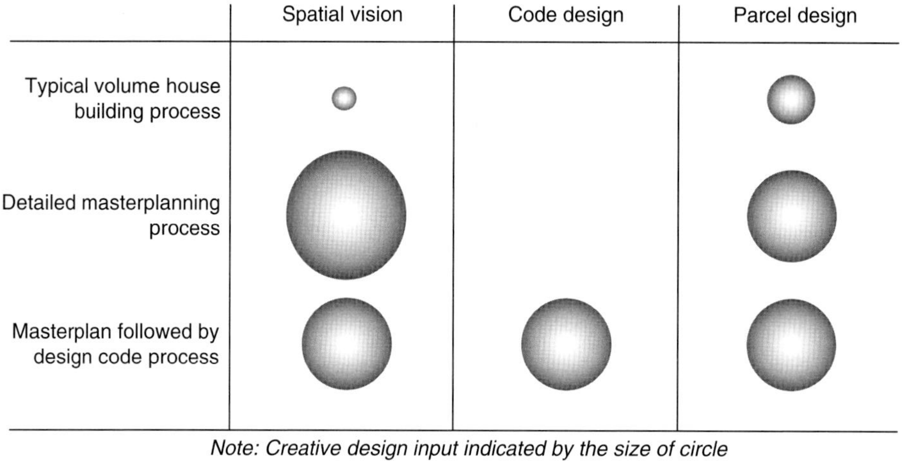

	Spatial vision	Code design	Parcel design
Typical volume house building process	◦		●
Detailed masterplanning process	●		●
Masterplan followed by design code process	●	●	●

Note: Creative design input indicated by the size of circle

Figure 3.3   Design input and development processes compared.

determines the precise characteristics of design codes. The case study code documents, for example, varied in length between 25 and 100 pages. While some aspects were highly prescriptive (e.g. building lines), others were dealt with much more flexibly (e.g. architectural treatments).

The extent to which codes are capable of modification during their life was also a matter for local decision, with formal processes of code review or the issuing of code supplements common in order to give greater flexibility between development phases and to enhance those parts of codes that proved less successful. Reflecting the balance that needs to be struck, Walters (2007: 94–5) warns:

> The fear is always that codes will become overly prescriptive, but the experience shows that if codes back away from the levels of prescription necessary to achieve urban order and clarity in spatial layout, they run the real danger of becoming too flexible and allowing bad design to flourish alongside more creative interpretations.

Mediating the tyrannies

What is universal, however, is the potential for code production to act as a collaborative capacity-building process and, in so doing, to challenge the types of praxis that underpin the three tyrannies. Thus, the research programme showed how coding brings together a wide range of individuals and organisations with a part to play in delivering development, and that these roughly divide into two groups: the 'coding team', which comprises the full range of technical stakeholders (professionals) involved in producing and using the code; and, 'wider interests', such as the local community (see Table 3.1).

Table 3.1 Stakeholders' roles within a typical coding process.

Groups	Interests	Stakeholders	Key stakeholder roles include:
Coding Team	Land interests	Landowner	Establishing aspirations from the start for a high quality development, using freehold rights throughout to guarantee delivery against the design code
		Master-developer	Initiating the site-based vision and code design process through appointment of high quality designers, and subsequently assessing parcel development proposals against the code
		Funding agency	Using landownership and funding powers to deliver the requisite skills, resources and know-how for a high quality coding process, and effective assessment and enforcement
	Design interests	Masterplanner/ framework designer	Preparing the masterplan or development framework as a strong vision for the long-term development of the site(s), reflecting any existing policy and guidance, local consensus on the vision and the client's brief
		Code designer	Coordinating different interests as a basis to prepare the design code as a means to implement the essential principles contained in the masterplan/vision
	Development interests	Parcel developers	Developing proposals and achieving consents to deliver on site a development parcel within the masterplan/vision
		Social housing providers	If involved, developing proposals and achieving consents for the delivery on site of a development parcel – or part thereof – within the masterplan/vision
		Parcel designers	Creatively interpreting the code and masterplan to develop high quality designs for individual land parcels and their constituent buildings, spaces and areas
	Public interests	Planning authority	Establishing aspirations from the start for a high quality development, initiating or playing a role in initiating the masterplan/vision and design code, and administering the development control and any enforcement processes on the basis of the code
		Highways authority	Playing a role in design code production, revising and updating existing highways standards as necessary, and assessing and adopting the infrastructure that results
		Environment agency	Approving discharge from drainage facilities (i.e. sustainable urban drainage – SUDS), and advising on incorporation in the design code
		Building control	Approving parcel proposals against the national building regulations, and advising on incorporation and adaptation for the design code
Wider interests	Private interests	Utilities providers (including water)	Adopting service infrastructure, and advising on incorporation of requirements in the design code
	Community interests	Local politicians	Establishing design aspirations in advance of development interest, approving masterplan/ vision and design code and delegating authority to officers to manage the delivery
		Existing community	Engaging in the masterplanning/vision-making process through serious and significant involvement
		Future occupiers	Becoming involved through normal planning processes and engagement in long-term management and maintenance processes on the basis of the design code

The coding team can be further divided into four sets of interests – land, design, development and public interests. A critical role of successful coding processes is in providing the space for this range of stakeholders to understand and engage with the intersecting roles and prime motivations of all the others – in building trust and capacity within the team. These motivations varied across the case studies, but collectively included:

- the delivery of high quality design to support the creation of sustainable places – the primary objective;
- optimising investment returns – a necessary precondition;
- creating certain and efficient development process to facilitate the necessary investment;
- delivering planned development capacities (e.g. numbers of housing units and associated uses);
- achieving key technical design parameters, while avoiding their over-dominance in design outcomes;
- establishing consensus over development, by delivering on all of the above.

To succeed, coding processes must address these collective aspirations. While key land and public interests, such as planning, are likely to be involved in one way or another from the start, others, such as parcel developers or highways authorities, will only be involved later on. It is thus imperative that those involved from the outset establish a firm basis upon which to work with other parties as they join the process further down the line. The pilot schemes suggested that this can best be done when all parties collectively consider and address the full range of motivations from the start, and where this did not happen tensions arose.

Not every scheme subject to a design code follows the same process. Whether, for example, public or private sector stakeholders lead the process may determine who takes which role within the coding team. Certain roles can also be combined in single stakeholders, for instance: local authorities with appropriate skills in-house may take on the role of code designer; landowners may act as the master developer; and the master developer may subsume the role of parcel developer. Design roles can also be combined. In some of the case studies the masterplan (vision) designer was often the same as the designer of the code.

An early and vital role of any coding process thus involves putting together the right team with the right skills and resources, and commitment to the use of a coded approach. This process avoids selecting stakeholders stuck in the sorts of confrontational mindsets discussed above. Instead, stakeholders are selected who are willing and able to negotiate their role and contributions to the development process within the confines established by the code. Design codes thereby establish a zone within which productive negotiation (rather than compromise) occurs, internalising this within the development team rather than externalising it as open conflict. Tyranny is thereby replaced by understanding and a desire to address collective aspirations.

Many minds remain set

Despite evidence from the research, many minds remained set, including some signature architects with their headline-generating potential. Will Alsop quickly proclaimed that: 'Design codes will stifle our imagination.' Similarly, Richard Rogers claimed: 'Codes are for pen-pushers and penny-pinchers who have not a clue about design and want to find their way through the planning system.' (quoted in Bennett 2005). On the market side, while recognising the potential of codes, to, for example, 'level the playing field' between developers (Paul Newman of Paul Newman Homes quoted in English Partnerships 2007a: 3), representatives of the real estate professions continued to express concern about the potential of such detailed guidance to reflect commercial considerations, to be flexible in the face of demand issues and to speed up the development process (Barnes 2004).

A survey of architects' attitudes to regulation generally confirmed these predominantly negative associations with design coding, with 39% of architects recording hostility to their further use and 38% being agnostic (Street 2007: 11). Clearly these historic confrontational mindsets are difficult to dislodge, with the danger being that such architects will exclude themselves from the volume housebuilding market for another generation.

Despite this, a minority of architects have been open to their use (22% in the survey above), and despite an earlier Royal Institute of British Architects (RIBA) Practice Note that urged caution on the use of design codes and warned: 'Design codes risk pattern-book housing' (RIBA 2005), following the launch of the research described in this chapter, the then RIBA president concluded that: 'In the right circumstances and with the right expertise, they can speed up the planning process and deliver excellent results.' (quoted in Bennett 2005). The architecture profession's division on this subject was, however, further illustrated when the RIBA changed its position yet again, and at the initiative of the subsequent president argued that codes would be a 'dead hand to innovation' (Gates 2006).

Conclusion

No one sets out to create poorly laid out, characterless places, neither do they try to exclude good designers from the residential development process or to prevent developers making a reasonable return on their investment. Despite this, too much of what has been built in the recent past displays the former characteristics, while the latter perceptions remain widespread among affected groups. As the research referred to in this chapter suggests, site-specific design codes have great potential to assist in overcoming these problems, with potential benefits including:

- better-designed development with less opposition locally and a level playing field for developers;
- the enhanced economic value that a positive sense of place and better quality design can bring;
- a more certain planning process and an associated more certain climate for investment;
- a more coordinated development process built on consensus instead of conflict.

Furthermore, in regulating future urban development, design coding does not stifle the potential for creativity and value generation and it may even enhance these critical contributions to place-making.

Multi-stakeholder site-based codes can thus help to bridge the gap between creative, market-driven, and regulatory modes of praxis – the three tyrannies. In doing so they are not simply regulatory tools for the control of private interests by public ones, or even of some private interests (developers) by others (landowners) but are also tools for guidance and consensus building within a zone of productive negotiation rather than one of conflict and compromise. Design coding provides a medium through which to shake off narrow sectoral perspectives – the tyrannies – and in the process force the creators of the built environment to see the process as a collective and holistic endeavour.

Some stakeholders will never – for largely ideological reasons – accept any form of regulation as a positive contribution to the development process, but the empirical evidence shows that design codes have the potential to overcome the tyrannies by setting the development process within a far more positive context of productive negotiation. This is significant because it demonstrates how it is possible to deliver creativity and value within a complex multi-stakeholder development process, while successfully regulating urban form, and building capacity and understanding within the development team.

The reality of design codes thus differed from many assumptions, a reality seen in many of the most interesting English housing developments in recent years, including Hulme (Manchester), Greenwich Millennium Village (London), Newhall (Harlow) and Upton (Northampton). Although not universally praised, these developments (all case studies in the research reported here) represent major steps forward from the standard volume-built developments that would have been the alternative. A similar experience is evident in the USA (see Parolek *et al.* 2008: Section 4). It is thus possible to conclude that, when used in the manner described above, design codes are valuable tools to regulate the essentials of urbanism, while leaving room for design creativity and enhanced market value.

For its part, the research demonstrated that architects (often eminent) and developers (including national volume builders) have been willing to contribute to successive phases of projects within the schema laid down by design codes and, despite initial reservations, have afterwards overwhelmingly given a strong endorsement to the process (DCLG 2006b: 15). As Elizabeth Plater-Zyberk (in Scheer & Preiser 1994: vii) has argued '… control and freedom can co-exist most effectively when incorporated in regulations that precede the act of design, framing parameters of a given programme, rather than conflicting in judgement exerted on the completed design.' As the experience of design coding suggests, whether in creative, market or regulatory roles, stakeholders benefit profoundly from positive engagement with each other. In the UK, recognition of the potential of design codes is now reflected in their adoption in government policy (DCLG 2006c: Annex B).

Note

1. A version of this chapter was previously published as Carmona (2009).

4

Proactive Engagement in Urban Design – The Case of Chelmsford

Tony Hall

Introduction

For an understanding of how urban design policy instruments can impact upon developers' decision-making with positive outcomes, the Chelmsford story is an interesting one. This interest stems from a remarkable turnaround that took place there in the late 1990s. What had been an average and unprepossessing town became one that was liveable and sophisticated. A substantive and continuing urban renaissance had begun. Whereas, for many, the town may not have been seen as in any way remarkable in terms of professional practice, by 2003 it was clearly in the forefront. High standards of design had become the norm across the Borough, a position recognised by the award of Beacon Status for the Quality of the Built Environment by the Government in 2003. This good practice was also attested to in studies by the Commission for Architecture and the Built Environment (CABE), including their *Housing Audit* (CABE 2004c). It applied not just to houses but also to the commercial life of the town, especially shops. Chelmsford even achieved an entry in the *Good Place Guide* (Billingham & Cole 2002). A full account of how this was achieved has been published (Hall 2007).

The turnaround was, in essence, a regime change that led, ultimately, to improvements in the built form, although it can be best understood as a sequence of interrelated step changes. The first step occurred at the political level with a new resolve to refuse planning permission for proposals that

Urban Design in the Real Estate Development Process, First Edition. Edited by Steve Tiesdell and David Adams.
© 2011 Blackwell Publishing Ltd. Published 2011 by Blackwell Publishing Ltd.

were poorly designed, which, for major proposals at that time, was most of them. This step was consolidated by the upholding of refusals on appeal. To consolidate such decisions further into a long-term programme, they had to be expressed and implemented through the work of the Council's professional officers. This was brought about through both staff changes and the heightened confidence that comes with increasing success. Although it had at its heart the appointment of a team with the necessary specialist skills, the changes were not confined to this step, and embraced a large section of the officer corps. The officer teams then prepared policy and negotiated with applicants. This then impacted upon the developers. They began to do things that they had not done before and were not doing elsewhere. Their behaviour underwent a step change also. The consequence was that what was built was built better. This was the final step.

Making the turnaround

Chelmsford Borough has a population of approximately 150,000 and is situated 50 km north-east of London in the centre of the county of Essex. Much of the 20th century urban development of south and central Essex has been rather uninspiring, usually seen as the butt of jokes rather than as a beacon of achievement. Design in the town during the 1960s and 1970s was far from satisfactory. Nevertheless, the town continued to grow and prosper. As a result of both government and County Council policies, Chelmsford was subject to a substantial and ongoing house-building programme and consequent increase in population. Decline in manufacturing industry was more than compensated for by the expansion of service employment. The fact that the cycle of development was ongoing and proceeding at a substantial pace had always offered the prospect of a better future, if only the development process could be properly steered.

In 1996, a new political administration started the process of achieving higher standards of design and sustainability in the built environment. The first significant changes to planning policies came in 1997. Not only was a borough-wide local plan (CBC 1997) finally adopted, but Chelmsford Borough Council (CBC) also adopted the revised Essex Design Guide, (ECC 2005) as supplementary planning guidance. These two events provided a foundation from which further progress in design control in the Borough could be made. The process of creating a more effective structure for the council's operations was also begun, at both officer and political levels, including the building up of a team of professional urban designers. Efforts to change the corporate culture, with greater inter-professional working were also begun.

As Chelmsford entered the new millennium, a proactive approach to design control was in place. The position had been reached where every new development was expected to achieve the required standards of design. The Council's urban design team was approaching its full strength of five professionals and was applying its accumulated experience in negotiation to each proposal that came forward. As the staffing position on urban design gradually improved, so the rate of production of detailed site-specific briefs increased. The degree of prescription and delineation of desired physical structure also increased. Each site where major development was expected, now had a design brief well in advance, which outlined the location of blocks and the character of urban spaces. Overall, this turnaround took six years to achieve. This was a considerable task which was not just a matter of policy content but also of resources and process.

The proactive approach

Urban design is not normally a statutorily required function of a planning authority. However, embracing it as a planning activity radically changes the way a local authority approaches the statutory processes of plan making and controlling development. In practical terms, a local planning authority's urban design role is promotional. It does not design the built environment as such, but anticipates and encourages development, influencing and guiding those who make the investment. Potentially, all the planning tools at a local council's disposal have substantial scope for positive, creative influence, through briefing, policy statements and agreements. Chelmsford Council saw its role as setting design objectives based on an understanding of both the strategic picture and the site opportunities. This meant sometimes leading, sometimes partnering and sometimes scrutinising. It required an approach that was *proactive*, in contrast to the *reactive* stance often associated with the control of development.

But being proactive was not value-free. At Chelmsford, place-making became a basis for requiring quality through planning approvals. Adoption of design principles ensured that new development created a sense of place, respected its context and met functional needs. The overall aim was to make places by envisaging, shaping and managing change. It meant thinking of places and communities at different spatial levels: the town, the neighbourhood and the street, taking account of the physical and intangible qualities that go to make a place. Making places involved specifying location and linkages, uses and density as the context for design, with the quality of the public realm used to glue the whole together.

Progress cannot be made by relying solely on the tactical use of procedures, permissions and agreements. They can be successful only when set in the context of design guides and site-specific guidance. Published policy was, therefore, essential for a proactive approach. It enabled all parties in the development process to know the position of the planning authority at an early stage and to know it clearly. This aspect of design control was of prime importance as it was the means by which all relevant aspects of a planning authority's policy were conveyed to a potential developer at the time when planning permission was sought. It had three components:

(1) A clear, physically-based spatial strategy.
(2) Adoption of a general design guide.
(3) Briefs for all significant sites.

The physically based spatial strategy was conveyed through a new development plan embodying a long-term vision, especially in the town centre. Its policies related the intensity of development to accessibility, in pursuit of the reduction of the need to travel and travel by sustainable modes. These accessibility principles led logically to the promotion of an urban renaissance involving the intensive use of town-centre brownfield land. They also led to the need for access to open green areas, both within the redeveloped areas and through 'green corridors' linking them to the suburbs and countryside.

Vehicles for conveying spatial strategy will vary over time and from country to country. The development plan system that applied in Chelmsford during the period described is no more and the one that is current at the time of writing will inevitably be replaced in due course. Nevertheless, whatever the actual details of the system, the need for the incorporation of design goals and strategies into some form of development plan will remain. It is a need that would apply in all countries irrespective of the procedural nature of their planning systems.

The general design guide, in this case the *Essex Design Guide* (ECC 2005), provided guidance on generic aspects of urban design that applied across broad areas, such as residential neighbourhoods, throughout the Borough.

The planning brief was the foundation of the proactive approach and the principal vehicle for setting out design expectations for a site. Wherever development was expected, or was being promoted by the Council, planning briefs set out principles and guided design. They often helped to unlock complex urban sites. If done quickly, they influenced value, increased certainty and established a design approach before negotiation took place.

Different types of brief were devised to suit different circumstances. The typology adopted at Chelmsford was:

- *Area strategy* – a long-term strategy for change for a wider area, such as an urban quarter or series of linked development sites.
- *Urban design framework* – an integrated design approach to a number of related sites and public spaces.
- *Masterplan* – a definite structure of routes, building blocks, spaces and uses for a large development area, often with an implementation programme.

- *Planning brief* (sometimes called a *design* or *development brief*) – guidance for the development of a specific site containing detailed guidance on land use, access and urban design and planning obligation requirements.
- *Concept statement* – a short statement of the preferred layout and design approach to a site, produced quickly by officers, pending Council approval.
- *Character appraisal* – a definition of the special architectural and historic interest of an area providing the basis for more detailed advice on design guidance and enhancement proposals.
- *Village design statement* – a description of the positive and negative elements of a village produced as a snapshot by a local community, which might ultimately adopted by the Council.

All the site-specific types of guidance, in line with standard planning methodology normally contained:

- a review of the purpose, status and setting of the guidance;
- a site appraisal;
- the policy context;
- the design principles to be applied to the particular site.

In addition, a proactive approach required:

- diagrams of the desired physical structure, blocks, frontages, access and uses;
- guidance on issues relating to implementation.

The distinctive aspect was the lengths to which the Council went to address the physical structure of the desired development in its site-specific guidance. Perimeter blocks, active frontages and location of open space were all normally shown in outline. The reason for their inclusion was that there was, in reality, little room for manoeuvre if all contemporary design principles were to be correctly followed. Perimeter blocks tend to have certain standard sizes with limited variation. The constraints on most sites were such that there was often only one, perhaps two, ways of fitting them in if proper frontages were to be maintained. Once the local open space requirements had also been calculated, both in terms of quantity and necessary dimensions for particular recreational activities, then the options were further limited. In these circumstances, it saved a great deal of time and trouble if these limited options were conveyed to potential developers in advance. The experience at Chelmsford was that, in the event, developers – and potential developers – reacted very positively to proposals at this level of detail. Their position was that if the Council had a view then they wanted to know it as clearly, and as far in advance, as possible.

The need for negotiation

Although publishing clear policy and guidance was a necessary condition for a proactive approach it was not a sufficient one. Ongoing negotiation with developers, their professional agents and other parties was also necessary. By 2002, all major development proposals were handled by a team of an urban designer, development control case officer, traffic engineer and such other professionals from arboriculture, law, housing, parks and leisure as might be relevant. Although time-consuming, negotiation was also rewarding if approached in a positive, constructive and creative manner and with a clear idea of what was to be achieved.

Proactive design negotiations required time and teamwork. Checklists covering issues, objectives and design principles were found to be useful. It was usually necessary to:

- establish an understanding of the setting, movement network and site;
- establish a contact person, design objectives and timetable;
- insist on the use of an architect;

and to end up with diagrams establishing:

- shape and place of blocks in context;
- outside space – public and private realms, paths, edges;
- highway design emanating from these;
- building fronts, corners, roofs;
- building elevations and materials.

Two examples

Beaulieu Park

An example that illustrates how the proactive approach was developed and operated in a greenfield setting is that of Beaulieu Park, an urban extension on the north-east boundary of the town, initially of 400 dwellings. It was a site where the changes in policy at local and central government levels were played out over a lengthy period. An initial planning brief (CBC 1996) had been approved by the Council. It was typical of the more general type produced by the Council's officers during the early 1990s and gave little detail on physical form beyond pedestrian and vehicle access and location of playing fields and parkland. The expectation at the time of both the developers and the Council's officers was that the initiative on design lay with the housebuilders, reflecting central government policy during the previous

Figure 4.1   The first stage of Beaulieu Park with large detached houses with neoclassical features fronting the development. Reproduced by permission of Tony Hall.

decade. Fortunately, though, a number of written design principles, including frontage to roads, were also included. The lead developers then proceeded by means of their own masterplan. This set out a skeletal road network, but not blocks, and the location of the principal areas of public open space. A variant of the masterplan partitioned the site into separate parcels of land to be developed at different times and, in some cases, sold to other developers.

The first two stages of the development, from 1997 to 1999, coincided with the adoption by the Council of the revised Essex Design Guide (ECC 2005) in 1998. Unfortunately, the developers and their professional advisors did not display, at that stage, a proper understanding of its intentions prior to its adoption by the Borough, even though it had been out on consultation, and then published by the County Council, some years previously. They also showed little awareness of the implications of emerging central government policy on design. The first stage of the development consisted of very large detached houses in a pseudo-classical style at around 20 dwellings per hectare (dph) (see Figure 4.1). This followed the desire of housebuilders at the time to 'front' their schemes with what they considered to be their most impressive houses, relegating smaller properties, including the affordable housing, to the rear of the site. The next stage of the development, fitting in housing behind the grander avenues, came in late 1998 and also comprised fairly large detached houses, not in an Essex style. Much negotiation ensued and, eventually, a compromise was reached, and this part of the development was completed in 1999.

After 1999, both procedures and outcomes began to improve markedly from the Council's point of view. The developers were now adopting the higher density layouts which conformed to a greater degree to both the emerging central government policy and the philosophy of the Essex Design Guide (ECC 2005). This also had the great advantage for the developers of providing significantly more dwellings than had originally been proposed. Matters had, though, been made more complex by the parcelling up and selling off of most of the rest of the site to other housebuilders. On the Borough Council's side, the emergence of a stronger design team was now producing results from a stronger negotiating presence. As the development progressed, so the standard of layout could be seen to improve. Although there was still a preponderance of larger houses and neoclassical styles, the intermediate stages of the development, to the south and east of the site, had a greater degree of continuous frontage, densities of at least 30 dph and parking to the rear of dwellings. The paving of roads and footpaths became more informal.

By 2000, the northern portion of the original Beaulieu Park site had not yet been developed and there was an opportunity for the Council's urban design team to prepare its own masterplan for it. This new document (CBC 2001) was part of Chelmsford's new generation of planning guidance. The text provided a systematic appraisal of the site and included the new, and strongly prescriptive, masterplan diagram specifying the location of blocks, frontages, pedestrian routes and local open space. A variant of this diagram, shown by Figure 4.2, identified the character areas that were to be provided within the urban form (Hall 2008a).

The result was that the urban form of Beaulieu Park North was different not only from the first stage, but also from the intermediate stages. Gone was the use of larger dwellings and neoclassical styles. The houses were smaller, almost entirely in neo-vernacular style and continuity of frontage was maintained throughout as illustrated by Figure 4.3. There was also a reasonably seamless integration of social housing.

The point to note is that in the early 1990s the developers were used to taking the initiative in layout and dwelling design, and their layouts of their standard house types reflected their own perception of what would be good for sales. By 2000, the initiative in design had been taken by the Council and its officers and its policies were supported by central government policy which had, by then, explicitly caught up with progressive thinking at the local level. The result was, in reality, even more profitable for developers as, not only did the houses sell, but there were more of them.

A similar story was acted out for a housing scheme at Great Leighs in the north of the Borough where a delay in the development from 1996 to 2001 enabled the initial very general brief to be replaced with a highly detailed masterplan negotiated and agreed between the Council's design team and the developers (Hall 2007; 2008b). The resulting development conformed to both the Essex Guide and the Council's desire to see a seamless integration of social housing.

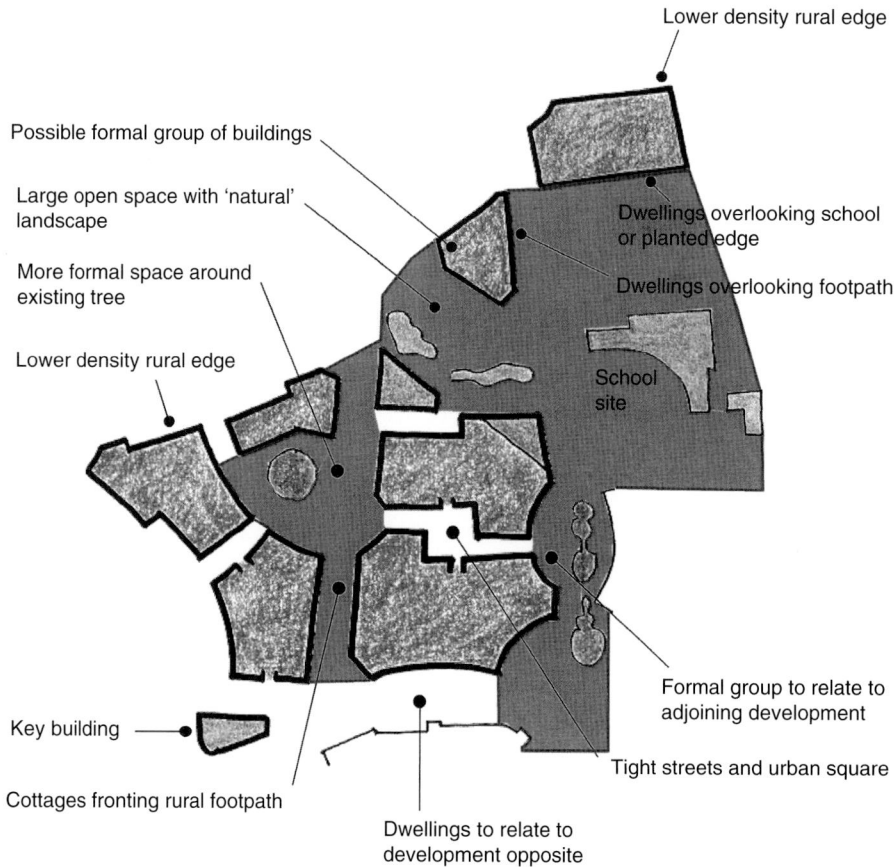

Figure 4.2   A diagram from the Borough Council's masterplan for the northern portion of Beaulieu Park (CBC, 2001) identifying the character areas that were to be provided. Note the complete specification of blocks and frontages. Reproduced by permission of Chelmsford Borough Council.

Chelmer Waterside

The second example is taken from the redevelopment of extensive brownfield land to the east of the town centre, lying beside, and between, the River Chelmer and a canal basin, that was to become known as Chelmer Waterside. The land between the river and canal had once been the site of the town's gas-works and was used mainly for surface car parking. Apart from a functioning wood yard and scrap yard, the canal basin was surrounded by derelict ware-houses which were not only unsightly but obscured the view of the water.

Before 1996, even though a brief for land around the end of the canal basin (CBC 1994) had been prepared, officers had found it difficult to interest devel-opers. It must remembered that this was shortly before the government's

Figure 4.3   A street scene within the northern portion of Beaulieu Park as completed. Note the continuous frontage, as required by the Essex Design Guide (ECC 2005), and neo-vernacular style – net density is 35 dwellings per hectare. Reproduced by permission of Tony Hall.

promotion of brownfield development and shortly before the evidence of a high degree of demand for town-centre flats in the town became manifest. Volume housebuilders generally based their business plans on what they had sold before and did not undertake the research that would have revealed the size and nature of the new markets. The important point to note is that the vision lay with the Council, not the developers and their advisors. Another policy consequence of this vision was that proposals for low intensity uses in the central area were discouraged and, where necessary, refused.

In 1997, the housebuilding firm, Higgins, agreed to have a go on land at one corner at the end of the Basin. The scheme comprised 41 flats at a density of 44 per hectare. They used their firm's standard dwelling types, in this case blocks of flats with a T-shape plan as can be seen on the right-hand side of Figure 4.4. Great efforts were made by officers in negotiation to achieve sympathetic roof shapes and building materials, in this case brick and slate in keeping with the historic period of the canal basin. The stylistic rationale was that, in addition to the canal itself, there were some period buildings that it would be advantageous to retain and for the new development to be in sympathy with. The agreed design would not have been permitted if it

Figure 4.4 The end of the canal basin at Chelmer Waterside: to the right is the developer's first stage of the redevelopment showing their standard flats with some added stylistic improvements; to the left is the second stage, architect-designed for the site and with mixed uses. Reproduced by permission of Tony Hall.

had been proposed under the regime that applied a few years later but, at the time, officers were only too glad for a developer to agree to take on the project and agree to some measure of aesthetic control. The remarkable outcome of this scheme was that all the flats sold instantly, much to the surprise of Higgins and to the gratification of the Council and its officers whose judgement on trends and potential in the property market had been vindicated.

An entrepreneurial local restaurateur then proposed an entirely new and substantial restaurant on the opposite bank of the canal basin. Although of modern construction, the new restaurant had a sympathetic roof shape and materials and incorporated an existing industrial building for use as banqueting facilities.

Buoyed up by the success of the sales of its first scheme on the canal, Higgins embarked upon a second phase which was to represent a decisive step forward in the way such development was carried out. This was to be an architect-designed, mixed-use scheme tailored to the site. The land in question was that between the first scheme and the restaurant. There was again a very substantial amount of successful negotiation, but this time it was pitched at a much more sophisticated level, in the light of both the emerging policy framework and the successful sale of the previous phase. The resulting scheme can be seen on the left-hand side of Figure 4.4. It shared with the previous one the theme of 19th century dockland aesthetic but it now had active frontages to the public road, a mix of uses and buildings wrapped round the canal basin with continuous shallow-plan form.

As the canal-related developments proceeded, their very success drew attention to the need both for a comprehensive strategy for the whole Chelmer Waterside area and for site-specific briefs for its component parts. In 2000, the new urban design team prepared such a document and, following an extended period of consultation and negotiation, the Council adopted the Waterside Strategy (CBC 2002a) two years later.

Higgins subsequently acquired a scrap metal yard at the other end of the canal basin near its entrance lock. This site fell within the coverage of a very detailed brief (CBC 2002b) prepared within the overall strategy. The brief both helped to unlock the site and direct the shape of development. It contained a diagrammatic plan, shown in Figure 4.5, indicating a shallow plan-block curving in a semicircle around a new marina. Far from feeling constrained by such prescription, the developers copied it, as can be seen from the aerial view of the completed scheme in Figure 4.6. The new block was designed for the site by the same architects who had been responsible for the second phase. While a style reflecting the canal's 19th century context was encouraged at the head of the canal basin, a more contemporary approach was considered appropriate at the other end as no existing buildings were being retained. The scheme incorporated 106 flats, at a density of 160 dph, with 25 per cent social housing. It showed advances on Higgins' first two phases with larger dwelling sizes, windows and balconies, the latter giving significant private open space to each flat. The building took full advantage of its site and connected well into the footpath and cycle network. Although confined to one wing, the social-rented accommodation was not distinguishable from the outside and offered a high standard of amenity.

The important point to note is that the Council was not just promoting, and obtaining, a higher quality of design but that it was also making its own interpretation of trends in the property market and the opportunities they afforded. It was thus providing a sense of vision and a lead to developers. A similar story was played out on a number of other sites within the town centre where production of briefs that were highly prescriptive in terms of physical form required developers to move from their standard dwelling types to architect-designed, mixed-use schemes that were fully integrated with their surroundings (Hall 2007; 2008b).

Reflections on the developers' response

It proved possible, through negotiation, to change developers' practices. The Council was able to get housebuilders to appoint good architects, to modify or drop standard house types, and to design new house types and one-off buildings. It was necessary to be prescriptive, to scrutinise, to challenge, to

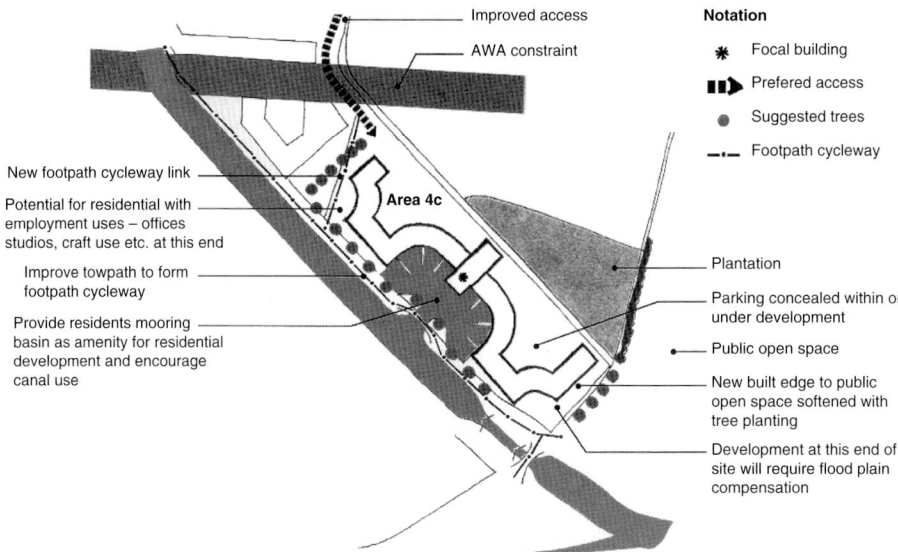

Improved access

AWA constraint

New footpath cycleway link

Potential for residential with employment uses – offices studios, craft use etc. at this end

Improve towpath to form footpath cycleway

Provide residents mooring basin as amenity for residential development and encourage canal use

Area 4c

Notation

✳ Focal building

I▮▷ Prefered access

● Suggested trees

—·— Footpath cycleway

Plantation

Parking concealed within or under development

Public open space

New built edge to public open space softened with tree planting

Development at this end of site will require flood plain compensation

Figure 4.5   Diagram included in the brief for the north-east bank of the canal basin near its entrance lock (CBC, 2002b): note the specification of the building location and proposal for a marina. Reproduced by permission of Ordnance Survey on behalf of HMSO: ©Crown Copyright, all rights reserved. *Source:* Chelmsford Borough Council.

Figure 4.6   Aerial view of Higgins' scheme for the north-east bank of the canal basin as completed: note the correspondence to the diagram in Figure 4.5. Reproduced by permission of Peter Rogers.

keep negotiating and to spend time on the public realm. It was necessary to encourage designers to be rigorous and ask them for design statements. It was the experience at Chelmsford that quality developers wanted the Council to make its requirements clear and were supportive of this process. To understand why this happened it is helpful to consider the developers' position in regard to both the greenfield and brownfield contexts.

Greenfield housebuilding

For greenfield housebuilding, land buying – and the contribution of the land buyer – is of crucial importance. This is where the real market is and it is a market between the housebuilders. Land is often purchased, both outright and in the form of options, a long time in advance of planning permission and long before any sales and design decisions are faced. These considerations are not only down the track but are also handled in a different part of the company. At Chelmsford, one major developer bought very large amounts of land over 20 years before planning permission was granted and in advance of allocation in a plan. This is where they make their money. It not only has nothing to do with design but it makes it very difficult for the firms to walk away easily from a particular locality in which they have invested heavily over a long period.

The housebuilders' initial objections to the Council's design policies related to the perception of what would be good for sales. What they wanted to do, but were not allowed to do, was to have:

- detached instead of terraced;
- their best and largest detached on the most prominent frontage;
- social housing squeezed into a single plot at the back instead of seamless pepper-potting.

However, what both sides knew all along was that whatever they built was going to sell. After all, that is how they made their money and why land buying was the crucial stage.

The profit margins were substantial. The evidence for this was from the Section 106 agreements. Although the developers would try to pay as little as they could, the amount of money they could come up with, if it was the price of planning permission, could be substantial. To take one example, the housing at Great Leighs (Hall 2007; 2008b) was conditional on a half-payment for a bypass. Difficulty with the public sector funding their half, delayed the scheme (fortuitously, as it turned out). The developer's payment was on top of all the other requirements (pubic open space, schools, social housing etc) and the size of it in relation to the number of dwellings surprised even the most experienced officers. Any variation in costs that might have arisen from changes that might have affected production and sales was, therefore, minor when compared to the overall profitability of the scheme. Even if the Council's approach had imposed costs (it did not because they got more houses in) they would not have formed a significant part of the decision-making process overall. For the Great Leighs example, and many others in Chelmsford, the obstacle to good design being proposed by the developer at the outset was not financial but the initial lack of expertise and imagination on the part the housebuilder and their architects.

Brownfield development

This is where commercial risk was, indeed, the big issue. However, it was not so much about good design as the developers' inability to understand market forces and to forecast trends. As with estate agents (and many other lines of business) their self-proclaimed expertise was largely a matter of following everyone else. This problem was aggravated by the organisational separation of land buying from sales, previously referred to. At Chelmsford, they resisted, for a very long time, the idea that office demand had declined and would be replaced by flats. Once this had happened, though, they all jumped on the bandwagon. They resisted building large expensive flats. They resisted building on waterside brownfield sites in town centres. It was the Council and its officers who correctly forecast and pressed for all these.

There were many developers who wanted to build low-intensity uses in the town centre (forgoing profit, it should be noted) but were refused. Note that all this was not a matter of how the developers saw, or handled, risk but an ignorance of the actual risks. Rather than a carefully calculated decision-making process, it was non-decision-making, i.e. doing what was done before. It is true that there are a large number of planners who do not understand these matters, but they should. It is essential for the professional role of planners to have this capability because the developers may not. This applies not just to urban design but to all other aspects of planning.

Why did they comply?

Why did the developers decide to go along with Chelmsford's policies? They had no choice. They were required to do so on pain of refusal of planning permission. Given that, the proactive approach was a way of saving everyone's time and money by making it very clear in advance exactly what was required of applicants. The most successful strategy in coping with the Council's requirements was for them to employ good specialist architects. This marginally increased costs but the returns were higher. It also saved time in gaining approval and, therefore, saved money. However, the developers did not necessarily pursue the same good design elsewhere, where they were not compelled to do so, and would revert to their old ways at Chelmsford if the pressure was not kept up. In other words they did not show a readiness to 'learn' as organisations.

Why then did they not boycott Chelmsford? The answer is that competitors would have stepped in. Given the extremely high value of land throughout south-east England, the pain of being made to do something different did not outweigh the rich rewards. There was a tendency for developers who were blocked by the Council (or delayed for some other reason) to sell the land on. However, there was never any shortage of takers. There also appeared to be an element of copying of competitors. Once one firm was making money though high quality design then all the others wanted to be seen to be doing the same in that location. Moreover, there were the prior landholdings mentioned above that certainly affected some developers. Another reason why some could not easily boycott the local planning authority's area is that they had invested in regional and local offices in conjunction with the land buying and which would then handle the subsequent stages of the process.

Did the Council's design policies impose any financial disadvantage upon developers, whether in the form of direct costs, risk or any other form? The experience at Chelmsford was that the answer was definitely no. No developer produced in negotiation the slightest evidence of any real net costs over the whole process. Most of them appeared to know in advance that this was the answer. Once the situation was clear to them, they complied. The situation was much more akin to bargaining in a third-world market than organisational decisions based on cold financial calculation. Their initial reluctance was based more on human and organisational factors than financial ones.

What was also notable was how quickly developers adapted to the situation once the guidance was definite and explicit. Conflicts between the Planning Committee and developers occurred in the mid to late 1990s, before this was the case (Hall 2007). From 2001 onwards, there were almost no appeals against refusal of planning permission on design grounds. However, even with the very clear guidance, there was still an important role for negotiation. This went way beyond the processing of the formal planning applications. Two activities outside the formal process were critical for raising quality. Both pre-application negotiation and post-permission vigilance, monitoring progress during detailed design and construction, paid dividends. From the developer's point of view, the dividend was that greater speed and certainty overall reduced their costs.

It must be made clear though that there would have been almost no good design if there had not been the background threat of refusal backed up by dismissal of the appeal. The reluctance of developers to comply voluntarily or, preferably, to take a lead in good design themselves, was not for financial reasons but because they did not understand the issues: more a matter of 'knowledge averse' than 'risk averse'. The proactive approach was an educational process rather than a financial compact.

Conclusion

What then can be learnt from the experience at Chelmsford? Experience there showed that the planning authority could change developer practices. Through negotiation the planning authority achieved neighbourhoods based on legible routes and meaningful spaces to generate a sense of place with well-integrated affordable housing and non-residential uses and quality public realm.

One of the most significant lessons was the way that increasing planning intervention gave scope for more, not less, quality architecture. Over time, there was a steady increase in the quantity, and degree of prescription, of published planning policy relating to design control. Use was made of policy in national guidance, design guides, local plan policy and site specific briefs. As these became more detailed, clearer and more purposeful, so the quality on the ground improved. Before the introduction of the explicit controls, what was built was the standard developer product with minimal architectural input. With strong planning intervention, architect-designed schemes, tailored to the site, became the norm in the town centre and common elsewhere. This applied to the design of shops and offices as well as housing.

When the process of effective design briefing and pre-application discussion was working properly, the processing of the application became largely a formality. Discussions started long before a planning application was submitted, and the brief was written before the discussions started. They reflected a need to see how different sites fitted together and related to development over a larger area, even the town as a whole. This required considerable long-term vision regarding both the physical form and the formal process that brings it about. All this could not have been achieved without investment in sufficient staff with the required expertise. Not only was an urban design team of professionals needed but the proactive process required cooperative working, as opposed to merely consulting, both between the different professions within a planning authority and with the agencies involved in the development process.

Although the experience related here took place in a context of high land values, there is no reason to suppose that the type of policies applied in Chelmsford would not be equally successful where land values are low. The tragedy is that, in areas of economic decline, councils may be reluctant to press developers to produce higher standards in case they go away. However, as has been explained, good design is certainly not less profitable – more often more so. Moreover, as is often pointed out elsewhere, it can add value within the process of regeneration. Reluctance on behalf of both parties to pursue higher standards is more in the mind than in the pocket.

The experience in Chelmsford showed how the gradual increase over time of both the quantity of published policy and its degree of prescription resulted in better quality of architecture and a more vibrant public realm. It was not something that should be seen as peculiar to Chelmsford or to the period in question. It has wide applicability. Chelmsford was very typical of many towns within the more prosperous parts of north-west Europe and other parts of the developed world. Because it had not been particularly well endowed, by British standards, with architectural heritage, its experiences could be seen as all the more relevant to other planning authorities. If this town could do it, then why not others?

5

Plot Logic: Character-Building Through Creative Parcelisation

Tim Love and Christina Crawford

Introduction

Most new urban development is planned based on a hierarchy of streets, resulting in blocks that provide the opportunity for land subdivision into real estate parcels. There is nothing particularly new about this strategy: the urban morphology of Haussmann's Paris was predicated on the star-shaped street pattern, with the blocks and individual plots a mere residual effect of the street configuration (Panerai *et al.* 2004: 18). It is the dimension and configuration of these resultant parcels, as well as their specific relationship to street systems, that determine their relative value and their ranking in an incremental build-out of the district, either by the master developer or sub-developers with oversight by the master developer team. This model of urban planning, with streets conceived first and the blocks resulting, is driven by the logic of streets and infrastructure, and supported by urban planners who promote the 19th century ideal of urbanism. In this version of the city, the streets and civic spaces of the city are defined by a continuous street wall of building faces; the public realm is conceived as a series of beautifully shaped outdoor rooms. In theory, the collaboration of infrastructural planners and architects on this vision of the city is ideal: streets are carefully designed to meet the projected traffic needs of development build-outs and design guidelines are established to assure an orderly built environment.

Urban Design in the Real Estate Development Process, First Edition. Edited by Steve Tiesdell and David Adams.
© 2011 Blackwell Publishing Ltd. Published 2011 by Blackwell Publishing Ltd.

But in practice, this model of development, especially on the large scale, has not met its promise. Many critics contend that both Battery Park City in New York City and Canary Wharf in London lack the authentic character and cultural and economic diversity of the 'real' city, despite the care with which both projects were conceived and executed. The desire was for diversity; the result is architectural and scalar homogeneity. There are many contributing factors to the sterile quality of the places created through the Battery Park City model of planning, from the professional yet mediocre quality of the architecture, to the draconian design guidelines that often stifle innovative and incremental contributions to the urban realm. Although issues of character abound in such cases, the Battery Park City model of urbanism is the primary operating contemporary approach; even masterplans that champion much more expressive architectural elements have the same fundamental masterplanning logic.

What remains unexplored in this model of urbanism is the fundamental relationship between prevalent building codes, block size, parcel size and intended building typology of the build-out. In current planning practice, these regulatory relationships are passively considered, given the dominant role of the building as either an edge to the public realm or a dramatic punctuation on the skyline. Rarely is the parcel map itself presented as part of the masterplan vision, regardless of the fact that it is the primary tool by which development and city-making are driven. The underlying structure of a district, however, is written in its attitude toward block and plot sub-division. The size and distribution of the parcels indicates the typology of buildings that can reasonably participate in the build-out. A careful parcel map, along with a set of regulatory guidelines, can and should be used as the primary tool with which to craft the character of successful new urban districts.

Setting the rules

The design of a new urban district is the result of a negotiation between several important players including public officials, who have a direct influence on shaping and approving a masterplan and then regulating its build-out, the master developer (who, in some cases, may be a public entity), the masterplanner, parcel developers, and the architects of specific parcels. In contemporary practice, several goals are likely to be shared by all of the parties, including walkable streets, a mix of transportation options, and enough controls to create an ordered and humane public realm. Among the above participants, the public official, master developer and masterplanner have the potential to control the ultimate character and build-out of the district through a series of rules that are established in the pre-development phase. The street grid, block size and smaller subdivisions of land are typically solidified in this earliest stage; zoning and other design guidelines are also established early. These dimensionally specific plots, in concert with the various text-based guidelines, then constitute the playing field and set of rules that the final actors – sub-developers and their architects – must live by, all instituted in the service of a successful urban realm.

Even in the earliest stages of a project, when the rules are being established, conflict can occur between the master developer and the masterplanner, often around the issue of flexibility of the build-out. The master developer will often seek to maximise market flexibility by demanding relatively large building plots, few constraints on the programme mix of specific parcels, and soft design guidelines. Of all of these issues, plot size may have the most impact on the future quality (and success) of high-density urban development. Sub-developers and their architects, cumulatively the players with the greatest potential to tangibly affect the quality of an urban district, are those whose actions are most tightly circumscribed by the underlying parcel map that charts future build-out.

Parcelling and subdivision strategies

The configuration of the parcel in relation to the block and street has an important impact on the resulting quality of the urbanism. Generally, parcels are configured in four ways relative to the normative blocks of a city district (see Figure 5.1), moving from the largest and most flexible, to the smallest and most prescriptive:

1.   District-based

In the first approach, land is released as a parcel containing several blocks. This strategy is geared to mega-development with relatively large-scale developers taking on significant pieces of the build-out. The guidelines for these large-scale parcels run the gamut from prescriptive to laissez faire in terms of internal street layout. On the prescriptive end of the spectrum, the internal street layout and overall urban form are defined by the master developer/masterplanner. In a looser approach, there may be requirements for a street edge and street access points into the development, but the internal street layout is left to the discretion of the sub-developer. In each case, the sub-developer pays for the street infrastructure internal to the parcel.

2.   Block-based

In the second land-release approach, the urban block, bounded on all sides by streets, is the parcel and unit of transfer. This approach often leads to a rational grid pattern, leading to the type of urban fabric postulated by Rem

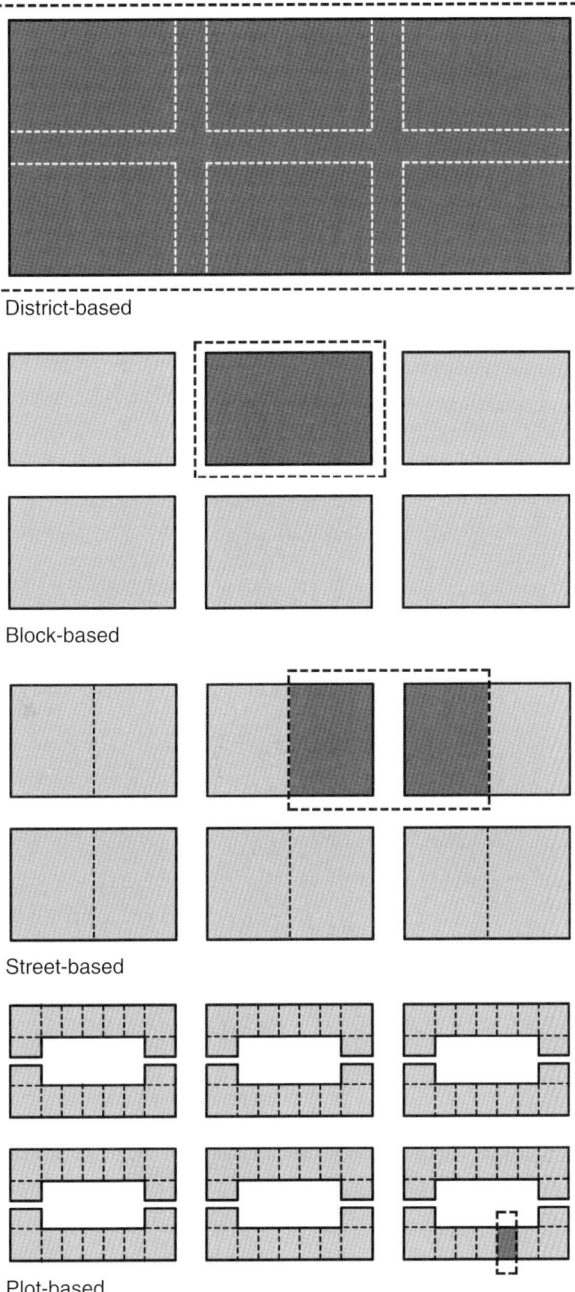

District-based

Block-based

Street-based

Plot-based

Figure 5.1 Parcelisation strategies: new city blocks are subdivided into individual building parcels using four primary strategies that range from large, district-based parcelisation to small-scale, plot-based division. *Source:* Utile, Inc. Architecture + Planning, based upon prototypes by Steve Tiesdell.

Koolhaas in his artwork *City of the Captive Globe* (1972). Even relaxed from this extreme rigidity, most contemporary large-scale development follows this general pattern. In this approach, the master developer provides the street infrastructure for the entire development.

3. Street-based

In the third approach, a parcel is comprised of two half blocks with a block-length of street included in the centre of the property. This approach makes the street the centre of the design rather than the edge of developer's site as in the first block-based approach. Unlike a block-based parcel scheme, this approach requires the sub-developer to build the infrastructure of the street within the parcel, thus reducing the upfront infrastructure costs to the master developer. In the case of Amsterdam South, the parcel allotted to a sub-developer comprised two half blocks separated by a street; these half blocks are then laminated to one another and aggregated to make the city.

4. Plot-based

In the final, most fine-grained and prescriptive parcel configuration, a block is divided into several parcels, each of which can be released to a different sub-developer. In this case, relatively more prescriptive guidelines must be required to establish rear yard setbacks, building heights at shared property lines, street-front qualities etc. In addition, rules may be established that limit the number of parcels that a single sub-developer can acquire on a block and/or rules that limit the number of contiguous parcels that can be developed by a single entity. Provided that design guidelines are not too stringent, it is this final land-release iteration that may lead to the most diverse urban fabric, as each parcel will be the result of the collaboration and aspirations of a different developer/architect team. The master developer is responsible, in this case, for all larger infrastructural costs.

The primacy of the urban realm

The prevailing lack of interest in parcelisation is likely the result of the primacy of the urban realm in contemporary planning and architectural discourse, which relegates the particular quality or nature of the building fabric to secondary status. This emphasis on the space between buildings has been taken up by two particular design protagonists: New Urbanist planners and landscape architects. For planners adherent to the New Urbanism movement in the USA, or those sympathetic to the Poundbury model in the UK, spatially figurative streets and spaces hark back to a time when the street was a social condenser: a space in which collective activity thrived and the vehicle was secondary. In creating pleasant streets and sidewalks, bounded necessarily by buildings, a better 'place' will result. Landscape architects in the emerging sub-discipline of Landscape Urbanism, on the other hand, are interested not in the people-collecting potential of these in-between spaces, but rather in the linear systems that offer a setting for urban natural habitats, ecologically sound water management, and multimodal transportation. In both models of contemporary urban design, the building fabric is mostly an inert mass that only gains meaning in relationship to the collective spaces of the city. Within the ideological framework of New Urbanism, for example, building edges are shaped to define figurative spaces and programmed with uses that generate and attract people to the public realm. In new models of sustainable urbanism, buildings generate storm water, higher temperatures as a result of the heat island effect, and greenhouse gas emissions. The public realm (as the virtuous complement to development) is there to ameliorate building-generated problems and bring an ecological balance back to the city.

Part of this lack of attention to the role of buildings – and the parcels on which they sit in a larger urban plan – might stem from disciplinary boundaries that persist between urban planning, which is focused on the policies and regulations that shape the city, and urban design, which is focused on the specific physical qualities of the built environment. This disciplinary rift has led to a strained relationship between the policies that set the ground rules for city-building, and the ultimate tangible urban fabric that results. Planners create the text-based rulebooks that set the ground rules for city-building, and urban designers arrive on the scene later, take the rules as presented, and try to craft quality places out of (or in spite of) the regulations. Often, the regulators and implementers feel themselves to be working at cross purposes, in an antagonistic relationship that prevents new collaborative modes of urban design emerging that are more germane to the economic and political realities of city-building in late capitalist societies. Particularly, there is a need to link the logic of the land speculation, as manifested in the plot configurations of new urban development, with the kind of physical city that is desired.

Specifically, the size, shape and interrelationship of the plots in a new urban development need to be based on the specific form of the building types that are envisioned to fill out the plan. In most of the subdivision strategies outlined above, the parcelisation of large development areas into building-sized plots is framed first and foremost by the overall pattern of a street network – a network that is often dictated by the needs of transportation systems. Plot shapes and sizes are also fixed by real estate valuation strategies based on an analysis of potential land value against the cost of infrastructural improvements. In suburban development, this analytical process privileges sites that are relatively deep and narrow, as the street frontage is much more valuable than the land within the inner block. In most urban developments there is a cursory check of the fit between plot and potential building types, but only concerning the most basic dimensional criteria for different potential uses. We would argue instead, for an urban planning and development approach that begins with the conception of the building types – that is, with the plots, streets, blocks and other infrastructural components growing out of the particular characteristics and infrastructural needs of the building units. To build this kind of particularity into an urban design, the most rudimentary tool is the subdivision of land: the parcel, or plot, which in turn supports a carefully calibrated range of building types. It is an inside-out logic that preconceives city-building from the more intimate scale of the individual building outward, and requires deep understanding of the scale, types and diversity of buildings that accrue to make quality urban places.

The pitfalls of flexibility

Typically, parcels are sized for maximum market flexibility. To support the type of flexibility to which larger developers aspire, only two parcelisation strategies can be considered: the district-based or the block-based model. To reach extreme potential build-out (and profit), the largest, most demanding programme drives dimensionality: in this case the typical office floor plate of a contemporary commercial building. Large-scale urban development today is largely geared towards capturing a global market share of the financial service and bio-technology sectors. To meet these demands, the preferred floor plate dimension of commercial buildings continues to grow.

When maximum flexibility is the primary marketing strategy for large-scale development, then only super-sized parcels are planned; the greater assumption is that smaller building types such as multi-family housing, hotels, retail and mixed-use versions of all of the above can be accommodated within the mega-parcel. There are three main consequences of this approach. There are scalar and character challenges, projects so large as to limit competition within the development community and astronomical project payback premiums to fund steel or reinforced concrete construction, the default construction type for high-rise buildings. All of the above consequences conspire to create the dull quality of street life in the Battery Park City model.

First, the scalar challenge. If the ideal large tenant – the biotech company, the financial firm – is captured, then the urban plan accommodates only one building per block. While seemingly logical from a building design standpoint, since there are no difficult party-wall edges to deal with, the consequence is a development mono-culture on each block, no matter how artfully the ground-floor programme is mixed. The constellation of uses inserted into any of these singular behemoths seeks to provide balance within the building, and is for discrete users, not the larger district in which it sits. Complicated financing for these large-scale developments seeks to balance risk and justification of specific quantities and configurations of programmatic components, based on similar successfully implemented projects on neighbouring blocks, and they will therefore tend to be more similar than different. The result is a city comprised of development mono-cultures across the street from development mono-cultures, without much divergence in their character and programme.

An added negative scalar effect of the one-large-parcel-per-block paradigm is that smaller programmes – housing and retail, for instance – require convoluted massing solutions to define the edges of the block. Out of this struggle, building types have emerged that are variants on the podium and tower scheme, or perimeter-block and tower scheme, depending on the size of the block and the targeted density of the development. Vancouver, which sought to rapidly increase residential density within the downtown core, took these mega-parcels and invented a podium and point tower residential type that has been exported to other cities with common mega-parcel issues. The financial premium of building point towers on large blocks, however, led to a dissatisfying lack of economic diversity in this section of the city, and to overuse of the formerly innovative massing solution (see Figures 5.2 and 5.3). Vancouver is now looking for direction from its architectural community to develop alternative building types that can still work within the underlying framework: the mega-parcel.[1]

The second consequence of large-parcel development plans is lack of developer diversity: only one type of developer and builder can participate in the build-out of these oversized blocks. For development schemes conceived and promoted by large-scale development concerns like ING in the Netherlands, and Forest City Ratner in the USA, the logic for this approach is self-evident: it limits the competition. But for public and public–private initiatives such as Battery Park City, Canary Wharf and Boston's Seaport District, the ideal circumstance would be to leave the field open to a host of qualified developers. Because of the unwieldy size of each development opportunity, the build-out of many of these plans has taken decades longer to occur than originally projected, or worse yet, has led to a number of permanently stalled or abandoned projects in the wake of the financial crisis that began in 2008. Too much complicated financing is required to bring these mega-projects to life, and in a risk-averse economic climate, this scale of development becomes virtually impossible to achieve. Over-ambition and singular site control leaves cities at the mercy of large developers; incremental development, in such a circumstance, is almost impossible.

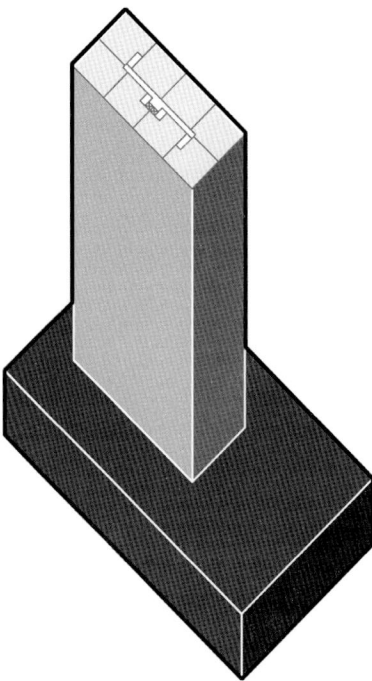

Figure 5.2 Vancouver podium building type: in an effort to insert residential uses into Vancouver's typical large-scale block, the City encouraged the development of a new building type, a slim residential tower that rises above a street-defining podium. *Source:* Utile, Inc. Architecture + Planning.

Figure 5.3 Waterfront view of downtown Vancouver: the Vancouver type is now overly prevalent in the downtown, leading the design community to look for new typological solutions for the City's large-scale blocks. Reproduced by permission of Keith D. Tyler.

   The third and final downfall of the large parcel planning prototype is that the block-sized building is, by default, a steel or reinforced concrete building. Purchasing, or leasing, a block of a city needs a significant return on the initial investment. While zoning of individual cities seeks to limit density to a reasonable standard, there are often side deals that a city will strike with a developer to gain public amenities in exchange for greater density. Profitable designs are tall, broad, and always work to maximise spaces for greatest ultimate leasable area. This means that steel will be integral to the design, elevators will be plentiful, and that all of that cost will be offset by the greatest possible density. If the planning scenario were to allow for mixed- and modest-sized parcelisation in addition to the necessary (and in certain cases desirable) large parcel blocks, a healthy mix of construction and material types could be feathered into the city.

   City governments are often complicit in maintaining the large-parcel status quo. While large projects can be publicly controversial and highly scrutinised, they place less stress on the system in comparison to a finer-grained subdivision model in which hundreds of owners/developers are filing for reviews and approvals. Ultimately, it is simpler for the local government to support a parcelisation strategy that at least leaves the door open for a singular entity to come to the table; it is a better risk, in some ways, than dealing with many small enterprises (often less sophisticated), who need to be more closely managed. It must be understood, therefore, that ensuring higher quality places within the city may require increased oversight from the governing municipality.

Economic viability of low-scale, densely distributed buildings

Over the past decade, the international demand for steel, and its escalating commodity price, has caused steel and reinforced concrete frame buildings to be relatively more expensive than load-bearing masonry building in western Europe and wood frame buildings in North America. Due to this material cost discrepancy, there is a leap that a building or urban project must take, once the building code threshold for the lower-cost materials has been exceeded. Five to six storeys is the limit for lower-cost concrete block in Europe; in North America, four to five storeys is the maximum building height possible with wood construction. Beyond these limits, a project must use more expensive material – steel, reinforced concrete – which immediately forces a financial offset in increased density. To close the expenditure-to-return gap, a project that might, for contextual reasons, wish to be eight storeys becomes eleven storeys.

   The building code for comparable densities in the USA and Canada is based on the vernacular of wood frame construction. Given the more recent history of large-scale development in these countries, beginning with Battery Park City in New York City in the 1980s and culminating in the real estate boom of the 1990s and 2000s, there are no laudable precedents of privately financed large-scale developments that leverage the social and economic advantages of high-density wood-frame construction in urban areas.

Part of the answer may be the economic and cultural divide between the large-scale urban developers working in American cities and production housing developers such as Toll Brothers and Linear building large-scale suburban housing projects. The other reason may be cultural. In the 1990s, the federal government in the USA initiated Hope VI, an initiative to rehabilitate or replace early to mid-20th-century public housing. Many of the brick and concrete complexes were in severe disrepair and were planned upon a policy of urban segregation. In an effort to re-knit the communities back into the urban fabric, many mid- and high-rise buildings were demolished, replaced with high-density, wood frame vernacular houses, replete with individual stooped entries, gabled roofs and bright coats of paint. This new housing solved some cultural issues among low-income residents – including an increased sense of personal responsibility for upkeep – but one of the unexpected negative results of the programmes is that wood frame development in urban areas may now be too closely associated with publicly financed housing projects.

Although several of the projects developed under the programme sought to maximise the densities possible within the framework of the building code for wood frame construction, the design priorities for the projects was focused on vernacular imagery and traditional patterns of neighbourhood planning. More recently, community development corporations and private non-profit developers with special regulatory authority to build affordable and 'workforce' housing are beginning to make inroads in this area, but not at the scale of previous generation Hope VI projects or with the density and urban aspirations of European examples.

The agenda for a robust lower-scale urbanism in North America needs to begin with the invention of the residential building types themselves, with an eye to their potential aggregation into urban blocks and districts. Once successful and innovative types are established, an attitude toward intelligent parcelisation can follow, likely based upon the plot-based model to allow for a variety of developers to be engaged.[2]

Alternative models

Given the negative consequences of the mega-parcel model, there needs to be a greater bandwidth of parcelisation options – incorporating all four strategies outlined above – that seek to balance the advantages of large and flexible parcels with modest parcels that will attract capital investment at a smaller scale and create a city with more physical diversity. But with smaller parcel sizes, the consequences of probable and possible building types cannot be left to the market (and chance). Rather, masterplans will need to be built up with a specific idea about the possible building types embedded in their very logic, ranging from highly dense low-scale buildings that can thrive on small parcels, to more innovative types to fill out the mega-block, as it will inevitably persist in some contexts.

Several recent urban development plans have critiqued the primacy of the large parcel, single-block development paradigm. If the past few decades have illuminated the risk factors in sizing parcels to the maximum possible future use, and creating a city that forwards flexibility as the determining criteria, then the antidote must be found in careful specificity. All the case studies below share two commonalities: the parcel map was clearly defined with a mix of plot sizes and often multiple parcels on a single block, and they took as their unit of measure a specific building type to establish reasonable dimensional standards at the parcel level. Many of the sub-developers and architects who participated in the build-out of these case studies also found ways to take advantage of local codes, innovating building types that are as dense as possible while still keeping within regulatory limits. In the following examples, scalar variety was clearly a goal of the masterplan, and in each case the programme was largely predetermined. When the programme is set early enough in the project, parcelisation can be an outgrowth of general building size and typology. The examples display a range of masterplanning entities, ranging from municipalities (in which zoning bylaws and other policies are the tools of enactment) to private developers, who see diversity and urban texture as a key selling point.

Hammarby Sjöstad

Hammarby Sjöstad, initiated in 1995, is a dense, largely residential new neighbourhood on the formerly industrial port lands of Stockholm, Sweden. The public goal of the project was to create an 'eco-neighbourhood' whose masterplan would incorporate environmental technologies and promote a sustainable lifestyle. Rather than allow private developers to determine the parcelisation of the neighbourhood, the masterplan design and development was spearheaded by two city agencies: the City Development Administration and the City Planning Administration. The plot-based parcelisation strategy was used for two primary reasons: to ensure that the built-out scale of the new neighbourhood would erase the memory and character of the industrial scale that previously occupied the area, and to make the individual parcels small enough to permit a large number of small developers to participate. To date, over 40 development entities, both public and private, have completed buildings within the precinct. According to the City of Stockholm, the comparatively large number of development participants led to a healthy competitive atmosphere that fostered architectural and sustainable innovation, and a higher standard of construction.

There was one crucial difference from the standard plot-based scenario that causes the Hammarby Sjöstad example to stand out. Rather than placing the burden of all infrastructural financing on the master developer – in this case, expensive remediation of contaminated sites – the City allowed sub-developers to choose how and when to participate in the cleanup. The first option allowed for the developer to contribute early to the cost of remediation in exchange for reduced land cost. Option two allowed the participant to pay market rate for a remediated site. Most developers opted for the early-in option, which helped the City pay for the cost of remediation in real time. Another major benefit of the reasonable size of each individual development lot was that the capital outlay for an otherwise overwhelming remediation effort was spread among an assemblage of participants.

Hammarby Sjöstad is largely a residential neighbourhood; thus multi-unit housing buildings constitute the standard type. No matter their specific architectural expression, the vast majority of the residential buildings leverage the maximum allowable height and configuration for a single-stair/single-elevator point-load residential building to make the densest, and therefore most profitable, individual development. Most of the buildings in the development push the limits of the code by placing duplex units at the fifth floor of the shared circulation to gain an additional sixth storey within the governing regulatory framework. The second floor of this penthouse duplex is often stepped back to allow the canal- and street-fronts to retain an intimate low-rise scale. Left to their own devices in a competitive environment, the sub-developers and their architects found ways in which to innovatively create projects that exhibit high design quality within a tightly prescribed dimensional and regulatory framework.

Malmö Bo01

Sweden's entry to the European Housing Expo, 2001, is the largely residential planned district of Malmö Bo01. In the earliest planning documents for the project, the City of Malmö joined with potential development partners to articulate a formalised vision for the new *City of Tomorrow*, a tabula rasa ecologically sustainable neighbourhood. Explicit in their vision was a desire for authentic urbanity: '... the City of Tomorrow will be an ecologically sustainable, densely built-up inner city.' (Bo01/ City of Malmö 1999: 12). In addition, the planners indicate that diversity is a key motivating factor in the design of the community, not just demographic diversity, but assortment in terms of '... everything from the design of urban spaces and parks to the selection of dwelling sizes, types of building and floor plans' (Bo01/ City

Figure 5.4 Malmö Bo01 Streetscape: the diverse ground-level experience within the neighbourhood is created by a casual site plan and irregular parcel geometry. Reproduced by permission of Steve Tiesdell.

of Malmö 1999: 17). While the bulk of the new neighbourhood is residential, there are a host of support services that provide programmatic, and therefore the seeds of scalar, difference within the fabric.

Västra Hamnen (the Western Harbour) is a self-sustaining neighbourhood on the western edge of the larger Malmö Bo01 planned district, and its first phase of construction. The quarter is comprised of a diverse collection of buildings casually related to each other in a picturesque plan composition (see Figure 5.4). The disposition of parcels, and ultimately buildings, was predicated on two complementary desires. First, the buildings were carefully oriented to protect the interior of the neighbourhood from prevailing winds sweeping off the harbour; taller buildings were placed at the waterfront for the same wind-blocking effect. Here, the master developer began with a block-based parcelisation strategy that took the multi-unit courtyard housing type as the standard building block. But, unlike many block-based examples, the orthogonal grid was skewed in response to environmental concerns. The resultant blocks were scaled to small and oddly shaped plots, requiring customised architectural responses rather than the off-the-shelf solutions favoured by market-driven developers. Second, the city planners established

Figure 5.5   Malmö Bo01, Turning Torso Tower: large parcels carefully inserted into the interior of the masterplan meant that larger-scale buildings, such as the tall residential tower, could also be part of the development mix. Reproduced by permission of Steve Tiesdell.

early the aesthetic criteria that each building grouping be unique in form and material. These requirements were not resisted by the sub-developers. On the contrary, the irregularity of the parcel geometry forced variable form and material differentiation lent each project unique qualities that allowed for market differentiation. The result is a plan that celebrates variety and leverages the ability of the market to create a more natural kind of urban discordance.

Vertical variation was also built carefully into the plan. Taller buildings were placed against the water's edge, to shield the inner core of the neighbourhood from harsh harbour winds. Moving away from the water, the neighbourhood parcel sizes increase on a modest gradient to allow for larger buildings to share adjacencies with smaller-scale buildings; the masterplan ensured that larger-scale buildings were not *precluded* from inclusion in the district. One development that shows the capacity of such a parcel-size gradient is the 190-metre, 54-storey 'Turning Torso', a torquing point tower designed by architect Santiago Calatrava (see Figure 5.5). From a conceptual and compositional standpoint, the tower is a success: it demonstrates that large-scale buildings can co-exist adjacent to mid-rise development. While the Turning Torso is a landmark structure, it is none-theless an example of a single-block mega-development that ultimately lacks the social-connectedness of the other smaller-scale blocks within the neighbourhood.

Madinat Al Soor

The plan of the Madinat Al Soor district, part of the Office for Metropolitan Architecture (OMA)'s ambitious plan for Waterfront City in Dubai, sought a similar organic result to that being achieved in Malmö (see Figures 5.6a and b and 5.7). Whereas the majority of Dubai was being developed on a Battery Park City urban model – mega-blocks that host one building, often a hyper-scraper – Madinat Al Soor was to approximate the aggregative urbanity of a traditional Arab city, but with contemporary architectural expression. While the initial planning for the proto-Arab neighbourhood may have been OMA's tongue-in-cheek response to the ubiquitous Dubai tower, the developer immediately saw the merit of purposeful market differentiation. The developers surmised that the street-level intimacy and scalar variability between adjacent buildings was precisely what the rest of Dubai was lacking.

In this case, a singular building typology – with many variations and an organic disposition – was the primary tool by which a pleasing randomness was ensured. The building block for this plan was the traditional Arab court-yard type, one in which units or leasable spaces wrap a privatised exterior space. In the Al Soor plan, this type was dimensionally tweaked, aggregated and made to host a variety of uses, from residential to retail, to office. For office use, the courtyard type had to morph from a low-rise to a high-rise object (at 13+ storeys), so that the courtyard became, effectively, an exterior atrium. Once the building blocks and the programme mix were set, the parcelisation simply post-justified the building massing and programme mix. The highly specific plot plan was a key drawing in OMA's masterplan. In this instance, the owner of the project and client for the design, Nakheel, reserved the right to act as a sole developer for the project, but the plan was devised to allow for attenuated phasing, and for Nakheel to choose the lesser role of master developer for a large number of smaller construction entities in the future. While they had yet to determine how, and in what increments, the land would be released, the building-specific plot plan would allow for anything from the district-based to plot-based strategy to be enacted (in other words, with the plan as designed, the full range of land-transfer strate-gies could be realised). In the roll-out of this project (never built), the highly specific parcel boundaries were coupled with a relatively loose set of design guidelines, a combination that was to allow the natural forces of the market to create aesthetic diversity.

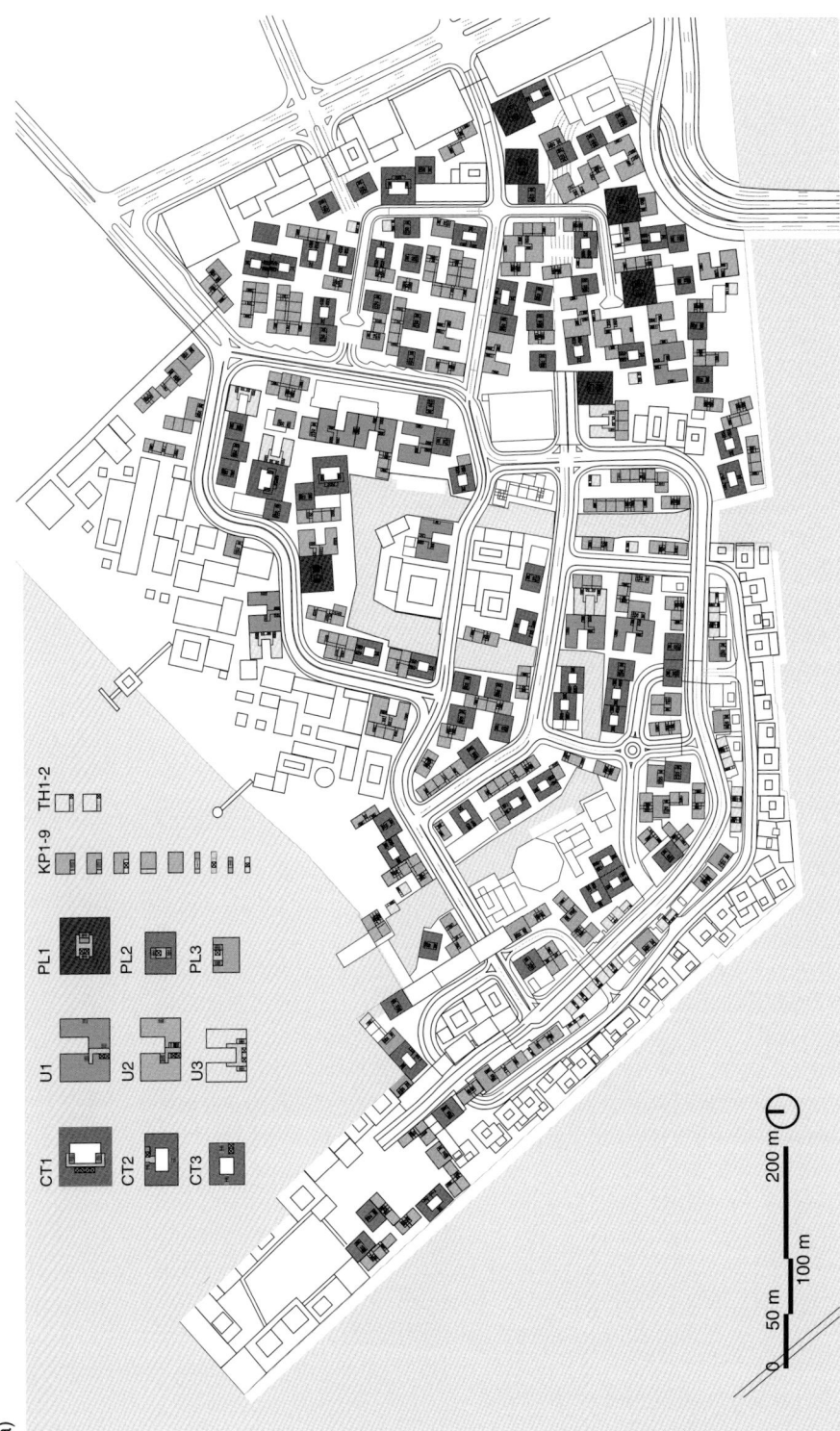

CT1 U1 PL1 KP1-9 TH1-2

CT2 U2 PL2

CT3 U3 PL3

0 50 m 100 m 200 m

Figure 5.6 (a) Madinat Al Soor District Plan + Madinat Al Soor Parcel Plan: the organic quality of the district plan was ensured by the casual disposition of a limited number of building types. Individual parcel division resulted from specific building footprints. *Source:* Utile, Inc. Architecture + Planning.

(a)

Figure 5.6 (b) Madinat Al Soor Parcel Plan. *Source:* Utile, Inc. Architecture + Planning.

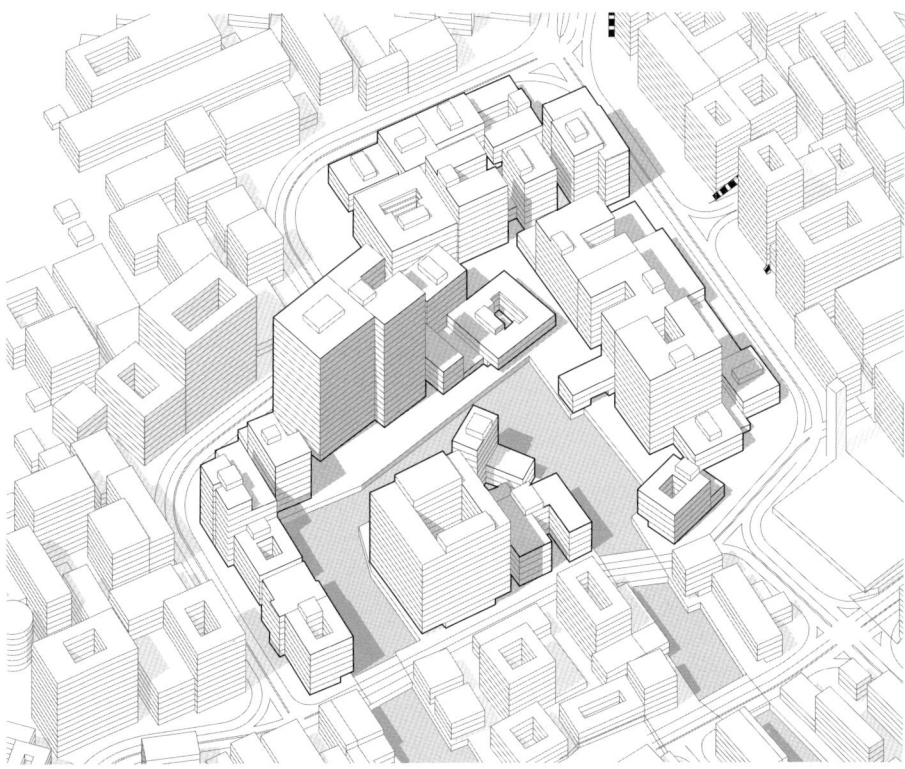

Figure 5.7   Madinat Al Soor Massing: an aggregative neighbourhood character was the result of high degree of variety in parcelisation and height. *Source:* Utile, Inc. Architecture + Planning.

Borneo Sporenburg

Urban plans based on a more normative orthogonal grid have shown that small-scale parcels, design guidelines and the market can create the desired effect of urban variety. The narrow row houses on Borneo Sporenburg (1993–1996), part of the Amsterdam's eastern docklands, have been championed by urbanists and architectural critics because of the variety of architectural expression yielded by a building code that required specific solutions for light and air and on-site parking (see Figure 5.8). Important to the logic of the project was a realisation that high densities could be achieved with individual houses compactly arranged and smaller-than-typical street widths (not only to raise density but to encourage a more robust pedestrian realm). In total, 100 architects designed within the masterplan set forth by Adriaan Geuze of West 8, creating new prototypes within the framework. The overall experience of the project – especially from the water, onto which the majority of the dwellings look – is one of textural variety. Large plots were also sprinkled throughout the repurposed docklands, interrupting the march of low-rise townhouses. These play host to mid-rise multi-unit buildings that help to

Figure 5.8 Borneo Sporenburg Canal View: very small plot sizes and a regulation precluding the aggregation of lots into larger development parcels results in an urban facade with rich textual variety. Reproduced by permission of Steve Tiesdell.

increase overall density, but that also play an important urbanistic role: to diffuse scalar monotony.

Borneo Sporenburg is financially feasible partly because the sub-developers use lower-cost construction materials at the very edge of building code compliance in terms of height. In should also be noted that the planning maximises horizontal density. Narrower streets, frequent, but small open spaces and shared party walls all contribute to profitable low- to mid-rise development. In addition to the direct influence of regulatory thresholds on the financial logic and physical manifestation of urban proposals, since 1945 new development in the social democracies of northern Europe has been built in relatively dense low-rise patterns. The USA, rife with suburban densities, has little such experience, and therefore has further to go to realise the potential of more tightly packed yet urbane development.

Borneo Sporenburg may offer a more applicable model for mixed-scale development in North America, Great Britain and Europe than the examples of Hammarby Sjöstad, Malmö and Madinat Al Soor. It proposes a highly rational and transferable planning logic that builds in specificity and variability of parcel size so that a range of scales of development are not only possible, but also required. Used in different combinations and arrangements, this mixed parcel-size approach may be the right model for large-scale urban districts, not only because of the authentic urban character that results, but because of the mix of developer entities and construction technologies that will contribute to the build-out of the city.

Conclusion

The return to the city – a late 20th-century phenomenon in the USA – has proven that density and economic, demographic and architectural diversity are bankable assets to be emulated and capitalised upon. So how are these qualities, inherent to the existing city, created from scratch? The answer is by ensuring that the right balance of regulatory controls is established in the underlying structure of the neighbourhood from the beginning. A range of regulatory tools are available, from Euclidean zoning approaches that limit uses and densities to highly specific design guidelines that fix building set-backs and cornice heights, window types and materials. As our examples suggest, carefully dimensioned, shaped and arranged building plots that anticipate the thresholds of prevailing building codes can result in a success-ful urban framework for new development. Whether and when to use any one of the four subdivision strategies articulated above – ranging from district-based to plot-based scale – should be understood as a decision that will deeply affect the character of any new district.

Each strategy will be viewed differently by the development commu-nity. While it may be expected that too many controls, be they parcel-size or regulatory guidelines, may drive away some developers, many others will appreciate the certainty that well-defined controls provide a project. In financial terms, the clearer the possibilities of a site, the more accurate a pro forma and the more secure the investment outcome. Architects may also initially chafe at tightly defined controls. But, as the example of Borneo Sporenburg demonstrates, properly framed constraints that stop just short of specific aesthetic prescriptions provide a carefully calibrated framework in which innovation can occur. In such a setting where the design problem is not a simple one, and innovation is rewarded, architects prove their worth.

To create a successful, high quality urban place, a balance must ultimately be found between allowing the market to set the standards, and exercising a measure of control that can predict with some certainty the building typolo-gies that will inhabit the plan. By acknowledging that the building, and not the street, is the primary unit by which the market creates urban character, it is imperative that urban designers, in close collaboration with real estate experts, design the subdivision of the land, based on an anticipated range of building types, to create a framework for future urban variety and vibrancy.

Notes

1. In 2007, the Architecture Foundation of British Columbia and Royal Architectural Institute of Canada co-sponsored an open architectural ideas competition entitled 'poto-type' (podium/ tower typology). The purpose of the competition was to question the ubiquitous podium/ tower solution in downtown Vancouver, given that '... proliferation of this architectural mono-type could potentially create social and economic disparateness while weakening neighborhood identities'. The competition brief and the winning schemes can be found at www.poto.ca.
2. Utile, the architecture firm and think tank where the authors practise, has been focused on this agenda for the past five years. Design research at the firm, and in housing studios at the Northeastern University School of Architecture in Boston, has shown that high quality units can be designed within zero-lot-line wood-frame row house and courtyard buildings.

6

The Business of Codes: Urban Design Regulation in an Entrepreneurial Society*

Nicholas J. Marantz and Eran Ben-Joseph

The realtors have learned that nothing does more to create and stabilise value than wise city planning. They have realised that they cannot regard their business as a profession if they simply transmit values as they find them and fail to apply scientific principles in building cities.
J. C. Nichols, Director, National Association of Real Estate Boards
City Planning, Vol. 1(1), 1925, p. 34.

Introduction

Developers have always played a central role in urban planning and land use regulation in the USA. From the early years of the 20th century, real estate industry leaders saw the regulation of city planning and development as a boon to their trade (Weiss 1987). Developers assumed a crucial role in the design and implementation of regulation, because they understood the potential for legal rules to boost property values, safeguard investments and control competition.

This chapter explains the role of the real estate industry in the regulation of development in the USA and explores this history's implications for future innovation. The first part, *Zoning America*, describes the foundation of contemporary American real estate development controls. It explains how

* Partial funding support for the research reported in this chapter was provided by the National Science Foundation.

Urban Design in the Real Estate Development Process, First Edition. Edited by Steve Tiesdell and David Adams.

efforts to reform America's cities gave developers the opportunity to push for favourable regulation. The second part, *Developing America*, shows how large-scale developers decisively influenced the form and content of such regulation in the 20th century. These developers sought certain forms of regulation and ensured that the responsible federal agencies were staffed with their confederates. Asking how regulation affected these developers would be somewhat misleading, because they exerted great control over regulation. We therefore seek to understand why large-scale developers sought certain types of regulation, and how the results have affected the built environment. The third part, *Designing the American future*, contextualises contemporary American development regulation in this history. It discusses recent innovations such as form-based codes and the Leadership in Energy and Environmental Design Neighbourhood Development (LEED-ND) rating system, and assesses their prospects in light of the history outlined in the first and second parts. This history suggests that regulation of the built environment invariably reflects struggles over resource allocation and social identity. Obscuring this essential feature of regulation with a technical discourse of tools may hamper efforts to encourage the development of vibrant places.

Zoning America

The beginning of the 20th century launched a distinct epoch in the regulation of America's built environment: the era of zoning. Until the first decade of the 20th century, government regulation of the built environment depended on longstanding common law nuisance doctrine. A nuisance is a '… condition, activity, or situation (such as a loud noise or foul odor) that interferes with the use or enjoyment of property' (Garner 2004: 1096). By the 19th century, the maxim *sic utere tuo ut alienum non laedas* – 'so use your own property as not to injure that of another' – had become enshrined in British and American court decisions (Smead 1935). Since at least the 15th century, for example, the common law permitted a homeowner to recover damages from a neighbour who maintained a malodorous brood of hogs (Tyrwhitt 1826: 102–08).

Throughout the 19th century, many American cities adopted ordinances codifying such prohibitions on specific 'noxious' land uses (Ellickson & Been 2005: 75). State courts routinely found these statutes to be valid exercises of a city's 'police power' to protect public health, safety and general welfare (Ellickson & Been 2005: 75). (Under American federalism, the states retain the right to exercise the police power and they typically delegate much of it to local governments (McQuillin 2009, sec.24:34).) Such codification did not, however, alter the general character of public regulation of real estate development, which remained confined to the prevention of traditional nuisance.

As the 20th century dawned, dramatic changes were sweeping American cities, leading to dissatisfaction with the regulation of urban form. A swell of immigration in the latter half of the 19th century meant that, between 1870 and 1900, the US population nearly doubled (US Census Bureau 1993). This increase accrued disproportionately to cities (US Census Bureau 1999),[1] where it compounded concerns about overcrowding and stoked anti-immigrant sentiment (Lubove 1962: 11–20, 51–55). At the same time, technological advances, ranging from the advent of the steel frame structure and the elevator to the widespread distribution of electricity, promised to reshape urban America (Toll 1969: 47–55).

These trends were most evident in New York City, where, in response, progressive reformers and powerful property owners allied to press for more comprehensive regulation of the built environment (Toll 1969: 147–48). Concerned that a proliferation of manufacturing lofts would decrease their property values by introducing hordes of immigrant labourers, holders of prestigious Fifth Avenue real estate sought to prevent the encroachment of the burgeoning garment industry (Toll 1969: 113–16, 175–79). Landlords in lower Manhattan, meanwhile, hoped to restrict skyscraper development to stave off a glut of office buildings competing for natural light and tenants (Toll 1969: 153–54). Reformers saw a shift in regulation as a means of improving public health, enhancing fire safety and facilitating development of the City Beautiful (Toll 1969: 117–38).

To achieve these aims, the alliance of businessmen and reformers chose the mechanism of zoning. It is not immediately apparent why they made this decision, for zoning is a blunt instrument, which divides a city into districts with differing restrictions on land use, setback and building envelope. (American zoning is now commonly known as Euclidean zoning after the US Supreme Court case that affirmed the constitutionality of the practice – Village of Euclid v. Ambler Realty Co. 1926).

According to a leading treatise, 'Zoning exists to carry out three primary functions:

(1) to regulate the use of land, and the use of buildings and other structures;
(2) to regulate the size of buildings and other structures; and
(3) to regulate the location of buildings and other structures, in relation to lot lines and to other buildings' (Williams & Taylor 2003, sec.17:3).

Thus, zoning does not address the issue of civic beauty, and it influences urban form only at the most basic level. Yet zoning was seen as a desirable instrument for two reasons. First, given the constraints of the US Constitution (and the constitutions of individual states), it was the cheapest option. Second, according to its proponents, zoning had worked in Germany and could be successfully imported to the US.

The police power, eminent domain, and the cost of regulation

Initial American efforts to regulate building form relied not on the police power, but on the states' inherent power of eminent domain. The 'takings' clause of the Fifth Amendment to the US Constitution stipulates that '… [no] private property [shall] be taken for public use, without just compensation. By implication, the US Constitution does not prohibit the taking of private property '… for public use', so long as the government provides 'just compensation'. Early urban design regulations enacted by state and local governments were drafted to comply with this portion of the US Constitution and analogous state constitutional provisions. In 1898, for example, Massachusetts adopted a law imposing height limitations on buildings around Boston's Copley Square. The law passed constitutional muster because, the Massachusetts Supreme Judicial Court found, '… it seems to have been intended as a taking of rights in property *for the benefit of the public* who use Copley Square. It adds to the public park rights in light and air, and in the view over adjacent land above the line to which buildings may be erected' (emphasis added) (*Attorney General v. Williams 1899: 478; Williams v. Parker 1903*). Soon after the Massachusetts law was found constitutional, other jurisdictions adopted similar regulations based on the power of eminent domain (Barbre 1972).

But eminent domain entailed compensation, making it a costly tool for governments seeking to regulate the built environment. Proponents of zoning such as Edward Bassett, a pivotal figure in the development of the technique, believed that using the police power to regulate the built environment presented no such problem (Bassett 1922: 320).[2] (Distinguishing between exercise of the police power and the power of eminent domain has subsequently become one of the most difficult problems of American planning law (Ellickson & Been 2005: 134–209).) Advocates such as Bassett drew support from an influential treatise by University of Chicago law professor Ernst Freund. Freund argued that the deprivation of property pursuant to a legitimate exercise of the police power did not constitute a 'taking' subject to the Fifth Amendment. According to Freund (1904), so long as the regulation of the built environment was justified as preventing a harm (as opposed to conferring a benefit), no compensation was necessary (1904: 546–47). Based on this analysis, American zoning became characterised as an extension of nuisance law instead of an affirmative instrument for public benefit.

The German precedent

Zoning also appealed to its American proponents because of its apparent success in Germany. By the turn of the century, the practice had become a key component of German regulation of the built environment (Sutcliffe 1981: 32–34, Ladd 1990: 187–94). In 1891, Frankfurt adopted an ordinance dividing the city into different districts, each with specified permissible densities, heights and uses (Sutcliffe 1981: 32). German courts found the Frankfurt ordinance legitimate and, by the beginning of the 20th century, similar laws were in place in most of Germany's larger towns (Sutcliffe 1981: 33).

This trend precipitated even greater changes in German planning, as cities adopted increasingly comprehensive regulatory regimes for urban development. In the first decade of the 20th century, most German states enacted general planning laws empowering urban authorities to plan and construct streets, infrastructure and public space. Such laws typically enhanced municipal power to acquire land for public purposes and to compel the sale of such land if necessary (Sutcliffe 1981: 33–34).

Thus, once German cities had adopted zoning, they recognised the need for concomitant authority to regulate the development of the built environment. The governments of the German states then conferred greater power on cities so that they could carry out the task of planning. This led to the recognition of planning '... as both a useful and a practicable municipal activity', and the term *Städtebau*, which Josef Stübben and Camillo Sitte had used to describe their practice, joined German vernacular to describe the new activity (Sutcliffe 1981: 34).

A number of influential Americans were smitten with the German system. At the First National Conference on City Planning in 1909, held in Washington DC, Frederick Law Olmsted Jr, son of the great landscape architect and a central figure in 20th century American planning, extolled the virtues of German city planning (Committee on the District of Columbia 1910: 63–70). Frederic C. Howe, one of zoning's most active proponents, published a slew of articles in popular magazines praising German cities as incomparable in the modern world (Howe 1910a) and urging America to follow the German model of regulation (Howe 1911a: 486).[3] (Howe presented a similarly favourable assessment to the Third National Conference on City Planning (Howe 1911b).) Howe's and Olmsted's homilies were hardly unique. Influential publications ranging from the *Atlantic Monthly* to the *New York Times* printed pieces recommending importation of German built environment regulation (Godfrey 1910a, 1910b, Williams 1913a, Baxter 1909).

Ideas varied regarding what such importation would entail. The answers ranged from a thoroughgoing revision of American urban government, to the simple addition of zoning power to the palette of urban regulation, to uncertainty.

Howe, among others (see, for example, Brooks 1915: 222–234), believed the German example militated in favour of drastic expansion and transformation of the legal powers available to American cities. German cities had far more at their disposal than the mere power to designate land uses, mandatory setbacks and maximum building envelopes (Sutcliffe 1981: 22–35, Ladd 1990: 186–235). 'The German city,' Howe contended, '... is free – free to dream big dreams, and when they are ready for realisation, to achieve them and enjoy the fruits thereof. The American city, on the other hand, is in chains' (1911a: 486). Whereas state governments largely barred American cities from commercial undertakings, Howe noted, many German cities owned a considerable amount of land and actively engaged in speculation. Howe conceded that the electoral structure of urban government in Imperial Germany, which apportioned voting power based on income, was fundamentally undemocratic (1910b: 13796). He nevertheless hoped that American cities and states would adopt a wide array of reforms – from new civil service rules to different tax laws – so that they would more closely resemble their German counterparts (Howe 1911a).

Other proponents of zoning envisioned a far more limited role for German innovations. Frank Backus Williams, for example, equated zoning with German city planning and advocated the importation of this single tool only (Williams 1913a, 1913b). Zoning, Williams said, '... *does* ... lessen congestion in overcrowded Germany; it *does* make city land more useful and valuable; it *does* tend to prevent the useless and costly changes in the character of localities; it *does* stabilise values; it *does* make living conditions more comfortable and convenient and business more economical and efficient' (Commission on Building Districts and Restrictions 1916: 203) (emphasis in original). Williams may have had an ulterior motive for reductively ascribing the benefits of planning to zoning. As special counsel to the New York Heights of Buildings Committee, Williams had to resolve two fairly narrow problems: limiting the profusion (and height) of skyscrapers and halting the incursion of factories onto Fifth Avenue (Toll 1969: 150). Zoning alone could (and perhaps did) serve these goals, even though it did not fulfil its proponents' grander claims.

Although Olmsted, like Howe, suggested that the shape of German cities owed much to their extensive regulatory powers, he hesitated to embrace the German model. Olmsted understood German city planning as a holistic practice, observing:

> [A] city plan in Germany includes in one unified project not only a surveyor's plan for the layout of streets, and so forth, but the whole code of building regulations, health ordinances, police rules, and system of taxation in so far as they have a direct influence upon the physical development of the city (Committee on the District of Columbia 1910: 66).

Olmsted saw German urban planning as an impressive response to the problems confronting German cities. Yet, he suggested that these lessons might not travel well across the Atlantic, noting that '... although we have an immense amount to learn from Europe, and especially from Germany, in regard to city planning, it would be very foolish for us to copy blindly what has been done there' (Committee on the District of Columbia 1910: 70).

During the first decade of the 20th century, the nascent planning profession had reached a broad consensus that German regulation of the built environment was worthy of some form of emulation. Yet opinions diverged widely concerning how, precisely, America should adapt the German model. Should American cities implement zoning alone? Or some more comp- rehensive form of regulation?

American ideals

Zoning's initial American proponents had diverse interests, ranging from maximising real estate values to ameliorating the living conditions of the poorest urban residents. In the latter camp, two key figures were Frederic C. Howe and Benjamin C. Marsh. Both played vital roles in bringing German zoning to America. Howe cut his teeth as a crusader for municipal reform in the administration of Cleveland mayor Tom Johnson, then moved to New York where he became a prolific author (Rodgers 1998: 139–140). Marsh, the executive secretary of the Committee on Congestion of Population, a New York reform group, organised the First National Conference on City Planning, held in Washington, DC in 1909 (Peterson 2009: 126–27). In the same year, he published *An Introduction to City Planning: Democracy's Challenge to the American City* (Marsh 1909), which historian Daniel Rodgers has dubbed '... the first clear description of German city planning measures to reach American readers' (Rodgers 1998: 182). One chapter of Marsh's book con- sisted of a translation from Josef Stübben's treatise *Der Städtebau*, and Marsh devoted another chapter to city planning in Frankfurt (Marsh 1909: 40–61).

Howe and Marsh had ambitious, if slightly divergent, agendas for urban American. In embracing not only zoning but also a panoply of powers for American cities, these men sought to redefine the role of urban government. Howe '... reached out for the social city ... a place marked by collective action and ... the ineluctable interdependencies of living cheek by jowl in a growing community' (Barron 2003: 2309). Like Howe, Marsh sought for cit- ies the power to levy taxes on the 'unearned increment' of land values increased through urban growth. Such a tax would permit cities to capture some of the financial benefit that was due to municipal expenditure and would deter private real estate speculation (Howe 1905: 169, Marsh 1911). But whereas Howe celebrated urbanisation, noting that '... to an ever-in- creasing mass of the population, opportunities are crowding one upon another' (Howe 1905: 25), Marsh was deeply concerned with congestion, despairing 'that such an overwhelming proportion of the population should be jammed into a few great cities' (Marsh 1909: 6). Although their social agendas seemed to embrace opposed values, their morphological ideals for the city were strikingly similar. In describing the virtues of density, Howe pointed not to Germany's densest metropolis (Berlin), but to smaller-scale cities such as Düsseldorf and Frankfurt (Howe 1910a). Marsh (1909) cited the latter as a paragon of urban deconcentration (Marsh 1909: 46–61).

Both men shared a concept of urban government that diverged markedly from prevailing American thought. Howe saw the city as an organism – '... a conscious, living thing with a big life of its own and a definite mission to perform' (Howe 1913a: 155). Yet he also described the city in terms typically reserved for private corporations. In America, he wrote, '... the city is a political agency of the State' (Howe 1913a: x). The European city (particularly the German city), by contrast, was '... a business corporation organized to realise the maximum of returns to the community' (Howe 1913a: x). Marsh articulated a similar vision of the role of urban government, advocating land purchasing power for American cities not to promote 'municipal socialism', but as '... a business undertaking on the part of the American city' (Marsh 1909: 36).

Developing America

Howe and Marsh both had substantive visions for the American city, encompassing not only urban form, but also the social, economic and political structure of urban life. Although they did not hide these visions in their writing or their speeches, the introduction of zoning into American land-use law ultimately undermined fundamental features of their agenda. This occurred through a two-stage process. Initially, other proponents of zoning, such as Williams and Bassett, endorsed the technique as a means of accomplishing specific goals for the City of New York having little to do with the agenda espoused by Howe and Marsh. Later, with the help of Frederick Law Olmsted Jr, major American developers would promote the implementation of zoning throughout the country to protect their investments. Like much regulation, then, zoning served as much as a tool of business as of the government. Bassett, Williams, Olmsted and other key players in American real estate development abstracted the practice from its original context, resulting in urban places differing dramatically from the cities that so impressed Marsh and Howe.

The initial American zoning ordinances were actually quite similar to those in Germany (Logan 1976: 383). But zoning was not accompanied by the other German planning techniques, and this selective importation likely contributed to a different outcome in America. It is far from clear that all of the German techniques could have been carried over to America. Even if they had been, it seems improbable that they would have functioned in the USA as they had in Germany.

Zoning prevailed in the USA because men such as Williams successfully portrayed it as a neutral tool to solve urban woes and to boost real estate values. Williams ascribed the benefits of *Städtebau* to zoning alone (Commission on Building Districts and Restrictions 1916: 203). By substituting a technical discourse of tools for a debate concerning the allocation of rights and the structure of society, the men who fashioned New York's 1916 zoning ordinance deployed the technique to keep factories off Fifth Avenue and control the city's skyline (see Figure 6.1).

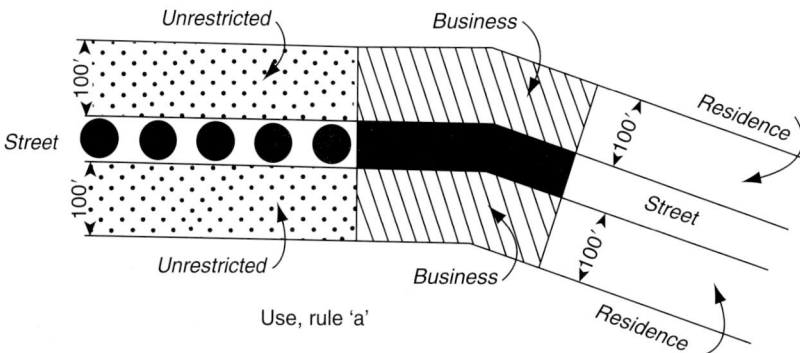

Figure 6.1 New York 1916 Use District Map (partial) illustrating city planning laws and regulations: New York's 1916 districting formed the basis for American zoning. *Source:* New York Public Library.

Once New York overcame the initial legal and political hurdles of implementing zoning, America's leading real estate entrepreneurs embraced the practice in developing the nation's burgeoning suburbs. These men were large-scale 'community builders' who, as Leo Grebler put it, developed self-contained '... communities with specially designed street patterns and commercial and other facilities' (1950: 62). Grebler contrasted these men with '... the fly-by-night operator, who takes an occasional fling at housing production' (1950: 62). The 'fly-by-nights' generally produced relatively shoddy housing, undercutting the community builders on price and diminishing the value of the community builders' developments by decreasing the overall quality of the housing stock in a given neighbourhood. As Marc Weiss has documented, the fly-by-nights were '... a source of scandal and market instability that community builders hoped to eliminate as competitors through government regulation and private trade association arrangements' (Weiss 1987: 5). Zoning was the most prevalent government regulation that the community builders embraced (Weiss 1987: 5).

In turning to zoning as a means of market control, the community builders enlisted the power of the federal government. During World War I, the community builders worked closely with the federal government through their flagship professional organisation, the National Association of Real Estate Boards (NAREB).

> [F]uture NAREB President Robert Jemison, Jr ... directed housing and land development for the Housing Division of the Emergency Fleet Corporation. When the USA Housing Corporation (USHC) was created in June 1918, several NAREB leaders served as officers and directors of the corporation, and ran its Real Estate Division, which provided subsidised financing for private residential developers building 'priority' war worker housing (Weiss 1987: 59).

Olmsted, whose firm had previously planned subdivisions for NAREB members, directed the USHC's Town Planning Division, which assisted private developers working for USHC and built public housing for war workers (Weiss 1987: 59).

This close relationship between the federal government and the community builders persisted into the 1920s, when the US Department of Commerce led the effort to promote zoning. In 1916, New York City adopted America's first comprehensive zoning ordinance (Bettman 1923: 834), after producing thorough reports defending the legality and utility of the practice (Heights of Buildings Commission 1913, Commission on Building Districts and Restrictions 1916). In 1921, John M. Gries, Chief of the Division of Building and Housing in the US Department of Commerce, convened a '... committee to consider the question of zones' (Chused 2001: 598). The committee, intended to promote the spread of zoning in the USA, included Olmsted and veterans of the New York campaign such as Edward Bassett (Chused 2001: 598–99). In 1922, the Department of Commerce published *A Zoning Primer*, an explanation of zoning aimed at a wide audience (Department of Commerce, Advisory Committee on City Planning 1922). Gries received requests for over 50,000 copies '... [w]ithin a few days' of the book's release (Chused 2001: 599, n.14). In 1924, the Department of Commerce published *A Standard State Zoning Enabling Act*, which provided a template for state governments to grant municipalities the authority to enact zoning laws (Knack *et al.* 1996: 5–6). It sold more than 55,000 copies (Department of Commerce 1926: 3). By 1926, the year in which the Supreme Court held zoning constitutional, 422 US municipalities had adopted zoning ordinances (Gries 1926). By the end of 1927, 29 states had adopted zoning-enabling legislation based either entirely or in 'large part' on the Commerce Department's model (Department of Commerce, Division of Building and Housing 1928: 10).

The interests of NAREB's members differed substantially from those of Marsh and Howe. Whereas Marsh and Howe sought social transformation, the NAREB members desired market control. Olmsted had recognised this difference in 1909, when he launched an effort to push Marsh from his leadership position in the city planning movement. At the time, Olmsted was planning the Forest Hills Gardens subdivision in Queens, New York for Edward Bouton, who would go on to form NAREB's City Plan Committee in 1913 (Peterson 2009: 128, Weiss 1987: 50, 58). Having participated in the first National Conference on City Planning in 1909, where he praised the German model without embracing it, Olmsted believed that the value of the Conference depended upon whether 'Mr. Marsh or a saner person' organised it (Peterson 2009: 128). Opposing Marsh's efforts to inject social reform into the field of city planning, Olmsted stated that he wanted '... to relieve the conference of the danger to which it will be subjected by the well-intentioned Mr. Marsh if he is not forestalled.' (Peterson 2009: 128). In 1910, Olmsted engineered an election that pushed Marsh from his executive role in the Conference, filling Conference committees with men sympathetic to Olmsted's positions (Peterson 2009: 129–30).

The community builders were interested less in the future of America's cities than in the fate of their property investments. Zoning could help the community builders consolidate an oligopoly position. As NAREB member J. C. Nichols put it:

> Now, if in developing our subdivisions, we can limit the quantity of certain classes of property, if we can create the feeling that we have a monopoly of that class of property around a little plaza or square, if we give the prospective buyer notice that if he doesn't buy that property today somebody else will buy all that is left of it tomorrow, we are assisting in the sale of that property, and the man that has it won't give it up except at an advanced price, and we can raise the prices of the adjoining property (Weiss 1987: 65–66).

This priority of the community builders suggests why zoning, not planning, became the dominant feature of government regulation of the American built environment. The community builders saw zoning as a means of protecting their own planning activities.

Zoning, as Jon A. Peterson notes, '… had been established without referring to a city plan for guidance. It had not been shaped by a larger view of the public interest' (Peterson 2003: 314). In 1928, Harland Bartholomew, who had risen to national prominence as secretary to Newark's City Plan Commission, argued that a zoning ordinance adopted without a city plan '… becomes largely an instrument of expediency, subject to constant and often whimsical change.' (Peterson 2003: 314). When Bartholomew made this observation, 754 municipalities in the USA had adopted zoning ordinances, but no more than 200 cities had ever even attempted to formulate a general plan (Peterson 2003: 314). In Germany, zoning had accompanied government planning. In America, zoning was a substitute for government planning.

By mid century, the situation had scarcely changed. In an influential 1955 article, Harvard Law School professor Charles Haar observed that many jurisdictions did not require planning and that, even in communities legally mandating planning, zoning typically came first. Almost half of all cities with comprehensive zoning ordinances had adopted no masterplan. Cities requiring masterplans typically fared little better, frequently allowing planning to take a subsidiary role to zoning. Section 3 of the Commerce Department's *Standard State Zoning Enabling Act* indicated that zoning ordinances should be made 'in accordance with a comprehensive plan.' Yet, due to the widespread disregard for planning, judges generally interpreted this requirement as '… meaning nothing more than that zoning ordinances shall be comprehensive – that is to say, uniform and broad in scope of coverage' (Haar 1955: 1157).

In part because of this lack of public planning, the 'variance' – a seemingly minor component of the *Standard State Zoning Enabling Act* – assumed inordinate significance. The *Enabling Act* had given local boards of adjustment power to grant relief from the strictures of zoning on a case-by-case basis:

> The board of adjustment shall have the … power[] … [t]o authorise upon appeal in specific cases such variance from the terms of the ordinance as will not be contrary to the public interest, where, owing to special conditions, a literal enforcement of the provisions of the ordinance will result in unnecessary hardship and so that the spirit of the ordinance shall be observed and substantial justice done (Department of Commerce 1926: 10–11).

The variance procedure, then, could override a zoning ordinance in exceptional circumstances. By the latter half of the 20th century, however, critics were charging that the '… variance procedure, conceived as the 'safety valve' of the zoning ordinance, ha[d] ruptured into a steady "leak"' (Shapiro 1969: 9). A good deal of evidence has been adduced to support this claim, demonstrating that local zoning boards typically grant between 50 per cent and nearly 90 percent of variance requests (Ellickson & Been 2005: 294).

Zoning may not have facilitated predictable public land development practices, but planned communities *were* proliferating. The planning, however, was not a government function. Since the beginning of the 20th century, the community builders had pushed for homeowners' associations, or 'private governments', to control planned subdivisions, which came to be known as 'common interest developments' (CIDs). Property ownership in a CID was generally a prerequisite for suffrage in its homeowners' association. J. C. Nichols of NAREB pioneered this form of development in 1914 with the Mission Hills development in Missouri (Worley 1990: 166–68). Nichols explicitly sought to create exclusive enclaves through '… the control of a considerable area of land, so as to establish harmonious surroundings and give permanency to the character of the neighbourhood' (Nichols 1914: 132).

Like zoning, the CID vehicle gave the community builders greater control over the neighbourhoods that they constructed and created the potential for increased profits. Also, like zoning, CIDs drew on a legacy of European social planning – this time Ebenezer Howard's Garden City. But whereas Howard's Garden City was to be a limited-dividend company that would ultimately provide for a local welfare state (Howard 1898 [2003]: 44–45, 54–57), the CID was purely a mechanism for builders to control how their

Figure 6.2 Common interest developments such as Seabrook, Washington, have enabled developers to maintain profits and have introduced flexibility into the design process. Developers' ability to operate outside standard subdivision regulations allows the introduction of design solutions including clustered buildable land, smaller lots, reduced setbacks, and commonly owned open spaces managed by the homeowners. Reproduced by permission of Seabrook Land Company.

developments looked and, to a large extent, who lived there. CIDs proliferated only fitfully during the first half of the 20th century, hampered by the Depression and the two World Wars (McKenzie 1994: 56–57). The building boom that followed World War II, however, prompted developers' renewed interest in CIDs. Large-lot suburban development sharply reduced the supply of land, contributing to a steep increase in land costs as a percentage of housing unit price (Mayer 1978: 13). CIDs were a mechanism to cope with these rising costs. With a CID managing a cluster subdivision or planned unit development, a developer could '... shrink lot sizes ... [while] satisfy[ing] the need felt by home-buyers and public agencies to preserve some ambience of nature. Using smaller lots and commonly owned open spaces managed by homeowner associations, builders could create low-cost amenities like parks and tennis courts without increasing the size of the overall development' (McKenzie 1994: 84). (see Figure 6.2)

When selling relatively dense development to middle-class families seeking the suburban ideal of big lawns and picket fences proved problematic, the community builders turned to the federal government for assistance (McKenzie 1994: 81–82). Created by the National Housing Act of 1934 in order to stabilise housing finance, the Federal Housing Administration (FHA) was a government agency with extremely close ties to the community builders. Because the FHA insured home mortgages, its underwriting guidelines exercised extraordinary influence over the patterns of urban (and suburban) development (Ben-Joseph 2005: 70–74, Jackson 1987: 203–18, Weiss 1987: 145–58). Marc Weiss, who has documented the extent to which NAREB stalwarts comprised FHA's leadership, observed that '... [t]he community builders who led NAREB enthusiastically welcomed FHA's powerful interventionist role,' in part '... because FHA was largely run by representatives of the real estate and banking industries' (1987: 145–46).

Because low density was a large part of suburbia's allure, following World War II the community builders relied on FHA's influence to de-stigmatise the relatively high density of CIDs by promoting cluster developments as exclusive enclaves. The exclusivity associated with the low density of suburban development attracted many residents (Dobriner 1963). The proximity introduced by cluster subdivisions threatened this facet of the suburban experience (McKenzie 1994: 81). In 1962, Byron R. Hanke, the chief of FHA's land planning division, took a two-year leave from the agency to work for the Urban Land Institute, a NAREB spin-off organisation devoting considerable energy to CIDs (McKenzie 1994: 91–92). In 1963, the Urban Land Institute issued a report entitled *Innovations vs Traditions in Community Development*, noting the opportunities that CIDs provided for exclusion:

> Existing as private or semi-private areas they may exclude undesirable elements or trouble-makers drifting in, youngsters who 'take over' facilities and push out residents. Those not living close by and unable to benefit from small local parks should neither be required to support such areas by public taxes nor allowed to invade the quiet and privacy of those enjoying the benefits created by private methods (McKenzie 1994: 88).

The same year, the FHA issued a manual entitled *Planned-Unit Development with a Homes Association*, indicating that the agency would insure only those cluster subdivisions controlled by the sort of exclusionary homeowners' association envisioned by the Urban Land Institute (McKenzie 1994: 89). Hanke played a central role in the FHA's decision to insure such developments (McKenzie 1994: 92).

The efforts of the community builders and the FHA paid off. By the end of the 20th century, some 47 million Americans – one-sixth of the population – lived in CIDs (Ben-Joseph 2004: 132), and zoning exerted a pervasive influence on the form of American cities and towns. The legacy of these phenomena is the subject of the next part.

Designing the American future

Euclidean zoning remains a potent force shaping America's built environment. Jane Jacobs, author of the most enduring critique of zoning from a design perspective, described the conditions necessary '... [t]o generate exuberant diversity in a city's streets and districts' (Jacobs 1961: 150). According to Jacobs (1961: 150–51), '... the district, and indeed as many of its internal parts as possible, must serve more than one primary function; preferably more than two,' and '... there must be a sufficiently dense concentration of people, for whatever purposes they may be there.' Euclidean zoning directly conflicts with these goals: it was designed to separate uses, '... lessen the congestion of streets ... [and] prevent the overcrowding of land' (Department of Commerce 1926: 6).

In the wake of Jacobs's critique, the planner's palette expanded to encompass techniques such as incentive zoning, design review, site-plan review and overlay zoning. These tools were intended to overcome the problems of Euclidean zoning that Jacobs identified, but have achieved mixed results. In incentive zoning, developers make concessions (usually to provide some putatively public amenity) in exchange for permission to build at higher densities than allowed as-of-right by underlying zoning ordinances. Such arrangements have produced a glut of desolate urban plazas and under-used pocket parks (Weaver & Babcock 1979: 58–60, Kayden 2000). Anecdotal evidence suggests that case-by-case design and site-plan review procedures have enabled municipalities to raise the bar for design in some cases, generally to promote historic preservation or to regulate individual, large-scale developments (Scheer & Preiser 1994: 85–143, Wickersham 2001: 556–57). But, because such procedures place additional demands on developers, they are only practical in strong real estate markets. Reviewers, moreover, may abuse their discretion to deter development by reference to vague aesthetic standards (Blaesser 1994). Finally, because these procedures are inherently ad hoc, they may undermine coherent urban design strategies (Barnett 1974: 42–43). Overlay zoning districts, where underlying zoning restrictions may be relaxed, have enabled the builders of suburban planned unit developments to increase densities and improve design outcomes in some cases (Ben-Joseph 2004). Such developments, however, are frequently managed by homeowners' associations. Critics of such private arrangements contend that CIDs contribute to spatial segregation and undermine participatory democracy by intensifying conflict among neighbours, disenfranchising renters and dividing cities (Barton & Silverman 1994).

Attempting to improve on these innovations, architects Andrés Duany and Elizabeth Plater-Zyberk have mounted one of the most prominent assaults on Euclidean zoning. As founders of the Congress for the New Urbanism (CNU), Duany and Plater-Zyberk have championed the aspects of urban form that Jacobs cherished. Two regulatory instruments developed by CNU affiliates – form-based codes and the Leadership in Energy and Environmental Design for Neighbourhood Development (LEED-ND) rating system – merit particular attention for the impact they may have on developers' decisions shaping the built environment. Unlike Euclidean zoning, form-based codes do not focus on land use, and instead use ample illustrations to '... mak[e] building type, street type, or a combination of the two the primary regulatory elements' (Congress for the New Urbanism 2004: 36). LEED-ND is the neighbourhood-scale component of the LEED family of 'green' building certification programmes administered by the US Green Building Council (USGBC), a non-profit organisation funded largely by the building trades. According to the USGBC (US Green Building Council 2010a), LEED-ND '... integrates the principles of smart growth, urbanism and green building into the first national system for neighbourhood design. LEED certification provides independent, third-party verification that a development's location and design meet accepted high levels of environmentally responsible, sustainable development.'

The New Urbanist campaign shares some striking similarities with early 20th century efforts to promote zoning. Just as zoning's proponents drafted advocates from academia, politics and the professions, CNU's board includes professors, elected officials, lawyers and engineers, in addition to members of the design professions (Congress for the New Urbanism 2010). Whereas some of zoning's most ardent advocates stressed the virtues of urban community that they professed to have found in Germany, the New Urbanists evoke neighbourly pre-Euclidean American towns (Duany & Plater-Zyberk 1992). Just as reformers made common cause with developers to implement zoning, the New Urbanists have sought the imprimatur of some of America's largest-scale developers (Pyatok 2000: 806) and local business organisations (Polikov 2008). And where the proponents of zoning in New York intimated that their favoured technique would recognise and preserve the 'natural' form of the city (Toll 1969: 164), Duany has suggested that New Urbanist techniques reflect some inherent urban-to-rural gradient (Duany & Talen 2002a: 1453, 2002b).

As with zoning, which was proposed to reduce congestion, protect residential environments and promote market stability, the techniques of New Urbanism are said to solve a wide range of problems: social exclusion, environmental degradation and aesthetic abomination (Congress for the New Urbanism 1996). Like the proponents of zoning, then, New Urbanists contend that their preferred techniques are capable of advancing a social agenda and promoting the interests of developers. Whether these techniques can (or will) accomplish *both* ends remains an open question.

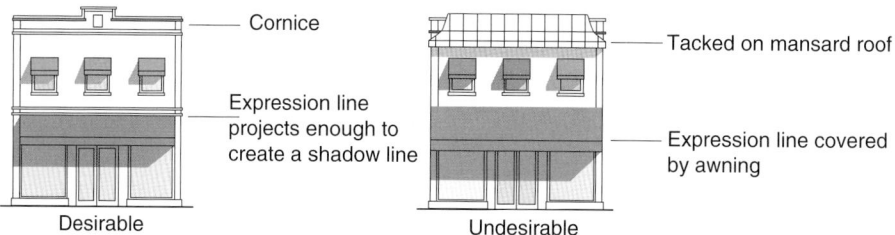

Figure 6.3 Form-based codes and architectural regulations from Hercules, California specify requirements for all building facades except single-family houses. The rules include mandatory expression lines delineating the division between the first and second stories and requirements for cornices at the top of the facades. Written rules set out minimum dimensions and permitted finish materials. *Source:* City of Hercules.

Form-based codes

Duany and his associates seem to see form-based codes as one of their most important tools. Like Euclidean ordinances, form-based codes establish setbacks and building envelopes. But instead of proscribing uses as in Euclidean zoning ordinances, purely form-based codes define place by using diagrams and illustrations to *prescribe* certain design attributes, such as roof gables or the arrangement of structures. Such laws may be gaining support, but to date only a handful of municipalities have instituted mandatory form-based codes (PlaceMakers 2010). In 2004, the California legislature passed a law intended to facilitate the use of form-based codes (Cal Gov Code §65302.4), and in 2009 the city of Miami passed a form-based ordinance scheduled to become effective in May 2010. (The ordinance imposes significant use-based restrictions, and its fate is somewhat uncertain (Miami 21 Code 2009, Musibay 2009).) (see Figure 6.3)

In practice, however, it is not entirely clear where Euclidean regulation ends and form-based codes begin. By improving the illustrations in development codes, form-based codes can clarify the physical effects of regulation. Non-regulatory solutions, however, could accomplish the same goal. For example, the Visual Interactive Code, a computer-based system, enables users to convert land use regulations and planning data into an intuitive visual format (Ben-Joseph 2005: 185).

While local governments could simply add specific design prescriptions to existing Euclidean zoning ordinances, and supplement these ordinances with illustrations, some proponents of form-based codes have more ambitious goals. First, as the Congress for the New Urbanism has indicated, form-based regulation is intended to supplant use-based regulation, at least to some extent. Second, the form-based codes proposed by Duany and his associates condition permitting on compliance with aesthetic controls. These aspects of form-based codes may run afoul of the political economy of American local government.

If form-based codes would deprive local governments of power, municipalities are unlikely to embrace this new regulatory tool. Through the actions of NAREB and the Commerce Department, municipalities obtained the power to regulate land use proactively. This is, arguably, the most economically valuable power available to municipalities (Briffault 2002: 262–68). Because local governments have few other legal powers at their disposal (Frug 1980: 1062–67), the power to regulate land use is particularly precious to them. To the extent that form-based regulation replaces use-based codes, requiring municipalities to cede control of land use and allowing developers to determine the mix of uses independently, it seems unlikely to gain traction.

It is also unclear whether the development industry will support the public adoption of form-based codes. Many of the most notable New Urbanist developments are CIDs, in which the property owners privately agree to certain design standards. In such settings, developers and homeowners may see form-based codes as an expedient for controlling the physical character of their development over time. Miami's experience, however, illustrates the challenges confronting government adoption of form-based codes. At the time of writing, the city's new mayor, who opposed the code when he was a member of the City Commission, has delayed its implementation and, through a spokesperson, expressed an intention to 'tweak' the code (Musibay 2009). Many of the city's most prominent designers and developers also oppose key provisions, owing to concern that the code will impair the quality, originality and profitability of new construction (AIA Miami 2008, Rabin 2009).

Even if form-based codes are publicly adopted on a broader scale, there is reason to believe that they will not have the desired impact over the long run. Just as the *Standard Zoning Enabling Act* included a variance procedure, many …

> … New Urbanist design codes … include a variance concept that reflects the same optimism that once pervaded traditional zoning, namely, that with prestated land use classifications and rules, the system would be virtually self executing, with variances being the rare exception, and then only justifiable on the basis of 'particular hardship' (Blaesser 2008, section 8:41).

The Miami code, for example, includes a variance provision that almost precisely follows the language of the Standard Zoning Enabling Act (Miami 21 Code, section 7.1.2.7.a 2009). If the 'steady leak' of the Euclidean variance is any precedent, then the finely calibrated morphological controls sought by the New Urbanists may be difficult to achieve.

*Leadership in energy and environmental design
for neighbourhood development*

The New Urbanists may find a more promising platform in LEED-ND, the product of their collaboration with the USGBC and the National Resources Defense Council, an environmental non-profit organisation. Like the USGBC's LEED systems for smaller-scale projects, LEED-ND would audit development projects for environmental sensitivity in a variety of categories:

- *Smart location and linkage* encourages communities to consider location, transportation alternatives and preservation of sensitive lands while also discouraging sprawl.
- *Neighbourhood pattern and design* emphasises vibrant, equitable communities that are healthy, walkable and mixed-use.
- *Green infrastructure and buildings* promotes the design and construction of buildings and infrastructure that reduce energy and water use, while promoting more sustainable use of materials, reuse of existing and historic structures and other sustainable best practices.
- *Innovation and design process* recognises exemplary and innovative performance reaching beyond the existing credits in the rating system, as well as the value of including an accredited professional on the design team.
- *Regional priority* encourages projects to focus on earning credits of significance to the project's local environment (US Green Building Council n.d.) (see Figure 6.4).

Although the LEED-ND rating system remains a pilot project at the time of writing, if it follows the trajectory of LEED systems for individual buildings, then municipalities and states may require LEED-ND certification for certain kinds of projects or may offer tax or fee rebates for certified projects.

The LEED systems are variants of building assessment systems that have long been a feature of real estate development in the USA. In the American legal tradition, state or local governments have typically legislated building quality standards (Seidel 1978: 75–80). It would be misleading, however, to suggest that these jurisdictions *write* their own building codes. Instead, state and local governments typically adopt (in whole or in part) model building codes created and updated by independent, non-profit standards organisations. Although governments may pay a nominal fee for the codes, the standards organisations receive their primary financial support from the building trades or the insurance industry. Organisations promulgating fire codes were founded by insurers in the 19th century to reduce risk and improve actuarial accuracy (Teaford 1984: 199–202). Members of the building trades promote their own uniform codes because standardisation enables them to achieve scale economies. Codes sponsored by the building trades

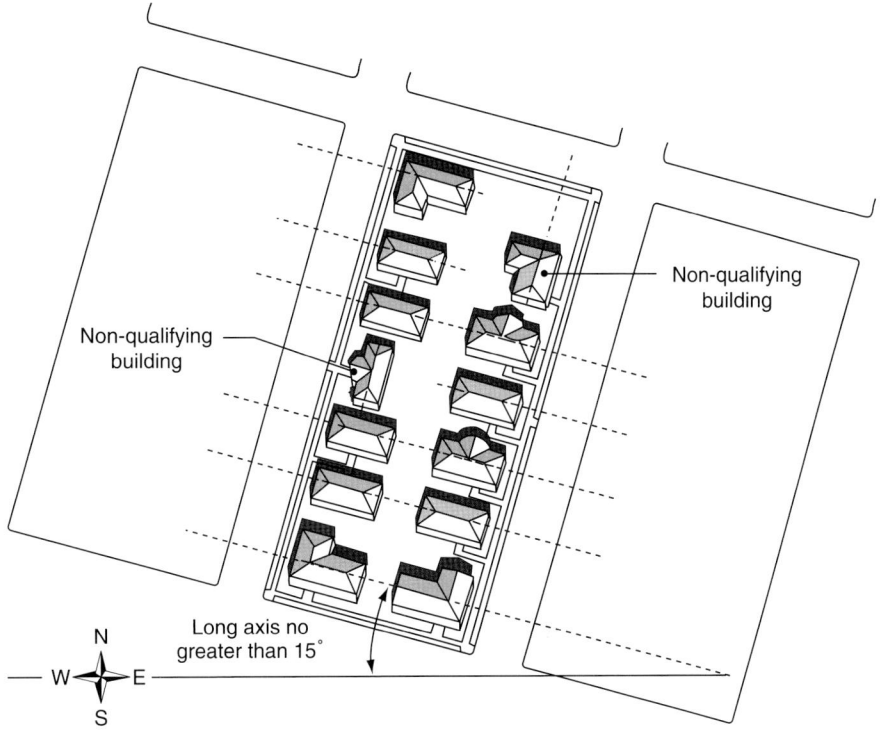

Figure 6.4 LEED-ND credits and ratings address development features such as location and linkage, infrastructure, neighbourhood pattern and building disposition: for example, developments that meet specific criteria in response to solar-orientation will receive points for their LEED rating. Reproduced by permission of United States Green Building Council, Inc.

came into existence, in part, to compete with the fire insurers' codes, which raised the costs of construction and discouraged use of flammable materials including wood (Ventre 1973: 238). Dominant players in the building supply industry may try to shape these regulations to exclude the products of less powerful rivals (Ventre 1973: 225–392, *Allied Tube & Conduit Corp. v Indian Head* 1988).

The USGBC's sponsors include many of the most prominent firms in the building trades and the energy sector (US Green Building Council 2010b). Given the increasing popularity of LEED systems for assessing the environmental sensitivity of real estate development, these firms have a clear interest in influencing the content of the standards. This alliance of interests suggests that LEED-ND stands a reasonably strong chance of gaining traction.

The LEED-ND system, however, faces significant competition from important players in real estate development. The National Association of

Homebuilders (NAHB) and the International Code Council (ICC) have joined forces to promote their National Green Building Standard, a system that competes with LEED-ND. Like the Urban Land Institute, NAHB was formed as a spin-off of NAREB and was intended to focus specifically on the interests of the largest-scale community builders (Weiss 1987). The ICC was formed in 1994 through the merger of the three major model code organisations sponsored by the building trades (International Code Council 2010). NAHB is concerned that member profits might suffer if developments must conform to the New Urbanist ideal of 'Traditional Neighbourhood Design' (TND), entailing compact, mixed-use neighbourhoods. NAHB has noted that, even though developers apply TND principles with increasing frequency, 'the vast majority of new developments incorporate very few TND principles in their community design' (NAHB Land Development Services Department 2007: 1–2). TND principles privilege density. But because most new residential construction occurs in 'suburban and exurban greenfield locations', NAHB is concerned that 'a heavy bias toward TND development could exclude much new development from being eligible to meet the criteria being established by LEED-ND' (NAHB Land Development Services Department 2007: 2). NAHB has encouraged its members to use its own code, which is more solicitous of lower-density construction. It remains an open question whether states and municipalities will adopt both LEED-ND and NAHB's National Green Building Standard, choose between the two or adopt neither.

Conclusion

The trajectory of American land development regulation suggests that cautious optimism may be appropriate for innovations such as neighbourhood design standards, although the prospects for form-based codes (at least in their pure form) seem somewhat dimmer. From Frederic Howe to Andrés Duany, proponents of urban change have long called for better government regulation on the built environment. And while their messages have influenced the debate, they have achieved success only to the extent that their ambitions aligned with the most powerful figures in real estate development. In the process, as the case of zoning demonstrates, their original regulatory intent may be undermined.

Duany has become a central figure in debates about the urban future because he has cannily marketed his ideas to key constituencies of policy change: businesspeople, professionals, public interest groups and the politicians who represent them. He has thus assumed the role of the policy entrepreneur, '... identifying problems, networking in policy circles, shaping the terms of policy debates, and building coalitions' (Mintrom 1997: 739).

If Duany's project echoes Howe's idealism, it also reflects Olmsted's sober pragmatism. Like Olmsted, Duany has enlisted large-scale developers in his cause. And, just as Olmsted entered government service as director of the USA Housing Corporation's Town Planning Division, New Urbanists have penetrated the upper echelons of the federal policy-making apparatus. In July 2009, Shelley Poticha was appointed Senior Advisor for Sustainable Housing and Communities at the US Department of Housing and Urban Development (HUD) (HUD News Release 09–130 2009). Prior to her federal government service, Poticha was involved in formulating the pilot version of LEED-ND (US Green Building Council 2007: 3) and was the Executive Director of the Congress for the New Urbanism (HUD News Release 09–130 2009).

A century after zoning ascended to a dominant position in the regulation of America's built environment, the country may be poised to revisit its control of real estate development. Zoning was initially adopted in response to unprecedented challenges confronting America's largest city – a dramatic surge in population coupled with rapid innovation in building technology. Climate change now poses a far more menacing threat than the problems facing New York 100 years ago. And the regulatory response seems likely to encompass some elements of the New Urbanist agenda.

Tools such as LEED-ND are components of a broader strategy to provide incentives for development reflecting New Urbanist principles. Legislation pending in Congress, entitled the *Livable Communities Act*, would fund coordination of existing land use and transportation planning processes, promote inter-jurisdictional collaboration and provide grants for projects that would encompass mixed use development and reduce car use (S. 1619 2009, HR 4690 2010). The programme would be controlled jointly by HUD, the Environmental Protection Agency and the Department of Transportation. Appropriations legislation that has already been enacted into law allocates US$150 million to planning grants for projects that would be eligible for funding under the *Livable Communities Act* ('Consolidated Appropriations Act 2010' 2009). Shelley Poticha, in her capacity as Director of HUD's Office of Sustainable Housing and Communities will oversee the planning grant programme (US Department of Housing and Urban Development 2010).

It is far too soon to tell whether such a strategy will fundamentally alter the form and pattern of development in the USA. Regional solutions to the problems of American planning are clearly necessary, yet they have been proposed for nearly a century and have proved largely elusive (Wachs & Dill 1999). If such solutions are to have meaningful impact, they will necessarily entail political conflict about social identity and the allocation of resources. As the history of zoning suggests, obscuring this conflict with a technical discourse of tools may hinder the development of vibrant, dynamic places that enrich life.

Notes

1. Between 1870 and 1900, the population of the 50 largest American cities increased from 5,775,778 to 15,247,946.
2. 'Fireproof requirements, plumbing rules, tenement house laws, strength of construction requirements, all come within the police power. *They are exercised without compensation being made to the private owner subjected to regulation.* ... The police power can as well be employed for zoning as for uniform sanitary and fire protection laws.' (Bassett 1922: 320) (emphasis added)
3. '[I]t is to Germany ... that we must go for our models.' (Howe 1911a: 486). See also Howe 1910b, 1910c, 1911c, 1912 and 1913b.

7

Good Design in the Redevelopment of Brownfield Sites

Paul Syms and Andrew Clarke

Introduction

As Tiesdell and Adams contend in Chapter 1, '... the designer's opportunity space is generally larger on more constrained brownfield sites than on less constrained ones'. Although mainly true, the 'designer' or 'place-maker' in this context is likely to extend well beyond the normal perception of urban designer, architect or town planner, to include other disciplines that may have little or no involvement in the design process on greenfield sites. These other disciplines include, for example, environmental consultants, archaeologists, ecologists and soil remediation specialists, all of whom compete for a share of the designer's opportunity space. Their input may significantly constrain the work of those professions more normally regarded as the 'designers' in development projects and restrict what design concepts are considered feasible.

Within this context, this chapter focuses on how policy and regulatory tools can be used to stimulate or encourage better quality design at brownfield locations (see Box 7.1 for a definition of brownfield land). The chapter takes a deliberately broad view of what constitutes a stimulus tool, defining it as...

> ... a mechanism employed by a governmental body, either central or local, or a quasi-governmental agency, to encourage an actor or group of actors, for example both public and private sector developers, to undertake development projects on sites, or in locations, that the actor would not otherwise

Urban Design in the Real Estate Development Process, First Edition. Edited by Steve Tiesdell and David Adams.
© 2011 Blackwell Publishing Ltd. Published 2011 by Blackwell Publishing Ltd.

Box 7.1   Definition of brownfield land

A number of different definitions and understandings of the term 'brownfield' are in existence, and these often differ from country to country or between jurisdictions. In some instances, the definitional approach finds its origins in environmental protection, whereas elsewhere the term may be used primarily in relation to land use. Having regard for the international audience for this book, it is important to define what we mean by the term 'brownfield' in this chapter. Syms first defined 'brownfield' in the UK context in a conference paper in 1993 and then in a book chapter in 1994, as 'any areas of land which have previously been the subject of a man-made or non-agricultural use of any type. This would include industrial uses such as chemical works, heavy engineering, shipbuilding and textile processing, together with unfit housing clearance sites and docklands, both inland and coastal, as well as mineral extraction sites and those used for landfill purposes.' (Syms, 1994: 63) As will be appreciated, this is a very broad definition, especially when viewed against a contemporary US definition: 'brownfield: abandoned, idled or underused industrial and commercial facility where expansion or redevelopment is complicated by real or perceived environmental contamination.' (Fields, 1995).

  The US definition, which is generally applied throughout North America and in a number of other countries, therefore links brownfield with specifically industrial and commercial sites, synonymous with contamination, whereas the UK approach includes housing sites and land that is lying derelict without there necessarily being any concerns regarding contamination. The UK understanding of the term brownfield is the one generally used in UK policy measures and in this chapter.

---

consider and/or to undertake better quality development than would otherwise occur without the stimulus.

Now that state subsidy of individual development projects, at least in the European Union, is likely to be seen as anti-competitive by the regulatory authorities, the chapter pays particular attention to how 'design-based' guidance and other policy instruments can be implemented at the local level to encourage developers to invest in design expertise.

  The chapter first considers how the redevelopment of brownfield land has achieved such policy significance in England. It explains how, since England is one of the mostly densely populated countries in the world, achieving the effective and efficient reuse of land has been central to public land-use policies for the past decade and a half.[1] The chapter then moves on to review and categorise different types of stimulus tools, while exploring how the implementation of design guidance and policies can be used to stimulate higher design quality at brownfield locations.

So far as all policy and regulatory tools are concerned, the chapter describes the position in England that existed immediately prior to the General Election held in May 2010. By July 2010, the new Coalition Government had already signalled its intention to scrap, or significantly revise, a number of the existing planning and housing policies. The future existence and roles of some of the delivery agencies was also open to question.

Redeveloping and reusing brownfield sites: the policy and regulatory context

Ensuring the effective and efficient redevelopment or reuse of brownfield sites is central to land-use policies in the UK – and especially in England, which has a population of around 51 million people. Although densely populated, the majority of this population is concentrated in several large conurbations and major cities, the growth of which has been constrained by more than 60 years of planning control and green belt policies. Over the past decade, there has been a stronger focus on redeveloping brownfield sites for housing uses, to meet an ever-increasing growth in new household formation. This focus was manifested by the imposition in 1998 of a national target for at least 60 per cent of new housing in England to be provided on brownfield sites or through the conversion of buildings (DETR 2000, DCLG 2006c para 41). For several years, this target has been comfortably exceeded with out-turn percentages well in excess of 70 per cent. Indeed, in some locations, notably London, almost 100 per cent of housing has been provided on brownfield sites.

Since 2007, a significant reduction in greenfield development has accompanied this marked increase in new dwellings completed on brownfield sites (see Syms 2010, chapter 3). While some lobby groups, such as the Campaign to Protect Rural England (CPRE) and the Environmental Industries Commission (EIC) have called for the national brownfield target to be increased above 60 per cent, to say 75 or 80 per cent, some commentators have recently suggested that the brownfield emphasis is no longer relevant. Arguing that the '… brownfield-first policy has run its course', Aldred (2010: 9), for instance, acknowledges that the policy has '… been a remarkable success on its own terms' but postulates that there have been unfortunate, and unforeseeable, side-effects as councils '… have met the target by restricting development on non-brownfield sites.' He contends that this has reduced the total supply of housing land between 1995 and 2007, despite land prices rising by over 250 per cent, and suggests that '… after fifteen years of brownfield-first policy, the most suitable brownfield sites for housing have been developed' and that much remaining brownfield land '… is located in places without strong demand' (Aldred 2010: 10).

Over the years, many brownfield sites have come forward for development without any government stimulus. This is because their location, coupled with demand, enables the market to deliver the new housing without policy intervention. Elsewhere, however, especially in inner cities, developers responded to the 60 per cent target and to the policy pressures for higher density development. This increased average densities from 25 dwellings per hectare to between 30 and 50 dwellings per hectare (DETR 2000) and produced numerous high-rise blocks of one- and two-bedroom apartments, aimed primarily at the 'buy-to-let' market, creating an oversupply in many cities and large towns.

Many local planning authorities thus found themselves powerless to resist applications for very high density developments, which they would previously have refused on the grounds of 'over-development', while others actively encouraged high-rise 'landmark' proposals. Many such developments had little regard for the principles of good urban design, often making no contribution whatsoever to the public realm. One high-profile critic of higher density development, Sir Peter Hall, argued in 2005 in a footnote to an independent report of the Urban Task Force, that '... there is no overriding need to save greenfield land ... [and] the case on sustainability grounds for further raising minimum densities is non-proven; the requirement to first develop brownfield land in the growth areas would in practice lead to inflexibility which would almost certainly slow their development' (Urban Task Force 2005: 19).

Such controversy helped cause *Planning Policy statement 3 – Housing*,[2] to be modified in 2006 to include a stronger emphasis on urban design, reflected in its statement that 'Local Planning Authorities should develop housing density policies having regard to:

• The spatial vision and strategy for housing development in their area, including *the level of housing demand* and need and the availability of suitable land in the area.
• The current and future level and capacity of infrastructure, services and facilities such as *public and private amenity space, in particular green and open space.*
• The desirability of using land efficiently and reducing, and adapting to, the impacts of climate change.
• The current and future levels of accessibility, particularly public transport accessibility.
• The *characteristics of the area*, including the current and proposed mix of uses.
• The desirability of achieving *high quality, well designed housing ...*'
(DCLG 2006c para 46, emphasis added).

Such aspirations reflect a desire to see high quality developments built in keeping with their areas and provided with amenity spaces and an appropriate mix of uses. Rather than stipulating housing densities, the policy statement states that 'Local Planning Authorities may wish to set out a range of densities ... although 30 dwellings per hectare (dph) net should be used as a national indicative minimum ...' and suggests that where authorities '... wish to plan for, or agree to densities below this minimum, this will need to be justified ...' (DCLG 2006c: para 47). These changes have enabled local planning authorities to resist demands for very high density schemes not justified either by local housing demand or the area context.

In addition to land-use policies that seek to direct new development towards brownfield sites, an important fiscal policy, the Land Remediation Relief, was introduced in the 2001 Budget across the whole of the UK to encourage brownfield redevelopment. This is described more fully later on.

Irrespective of issues around housing provision, development densities and taxation incentives to assist redevelopment, not all brownfield sites are capable of redevelopment, whether for housing or any other use. A significant proportion of brownfield sites, for example, are in areas prone to flooding. The importance of these sites with regard to both their biodiversity and flood alleviation potential was recognised in the National Brownfield Strategy for England, the first 'overarching principle' of which states:

> When considering the allocation of land for future uses, the principle of 'redevelop or reuse' first shall be used alongside the PPS 25 (Development and Flood Risk) sequential test and reference to site's potential biodiversity value in accordance with PPS 9 (Biodiversity and Geological Conservation) (English Partnerships 2007b: 5).

Heritage considerations may also limit development on brownfield sites. In March 2010, the Government published a new *Planning Policy statement 5 – Planning for the Historic Environment* (PPS 5), the policies in which, where relevant, must be taken into account in development control decisions in England. PPS 5 aimed to deliver sustainable development while ensuring the conservation of the historic environment and its heritage assets, so that they may be '... enjoyed for the quality of life they bring to this and future generations' (DCLG 2010: 2). In practical terms, when considering the redevelopment of brownfield sites that may contain heritage assets, '... local planning authorities should require an applicant to provide a description of the significance of the heritage assets affected and the contribution of their setting to that significance' (DCLG 2010: 6). Compliance may well involve the prospective developer commissioning archaeological investigations, or other specialist assessments of the historic context of the site, and additional works to conserve or preserve the heritage assets. The additional time and costs involved, which must be factored into the development appraisal, potentially impact on developer's and the designer's opportunity space.

The redevelopment potential of brownfield land is also affected by the 'contaminated land legislation' contained in Part 2A of the Environmental Protection Act 1990. This requires local authorities to inspect their areas for the purpose of identifying land which appears

> ... to be in such a condition, by reason of substances in, on or under the land, that – (a) significant harm is being caused or there is a significant possibility of such harm being caused; or (b) pollution of controlled waters is being, or is likely to be caused.

The 'polluter pays' principle makes the person responsible for causing the pollution, or allowing it to occur, liable for the costs of making the site safe. Significantly, liability extends only to making the site safe for its existing use. On a vacant site, this might simply involve preventing contaminants from coming into contact with ground or surface waters, flora and fauna, or with any person entering the site. This might be achieved with a simple cap layer over the site (clay or concrete) and/or an underground barrier wall, leaving the contaminated soil contained within the site. Such treatment may fall well short of that required to prepare for redevelopment. In the absence of the original polluter, the current site owner may be held liable, while any developer may also become liable by unwittingly breaching any containment layers or barriers. There are various tests to determine liability under the legislation, as well as 'hardship' provisions, but these are beyond the scope of this chapter.

As these policies highlight, brownfield sites represent important national assets which should be reused in preference to further encroachment onto greenfield land. While conflicts over environmental and ecological issues may also affect greenfield sites, those concerning archaeological or historic matters are less likely to constrain greenfield development. Although such features can often produce benefits, for example through the creation of new or improved habitats and the conservation of heritage assets, all of which can enhance the long-term value, in the short term, they may well extend or delay building programmes, and increase costs and design constraints

Alongside policies making more effective and efficient use of brownfield land, creating sustainable places where people want to live, work or spend their leisure time has been another government priority. In May 2009, the Departments for Culture, Media and Sport, and Communities and Local Government jointly published *World Class Places*. This was a strategy document rather than a policy instrument, which acted as a market-shaping (information) tool by laying '... out the Government's approach to improving quality of place – the way the places where we live and work are planned, designed, developed and maintained – and the steps [it] will be taking to build on recent progress' (DCLG & DCMS 2009: 6).

The strategy defines 'quality of place' as '… the physical characteristics of a community – the way it is planned, designed, developed and maintained – that affect the quality of life of people living and working in it, and those visiting it, both now and into the future' (DCLG & DCMS 2009: 11). Alongside the many different factors that contribute to quality of place, it highlights how the physical characteristics of a local area can contribute to the quality of life of the people who live and work there. While not specifically directed at the redevelopment of brownfield sites, the strategy document acknowledges the shift to brownfield development, commenting that '… we are building less on greenfield sites and instead investing in regenerating run-down brownfield areas' (DCLG & DCMS 2009: 7). It also notes the Government's commitment to promoting brownfield, mixed use forms of urban development, that are inclusive and sustainable, built around the needs of pedestrians as well as car owners. The *World Class Places* strategy '… sits squarely within this broad approach' (DCLG & DCMS 2009: 37).

Having reviewed the importance of brownfield development within recent government policy, the chapter now turns to consider the policy instruments that have been used to stimulate or encourage brownfield reuse.

Stimulus instruments in practice

In this section, we outline the different stimuli that may influence, directly or indirectly, a developer's decision-making process when assessing whether or not to proceed with the development of a specific site, or in a general location. For the most part, a stimulus tool may be seen as providing the developer(s) with an economic advantage, although it is important to note that the direct subsidy of a development by a governmental body, in order to make it economically competitive, may well breach European Union rules on state aid. Other interventions may include the provision of site preparation works and off-site infrastructure. As discussed below, stimulus tools may also include such regulations and policy statements as guidance on the design and form of new developments and interventions at the site specific level by local planning authorities. We therefore look first at development stimulus tools, then at design stimulus tools before exploring how they might work in combination

Development stimulus tools

These typically encourage development to happen in a particular location, to happen sooner, to be of higher quality or for there to be more of it, etc. Development tools/instruments typically impact directly on developer behaviour by increasing reward, reducing risk etc.

As Tiesdell and Adams outlined in Chapter 1, the main development stimulus tools may be described as:

- direct state actions;
- price-adjusting instruments;
- risk-adjusting instruments;
- capital-raising instruments.

We now deal with each of these in turn.

(1) *Direct state actions* operate at the site- or area-specific level and are usually intended to overcome particular obstacles to development by the provision of public infrastructure and serviced sites, environmental improvements, assistance with land assembly/subdivision, etc. The National Coalfields Programme was an example of this. As implied by its name, this programme was aimed directly at those parts of England affected by closure of the coal industry. It commenced in March 1997 and directly intervened in 107 former colliery sites. By November 2008, public-sector investment had reached £435 million, levering in £772 million of private finance (see http://www.homesandcommunities.co.uk/coalfields_programme). The public sector investment was largely directed at remediating sites and providing new infrastructure by working with partners to create new homes, employment workspace, health and leisure facilities and new public open space. Since many coalfield sites suffered from extreme market failure, often to the extent that without direct intervention there would have been no market at any price, this was a 'direct state action' development stimulus tool, with potentially price-adjusting and risk-adjusting attributes.

(2) *Price-adjusting instruments* operate by adjusting the price of an activity to a developer by the imposition of site-specific taxes, tax credits/incentives/breaks or subsidies/grants etc. Traditionally, gap-funding grants fulfilled this role. These operated under several names, initially Urban Development Grant (from the early 1980s), Urban Regeneration Grant and City Grant, which was eventually combined with the Derelict Land Grant programme to form English Partnerships Investment Fund (EPIF).[3] Where such programmes contained an economic subsidy, they operated as price-adjusting stimulus tools by directly affecting development costs and/or revenues. Otherwise they acted as risk-adjusting tools, since public-sector participation reduced the yield expected on regeneration schemes. In 1999, the European Commission ruled that EPIF constituted illegal state aid, and the programme was discontinued in December of that year. English Partnerships subsequently agreed an EU-compliant replacement scheme, under which any enhancement in land value accrued to the public sector. Although available to regeneration agencies, it lacked a dedicated budget and saw little use.

(3) *Risk-adjusting instruments* work by adjusting the risk to the actor associated with an activity: for example, by creating a more predictable investment environment through demonstration projects; policy stability; investment actions; active place management etc. The operation of Derelict Land Grant illustrates this. This grant was primarily intended for use by local authorities to enable them to reclaim land where the cost of reclamation exceeded any enhancement in land value, with 100 per cent of the excess cost met by a central government grant (see Syms 1994: 78–80). There was also a similar private sector scheme under which 80 per cent of the excess cost was met by grant aid. In theory, this programme may be seen as a price-adjusting stimulus tool but in practice it was intended to ensure the restoration of damaged land to such a condition that it could compete on equal terms with undamaged land in the same vicinity. The programme was therefore more of a risk-adjusting tool, as the public sector shouldered any cost of reclamation exceeding the economic end value of the site. Nevertheless, a side impact could involve the general uplifting of prices in the neighbourhood through the removal of the 'blighting effect' caused by the derelict site.

(4) *Capital-raising instruments* operate by facilitating the availability of development finance or, alternatively, by enabling particular developers to access sources of finance previously inaccessible to them and/or to access it on more favourable terms. Land Remediation Relief works partly in this way. This is a fiscal measure aimed at encouraging corporate landowners to tackle the problems of contamination and dereliction on their unused, or under-utilised, landholdings. It aims to secure the voluntary preparation of land for redevelopment, with the landowner benefiting from Corporation Tax Relief at the rate of 150 per cent of the cost of qualifying expenditure. This stimulus tool may be best regarded as both a price-adjusting and a capital-raising measure, since it should produce an improvement in the value of the capital asset and, through the tax relief, an improved ability to raise capital for the site redevelopment.[4]

Design stimulus tools

In Tiesdell and Adams' elaboration of opportunity space theory, tools intended to encourage 'better places' operate by encouraging the developer to yield opportunity space to a designer. Thus, when a local planning authority raises its expectations about design quality, it creates a de facto design stimulus, since it makes developers more likely to consider design and place-making issues and to commission skilled designers for their project. Indeed, where design expectations are particularly exacting, the developer may well conclude that commissioning skilled designers is the most cost- and time-efficient way to obtain regulatory consents. In this context, a developer yielding opportunity space to a designer is not (necessarily) a 'Bad

Thing' for the developer, because the designer might make better use of the opportunity space to produce a better, more profitable/more rewarding project, or simply a means of securing quicker consents.

We can identify eight examples of such design stimulus tools, which we discuss in turn below, with reference to specific examples. As Tiesdell and Adams indicate in Chapter 1, such tools operate by making developers realise either they 'want to' provide better quality development, or that they 'have to' or that it is 'worth it' because of remunerative advantage. The eight tools are:

(1) design stimulus delivered or administered by the local planning authority;
(2) specific area and/or site design policy and guidance;
(3) local design policies;
(4) national policy tools and guidance;
(5) design review;
(6) 'By Design' enabling;
(7) where a public sector landowner requires particular design standards;
(8) existing place quality, local competition or developer aspiration driving quality.

We now deal with each of these in turn.

(1) Design stimulus delivered or administered by the local planning authority (LPA)   This requires a committed LPA with sufficient urban design skills to promote and secure design quality through development control on a case-by-case basis. Many authorities now have in-house urban designers to deliver this role, while others instead rely on limited input from consultants or on sharing resources with other authorities. It is crucial that planning authorities do not accept the easiest or cheapest solution or standard designs or solutions, as these are usually unrelated to context. Instead, requesting site analysis and requiring the design to be related and responsive to context acts as a stimulus to a more appropriate solution. This is a challenge to most 'entry level' designs. Understanding how far a developer can be pushed and encouraged towards better design is thus a key skill for designers.

Often the request for a more considered design and for greater skills commitment from the applicant results in both a better scheme and a more efficient and economically viable development. Simple matters like maximising contextual features such as canals or attractive views out of a site and relating the development to local vernacular and character are important messages. As Figures 7.1 and 7.2 illustrate, this approach has worked well in securing housing layouts that are much more appropriate for their context in East Staffordshire.

(2) Specific area and/or site design policy and guidance   These design quality tools are drawn up and implemented locally to address particular

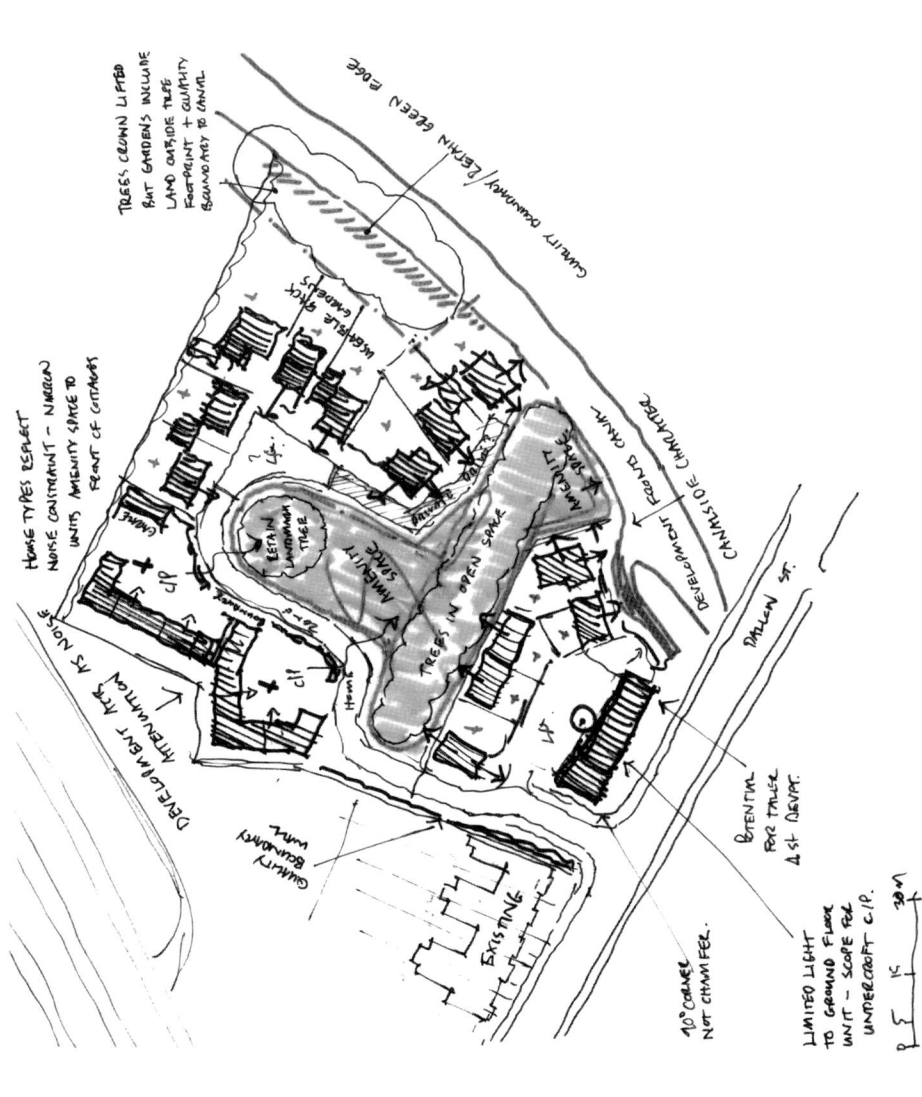

Figure 7.1 Land at Dallow Street, Burton-upon-Trent, East Staffordshire: Sketch design and layout ideas prepared at design review meeting by local authority urban designer working with developer's design team. Reproduced by permission of Taylor Young Ltd.

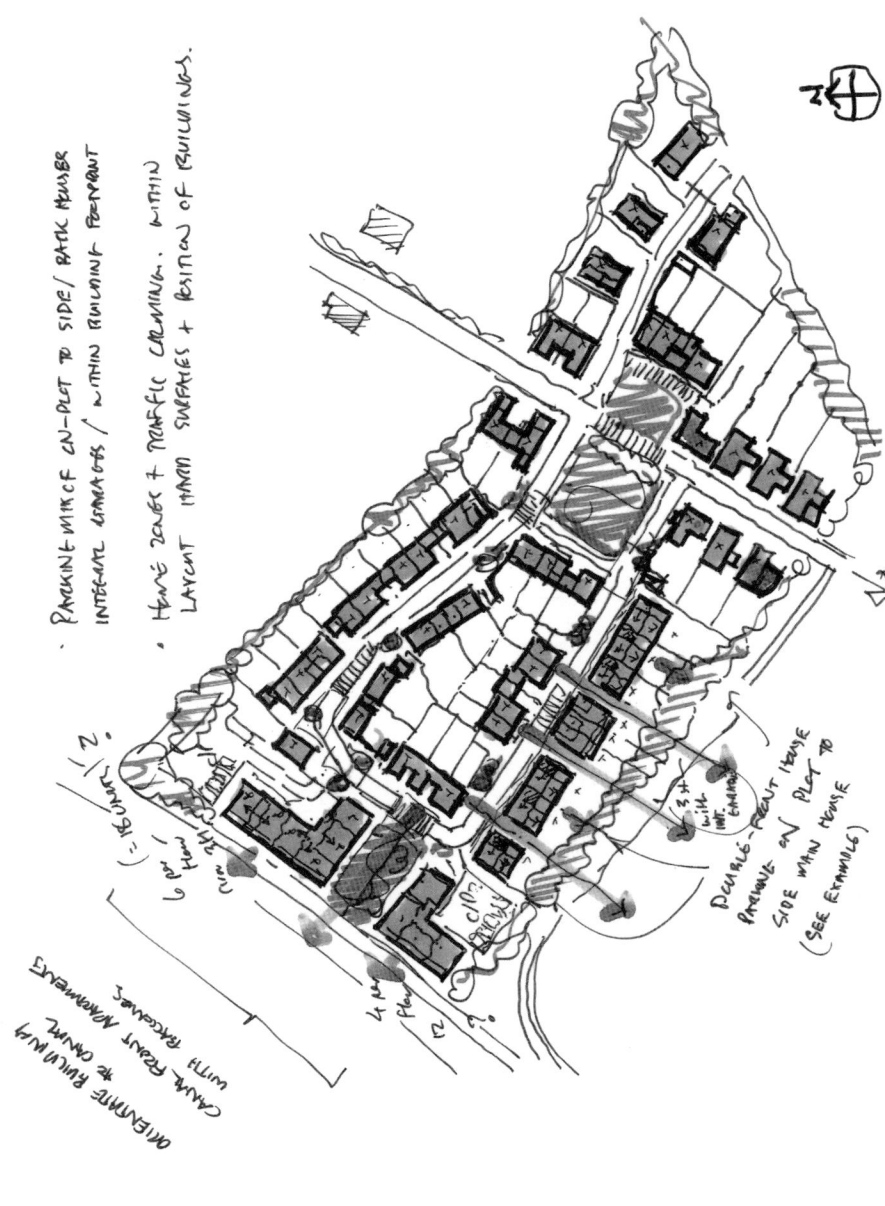

Figure 7.2 Land near Branston Water Park, Tatenhill, East Staffordshire: Sketch design and layout ideas prepared at design review meeting by local authority urban designer working with developer's design team. Reproduced by permission of Taylor Young Ltd.

Figure 7.3 Improving the existing public realm in St Helens. Reproduced by permission of Taylor Young Ltd.

site, area or thematic design and development challenges. They give planners, and particularly those working in development control, the ability to focus on key design issues and negotiate more effectively with developers and applicants. Good examples are George Street Quarter, St Helens and Didsbury Point, Manchester.

In St Helens (see Figure 7.3) a public realm design guide was prepared to support investment in buildings, shop fronts and streets and spaces. The guide helped to set the vision and quality standards for the place. It served both as a campaigning document, used to secure public investment, and a controlling document, used to establish a consistent approach to matters such as materials, design approaches, street furniture, lighting and colours. The guide was recognised as instrumental in securing consistently high implementation by all stakeholders.

At Didsbury Point, a design guide was prepared, alongside a masterplan, to guide the future detailed design of a major new residential and office development (see Figure 7.4). As a condition of outline planning approval, the guide was required in advance of, and to control, subsequent reserved matters applications. It then provided continuity throughout all subsequent phases of detailed design, development and implementation.

(3) Local design policies Since such policies need careful application through briefing, negotiation and design review, without skilled in-house designers or

Figure 7.4   Didsbury Point: A 'design guide' led approach to creating an attractive new street scene. Reproduced by permission of Taylor Young Ltd.

design-literate staff to administer and apply them, they will be less effective. If local authority staff lack the necessary training and experience to apply design policies to specific sites, it will fall to applicants to demonstrate how they have responded to policies. Such an approach can work, since it may be an explicit design stimulus in its own right simply to state, for example, that 'the council will expect skilled designers to be used and site analysis to be undertaken and linked to scheme proposals'. Of course the local authority will then need to assess whether or not these tests have been satisfied.

(4) National policy tools and guidance   These include, for example, Building for Life (BfL) (see http://www.buildingforlife.org/) run by CABE and the Home Builders Federation with Design for Homes. BfL sets out 20 criteria against which development proposals can be assessed, covering environment and community, character, streets, parking and pedestrianisation, and design and construction. It requires accredited assessors, who are in short supply, particularly in the private sector. However, CABE made a commitment to train one officer in each authority. Concern has been voiced about the use of BfL assessment criteria at the outline application stage, because not all aspects may be known at this early stage in the development design process. This problem may be overcome by introducing a 'light or strategic' version of BfL.

Bridgewater Place (View 2)

Figure 7.5 Redevelopment of a historic waterfront to the Bridgewater Canal at Leigh. Reproduced by permission of Taylor Young Ltd.

(5) Design review This includes, for example, national CABE design review and regional design reviews, and both of these put schemes under greater scrutiny and encourage a higher level of design quality and process. They are not about imposing specific solutions or styles. Their greatest value is for the panel to be taken through the design process, from analysis and constraints right through to the design response and proposals, in order to evaluate the approach and outcome in the round. Having planning officers and clients involved the actual design review (and in the preparation for it) is very helpful.

Almost always a design review will suggest some improvements, which do add value if undertaken positively and if real-life limitations are fully appreciated by the panel. To get most from this process a positive and open approach is needed. It offers real potential to add value and stimulate design quality, but often design review covers only a small proportion of larger schemes. The national and regional focus is starting to address this to some degree.

The examples in Figures 7.5 and 7.6 show Bridgewater Place in Leigh and Ashton Green in Leicestershire. These schemes won support respectively at regional and national CABE design reviews. Bridgewater Place is a major residential-led mixed-use development on the Bridgewater Canal in Leigh, Greater Manchester. Ashton Green is a sustainable urban extension including

Figure 7.6 Masterplan of Ashton Green, Leicestershire. Reproduced by permission of Taylor Young Ltd.

a new school and over 3000 new homes. As these examples show, it is important to commence the review process early in the evolution of the design. It is also essential for the developer and designer to share a thorough understanding of both the design ideas and the development objectives, to recognise internal and external development constraints and to remain open-minded.

(6) 'By Design' enabling   This approach involves communities and other stakeholders in evolving design ideas. It can be provided independently by CABE or, in some cases, consultants. The approach has been championed by The Prince's Foundation, which regards it as '*... collaborative planning*' and '*... one of the Foundation's key planning tools, and the framework by which [its] values are disseminated to influence future development of the built environment*' (see The Prince's Foundation website – http://www.princes-foundation.org/index.php?id=33).

At Ashton town centre in Greater Manchester, visioning, advocacy and enabling processes led by Taylor Young brought together key stakeholders within the public and private sectors to develop an urban design and place-making agenda for the town and position this within real-life commercial considerations. Although the outcomes were specific to Ashton, the processes of creative thinking and problem solving are transferable, and this can help unlock problems and stimulate activity and innovation. Through training and study trips, it is possible to provide those involved in the design and development process with improved skills to deliver better places. This might include funders, clients, project managers, planners and elected councillors. The key issue is to foster an appreciation of the value of good design and to learn 'what can be done' from studying the best national and international experience elsewhere.

(7) Where a public sector landowner requires particular design standards   The economic value placed by public sector landowners on any site crucially affects the likely design standards and may be regarded as both a development (price- and risk-adjusting) and design stimulus tool. In practice, the stimulus is delivered principally through site briefs and the procurement of development partners. Two case studies illustrate different outcomes, one positive – King's Waterfront, Liverpool – and one that, at the time of writing in mid 2010 has yet to have a positive outcome – the land at Gorton Monastery.

At King's Waterfront (see Figure 7.7) Liverpool Vision and English Partnerships (now the Homes and Communities Agency – HCA) were instrumental in delivering a major mixed-use development including a convention centre and arena, hotel and restaurant. A major residential development is still to be built. The public sector set the design agenda through design competitions and helped to manage the design and delivery process, based on a strong masterplan vision.

Figure 7.7   King's Waterfront Liverpool, showing the Echo Arena and, in the foreground the newly opened 'Liverpool link' from the Leeds and Liverpool Canal to Albert Dock. Reproduced by permission of Taylor Young Ltd.

The redevelopment of land at Gorton Monastery has been less successful (see Figure 7.8) Here, the HCA has championed high design standards at this landmark site in Manchester. The site adjoins the iconic Gorton Monastery (already restored as the result of tireless campaigning and considerable public funding), which provides a key design driver. However, the preferred developer has struggled to meet these high standards given difficult market conditions, and so, in 2010, the quality standards were reset. The concept of securing exemplar design through its landholding remains a key ambition for the Agency.

These two examples show significant differences in both the location and development form. King's Waterfront is located in a highly prominent area of the city, close to the 'Three Graces', and contains significant public realm and commercial uses. In contrast, the Gorton Monastery site lies in the old industrial area of east Manchester, now undergoing major regeneration, and is heavily reliant on the delivery of private sector housing.

(8) Existing place quality, local competition or developer aspiration driving quality   Developers who see a market opportunity for a high quality scheme with high-value end uses and users will be prepared to invest in

Figure 7.8   Gorton Monastery, East Manchester: Masterplan street scene. Reproduced by permission of Taylor Young Ltd.

a high quality development concept. An example of this approach is 'Wainwright's yard' in Kendal (see Figure 7.9). This is a mixed-use development anchored by a food store and carefully integrated in the grain of the historic town. The Conservation Area designation required quality development, but the retail assessment of the town also identified a market for high-end niche shopping. Since retail development of this type requires a high quality setting, the design approach was set to create a place of quality that could sustain a premium town centre 'offer'. In this case, the design quality of buildings and the public realm was a key part of the developer's ambitions and the development's specific attraction.

Bringing together development and design stimulus tools

If there is a distinction between development and design stimulus tools, then four situations are possible:

(1) No design stimulus and no development stimulus instruments – nothing happens.

Figure 7.9   Wainwright's Yard, Kendal: High end niche shopping in a conservation area. Reproduced by permission of Taylor Young Ltd.

(2) Design stimulus instrument but no development stimulus instrument – if development happened it would be of high quality, but, due to the lack of a development stimulus tool, no development happens (i.e. development is not stimulated).

(3) Development stimulus instrument but no design stimulus tool – perhaps plenty of development happens (i.e. it is stimulated) but it is of poor quality.

(4) Development stimulus instrument + design stimulus instrument – the ideal situation: development and design stimulus tools are complementary – i.e. the result is significant high quality development.

Some development stimulus tools could be changed into *development + design stimulus tools* by adding *design strings* to the basic development stimulus tools. For example, the 'entry cost' of developing on a serviced plot with infrastructure provided could be raised if the developer is required to conform with a design guide or code.

In practice, the response of developers to stimulus tools, whether development (economic) or design-related tends to reflect market circumstances.

Some brownfield developments are delivered as the result of market demand, with little or no need for intervention or incentives. The success of such developments is often dependent upon design quality. In contrast, developments that respond to public policies, such as brownfield land targets and higher densities, may not have derived from market research. This, when coupled with poor design, has led to the preponderance of one- and two-bedroom flat developments in many city centres.

Conclusion

In an ideal world, the base land value of a brownfield site would be adjusted downwards, even to zero or a negative figure, in order to accommodate all aspects of the design. However, property development rarely, if ever, takes place in an ideal world and, almost without exception, landowners will seek to maximise the price they receive for their land, even if it is contaminated or derelict. There is therefore inevitably a trade-off between meeting price expectations and design aspirations.

If a site is lying vacant and unused it is often difficult to ascribe a monetary value that will be recognised in the marketplace. Nevertheless, landowners may have a view as to its worth to themselves or to their businesses, which may be based on a historic asset valuation, used as collateral for bank borrowings. In the south of England especially, the latent brownfield site may still be in use. Even if that use is of low economic value, such as vehicle dismantling, surface car parking or container storage, it can still produce considerable income for the site operators/owners, often justifying valuations approaching, or even exceeding, development land values, once site remediation and infrastructure costs are taken into account. This then leaves the rather blunt instrument of compulsory purchase ('eminent domain' in North American parlance) as the last resort to assemble the site. However, many local authorities are reluctant to use their compulsory purchase powers, lacking both the financial resources and the human skills required to embark on the process that can be both costly and time consuming. Authorities are therefore likely to look to prospective developers to underwrite the process of site assembly, thereby further reducing the developer's opportunity space.

Good quality design coupled, where necessary, with fiscal or other incentives can provide the essential ingredients that can transform a marginal scheme into a successful property development. Paying attention to the standards of the design and, especially, producing an environment in which people want to live, work or visit can even create demand where it previously did not exist. Nevertheless, it must be recognised that in weak market conditions such demand may be fragile, and the developer will need to pay close attention to contingency provisions, including changes to the development mix, in order to ensure a successful outcome. Good design and flexibility therefore needs to be integrated into the project plan from its initiation. To summarise, achieving a successful outcome in the redevelopment of a brownfield site requires a delicate balance of many ingredients including environmental, ecological, historic, cultural and, of course, good design.

Notes

1. This is not to say that all development has to take place on brownfield land, or indeed that all brownfield sites are suitable for development. (For a more detailed discussion of the issues surrounding brownfield redevelopment, see Syms, 2010).
2. PPS 3 (and, before it, PPG 3) is the main piece of central government policy on housing development in England.
3. English Partnerships was established in 1993 as the national regeneration agency for England.
4. English Partnerships, as the national regeneration agency for England (now subsumed into the Homes and Communities Agency), worked with HM Treasury and HMRC on the revisions to Land Remediation Relief so as to include derelict as well as contaminated land and, in order to assist those responsible for its administration and the claimants of the tax relief, produced a Best Practice Note (BPN27) on Contamination and Remediation Costs (English Partnerships 2008).

8

Competitions as a Component of Design-Led Development (Place) Procurement

Steven Tolson

Introduction

One might think competitions get the right results. But is that correct? Is the winner of the Football World Cup competition necessarily the best team in the world? Perhaps not, as the winner could be determined by a whole raft of issues, decisions and events that might not result in the best team winning or might even bring about the best spectacle. Certainly all the teams that participate in the World Cup want to win but many realise that they lack the necessary skills and so have to devise a game plan for beating better teams. This may bring about a result that the competition organisers would rather not see.

Competitions mean different things to different people. To a designer a competition is a device that brings forward lots of creative proposals, and one might expect that the best one would win. To an estates surveyor, a competition will be seen as a device that should attract the best offer price. To a politician or public official, a competition might be seen as a device that is the most equitable and democratic process, and while it would be good to have the best solution, so long as the process is fair then such people will be happy that they have done the right thing.

Of course, the most creative proposal could also be the most expensive, and the client simply has not got the budget to afford it. Perhaps the most

Urban Design in the Real Estate Development Process, First Edition. Edited by Steve Tiesdell and David Adams.

creative proposal is seen as a beautiful solution but there might be technical doubts about whether it can actually be built. Perhaps the most beautiful solution could be built, and within the prescribed capital budget, but perhaps it is expensive to operate, and so on. Competitions are thus far more complex than one might at first think.

Notwithstanding these complexities, the use of competitions has become an increasingly popular method to deliver more place-aware, design-led developments. This process is not a panacea, however; it needs to be well managed, well organised and well conceived.

A competition is a process that has the potential to establish good practice but process alone will not create a successful outcome. Competitions that are poorly organised, managed and conceived will not only irritate and annoy developers, designers and local communities, but, more importantly, will lead to unnecessary delay, wasted resources and a loss of energy, enthusiasm and project commitment.

While architectural (design) competitions may be seen as the route to deliver a quality design solution, it does not follow that developer competitions will do likewise. There has to be a clear understanding of the motivations of the participants. One thing is clear: a developer rarely has the same motivation as a designer. One might expect an architectural competition to be organised by those who know a thing or two about design but in the case of design-led developer competitions, how many times does one find a developer being on the judging panel?

To achieve a good competition there needs to be a clear understanding of more than just matters of design, otherwise the developer will not be interested and will not engage. Those who do engage will be quickly turned off if the client group is ill-informed and lacks the necessary experience of how development works and what needs to be done to get the best out of those whose aspiration may differ from that of the clients. Competition sponsors need to understand that bidders are acting on a speculative basis, putting time and effort into a project where there is no guarantee of success. If the competitor is messed about and burdened with time delays, then commitment and vitality for the project will be lost. Losing developer interest will not only be prejudicial to the specific project but could also endanger confidence in future competitions. The key point is that if you want to organise a competition, make sure that you have people in the client team who understand development as well as design. Competitions should be seen as a selling exercise as well as a process. To successfully sell, one needs to be able to demonstrate credibility by being well informed about all design and development matters. It is essential to avoid just seeking to implement a vision by simply relying on procurement techniques that could get one along a critical path from A to B but fail to engage with the right people with the right solutions.

Transferring vision and plan on to the ground is arguably the most difficult task in the process of place-making. In the UK, designers supported by informed clients have become highly competent in producing good masterplans, but sadly we have been less able in delivering such plans. This chapter examines some of the delivery issues and general procurement methods that might assist in getting good plans into good places.

Almost inevitably those that bring about vision are not the ones to deliver that vision. That said, the success of projects depends less on process and more on visionary and inspirational leaders who are able to see the project through from inception to completion and can persuade all stakeholders to equally commit energy, passion and vitality to the project.

So who are the key players in the delivery of better places? Essentially they fall into two categories – the place promoter (client) and the deliverer (developer). To achieve a successful competition, it is essential to understand the motivation of these players, and also recognise that competitions cannot be set up and promoted in a vacuum. Ideals and vision objectives have to be tested against economic, as well as social and physical, criteria.

The place promoter

We should first draw an important distinction between public and private-sector landowners as place promoters.

Private sector landowner as promoter

Private landowners typically want the quickest and maximum receipts from the sale of their ground. The only exceptions are where landowners have other non-monetary objectives, for example, where they have a long-term investment in the new place; live adjacent to the project and wish to ensure that their retained asset value is either maintained or enhanced; wish to be associated with an award-winning quality development; or perhaps (even in the 21st century) are philanthropic.

There are not many examples of this, but arguably when such projects arise they have the propensity to become exemplars of well designed places. This is simply due to being a private interest with the freedom to exercise project delivery in any appropriate manner – in contrast to public parties who are required to undertake a project delivery through complicated bureaucratic processes that tend to lose sight of the project's objective. Bureaucratic processes are designed to obtain fairness and 'best value' – though it is doubtful whether a private owner would be motivated to do anything other than seek 'best value'.

Other than just promotion, a private owner could be involved to a greater or lesser degree. They could restrict their participation to being just an inspirational visionary who sets the rules of engagement and sells their interest once the developer has been identified or, at the other end of the scale, could act as a full participator by being a joint venture shareholder in the delivery of a good place. Typically, private landowners looking for the delivery of a good place are more likely to be individuals, families or some entity with charitable status. It would be very rare to find a private company selling land with any objective other than gaining the highest price for the proposed asset disposal.

Public sector landowner as promoter

There are, of course, a range of public sector organisations, such as national governments, local governments, agencies and public bodies such as the National Health Service, who own land surplus to requirements. While the National Health Service is more likely to require the maximum value from the sale of non-operational assets, local authorities and public development agencies engaged in programmes of regeneration and/or public housing delivery are more likely to consider high quality design solutions to achieve better places. We will look at how such public organisations might set about achieving their objectives later in this chapter.

The deliverer and competition participant

Private sector developer

The private developer is likely to play a significant part in delivering better places. However, developers have different motivations from designers and place-makers. Private developers are largely motivated by maximising profit as quickly and safely as possible, and only a minority of developers are motivated by creating better places. In searching for profit, developers are looking for a route map that is uncomplicated, certain and can be delivered as fast as possible. That is, they are more likely to wish to repeat tried-and-tested formulae than to try out unfamiliar solutions not yet supported by substantive evidence. As it carries additional risks, the majority of private developers are not pioneering trendsetters. However, there are developers, most of which tend to be small scale, that are more informed about the wider place-agenda and set out to take advantage of commercial opportunities that the more traditional volume corporate developers seek to avoid.

It must be remembered that even if an enlightened developer wishes to participate in an exciting new place-making competition exercise, unless they are extremely affluent, they will need to gain the support of their financial lenders and the lender's advisor. Neither the lender nor the advisor is likely to be as enlightened and informed on the better places agenda as their customer.

Developer's objectives

To achieve a profit, a developer's prime objective is focused on accurately forecasting the value and cost of development and what underlying risks are attached to delivering the proposed project. Those developers who ensure that value and cost elements are rigorously researched will be better informed and more objective in their land acquisition deliberations than those with a methodology that is formed on the back of an envelope.

For a developer, the best assets are essentially those that can create quick receipts whereas the occupiers and investors of such assets and surrounding spaces will recognise that it is the establishment of the place and its recognition of quality that will influence long-term asset value. Clearly a place promoter is concerned with the longer-term realisation of the place but has often to rely on a developer who is more concerned with the short term.

However, a developer needs to understand the end investor's detailed requirements, which will reflect whether that investor is a landlord or an owner-occupier. To do this, there is a need to be confident that there is market demand and to know what the market is prepared to pay for the completed project.

While there are developers that are prepared to undertake both commercial and residential development, each of the activities has normally been undertaken by different players and organisations. Commercial developers, particularly those undertaking urban development that is bespoke in nature, will employ only a relatively small number of personnel within their organisations. This is because they prefer to rely more on external advice, particularly property practitioners who are actively engaged in the market on a daily basis. An investor's objectives of long-term asset growth should be broadly the same as that of the place promoter.

Other than specialist residential developers, housebuilders (they have now changed their name to a more consumer-friendly title as 'home builders') tend to undertake most of their operations in-house. This is due to volume builders preferring to procure their own consumer-proven standard products particularly in edge-of-settlement/greenfield locations. As planning policies have tightened in terms of greenfield land releases, pressure has increased for brownfield development, which may be supported by higher regulatory design objectives. We will return to housebuilding objectives later.

Valuation of commercial property is largely based on markets behaving in an objective manner. Commercial property values will reflect, amongst other things, the quality of the individual building, its flexibility and adaptability, its location, lease characteristics and the covenant strength of the tenant. Such criteria are relatively well understood and values can be readily established.

Difficulties, however, can arise when new mixed-use regeneration developments are promoted in places that lack any evidence for the promoted uses. Locations promoted for uses that fail to meet business operational and market criteria will struggle to gain support from lending institutions and their property advisors. Place-making competitions that promote mixed-use development solutions that are 'off-pitch' without supporting evidence or a robust rationale will fail to convince developers that their vision is viable.

If there is a lack of evidence to support such proposals, then it is highly unlikely that the developer will be able to get an independent valuation to support the proposals that will be required to secure debt funding. For example, planners may push for the incorporation of 'live work' housing within a development to give diversity in a mixed-use approach to development. While an interesting concept for small professional firms and craft businesses, working from home has not really progressed due to a small level of demand in particular locations. It may be desirable for an individual business person but those providing finance will be concerned with the saleability of the accommodation beyond the individual business prospects of the customer. The financial lender has to consider the security of the loan against the asset as well as the strength of the business proposition and general covenant strength of the customer.

In contrast to commercial uses, residential property values are influenced by subjective behaviour and perceptions that are informed by what is familiar and convenient.

Unfortunately there are few exemplars of good place-making practice so it is not familiar for the wider population. Better places can be delivered only if there is a good demand from consumers. Before this happens, the proposition has to be sold to a wider audience. Developers frequently claim that they merely produce developments that reflect and react to consumer behaviour. Clearly, a drive along any motorway in Britain will illustrate that new houses vary very little from Wick to Winchester.

Better places in continental Europe such as Germany, Scandinavia and the Netherlands are supported by a long history of good exemplars from expositions and research projects subsidised by the state. This 'seeing is believing' approach inevitably helps to sell ideas, and unlocks the critical barrier of consumer unfamiliarity.

Familiarity should breed confidence that will, with the right conditions, convert to a growth in value. A radical competition strategy, with a masterplan and architecture that promotes the unfamiliar, can thus lead to greater risk, as developers fear that the consumer will be wary of buying into something that is not understood.

Over the past three decades, suburban development has tended to move towards larger housing at lower densities. This has been mainly a product of easier access to larger levels of credit and an appetite by individuals to see a dwelling as an investment as well as simply a place of habitation. This move to larger houses in suburban settings that frequently lacked good place characteristics has become a 'familiar' housing form for purchasers. Understandably safe in the knowledge that buyers buy what is familiar, housebuilders have been content to provide such housing on a mass-produced basis.

However, in the past decade greenfield edge-of-settlement development land has become more restricted due to planning policies. This has resulted in more populated parts of the UK seeing a switch to more flatted dwellings in order for developers to become more competitive in acquiring land. The irony is that, in a recession, flatted development forms are likely to decline as developers go in search of lower-risk housing types.

Consequently, masterplans need to rigorously assess market demand to underpin the promoted uses. A lack of understanding of market demand and behaviour will present difficulties for those responsible for promoting the project and will discourage developers from participating in competitions. While it will always be a matter for developers to satisfy themselves on demand and the inherent value, promoters need to have a greater understanding of such matters if they are to create a greater quality of participation. Promoting clients need to be more informed, and if they can demonstrate greater clarity, the developers will be more positive as risks can be more readily assessed and quantified.

Having considered some essential value inputs to inform the masterplan, the client must consider the practical and cost elements that will help to inform project viability.

While those charged with place promotion may have researched 'best practice' from exemplar projects, their application on specific sites requires significant diligence in terms of meeting regulation standards, service infrastructure and geotechnical challenges. Of course, a good masterplan should consider these aspects and ensure that any plan is capable of being physically implemented. Sadly, this is rarely the case as masterplanners frequently move too fast towards illustrating their vision through a two-dimensional plan without regard to topography and what might lie below the ground.

Prior to any competition, it is better to be prepared by undertaking careful early research on site conditions and infrastructural implications than facing abortive work and redesigns simply because nobody bothered to check ground or infrastructure constraints.

Developer motivations and regulations

The key developer motivation is to obtain satisfactory statutory approvals that are economically viable in the quickest period possible.

Planning   The developer's prime focus is achieving a planning consent. It is one of the first mileposts in the development process. A planning consent effectively establishes the use and with it, value. However, the devil is likely to be in the detail. As property values grow and developments become more profitable, there is a tendency for the public sector to try to capture some of the growth in value through 'planning gain'. Interestingly, if planners and developers saw gains as place-making contributions rather than an opportunity to realise a wider aspiration, then perhaps planning gains could be focused and relevantly applied.

In a competition, planning gain is still likely to be a requirement. Typically, the place promoter may be the local authority housing department but it will not be able to limit planning gain obligations placed on its own council if this is an established planning policy.

Highways   The developer's second focus is achieving road construction consent/approvals.

Highway approval is essentially about meeting technical regulatory standards. It is these highway standards that set the key framework for place-making. The standards have historically tended to favour the motor vehicle. While safety is an important consideration, the standards largely considered how pedestrians fitted within a road hierarchy rather than being seen as the principal user of routes.

To return to the developer's key motivation of gaining statutory approvals, it is unlikely that developers will ever challenge a highway authority on the grounds of road design matters, even if they believe that there is a better design solution. Given the significant period that these guidelines have been in place, the resulting road typology has become ingrained in the housing layout form. This has led not just to a familiarisation with developers and road engineers but the form itself is well understood and familiar to the consumer.

Urban design campaigners have for many years pressed for a change in highway design. Thankfully, this campaign has brought about positive change with the introduction in England and Wales of *Manual for Streets* in 2007 (DfT 2007) and in Scotland, *Designing Streets* in 2010 (Scottish Government 2010). Prior to these important policy changes, masterplanning competitions struggled to overcome one of the greatest barriers to making good places.

Policy change alone will not reap immediate benefits as a change of such road forms to more pedestrian-friendly spaces is unfamiliar to consumers. As a result, it will take some time for people to gain confidence and understanding of the benefits of creating better quality space. For example, the introduction of Home Zones as people-friendly places still remains a matter of contention between some user groups and highway engineers. Whatever the outcome, there remains a doubt about what street form is appropriate. This creates uncertainty in the minds of developers. In real estate development uncertainty is just another word for risk.

The (end) place matters most

The user, owner/Investor

Places cannot be regarded as 'good' unless they are well used and enjoyed. Ultimately it is people's use, interaction and enjoyment within the place that will mark its reputation and ongoing success.

When creating plans, it is therefore important that vision and emerging forms should reflect proposals that are likely to be supported by all people, rather than simply a few. For example, recent higher density urban master-plans have placed great emphasis on high-density apartment living. This may be acceptable and demanded by young adults in search of the urban lifestyle but does not represent what families or older people may aspire to in terms of their habitation requirements. When markets are highly active and funding is readily accessible, developers and investors may be prepared to respond to plans if appropriate demand can be identified. When markets are trading at par or below par, however, development interest is more likely to be spread across sub-sectors to reflect the risk of being overly exposed within one specialist marketplace. As markets are cyclical, one could argue that sustainable places should reflect the longer-term needs of the total population.

Property investment players, whether they are landlords or owner-occupiers, seek long-term returns through good asset management and growth prospects. Place-making must therefore not be seen as an opportunity for experimentation or a representation of the fashion of the day but must be underpinned by good evidence-based research that informs place solutions that are capable of being sustained.

The competition

You might wonder, given that this chapter is about the use of competitions as a component in creating better places, why the focus has so far been about non-competition matters. It is simply that many competitions fail for a lack of understanding by place promoters of the developer's key issues and motivations. The first test for a competition is to gain as much developer interest as possible. To maximise competition entries, it is incumbent on the place promoter to understand and address some of the matters that have been outlined above. While the promoter may wish to improve on what developers conventionally deliver, the art of good salesmanship is to understand the motivations of the organisations whom they wish to persuade to participate in the project. One of the greatest challenges in the competition process is to convince developers to change their normal practices. However, the promoter must understand that asking for substantial and radical departures from the conventional developer approach is going to severely curtail interest and could jeopardise the project's success.

The promoter needs to build up the case to persuade the developer that, despite asking for a change in approach, the proposals are clear and the additional level of risk is manageable. Clearly, to be able to argue this, the promoter will need to understand risk rather than merely presuming that risk is the developer's responsibility. An enlightened and informed public promoter should be able to quantify the risk and be prepared to participate in such risk in order to achieve its goal of creating better places.

The instruments and processes of competition

An informed leader and champion It may not feature in the rules and regulations for competition procurement but experience shows that, as with life itself, without a good leader, the project will lack the necessary dynamic drive, leading to project failure. There should always be a clear leader for a competition who can orchestrate the process and enable their own team to perform. Equally, a good leader will be the chief salesperson who inspires developers to become involved in the competition. It is often argued that good leaders and champions are essentially born rather than processed. Sir Howard Bernstein, the chief executive of Manchester City Council, a leader and champion of significant reputation for getting things done, described himself as a 'municipal entrepreneur' which reasonably sums up what is required in the role of project leader and champion.

In the case of a public promoter, such leadership needs to be from the highest possible level both at public officer and political level. They need to be well informed to gain the respect and support of developers and stakeholders. Notwithstanding the challenges and risks, they need to be inclusive but decisive in making clear and quick decisions to maintain momentum, confidence and respect.

Sadly, good leadership is rare and, as a result, competitions often become a laboured process driven by rules and regulations and committees that lack vision and vitality. Leaders need to be good helicopter pilots who can survey the scene and drive the project from on high. Those who seek the worm's-eye view will not make good competition leaders.

The competition brief The success of the competition can be achieved only with a good-quality brief. A poor brief will produce a poor competition, and a shortfall in project outcomes. Too often a brief is an aspirational document, which is big on vision and graphic content but short on the technical practicalities and lacking a grasp of development processes and programming.

Earlier in this chapter developer motivations were described, and these matters need to be addressed at the time of the brief preparation. The brief must equip the development candidate with detailed information that addresses development considerations and design aspirations in order to have a better chance of success.

A brief that recognises market economies Promoters must ask themselves whether what they are promoting has market validity. An understanding of the market and an ability to justify what is being promoted is an important aspect in demonstrating confidence to the developer. Although it is a matter for developers to satisfy themselves on the detailed aspects of market demand, nevertheless, the brief should demonstrate a realisation of the marketplace and reflect 'real world' principles rather than be merely a utopian concept. That said, to make good places we need to see significant improvements and ambition not just from developers but also from public planners, road engineers and politicians. What is wanted is common sense, reflected in pragmatic approaches that are founded on doing the simple things well, rather than radical departures in practice. Such an approach has more chance of persuading a conservative consumer society to make small adjustments from their inherent values of comfort, convenience and familiarity.

A brief that embraces statutory requirements The brief should clearly demonstrate that the proposals have the support of the statutory authorities. For example, the brief should not just replicate the relevant pages from the current local plan but also spell out detailed aspects of what is, and what is not, acceptable in terms of both policy and design.

Ideally, the proposals should be backed up with the project having the benefit of supplementary planning guidance, which will clearly demonstrate what is acceptable. Too often competitions are left too open-ended, allowing developers to exploit the lack of clarity. Public promoters who leave matters open by transferring responsibility to their planning colleagues place undue and unreasonable pressure on the planning system and undermine fairness in competition. Leaving things deliberately open effectively invites developers to challenge planning policy in the hope that a more valuable submission can be gained.

Pressure may be placed on planners to relax their policy by agreeing to (say) a more valuable use. Such action brings about a competition that lacks fairness and is vulnerable to challenge by developers who have followed policy against those developers who choose to fight policy.

In preparing the brief, promoters should have gained complete 'buy-in' from the local planning authority thereby bringing absolute clarity on the planning position. A protocol between the place promoter and the planning officials will help guide a smooth passage through the statutory process. This is not to say that there should be shortcuts around the statutory functions but simply that an efficient process and a clear understanding will help oil the wheels of delivery, remove dubiety and developer gamesmanship. Place promoters must understand that while they may work for the same local authority, planning officials have to fulfil statutory obligations and therefore must maintain a level of independence and discretion in their actions.

In the case of private promoters, great care is needed to recognise that notwithstanding that the private promoter is looking to achieve a better design solution for the greater good rather than a personal good, there will be people in public office who instinctively believe that the private promoter is attempting to 'ride roughshod' over their role as planners and their statutory duties. It is imperative that the private promoter knows and agrees all detailed design elements within the competition brief. Failure to get the planners' support upstream is likely to create complications and delays downstream.

The role of the masterplan

Given the above comments on planning requirements, the promoter needs to decide whether the brief should include a masterplan or look to developers to promote their own masterplan proposals.

There are varied views on whether a masterplan should be provided and with what level of detail and prescription. My view is clear: a competition that invites developers to prepare masterplan proposals is a huge waste of resources and a lost opportunity. Developers that are given the task of creating a masterplan are more likely to see this as a process and a hurdle to overcome. There are very few developers who know about urban design and they certainly do not exist to play the role of place-maker. Developers are better at focusing on what they do best, that is filling in the framework with buildings. In addition, multiple masterplans within a competition environment create duplication. Due to inevitable competition time constraints, developer masterplans will never achieve the requisite level of research, considered design analysis and evaluation achieved by a rigorously researched and debated plan that is controlled and managed by the place promoter.

A project that promotes good place-making should have some form of masterplan or urban design framework as part of the competition brief to illustrate the vision of the proposed place. It is difficult to see how one can promote a good place without such a document and certainly the lack of a plan framework gives rise to later difficulties.

Stakeholder consultation First, it is well understood that the planning process and good place-making cannot take place without appropriate consultation with stakeholders. If the responsibility of preparing a masterplan is passed to the developer, it makes it very difficult for such a consultation to take place during the competition process. Typically, a competition might consist of four competitors, so it follows that four sets of separate consultation would be required, leading to confusion and possibly making promises that would not necessarily be fulfilled. In some cases, the promoter may exclude consultation until after the competition which compromises and prejudices the stakeholder consultation process to such an extent that the consultation becomes a 'lip service' creating an environment of exclusion. An excluded community that becomes cynical will be a disaster for the promoter and the deliverer.

Planning consultation Second, without a masterplan the planners will need to consider a variety of developer plan proposals which effectively will be seen as pre-application discussions. Understandably, planning officials are reticent about giving absolute opinions during the competition stage as they would be concerned at prejudicing themselves and their planning committee prior to a formal application.

Evaluating the masterplan Third, all competitions should be exercised fairly. The lack of a masterplan framework leaves all of the design work to the developer applicants making it difficult to evaluate on a 'like-for-like' basis. A failure to be able to evaluate fairly could lead to a subsequent challenge from a developer.

Risk and control Fourth, the passing of the masterplan process to the developer effectively passes early control to the developer. It is difficult to see how the place promoter can promote the creation of a good place when one of the key aspects of place-making has been passed to a party whose principal motivation is not about place.

A good competition should therefore have some form of masterplan or urban design framework established and preferably approved as supplementary planning guidance. A departure from this plan in any significant material way should disqualify any developer candidate.

What level of detail is required in a competition masterplan?

A key question for the promoter is to what level of detail should a masterplan framework be established prior to competition? There are arguments for a highly prescriptive approach which establishes a firm rule book of what can and cannot be done. This may be acceptable to the developer, providing such a proposal has been robustly tested with development and technical appraisals to demonstrate that such an approach can be viable. A prescriptive approach supported by good quality appraisal work can encourage developers as there is clarity in the process. In the late 1980s and early 1990s the Scottish Development Agency (subsequently, the Glasgow Development Agency), promoted the Crown Street Regeneration Project in Glasgow's Gorbals (see Figures 8.1 and 8.2). A competition was held, and the winning masterplan was implemented, with the Crown Street Regeneration Project laying out infrastructure and holding developer competitions for serviced sites. The masterplan and competition brief were quite prescriptive as to what could be delivered. This approach was the first of its type since that of New Town Development Corporations but, in this case, it was urban and high density. Such an approach was unfamiliar to many developers and as a consequence was not welcomed by a number of corporate-style operators. Thankfully, however, the promoter had the strength of conviction to proceed and, with the aid of grant assistance, was able to persuade enough developers to participate and deliver what is now regarded as a highly successful design-led housing regeneration project.

While Crown Street Regeneration Project worked on the basis of a prescriptive approach, generally most practitioners would argue for a greater level of flexibility, with an opportunity to develop variety and allow for future adaptability and expansion. The level of prescription within a masterplan depends on its general location and context and whether solutions are high- or low-rise.

The regeneration of Amsterdam's Eastern Harbour, including Borneo Sporenburg, included two masterplans developed with similar densities of around 100 dwellings to the hectare (see Figure 8.3). One solution was high-rise with a range of flatted blocks; another was low-rise, high density family housing interspersed with apartment blocks. The ability to develop a range of housing types, sizes and tenures provides consumer choice, allows wider multi-developer activity and generally helps spread developer risk.

Competitions offering too much flexibility will transfer control to the developer, and no matter what legal devices are put in place the promoter will lose their role, opportunity and effectiveness in delivering the place vision.

One key aspect is that the essential framework of any masterplan is movement and connectivity. Developers are interested in roads and footpaths only to the extent of ensuring that they satisfy statutory requirements. Indeed, it is normal for the public authority to take over the responsibility

Figure 8.1 New Gorbals Park, Crown Street, Glasgow. A place transformed by public investment with strong leadership, robust masterplan and a well-organised developer competition. Reproduced with permission of Steve Tiesdell.

Figure 8.2 Queen Elizabeth Square, Glasgow forms the second stage of the Crown Street Regeneration Project. The second phase competition, separately masterplanned, was helped by developers gaining confidence from the original project and a general recognition that New Gorbals was quickly establishing a reputation of being a good place to live. Reproduced with permission of Steve Tiesdell.

Figure 8.3 Low-rise high-density forms at Borneo Sporenburg, Amsterdam illustrate how variety can be achieved and can encourage family urban living. Having a range of housing types and sizes helped to spread the degree of risk for developers and investors while at the same time producing a more socially balanced population. Reproduced with permission of Steve Tiesdell.

of such functions on completion of the project. It is therefore wholly reasonable that the public authority acting as place promoter and ultimately responsible for such matters should have a key say in how the road and footpath routes along with all the other associated aspects are formed.

Equally as important is the form and distribution of open space. It is difficult to see how a place can be established and sustained without seeing both the open space and roads as being a fundamental part of how the place works. These aspects are the physical frameworks of the place. Most developers are less interested in such frameworks as they focus on the product that is directly for sale and provides project income. No matter how hard a developer tries, it is very difficult to persuade a purchaser that, in addition to the house and plot that they are buying, they are also buying part of the place. At the time of purchase, there is probably little or no landscape and it is difficult for purchasers who have no training in design to picture what kind of place will transpire when the landscape matures.

Of course, such observations may not apply where there is an informed developer who fully invests in the 'design-led' approach to development, or

Figure 8.4 The Drum, Bo-ness: a competition promoted and delivered by a private landowner, Grange Estate, who was looking to achieve a better quality design while maintaining a realistic view of developer's aspirations and consumer demand. Reproduced by permission of Cadell[2] LLP.

the project is relatively small and the framework already well established by neighbouring development.

Whatever the approach to masterplans, common sense should prevail, whereby masterplan frameworks have a degree of flexibility but also set well-defined rules as absolutes, while including guidance about other matters. This approach provides some latitude for the developer to manoeuvre within the planned framework. Such an approach occurred at the Drum Housing Project in Bo'ness, Scotland (see Figures 8.4, 8.5 and 8.6), where a private landowner, Grange Estate, appointed an urban designer, engineer and surveyor. Working with the client, the urban designer, established the design framework in collaboration with the civil engineer who provided technical inputs to roads and ground conditions along with the surveyor who advised on absolute rules and guidance and generally how far one might reasonably expect to go in terms of design and housing mixes, while maintaining developer interest. The result has been an exemplar award-winning housing development that met the landowner's objective of achieving a higher standard of design and at the same time produced the target revenue from land sales.

Figure 8.5 Phase 3, The Drum, Bo-ness, brought greater developer interest as a result of market confidence generated from the Drum's previous phases. This market reaction illustrates that consumers are wary of investing in something unfamiliar until they see bespoke products. Reproduced by permission of Cadell² LLP.

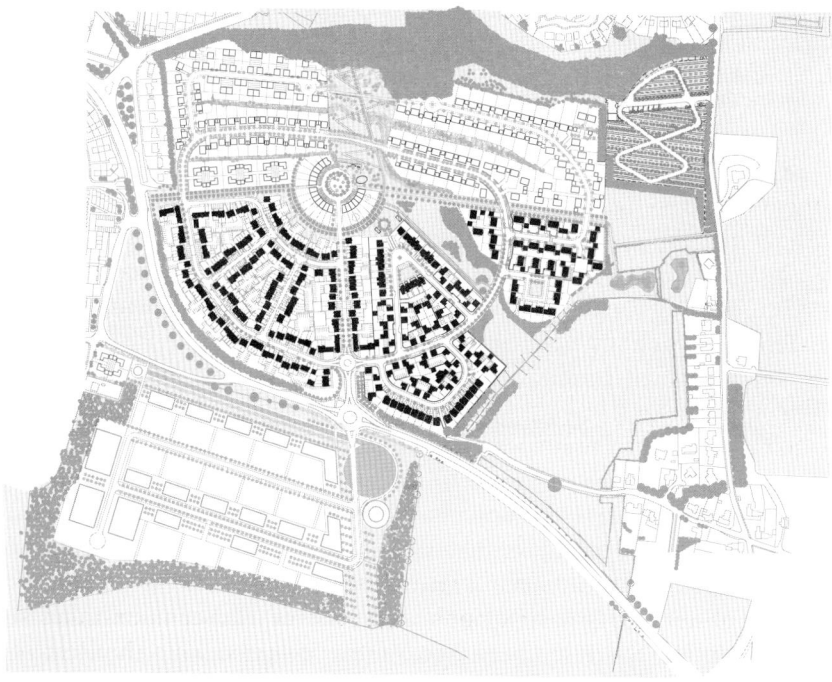

Figure 8.6 The Drum, Bo-ness masterplan designed by Cadell² was developed by a combination of sound urban design principles informed by an engineering discipline, an understanding of market economics and competition processes. Reproduced by permission of Cadell² LLP.

Just as it is impossible for a developer to make a 'home' it is equally impossible for a masterplanner and place promoter to make a 'place'. Developers, masterplanners and place promoters can only make frameworks for the home and place. It is for the user to fully establish these matters by building on to the framework and adapting forms and styles as time progresses. Providing there is a strong rule book and a sensible framework, then development should stand the test of people's inputs, interruptions and variations. Edinburgh's Georgian New Town Development is an excellent example of how a planned framework has been sustained and adapted to accommodate technological change and human behaviour (see Figure 8.7).

Technical Information   Place promoters often fail to provide sufficient technical information within their competition brief. Some promoters argue that it is difficult to prepare technical information without fully knowing what the project might entail. Equally some public utilities may not provide the necessary information until such time as a planning consent is in place.

Furthermore, many public promoters are risk averse and want no part in undertaking technical investigations that will be passed to developers. Passing information that can be relied upon for accuracy by the developer leaves the promoter at risk if such information is found to be inaccurate and the developer subsequently suffers a loss. Nevertheless, if the investigations are undertaken in a proper manner, and those undertaking the investigations provide appropriate warranties that are capable of being assigned, then such action should be acceptable and risk minimised.

Even if a promoter does not undertake such investigations, they are not absolved from risk. Clearly, if there is a lack of technical information, the developer will either have to conduct their own investigations or choose to qualify their submission. Large-scale investigations, such as ground and contamination reports, cost thousands of pounds and can take many months to undertake for survey, laboratory tests and analysis.

On very large competitions it has been known that, where a public promoter refuses to undertake such investigations, the developers club together and pay for the investigation collectively, with the winner paying the full price once the contract has been awarded. Such an approach is essentially an act of desperation by the developers when the public promoter should be taking on the responsibility for such investigations. One thing is clear: it is a complete waste of resources if the promoter refuses to undertake investigations, and each developer undertakes separate and duplicate exercises as part of the process. This duplication of effort and costs should be put to more positive use. Sadly this occurrence happens all too frequently.

Figure 8.7   Social activity and enjoyment in the newly rejuvenated St Andrews Square in Edinburgh's New Town. An excellent example of a new intervention in an established and well-respected place. Reproduced with permission of Steve Tiesdell.

If no promoter investigations have taken place, then developers may make numerous and different assumptions on a range of aspects. This will bring a lack of clarity at the competition's evaluation stage. If a promoter is unable to compare like with like, then significant difficulties can emerge.

While no developer is keen on legally challenging a public promoter on the fairness of approach, there may be challenges particularly where the project is of a large scale and lots of resources have been expended in what is a speculative winner-takes-all competition process. It is unreasonable for promoters to seek to hide behind small print that absolves them of responsibility. Actions that seek to avoid blame serve only to put developers off by creating a defensive environment and adversarial conditions that are counterproductive to the place-making objective.

Competition programme   The promoter should always reflect on what is a reasonable time frame for all parties to perform their tasks within the competition. Again this is about the promoter being sufficiently informed about the tasks and the length of time reasonably required by the developer for information gathering, design periods, financial appraisals and submission productions.

Uninformed promoters can be unaware of the extent of work required when preparing a submission proposal. The length of time an applicant is allocated to competition tasks should be commensurate with the information provided by the promoter within their brief. For example, if it is decided that a masterplan is a matter for the developer then clearly a significantly longer competition period will be required for the applicant to address such a matter. Similarly, if the promoter expects the developer applicant to undertake technical investigations then this can take a substantial amount of time and may, depending on complexity and timing, have to be made a conditional qualification to any submission proposal.

One matter is clear: the promoter should always seek to avoid or at least minimise submissions being qualified since this makes the evaluation of submissions difficult and vulnerable to challenge by unsuccessful applicants.

If insufficient time is provided to a developer applicant, then both quality and price may be prejudiced. Also, if the procurer asks the developer to perform quickly but does not mirror this speed in their own actions, then the developers will quite rightly lose confidence and interest in participating. Competitions should be fair and reasonable for all participants.

It is better to allocate more time at the competition stage than having to later negotiate with one party simply because there was pressure to get to an early decision.

The number of developer participants It has been stated earlier that public promoters have a tendency to be risk averse. This is not just in development conditions but can be applied to many facets of public operations where there has been an increasing threat of litigation and a public that is generally more informed about its rights.

A public promoter operating in such a culture is more likely to go for the easy and safer decision which is as risk free as possible. For this reason, it is essential that the project has leaders who can strip away the risk aversion and persuade their team to fulfil the challenge without feeling at risk.

Within this environment, the promoter needs to consider what kind of delivery structure should be put in place for the project. The easy and safe decision is for the promoter to select one developer candidate to pass on the responsibility of undertaking everything. However, is this risk free? First, the passing of the challenge to a sole provider leaves the delivery in one pair of hands. While good lawyers can devise developer obligations to ensure good performance, rules that are effectively adversarial create the danger of all participants walking around the site with the contract agreement under their arm and increase the likelihood that a dispute will occur. Second, transferring of responsibility also means the transfer of control from the promoter to the developer. Again contractual obligations provide some assistance but this is largely control from the back rather than the front foot.

Of course a lot will depend on the wider responsibilities of a public promoter but if a good place is to be delivered the state/municipality needs to consider its role beyond that of promoter. A good place will have parts that are going to be controlled by the state/municipality in the future such as streets and other pedestrian routes. Surely it would make sense for the state to have a direct role in their delivery rather than playing a more reactive role from the sidelines?

Lawyers may not agree with this approach but with the advent of tax incremental finance (TIFs) initiatives, the state is going to find itself increasingly involved in projects and therefore its aversion to risk needs to be reassessed.

In places such as Germany, Scandinavia and the Netherlands, the public-sector bodies take a more hands-on role to development. They do not necessarily see this as a cost exercise as they 'invest' in the delivery of the place by acquiring the ground, working with stakeholders in the development of the masterplan, providing all types of hard and soft infrastructure and then selling off serviced lots and plots to developers, housing cooperatives, social housing providers and individuals. The objective is that the receipts from the sale of the serviced sites pay for most, if not all, of the public sector costs. In effect, the public-sector place promoter takes on the role of place developer. While this is a commercial risk, it is largely within the public sector's control and has the best chance of delivering the best place outcome. An examination of the experiences in the Vauban project in Freiburg illustrates that the municipality managed to acquire the ground, masterplan the development and deliver the project of 2000 dwellings in only 10 years. Sadly such a scale of development in the UK would take longer. This is because it would not have comparable social infrastructure, it would not have an equivalent public transport network and it would fall well short of the high levels of sustainable construction and energy renewables that are urgently required to contribute to climate change targets.

Conclusion

So the key message for place-making delivery is that if one wants to realise good places, the promoter should not expect this to be achieved by simply writing a rule book, holding a competition and expecting the developer to do the rest. History has shown from Edinburgh New Town to Glasgow's Crown Street that the best solutions require the public sector to participate. Somehow, we have lost this participation and have been driven by political ideology that the market is best placed to deliver places. This does not appear to be the case in continental Europe. Sadly, to get more public participation will take time, since there is a lack of resource and development skill in the public sector. Indeed, it will take some brave politicians to make a radical shift by allowing the state to invest and actively engage in value-generating activity instead of monitoring the costs of others.

The message is clear, however: if we want good places then we need more municipal entrepreneurs.

9

Design Review – An Effective Means of Raising Design Quality?

John Punter

Introduction

In this chapter the emergence of design review is explored as a means of raising the design quality of development in the UK. The genesis of the now widely adopted processes and procedures is explored in the context of specific controversies concerning developers' use of, and response to, design review. Available evidence on the effectiveness of design review is assembled, and the contemporary challenges to its success are reviewed against a background of the varying levels of developer and local authority commitment to design quality.

Design review has various definitions depending upon the type of planning system to which it is attached and the purposes for which it is designed. Broadly defined it is '... the process by which private and public development proposals receive independent criticism under the sponsorship of the local government unit, whether through informal or formalised processes' (Scheer 1994: 2). However, design review can operate at the neighbourhood/community, local authority, sub-regional, regional or national level and, although the local authority is the most common host, it is not necessarily the primary recipient of advice. National design review is arguably oriented towards the development/design team and in reality only they can ensure real quality in design terms.

Urban Design in the Real Estate Development Process, First Edition. Edited by Steve Tiesdell and David Adams.
© 2011 Blackwell Publishing Ltd. Published 2011 by Blackwell Publishing Ltd.

It has long been recognised that negative development controls have their limitations, and that there is more potential for improvement in design quality if developers and designers can be encouraged to bring their schemes in for review at an early stage of design development. Notwithstanding this, design review is primarily intended to complement and refine the decision-making of municipal planners, or other officials who are responsible for the issuing of permits/permissions for development. However, there are different models and procedures from those that are fully integrated into local planning practice (most local panels) to those that are clearly separated (most regional and national panels) (Blaesser 1994: 46–49).

Origins, emergence and critiques of design review internationally

Arguably, the first review panels took the form of local aesthetic committees established in 1908 to draw up and implement aesthetic regulations in the Netherlands. In 1931 a national federation was established to support the work of what are now 130 such independent committees advising most of the Dutch local authorities on the design of development (van Weert 1999). German and Belgian cities have recently adopted variants of the Dutch model (Schaller 1999; Rombouts 1999). While the Dutch precedents had democratic impulses in giving lay people in the community a say in the design of projects, increasingly it was 'expert professionalism' which seemed to be more valued in review processes. In the USA, the growth of municipal design review to support conventional zoning controls was dramatic in the 1970s and 1980s, originating in historic districts, but rapidly spreading to cover the vast majority of major cities and towns by the early 1990s (Habe 1989; Shirvani 1990; Scheer 1994). Here a mix of citizen review, special boards and boards of local planners (with and without elected officials) developed, and pressures grew for reforms to make such panels more skilled and professional, and their decisions less subjective and less obsessed with elevations. Design review increasingly had to respond to its critics in the design and development industries and become more focused on major design issues and '… less of a diversion of political energy from environmental, social and economic problems and … genuine urban design' (Scheer 1994: 9).

In England, a Royal Fine Art Commission (RFAC) was established as a national design review body in 1924. Subsequently the Royal Institute of British Architects (RIBA) established local Architectural Advisory Panels in a fifth of all local authorities to assist local councils in their development control activities. While many subsequently lapsed, the reform of the RFAC in 1999, and its reconstitution as a Commission of Architecture and the Built Environment (CABE: charged with raising the profile of

architecture and urban design and the design quality of new developments)
has resulted in a dramatic increase in the practice of design review at both
national and regional levels across the UK. While CABE was expected to
review some 30–40 major cases a year, by 2004 it was commenting on
some 500 projects annually, and there was a subsequent proliferation of
local and regional panels which, by 2008, covered most of England.
Meanwhile Scotland (which had its own Royal Fine Art Commission),
Wales and (very recently) Northern Ireland have newly established national
design bodies (Architecture and Design Scotland; Design Commission for
Wales; Architecture and the Built Environment for Northern Ireland) each
with design review panels. For all these bodies, design review is a multi-
purpose activity. While its primary objective remains to improve the quality
of the most significant developments, design review is also an important
part of general intelligence gathering and supports the design research,
policy, education and skills improvement programmes of these national
agencies.

Design review has come under extensive criticism particularly in the USA
where its discretionary decision-making processes contrast with the traditional
administrative processes of control which use the clear, three-dimensional
volumetric controls embodied in zoning (Shirvani 1990; Scheer 1994). Common
complaints have been that design review is based on vague concepts (Hinshaw
1995) is frequently arbitrary and capricious (Poole 1987; Lai 1988), and fails to
include public comment (Habe 1989). Meanwhile academic researchers have
challenged the notion that the outcomes of design review are superior to those
of traditional administrative control processes (Nasar & Grannis 1999; Stamps
& Nasar 1997). Nonetheless, there is widespread agreement on the key principles and processes that ought to underpin design review, even if they remain
aspirational rather than deliverable given available skills and resources (Lai
1988; Punter 2007).

The growth of design review has not been as hotly contested in the UK
as it has in the USA, even though design control by local planning authorities (LPAs) was actively discouraged by central government until 1992.
However, in 2002–3 the design review practices of the CABE panel came in
for substantive criticism particularly from the London conservation and
local amenity lobbies. The architectural correspondent of the (London)
Evening Standard summarised its imperfections succinctly as '... unac-
countability, lack of transparency, cliquism, groupism, stylism.' (HoC
ODPM 2005: Q113), adding that

> ... the organisation's public image was being undermined by what appeared
> to be excessive and single-minded enthusiasm for particular kinds of
> development, and not necessarily the kind favoured by local residents or
> their democratically elected representatives (HoC ODPM 2005: CAB 14).

This re-emergence of the tension between 'expert' advice and local 'democracy' is a significant but often ignored issue in design debates. However, it is of fundamental importance to current planning policies, perceived deficits in community involvement, and to notions of an 'urban renaissance' whether it be debates about tall buildings, apartment developments, suburban intensification, sustainable design or the pervasiveness of NIMBYism (Punter 2009).

In the rest of this chapter the focus will be on the current system of design review operating across the UK, particularly upon national design review which is in turn shaping regional design review. It will explore how design review impacts upon developers' and upon designers' opportunity space, and how effective it is in raising the design quality of major developments.

The typology of design review in England, Scotland and Wales

In England, CABE now runs a bimonthly national panel which sees some 140 schemes a year either with or without the client or design team present. In addition to full panel review, design review officers also comment on other schemes in consultation with one of the chairs of the panel, and as many as 250 schemes may be reviewed annually in this way. In addition, CABE now runs a separate panel for new schools, the 2012 Olympic projects and the London CrossRail stations, but they are remunerated for these. There are six regional panels covering 270 LPAs, and nine sub-regional panels, all of which are now affiliated with CABE, and which conduct monthly reviews on similar lines. In addition, there are 63 local panels (mainly in southern England) some dating back to the 1920s, and 21 more are planned. All 18 Urban Regeneration Companies (public–private partnerships) have panels to vet their projects and associated developments. This means that 88 per cent of all English LPAs have access to a local-regional panel (all figures from Databuild 2008: 2–4: see CABE 2009). In Scotland and Wales, there are very few such local panels.

Architecture and Design Scotland (A+DS) has had a design review panel since early 2006, meeting more or less monthly, and it reviews nearly 50 projects a year (52 per cent of the schemes they have commented on). They also have an internal panel that provides a desk review of a substantial number of projects (30 per cent) while the remainder are reviewed by A+DS staff (13 per cent) sometimes with a panel member (5 per cent). The Design Commission for Wales (DCFW) has had a monthly design review panel since late 2003, reviewing some 60 schemes a year. All schemes go to full review, but DCFW is experimenting with an occasional 'desktop' review service where the development timetable does not permit a wait for a full review.

At the local level, the two most common types of panel are architectural advisory panels which report directly to the LPA development control team, and conservation panels (often amalgamated Conservation Area Advisory Committees) who are official consultees in the development control process, and who have a mix of lay and specialist advisors. In neither of these cases are developers and their design teams present, and the focus of the review is the design quality and the acceptability of the planning application. So the comments of both types of panel are direct inputs into the planning approval process rather than the design process itself, and often come too late in the latter to be effective. Their views may be briefly summarised in the officer's report which goes to the planning committee of the local council for approval, but they tend to be recoded in a cursory and very selective manner. Further review mechanisms include the retention by the development control team of a skilled design advisor, or the establishment of a team of skilled officers to provide additional review and advice, but these are beyond consideration in this chapter. However, a number of the big cities have established their own design panels more recently (e.g. Birmingham, Bristol, Glasgow, Sheffield) and these may prove to be a positive advance in review practice.

National design review: the genesis of CABE's procedures and processes

CABE has developed and refined its system of design review over the past decade, and it has developed the model that other national and regional bodies have adapted to their circumstances. It is now a statutory body, but it remains a non-statutory consultee within the planning process, meaning that it does not have to be consulted, and its advice is not binding. In a letter to all LPAs in 2001, the Government defined when CABE's design review panel should be consulted, suggesting reviews of proposals that are significant because of their size or public uses, their site or exceptional impacts upon the locality, and those that are important in shaping large scale future developments, or are '... particularly relevant to the quality of everyday life' (CABE 2002: 21).

In 2003, England's (CABE's) national design panel was challenged over the transparency, rigour and objectivity of its original design review procedures. These challenges emanated from concerns about potential conflicts of interest in the panel's deliberations given the development interests and working relationships of the CABE chair (a prominent London-based developer with a reputation for achieving design excellence) and most of the CABE Commissioners. The Government commissioned an audit of conflicts of interest in 2004 from legal consultants, and their 28 recommendations reshaped CABE structures and review processes (HoC ODPM 2005: Ev 51). The recommendations sought to ensure that CABE review processes conformed to the Nolan principles of public life (selflessness, integrity, objectivity, accountability, openness, honesty and leadership) and improved procedures for managing conflicts of interest (the chair of CABE was asked to step down, and the position can now no longer be filled by a property developer with significant commercial interests). Subsequently, these recommendations have reshaped all design review procedures ensuring that all panels are fastidious in recording all minor, and avoiding all major, conflicts of interest, are transparent in their operation and that appointments to the panel are the result of open and fair competitive processes.

A subsequent House of Commons Select Committee inquiry into the role and effectiveness of CABE recommended specific changes to design review practices including the publication of all informal advice issued by review staff to developers and local planning authorities and the discontinuation of 'pin-up sessions' (where the Design Review Committee chair met with staff to consider submitted drawings and subsequently issued comments on the scheme's design). They also recommended more detailed comments on schemes in the letters issued, a full record of attendees, clearer use of design criteria and opening up of meetings to the public (HoC ODPM 2005: 14–21) and all these have been implemented.

So significant changes have been made to design review practices and a new practice manual and a guide to setting up and running panels have now been issued (CABE 2006a,b; CABE *et al.* 2009) along with revised design criteria (see Box 9.1) and a statement on those issues which frequently undermine good design (see Box 9.2). Its post-2005 review processes have taken on board the recommendations of the Select Committee, doubling the frequency of meetings of the full design review panel but retaining reviews by professional staff 'in consultation with the chair of the design review panel' (CABE 2006a: 21). They emphasise '... consultation at the earliest possible opportunity' and that "... designers and promoters of projects ... approach it directly... though CABE will always aim to involve the local authority in discussions about the project' (CABE 2006a: 21). Its 77 panellists are drawn from the full range of design professionals appointed annually by public recruitment for a three-year period which may be extended. Selected CABE commissioners chair the panel and often act as observers.

CABE design review staff prepare briefing papers, display boards and models for a one-hour review session. A very brief introduction by the client is followed by a 15-minute presentation by the designer and some 40 minutes of questions and comments by the panel. The presenters and local authority receive a letter drafted by review staff and agreed by the panel chair within a month of the meeting, and if the project is a live planning application that letter is posted on the CABE website (CABE 2006a: 22–24).

Box 9.1 CABE's criteria for design review

Definition of good design

'... design that is fit for purpose, sustainable, efficient, coherent, responsive to context, good looking and a clear expression of the brief ... assessing quality is to a large extent an objective process. Ultimately, of course, some questions come down to matters of individual taste and preference. It is not often, however, that questions of this kind are important in deciding whether a project, judged in the round, is a good one. What matters is quality, not style.'

A building project matters to everyone who comes into contact with it or who is affected by it. Poor designs are unacceptable wherever they are proposed. Key questions include:

- *Client team* – Commitment to excellence? Realisation measures? Sustainability commitment? Realistic budget and programme? Range of skills? Management structure? Commitment to value not lowest cost? Appropriate procurement process?
- *The brief* – Clear brief? Clear aims and objectives? Budget and programme in place? Realistic brief in relation to budget and site?
- *Understanding the context* – Urban design analysis? Site context investigated and understood? Dealt with movement and physical characteristics? Urban design analysis informed the plan? Character considered? Positive contribution to the public realm? Clear distinction between public and private space? Positive and inclusive movement and legibility? Access to public transport?
- *Planning the site* – Appropriate site for the project? Masterplan flexible? Future development possibilities? Over-development? Landscape design integral and contextual? Maintenance plausible? Roads etc integral to landscape? Impacts of tall buildings?
- *What makes a good project* – Meet the brief? Satisfy all users? Improve operational efficiency of occupiers? Legible? Plans, sections, elevations and details fully integrated? Building structures, construction and environmental services integral? Adaptable extendible buildings? Whole-life costs accounted? Microclimate? Will it age gracefully? Will it become a cherished part of its setting?
- *The project in the round* – Commodity? Firmness? Delight? Design match aspirations? Viable? Adequate skills and quality of thought? Good value in short and long term? Clear procurement and delivery? Any innovations/risk-taking? Sustainability commitment? Improve local environment? Generous public realm? Design all of a piece? Does the project raise the spirits and add value? Has the design met the challenges of any historic building? Does the design match the quality of the context?

Source: Adapted from CABE 2006a: 5–18.

Box 9.2 CABE's 'alarm bells': common characteristics of poorly designed schemes

- Lack of evidence of client commitment to a quality outcome.
- Lack of evidence of clear, intelligent thinking in the design team.
- Lack of a clear brief.
- Contradictory aims and objectives.
- Lack of viability: projects that promise more than they can realistically deliver.
- No evidence of understanding the nature of the site.
- Adequate context analysis but no evidence of it informing the design.
- Projects which appear mean, pinching, obstructive in their approach to the public realm.
- Lack of clarity about what is private and what is public.
- Projects where it is hard to work out from the drawings what is actually proposed: confusion on paper is likely to correspond to confusion in reality.
- No effort to give clear and realistic illustrations of what the project will look like.
- No effort to illustrate the project in context.
- No effort to show an approach to landscape design where this is important.

Source: Adapted from CABE 2006a: 20.

Most other national and regional panels have developed similar criteria and processes, but being less well resourced than CABE they have to make certain compromises. In DCFW, there is only a single professional staff member and an assistant administrator to support design review, and lead panellists have to undertake site visits and briefings while all panellists contribute to report editing. However, an hour is devoted to discussion and the panel always invites the LPA to state their views on the development proposal under consideration (see DCFW 2005; 2007).

The chapter now turns to examine design review in relation to the research questions posed in the opening chapter of this book. The first of these is how design review affects the 'opportunity space' for design among developers and designers: the second is how effective design review is in raising design quality. Evidence is drawn from a wide range of sources but principally from the written submissions and proceedings of the ODPM Select Committee (HoC ODPM 2004a; 2004b; 2005) set up to investigate CABE's practices. These proceedings offer a rich vein of high-level comment and debate on the rigour, reception and value of design review from the perspectives of developers, designers, LPAs and amenity societies. It must be remembered that these are comments about particular processes that have subsequently been reformed. The intention is not to rehearse the debates of 2003–4 but to use the observations of these key actors on design review at large to explore the developers' and others' views on the value of design review.

How design review can increase the opportunity space for design

Design review processes can be considered as useful ways of increasing the opportunity space for designers within the developer's opportunity space (see Chapter 1). First they provide, free of charge, an expert design critique from a group of nationally or regionally respected and highly experienced professionals drawn from across the design disciplines. This is greatly appreciated by developers, designers and planners, who recognise the value of this kind of peer review. The Royal Institute of British Architects have described architects' experiences of CABE reviews as '... positive ... and the assessment as robust and occasionally extremely vigorous', and any criticism as '... useful ... well meant and well founded'. Architects particularly value the opportunity for 'challenging discussion' over design matters (HoC ODPM: 2004b; Ev 42).

Second the CABE reviews pay special attention to the client, the design team and the procurement method ensuring that the skills retained by the developer are appropriate to, and adequate for, the project. Special scrutiny is given to the client's commitment to design excellence and sustainability, and to potential value rather than cost, ensuring that the client's aims and objectives are appropriate to the site and that the budget and programme are realistic.

Third, the panel's advice potentially strengthens the hand of the LPA in its negotiations with the client/developer, providing them with the expert arguments and evidence to pursue design improvements, if necessary to appeal. Here the panel's authoritative advice is likely to be influential, though not necessarily decisive, in the inspector's decision.

The extent of the designer's opportunity space will be expanded if the projected development has come to the panel early in the planning process, but it will be significantly reduced the closer it comes to the point of lodging of the planning application. Just as best practice development control emphasises the importance of pre-application discussions to resolve design and development issues, so early consultation with the design panel dramatically increases the potential to positively influence design outcomes. The earlier the consultation, the less the abortive design work, the less prolonged the design negotiations, the lower the consultancy fees and the shorter the planning process.

Often the LPA refers major or problematic development proposals to the national panels, but not always early enough in the design negotiation process. This may be because they want to facilitate the development, or simply because they prefer to establish their own planning and design requirements.

Individual development control officers will often seek to achieve particular design outcomes and to exercise their considerable discretion through pursuing particular design principles, approaches or precedents, or preferred combinations of materials and finishes. Equally, the LPA may not have a strong design or place-making agenda. Sometimes a referral to a national or regional design review panel is the result of an impasse in design negotiations, or a strong local public reaction to a proposal, where an authoritative design view might facilitate an approval or refusal. That said, there are a significant number of LPAs who have repeatedly consulted CABE's panel, and who have made it an integral component of their control practice.

Similarly some developers make early consultations with national review panels an integral part of their development practice, using it to widen their opportunity space. Prominent examples include two of the largest British development companies, Land Securities and Grosvenor. The latter made repeated use of the CABE design review service in its Liverpool One city centre retail scheme (26 schemes by 16 different architectural practices) which won a nomination for the Stirling Prize in 2009.

> Whenever possible, Grosvenor has had informal discussions with CABE officers prior to submitting planning applications and before CABE formal reviews. Such discussions have been extremely useful in helping Grosvenor to ensure that it is achieving the standard of work to which we aspire and are being sufficiently creative. They have also enabled us to benefit from experience elsewhere and from arm's length consideration of some issues in which the project team have become immersed. We are aware that CABE's involvement has also acted as a spur to our designers (HoC ODPM 2005: 17).

So Grosvenor particularly value the dialogue with CABE staff. By contrast, they are less complimentary about CABE's formal review panels because:

> [i]nsufficient time and space is allocated for the proper explanation and discussion of very complex issues. Sometimes the lack of preparation and attention by some reviewers has not been worthy of the importance which clients and consultants attach to the reviews: nor commensurate with the weight that decision-makers attach to comments made at the reviews and to the published reports … reviews would be more effective and much more useful if a small number of relevantly experienced reviewers were able to give sufficient time to properly listen to explanations and to discuss proposals in depth (HoC 2005: 15).

Few developers are as publicly critical of full panel reviews, but the view that the time allocated for reviews does not allow adequate exploration of all the important design issues within a major scheme is widely held by developers and designers, and applies to all national panels. Developers and designers have the opportunity to focus the panel's attention on particular design issues, an opportunity that they do not always take. But there is no doubt that one-hour review sessions are a challenge to all parties, and a comprehensive critique may require a series of review sessions.

For other developers, external design review is not part of their standard development practice but an unwelcome source of further uncertainty and risk imposed by the LPA. In their evidence to the Select Committee, the British Property Federation argued that

> ... CABE ... are just a consultee, albeit a very influential one. Local Authorities are not bound to adhere to their decisions but more often than not they do, and as a result the design review panels are fast becoming a planning hurdle over which there is no appeal. The property industry is anxious that although CABE does not have the statutory power to stop a scheme, their opinion is being treated as definitive, and rigid adherence to it causes delays to projects ... (HoC ODPM 2005: 18).

But the managing director of the London arm of Land Securities did not see the process as presenting hurdles, but rather an opportunity to test out design ideas and explore how a scheme might evolve (HoC ODPM 2005: Ev 12 Q92). Arguably these two different perspectives on design review define the difference between investor-developers and trader-developers and their commitment to design quality. The former are directly approaching CABE, and using their design review service to improve the design quality and long-term viability of their projects, whereas the latter are principally concerned with the speed of approval and the minimisation of design/construction costs. This distinction is as critical to the effectiveness of design review as it is to the delivery of design quality generally.

The other dimension to this debate concerns the use made of informal reviews at an early stage of the development process, and whether these are being used to subvert the democratic planning process. It was two particular cases, where CABE informal design reviews endorsed proposals for major development by the property company directed by the first CABE chair, which unleashed allegations of conflicts of interest, and led to the independent audit and the subsequent Select Committee proceedings late in 2004. What emerged from the latter was a deep disquiet, expressed by four London amenity/conservation bodies, about the way that an informal review could tilt the scale in favour of a development before the scheme was even an application, and before any other interested party had been given an opportunity to comment. The critiques offered by these conservation bodies noted the way in which design review reports were being used to bypass public comment, ignoring local or even national planning policy, and even ignoring CABE's own advice on such matters as tall buildings. As one amenity body expressed it, citing two such informal reviews on their patch:

... the support which CABE offered to these schemes was relied on to a considerable extent at subsequent planning enquiries following appeals being lodged. It is unacceptable that these expressions of support should have the same weight as the properly considered views of locally based groups and the local authorities which represent their interests. It is also disturbing the way developers increasingly approach CABE (and the Mayor in London) to obtain support as a matter of course, before going to the local planning authority concerned, whose staff and members may then feel overwhelmed, or deterred from pursuing valid objections.

... The willingness of CABE to offer its support freely to development schemes at a very early stage, even before full impact studies have been produced, is considered to be irresponsible and unprofessional. Once such an expression of support has been made, it is then very difficult to back-track. Naturally such commitments are also made prior to local consultations being carried out to see what concerns the people directly affected by development proposals have, including neighbouring planning authorities. Of course, it is in the interests of the developer to get the Commission on board, but is it in the public interest? (HoC ODPM 2005: Ev 76 paras 5,6, & 13)

These criticisms were bolstered by a wider critique, articulated by prominent London conservation groups and SAVE Britain's Heritage, of CABE informal reviews for neglecting their own advice on tall buildings, for not fully considering the context of World Heritage Sites, for being strongly pro-development, and for down-playing conservation and context issues in their assessments.

These questions continue to be asked, albeit against a background of widespread support for CABE's and other bodies' design review service. The key issues as regards design quality are that the earlier that developers can avail themselves of the design review service, the greater its capacity to improve their designs. However, from the perspective of the wider public and the LPA, it is important that the developers' tactics and use of design review do not subvert a democratic development control process, and are fully interrogated by officers and councillors on the local planning committee.

The effectiveness of design review

The second major research question is the capacity of design review to raise design quality and its actual effectiveness. This remains the focus of considerable debate, and only now is the effectiveness of design review beginning to be closely monitored. As with development control at large, the very complex task of measuring the value added, or the harm avoided, by design review advice is unlikely to be within the resources of the organisation concerned, except perhaps in the case of CABE. Instead, all the national panels have undertaken some simple monitoring by surveying designers, developers and LPAs to ask them whether the design review advice has influenced their decision-making. For CABE some 91 per cent of LPAs who have experienced reviews consider such 'higher level' advice to be beneficial, recognising the objectivity/independence and the high level of design expertise it makes available (Meikle 2009: 10). Currently 70 per cent of those local planning authorities (85 per cent of the total) who use their design review service have '... *taken planning decisions in accordance with its advice*' (Richard Simmons quoted in Baillieu 2009: 7)[1]. However, this is not a very enlightening measure for as, Paul Finch, the first CABE chair of design review and now its overall chair, noted that

> ... in nearly 80 per cent of cases, people make some alteration to their scheme where we have suggested this is necessary, but generally that is to do either with fine tuning or occasionally with a fundamental re-think. On the whole ... people who have used our service ... find it useful ... in terms of numbers we see about one per cent of significant applications ... what we can hopefully do is just to give some pointers as to how certain schemes could be well done, in the full knowledge that the vast majority are not going to come our way (HoC ODPM 2005: Ev 24).

Experience in Scotland shows similar levels of acceptance of advice. A+DS monitoring suggests that 82 per cent of project teams take on board the advice offered by their design review, as do 77 per cent of LPAs, while 66 per cent of the latter incorporate it into their reports. However, only 52 per cent suggest it is influential at Planning Committee (A+DS 2009), figures which suggest that local views often override or ignore the 'expert' views. In Wales, DCFW monitoring provides more limited evidence but suggests lower levels of influence with 70 per cent of LPAs finding the advice useful, but only 40 per cent giving it significant weight in the control process, and only 14 per cent seeing it as influential at Committee. However, 66 per cent of design teams consider the advice has improved the project design (author's calculations from 2008–9 questionnaire responses). These lower figures can be explained by a more difficult development climate and correspondingly less proactive and demanding design requirements in the development control system in Wales (DCFW 2005; 2007: see Box 9.3).

However, many panellists and review staff consider that there should be more obligation on LPAs to respond to, if not take on board, the advice offered, and that this is the key to the effectiveness of design review at large. Only in the *Building Schools for the Future* programme in England has the review process been given more weight by the *requirement* that local authority project directors pay attention to comments and criticisms. Here, within

---

Box 9.3 Design Commission for Wales: critical design issues revealed by design review, 2003–2007

(1) The failure to present planning applications properly.
(2) The lack of proper analysis of context and site.
(3) The failure to use landscape architects early enough in the design process.
(4) The use of standard solutions when a bespoke approach was required.
(5) The failure to re-think standard highway design solutions.
(6) The need for a positive (and proactive) approach to residential intensification.
(7) The resistance to mixed use development.
(8) The vagueness of masterplans and their implementation mechanisms.
(9) The promotion of development in unsustainable locations.
(10) The failure to respond to sustainable construction imperatives.
(11) The failure to pursue socially inclusive design with adequate affordable housing.
(12) The poor design of tall buildings.
(13) The inadequacies of high density residential development.
(14) The inappropriate pursuit of the iconic building.
(15) Procurement methods which prejudice the delivery of design quality.
(16) The passivity of planning as regards design quality.

Points 1–10 were identified in reviews 2003–5; they were reinforced by reviews 2005–7 when points 11–16 were added.

Source: Adapted from DCFW 2005: 88–93 and DCFW 2007: 108–118.

---

a ten-point and five-level assessment process, only the top two levels are regarded as '… fit for purpose and acceptable' (CABE 2007c: 5).

Generally LPAs positively endorsed the role of design review. Four English local authorities gave strong testimonials as to the value of CABE design review to the Select Committee hearings in 2004. Ipswich, Newcastle, Manchester and Nottingham all saw the design review advice as a vital part of a wide range of positive support for LPAs seeking to raise design standards. Nottingham's testimony is particularly interesting because of its significant urban design achievements since the late 1980s (Heath 2009), despite working within a local development climate less than conducive to quality outputs. As their Assistant Director of Development noted:

> The Council is … currently subject to considerable development pressure … however the quality of the schemes coming forward is poor, or at best just acceptable … the quality of design is often lazy and unadventurous,

and the quality of details and materials frequently poor ... Nottingham has had a productive and valuable relationship with CABE since its establishment. We have found CABE to be very open, approachable, non-bureaucratic and unstuffy. It is easy to ring up and get useful advice, and officers are very ready to come up from London for meetings, site visits, workshops etc. This support and advice is extremely valuable to cities like Nottingham, which are dealing with very complex development issues for which they only have limited in-house experience and skills. It is especially important that CABE is able to give practical advice based on realistic understanding of the development industry and the marketplace. In my experience, their advice is genuinely appreciated by developer teams, and helps in finding practical solutions where the local authority and developer have reached an impasse ... design review sessions with developers ... have been particularly useful. I am impressed with the understanding and insights the Panel have given on complex schemes. This has been real added value which has significantly improved the quality of schemes, in my view (HoC ODPM 2005: Ev 25).

Evidence of how CABE has significantly shaped a range of different types of development is available in their *Design Reviewed* publications which include three systematic studies of review experience with town centre retail, masterplans and urban housing (CABE 2004d; 2004e; 2004f). These overviews analyse development and design trends and identify the strengths and weaknesses of contemporary development proposals. They highlight key questions which need to be asked about particular forms of development, and they offer valuable precedents which can inform both design and development control practices. In the case of town centre retail development (CABE 2004e), the overview documents the shift towards urban design-led solutions which are open street rather than mall focused, a major advance promoted by changes in the market as well as planning pressure. The overview of urban housing (CABE 2004f) identifies the complex design challenges which higher density development imposes on liveability, while the review of masterplans (CABE 2004d) highlights the key questions that need to be asked about all such plans. Regrettably, CABE has been unable to sustain and extend such syntheses. However, it publicises synopses of all reviews of projects that have reached the planning application stage on its website (www.cabe.org.uk/designreview).

Conclusions: design review and the quality of development control

Commenting on CABE's use of design review Hank Dittmar of the Prince's Foundation has concluded that:

The fundamental challenge for CABE is to improve the quality of design, and the way they have chosen to do this is through design review, which then has to be implemented by people in local authorities.

But that's difficult for the government, which doesn't have the money to train planners but has already made the planning system much more complex. So you end up with a situation where all of it – design panels and new standards for homes – ends up being administered by people reeling from the last edict (quoted in Baillieu 2009: 7)[2].

Dittmar underemphasises CABE's multi-faceted approach to the improvement of design quality, but he does recognise the size of the task confronting LPAs to complete new plans, embrace low-carbon design, monitor housing quality, further improve control efficiency and upgrade design skills at large, all with dwindling resources. Furthermore, he is right to emphasise that the broad effectiveness of design review remains almost entirely dependent upon the way that it is deployed and embodied in development control decision making.

That said, the principal determinant of design quality remains the commitment of the developer to design excellence and sustainability, and the skills of the design team retained to execute the project. This commitment may vary according to location, market conditions, time scales and personal/company circumstances, but the influence of both design review and development control will be largely determined by this predisposition. The contrasting approaches of investor-developers and trader-developers has been explored above, and similar contrasts exist between custom-built and speculative developments, and between bespoke and volume housebuilders. Many observers have noted the welcome emergence of a new breed of niche developers who have an interest in urban regeneration, conservation and sustainability alongside innovative architecture and urban design (Guy & Henneberry 2004; Punter 2010: 331–2). Evidence from the distribution of housing design awards reveals how a small group of housing associations, bespoke housebuilders and architect developers consistently achieve the highest design accolades (Biddulph *et al.* 2004), while 'Building-for-Life' monitoring in England reveals how the volume builders' products are largely responsible for the mediocre (53 per cent) and poor (29 per cent) design quality of new housing (CABE 2004c; 2005) which dominate the volume builders' output. The reality is that the majority of the development industry remains less than committed to high quality design.

All of this reinforces the conclusion that while design review can encourage better design in those projects it reviews, these will only affect overall design quality at the margins. The more projects in a locality that are reviewed the greater the potential for exerting a positive and more lasting influence, and this is why the development of regional panels is welcome.

But it is high-calibre local panels that are internal to the local planning authority that have the potential to be particularly effective. They can be embedded in both the Council's project development and development control processes from the outset to promote better design quality and sustainability. But even these are no substitute for a local-authority-wide, corporate commitment to good design, and a proactive development control service that is fully skilled and resourced.

Contrary to Dittmar's narrow view of CABE's activities, the national design bodies are well aware that design review needs to be complemented by a wide range of other activities that will promote quality urban design, directly assist the delivery of quality projects, and support innovation in sustainable urban design and construction. Equally, the national and regional design bodies recognise the need to continue to offer design training to planning officers and highway engineers in a variety of formats, and to maintain the flow of best practice advice on visioning, strategies, policy, guidance and control practices, while also encouraging higher public design awareness and greater community involvement. All of this is essential to contribute to the 'indivisibility of good design and good planning' heralded in PPS1 in England (DCLG 2005: para 33).

Notes

1. Reproduced by permission of Amanda Baillieu.
2. Reproduced by permission of Amanda Baillieu.

10

'Business as Usual?' – Exploring the Design Response of UK Speculative Housebuilders to the Brownfield Development Challenge

David Adams and Sarah Payne

Introduction

This chapter is concerned with the mass production of new housing by speculative builders and the extent to which its design can be influenced for the better by policy actions. As a starting point, it is important to remember that design is but one element of the speculative builder's business strategy and is by no means the most significant. Indeed, more attention is usually paid in speculative housebuilding to acquiring land, achieving government approvals, securing finance, organising construction and marketing the completed development than to matters of design (whether conceived as the appearance and functionality of the finished *product* or the problem-solving *process* by which it is delivered). Design is thus embedded within, and reflective of, the broader residential development process as well as the particular business strategy of each housebuilder. Both of these create an important contextual framework for design decisions, which changes over time in response to both social, economic and institutional circumstances and the particular development opportunities available at any moment.

The importance of this from the policy perspective is that actions intended to shape, regulate or stimulate residential design quality, or to build the

Urban Design in the Real Estate Development Process, First Edition. Edited by Steve Tiesdell and David Adams.
© 2011 Blackwell Publishing Ltd. Published 2011 by Blackwell Publishing Ltd.

capacity to do so, are unlikely to be successful unless related to a mature appreciation of their likely impact on the development process as a whole and the business strategies pursued by particular types of housebuilder. In this chapter, by connecting the pursuit of better-quality design by UK policymakers to their desire to shift the focus of housing development from greenfield to brownfield land, we seek to explore the extent to which speculative housebuilders, as adaptive business organisations, can be persuaded by policy actions to move away from mass or standardised designs towards customised or bespoke ones that might run with the grain of a place and demonstrate enhanced sensitivity to particular local contexts.

Speculative housebuilders are responsible for much of the new urban form of the UK. Unlike commercial (and to a lesser extent industrial) developers, speculative housebuilders consume extensive tracts of land, both within, and on the periphery of, UK towns and cities. Indeed, between 1990/91 and 2007/08, private developers built almost 2.95 million new homes across the UK, accounting for 85 per cent of all housing production (DCLG 2009). Significantly, this new residential Britain of the late 20th and early 21st centuries was disproportionately produced by a small number of very large companies. By 2000, for example, 71 per cent of all newly completed private homes across the UK were built by only 43 'major builders', each with an annual output of 500 or more units (Wellings 2001). The collective market share of the largest 15 of these companies, each producing 2000 or more units annually and classed as 'volume builders', had by then reached almost 50 per cent (Calcutt 2007). Consequently, the residential design quality achieved by speculative housebuilders, and especially by the largest companies, is both central to the prospects of securing that step-change in urban quality desired by policymakers as well as daily evident to millions of home owners first hand.

Yet, as one prominent Government report commented, '… too many housing estates are designed for nowhere in particular. They can be soulless and dispiriting. All too often they are not well-connected to local services and promote dependency on the car' (DTLR & CABE 2001: 5). Since the mid 1990s, policymakers across the UK have therefore waged a concerted campaign to transform the design quality of new residential developments. In this chapter, we draw on recent research conducted among major and volume housebuilders to enquire how far this campaign has changed the inherent design culture of the industry.

Our particular focus is on brownfield development, where earlier work had suggested that a more demanding market context and more difficult site conditions would cause speculative housebuilders increasingly to turn to skilled designers for successful and profitable solutions (Tiesdell & Adams 2004). We set out the context for our enquiry in more detail in the next section, where we review how the design critique of UK speculative housing products emerged from the mid 1990s and how this generated specific policy responses. We connect these with the parallel policy switch from greenfield to brownfield development and review emerging evidence from CABE on whether speculative housebuilders have made any real improvement in design quality in recent years.

The mediocre performance revealed by this evidence then causes us to look more closely at the business strategies and working practices of speculative housebuilders in order to understand the extent to which design is considered important within the industry. This leads us to report our own findings, from which we conclude that, ironically, the industry's apparent *product* innovations of recent years have been driven by the desire to avoid *process* innovations and so maintain 'business-as-usual'. The industry's continued reluctance to accord design a central place within its culture and strategies raises significant policy implications, especially in relation to the effectiveness of design regulation and the need for wider capacity building, which we explore in the concluding section.

The design debate around speculative housing development

The emerging critique of speculative housing design

By the early 21st century, the design quality of UK speculative housing development had come under concerted attack. The Scottish Executive's *Planning Advice Note 68: Housing Quality* illustrates this well, contending that: 'Many suburban areas lack character, identity or variety. Too many new homes look as if they could be anywhere. Thoughtlessly chosen standard house types and inappropriate materials look disconcertingly out of place.' (Scottish Executive 2003: 10)

Yet, until a decade earlier, governments had generally defended the right of housebuilders to produce whatever designs and layouts they considered 'the market' demanded, believing that minimal interference in the production specifics of new homes was essential to achieve the broader policy goal of greatly increased home ownership. Michael Heseltine, for example, shortly after having been appointed Secretary of State for the Environment by Margaret Thatcher in 1979, issued the now notorious Circular 22/80, which warned against 'the unnecessary imposition of design standards' by planners and councillors, and argued that since aesthetics were subjective, it was not the role of local authorities to impose their own tastes and fashions on developers (DoE 1980). This regrettable conflation of design standards with aesthetics, which Heseltine's statement reflected, plagued much of the policy debate around design for at least the next decade.

Ironically, the reversal of this market-led approach was initiated by one of Heseltine's Conservative successors as Environment Secretary, John Gummer, who voiced concern that 'ugly' housing estates that made places seem just like everywhere else, had become an important component of the growing public resistance to greenfield development (DoE 1996). By specifically asking what more could be done to raise design quality, Gummer sparked a debate that, in due course, produced intense policy interest in changing the design behaviour of speculative housebuilders.

Early contributors to that debate included Black (1997), a former developer himself, who spoke about the industry's reliance on a manufacturing, rather than design, process, its limited interest in the public realm, its 'build and walk away' trading ethos, and its lack of interest in local consultation. Fulford (1998: 128) added that this created '... a factory style box-building approach', while the Popular Housing Forum (1998) found the industry's customers generally considered their new homes to be cramped, boxy and lacking individuality. The Urban Task Force (1999) appointed by the incoming Labour Government, sought to turn around the UK's record of poor urban design through generating commitment to quality and creativity in the design of buildings, public spaces and transport networks.

The Urban Task Force report challenged not merely speculative housing design but the *design culture* of speculative housebuilders, evident in three particular deficiencies:

(1) Quantity appeared to matter far more than quality to speculative housebuilders (Carmona *et al.* 2003) and involved standardisation of production, with only limited changes made from place to place to the facade of standard house types, often for marketing reasons rather than to reflect particular place distinctiveness.
(2) Standardisation required limited design skills, so builders employed technicians not architects, who could even design housing layouts by computer without ever visiting the site to understand its problems, qualities, attributes and potential (Tiesdell & Adams 2004).
(3) This meant that little appreciation was given to the setting of new homes, with speculative housing estates failing to create successful streets, neglecting to provide attractive pedestrian routes and failing to appreciate their relationship with the wider landscape (Scottish Executive 2003).

Much of this design critique was directed at greenfield development, which until the late 1990s had dominated housing production. Tiesdell & Adams (2004: 39) summarised the criticism in the following terms:

On greenfield sites (and in the absence of external sanctions against doing otherwise) developers' strategic interest in design does not need to extend much beyond "kerb appeal", which, in practice, may amount to little more than different packing of standardised "boxes".

Despite such criticisms of poor or standardised designs, the continuing benefits of product standardisation (see later) and the resulting lack of strategic interest in design meant that there was little change to housebuilders' conventional approach to design, until at least the late 1990s. Indeed, standardisation remained an all too important business strategy for this risk adverse industry.

The transition to stronger residential design policy

Following its election in 1997, the Labour Government devoted considerable effort to transforming the urban design policy environment, in which the promotion of better designed residential developments featured prominently. Two main factors came together to strengthen residential design policy, namely the clearer articulation of policy aims in an attempt to shape market behaviour, and its more forceful implementation through both regulating market behaviour and building capacity to influence design thinking. Although driven forward primarily in England, the broad principles of this new approach were later reflected in policies adopted across the UK, and specifically by the Scottish Executive, north of the border. An early policy change sought to replace car-dominated housing layouts by emphasis on creating well-designed places served by traditional connected streets, rather than hierarchical road systems (DETR 1998). This was followed by a fundamental revision to Planning Policy Guidance 3: Housing (DETR 2000), which had five design policy objectives:

(1) The creation of environmentally and socially sustainable communities instead of single-use, socially zoned residential ghettos.
(2) Much greater emphasis on urban design, extended to cover residential areas, with townscape, social usage, urban form and functionality seen as important issues.
(3) Recognition of the importance of landscape design in promoting quality, enhancing drainage and increasing biodiversity.
(4) Legitimising architectural design as a policy matter, including concern for local building traditions and materials, energy efficiency and new building technologies.
(5) Encouraging local authorities to adopt appropriate design policy frameworks that require applicants to show how they have taken good design and layout into account (Carmona et al. 2003).

Significantly, Carmona *et al.* (2003: 126) drew important contrasts between the 2000 version of PPG3 and the 1992 version, which it replaced. They commented that:

> Looking back ... the impression given in the 1992 policy is one of lip-service to design ... Conversely, the 2000 version of PPG3 makes no mention of marketing needs as a driver of design solutions and places no obvious limits on the design aspirations of authorities ...

A companion guide to PPG3 entitled *By Design: Better Places to Live* (published jointly by the DTLR and CABE in 2001) elaborated in detail on how the principles of urban design could be applied to create better residential environments. Tellingly, none of the many case studies and examples used in the report commended the conventional suburban housing estate for so long produced by speculative housebuilders, although many drew attention to its deficiencies.

This new philosophy has remained at the heart of English design policy, with the latest guidance (DCLG 2006c: 8) proclaiming that: 'Good design is fundamental to the development of high quality new housing, which contributes to the creation of sustainable mixed communities.' Similarly, in Scotland: 'Creating high-quality residential environments is also a key Scottish Executive policy objective ... Developers should think about the qualities and characteristics of places and not consider sites in isolation.' (Scottish Executive 2003: 7 & 16)

Residential design policy has thus been reformulated to emphasise the making of sustainable communities, rather than the mere construction of housing estates. This reformulation has been driven forward by policy-shaping guidance at the national and increasingly local levels, where design now features far more strongly in development plans and frameworks, and where much greater emphasis has been placed on detailed design briefs and related supplementary planning guidance. Importantly, however, these sharpened policy-shaping instruments have been backed by the apparent reinforcement of design regulation, encouraged by the Government's statement in PPS 3 that: 'Design which is inappropriate in its context, or which fails to take the opportunities available for improving the character and quality of an area and the way it functions, should not be accepted.' (DCLG 2006c: 8)

Although there has been little resort to stimulus policies to promote better design (except perhaps in relation to historic buildings and where design conditions have been attached to regeneration grants) capacity building has featured strongly as a design policy tool, especially through the 'Building-for-Life' initiative. This was established in 2002 as a partnership principally between CABE and the Home Builders Federation (HBF), reflecting recognition by the housebuilding industry of its own need to significantly improve the design quality through cultural change and corporate commitment and by making greater use of an enhanced skills base. Significantly, the partnership has developed a national standard for measuring well-designed homes and neighbourhoods, through establishing 20 'Building-for-Life' criteria that '... embody our vision of functional, attractive and sustainable housing' (see http://www.buildingforlife.org/criteria).

These criteria can be applied through informal or formal assessment of individual proposed developments and are celebrated annually through the Building-for-Life Awards given to outstanding housing developments. A more representative picture, however, is evident from the audit process so far undertaken for 100 housing developments in London, the south-east and east of England (CABE 2004c), 93 schemes in the north-west, north-east and Yorkshire and the Humber (CABE 2005) and a further 100 schemes across the east Midlands, west Midlands and the south-west (CABE 2007a). These reports make salutary reading. Across England as a whole, only 18 per cent of new residential developments audited against the Building-for-Life criteria were rated as 'good' or 'very good'; 29 per cent were so poor that, according to CABE (2007a), they simply should not have been given planning consent.

In his foreword to the final report, CABE's Chief Executive commented:

> The housing produced in the first few years of this new century is simply not up to the standard which the government is demanding and which customers have a right to expect. Our research indicates that some things are improving. But the improvement is too little and too slow (CABE, 2007a: 3).

This raises two crucial questions about the comparative effectiveness of the various policy instruments so far deployed in the Government's attempt to transform residential design quality, which we subsequently address in relation to brownfield development within our own research, namely:

(1) How far can embedded behaviour within the private sector be fundamentally changed by a reliance on seeking to shape housebuilder behaviour, backed up as necessary by robust regulation of housebuilder behaviour?
(2) What role can and should capacity building play in fundamentally changing housebuilder behaviour?

The brownfield policy switch

Since 1998, when the Labour Government raised the proportion of new homes in England expected to be built on previously developed land or achieved through conversions to a target of 60 per cent by 2008, brownfield development has been seen as a central priority, even to the extent of a moratorium being placed on new greenfield release in regions such as north-west England. In due course, the brownfield emphasis combined with the policy emphasis on higher density development within PPG3 (DETR 2000), led to a wave of new apartment building across England, especially in the centres of major towns and cities (Unsworth 2007).

As Adams (2004) has argued, the brownfield policy switch represented a fundamental challenge to the tried and tested methods of most housebuild-ers, owing to the greater uncertainty in development appraisal caused by more problematic site conditions, the more restricted opportunities to secure land through options and conditional contracts combined with the greater need to piece together land ownerships and the limited range of con-tacts and networks that many housebuilders then had in brownfield land markets. Crucially, however, Tiesdell & Adams (2004) suggested that the innate complexity of brownfield land meant that developers would be more likely to turn to skilled designers to realise the full potential of each site.

Intriguingly, then, to overcome their own reduction in 'opportunity space' (or strategic freedom of manoeuvre) caused by the Government's brownfield emphasis, housebuilders might be persuaded to yield some of their remain-ing opportunity space to skilled designers. This would result in more indi-vidualised and bespoke developments better able to exploit the potential of brownfield land. In other words, attempts to shape and regulate housebuilder design behaviour might work most effectively in a brownfield context, where investing in skilled design would be a practical and financial necessity. Before we evaluate this possibility later in the chapter, we first summarise the most relevant aspects of the prevailing business model in UK speculative housebuilding as an important context against which to understand the industry's embedded attitudes and behaviour towards design skills.

The conventional approach to design and construction in speculative housebuilding

Design in UK speculative housebuilding is approached in two key ways: through products that housebuilders build and the processes used to deliver these. Emphasis has long been placed on the employment of traditional and relatively simple processes to deliver standard products. Design has thus been interpreted in quite shallow terms as a well-rehearsed *process* of laying out appropriate house types within a given area to deliver a set of *products* to a local market. This may involve some minor adjustment to the external appearance at each site, but normally there is little change to the footprint and functionality of each house type. It is indeed well documented in the literature that the UK speculative housebuilding industry is not renowned for its innovative capacity in either the development of its products or the processes it uses (see, for example, Ball 1999; Barlow 1999; Barlow & Ball 1999; Barlow & Bhatti 1997; Barlow & King 1992; Barlow & Ozaki 2003). Until recently, there has thus been little evidence in speculative housebuilding of deeper or more fundamental attempts to wholly re-engineer the design process to deliver better designed products.

The standard business model in speculative housebuilding reflects strong competition within the industry and reveals intense pressures to maintain profitability by cost minimisation. Over time, this model has produced two dominant business strategies: capturing land and ensuring construction efficiency. Operationally, the immediate concern of speculative housebuilders has been to generate positive cashflow since production times are relatively long and the market for new homes variable (Ball 1983). This means that speculative housebuilders must effectively manage the conflicting pressures of acquiring land, generating sales revenue and controlling production costs.

In this section, we explore how these factors have shaped the way housebuilders operate through instilling land acquisition and construction efficiency as a means of competitive differentiation and profit maximisation. We argue that, as a result, design is not intrinsically of strategic interest to most speculative housebuilders.

The critical importance of land in speculative housebuilding

Although land is the housebuilding industry's principal resource in the UK, the planning system controls its access and limits its supply (Barker 2004). Public sector regulation over the allocation and development of housing land results in an uncertain business environment for speculative housebuilders. The industry therefore allocates much of its resources to searching for, and acquiring, suitable development land and specifically to seeking its control by strategically building up 'land bank portfolios'. These comprise of development sites that:

- are in varyious geographical locations;
- are of different sizes and uses;
- are of different value;
- deliver different dates of profit realisation;
- have different levels of development risk (and potential reward);
- have different development timescales.

This business strategy allows housebuilders to operate their land acquisition activity as a conveyor belt – finely tuned to prevailing market circumstances while delivering the current strategic and financial priorities of the particular company. Such flexibility is intended to provide continuity of development and ensure a continuous revenue stream. Essentially, land banking offers corporate stability in an uncertain and risky business environment. Crucially, this strategy also allows housebuilders to capture any inflation in land values during the period that sites are 'banked'. Over time, housebuilders have learnt that land is a valuable source of inflationary gain. They may be tempted to delay development if they expect house prices to rise, as this would provide them with a valuable opportunity to secure a substantially increased profit margin on each house.[1]

Land banking is vital to maintaining output and maximising development gains in speculative housebuilding. Consequently, Barlow & King (1992) argue that good design and environmental quality is seen by most housebuilders as not contributing directly to the profit equation. The result is a 'land-focused' industry where housebuilders concentrate their competitive behaviour and strategies on land acquisition and cost minimisation as crucial elements of success. As we next discuss, pressure for construction efficiency has resulted in a marked reliance by most housebuilders on product standardisation, reflected in a distinct lack of innovative design capacity.

Design and construction efficiency in speculative housebuilding: the benefit of standardisation

The use of standard house types in residential design is the most marked example of how housebuilders aim to maximise development gains by minimising expenditure at any given level of output. Housebuilders consistently prefer to use standardised building materials and tried-and-tested construction methods to generate standard house types that can be readily reproduced at varying locations in an efficient and flexible manner (Hooper & Nicol 1999). Standard house types comprise two key elements: the structural footprint and the structural facade. By applying different facades to standard footprints, standard houses can be 'dressed' to match the requirements of any site and locality. This is illustrated in Figures 10.1a and b, which show two different ways in which a standard footprint for a four-bedroom detached property from the Manor Kingdom product portfolio can be 'dressed'.

Historically, the use of product standardisation has been popular in the design and development of mass greenfield estates and became a conventional design tool in providing development solutions to such sites. Because greenfield sites are typically larger than brownfield sites, have few constraints below ground or adjacent to the site and also have fewer (if any) existing structures to consider in design, housebuilders have been able to treat these sites as blank canvasses in design terms. This means that housebuilders can cram as many houses as possible onto the site in order to generate maximum house sales and drive up the return on capital employed. In the greenfield context, little regard is paid to how the layout of the site

(a)

(b)

Figure 10.1a, b These two photographs show how what is essentially the same internal footprint can be presented externally as two different house types. Taken from Manor Kingdom's Berkeley range, the stone-dressed frontage with dormer windows has been built at Newmacher in north-east Scotland, while the rendered frontage with the large bay windows has been constructed at Dunfermline in the central belt of Scotland. Reproduced by permission of Manor Kingdom.

relates to the existing or surrounding fabric. Design, both in terms of product and process, has therefore been of limited consideration in most conventional greenfield developments, since improved design was not seen as essential in delivering as many housing units as possible to ensure a healthy and viable development profit.

As this experience suggests, standardisation is compelling for housebuilders since design costs are greatly reduced, supplies purchased at bulk rates and the logistics of moving labour and materials simplified (Gibb 1999). Standardised house types enable blanket building control approval, which further limits pre-construction costs and enables accurate cost forecasting when land bids are prepared. Using standardised design also means that housebuilders can rely on designs known to have sold well in the past and learn which are most successful and popular. Opponents of standardisation have emphasised its inherent inflexibility and have called for innovation and better design of new homes built by the private sector. In the next section, we therefore present recent research exploring how far brownfield development has challenged design standardisation among UK speculative housebuilders.

Responding to the challenge of brownfield development

The research

The research presented here sought to examine the delivery and implementation of UK brownfield policy through an assessment of changing strategies of speculative housebuilders towards design and development. The conceptual basis for the research was drawn from institutional analysis and from core competence theory within the strategic management literature (Payne 2009).

The empirical research was undertaken in 2006 and conducted in two stages. The first sought aggregate data at an industry level through a postal questionnaire targeted at the 104 largest UK housebuilders (in terms of unit completions) from whom a 46 per cent response rate was achieved. The second captured disaggregated data at the company level through detailed interviews conducted with 10 sample companies operating in Greater Manchester or Central Scotland. The aggregate data provided a general overview of the attitudes, expectations and behaviours of UK housebuilders towards brownfield development. The disaggregated data presented the opportunity to explore firm-specific strategies for design in brownfield development.

The research showed that the brownfield development boom experienced in many British cities since the late 1990s was driven forward by 'pioneers' in the industry, who developed alternative and innovative design solutions for brownfield projects. However, these more specialist companies were a relatively small minority of housebuilders, and more than balanced in number by 'sceptics' who were inherently reluctant to take on brownfield sites. What made the difference to overall production was the middle group of housebuilders (who can be termed 'pragmatists') whose

Table 10.1 Typology of UK speculative housebuilders and their key features.

Type	Key features
Pioneers	• *Pioneers* were industry leaders in brownfield development. • Strategic and competitive focus was on the redevelopment of brownfield sites. • Most commonly regeneration specialists, e.g. Urban Splash. • Delivered 100 per cent of all their new homes on brownfield sites and had a land bank comprised of 100 per cent brownfield sites. • Had previously built all of their units on brownfield sites and intended to build all of their units on brownfield sites in the future.
Pragmatists	• *Pragmatists* were those housebuilders who had demonstrated increased use of brownfield land for housebuilding in the previous five years and who intended to continue using predominantly brownfield land in the future. • Delivered between 60 per cent and 89 per cent of their units on brownfield land and had a land bank comprised of between 60 per cent and 89 per cent brownfield sites. • Demonstrated positive changes in their 'brownfield behaviour' in the previous five years and intended to continue making positive changes in the next five years.
Sceptics	• *Sceptics* were those housebuilders who had continued to make only limited use of brownfield land in the previous five years and did not expect this to change in the next five years. • Delivered less than 60 per cent of all their new homes on brownfield sites and had a land bank made up of predominantly greenfield opportunities.

Source: Authors' own analysis.

familiar greenfield markets proved increasingly hard to access as planning restrictions tightened, and who saw an economic opportunity in switching production primarily to brownfield locations. Table 10.1 summarises the key features of these three types of housebuilder.

Whereas pioneers were attracted or 'pulled' by the market opportunity of brownfield sites, pragmatists and sceptics were driven or 'pushed' away from greenfield sites by tighter policy constraints. Crucially, the research found that, while pioneers searched for innovative design solutions, both pragmatists and sceptics worked hard to transfer product standardisation as a key design solution from their greenfield experience to brownfield sites. This was because construction efficiency remained a compelling strategic priority in maintaining an individual housebuilder's competitive edge. We shall now explain how and why this happened, and evaluate its impact in design terms.

Construction efficiency and the continuing importance of product standardisation

Construction efficiency became crucial to the profitability of brownfield development because housebuilders found themselves more constrained by the economics of the land and housing markets than at greenfield locations.

This was because on the one hand, land prices had to absorb the costs of 'abnormals', such as difficult ground conditions, and on the other, sale prices for completed dwellings were even more dominated by the second-hand market.

The continued importance of construction efficiency ensured that speculative housebuilders, with the exception of the pioneers, still relied on tried and tested conventional methods associated with standard product design in configuring brownfield developments. This did not usually involve the transfer of standard greenfield house types to brownfield locations, but rather the development of standard apartment types that could be positioned in many brownfield locations, with relatively minor facade changes. In design terms, this meant that most housebuilders made little attempt to weave new apartments into the urban fabric but instead expected that fabric to absorb their standard product.

As a result, they were able to reap the conventional benefits of product standardisation, such as controlling construction costs, managing materials procurement and providing the level of construction certainty necessary to reduce the risks of speculative residential development. In short, what may have appeared as significant *product* innovation by speculative housebuilders (development of urban apartments, rather than suburban houses) belied a determination to avoid *process* innovation and instead fall back on the embedded culture of standardisation. In management terms, rather than develop new core competencies for brownfield development, the pragmatists and sceptics interviewed opted to transpose across to brownfield locations existing competencies that had been well developed at greenfield sites. As this suggests, most housebuilders operate as *minimally adaptive* organisations, at least in the short term.

For this strategy to succeed at brownfield locations, housebuilders found that they had to sharpen their skills in both efficient plotting of their product and efficient use of materials. Plot efficiency enabled housebuilders to deliver high-density development, primarily composed of either standardised apartments or townhouses. Crucially, this made smaller brownfield sites more financially viable, generating a higher land offer. As Bridgemere West Scotland[2] (a pragmatic volume plc) explained, maximising the development potential through higher densities remained central to increasing brownfield revenues and so providing the landowner with a competitive offer. Caledonian Homes, a sceptical Scottish-based private volume producer, also emphasised the financial advantage of higher densities:

> ... we've made our houses efficient, i.e. you get a lot of square footage on quite a small footprint and that allows you to get more sales revenue out of the site and allows you to bid for a greater price on the land – so, in order to get that land, we use construction efficiency to make us finish Number 1 rather than Number 2.

Interestingly, the company attributed its use of standardised design solutions on brownfield sites to the pressure from landowners to receive the maximum value for their sites:

> All the landowner is interested in is maximising their land value; the way to do that is to make houses as efficient as possible and to get as many houses on the site as you can and make the non-developable areas as small as possible. You cram as many on to win the site, and that's the only way of winning it.

Controlling costs by using standardised product designs also meant that housebuilders could manage risk 'above ground' while concentrating their efforts 'below ground'. As Edzell North West, a sceptical volume plc, for example, made clear: 'With standard house types, which we've used a lot in the past, you know what it costs to come out of the ground, it's what is in the ground that's really the issue on brownfields.'

Most housebuilders managed to operate in brownfield locations simply by replicating new types of standard structural footprints, explicitly created for an urban environment. Few saw any real marketing advantage in bespoke product design. Product standardisation could normally take account of planning conditions that sought to regulate the external appearance of a development simply through facade alteration. This also cleverly allowed housebuilders to tweak their standard products in different urban environments. When required to use local materials by Calderdale Council, for example, Bridgemere North West, a pragmatic volume plc reported that:

> … we had to use the local stone and put slate roofs on all the units. But that's fine and we can do that with our standard footprints – we've done it before so we know the cost and where to get the materials from. It's not an issue for us. Our houses can be what you want them to be but we still have that certainty from the standard footprint, we can still control those build costs …

Since product standardisation had the inherent flexibility to respond to the differing facade requirements, it did not require a homogenous approach to external appearance, even though several brownfield developments by the same company might differ only superficially. Crucially, however, it did not require housebuilders to commission individual or bespoke designs for every brownfield site. As next discussed, such individuality proved the exception, rather than the rule.

The use of bespoke design solutions on brownfield sites

Although most speculative housebuilders still favoured product standardisation, the research found examples of bespoke design solutions on brownfield sites. Nevertheless, bespoke design was far from common, and generally depended both on whether the particular housebuilder was a pioneer, rather than a pragmatist or a sceptic, and on four site-specific issues, namely location, size, target market and the demands of the vendor/landowner.

Only pioneers saw bespoke design as core to their strategy. Vision Construction, a North-West-based pioneering regeneration specialist, made clear that because it was '... quite tuned into design', it realised the value of good design and therefore '... it's quite a strong part of the delivery of our developments'. This company developed a bespoke design solution around the unique demands of each brownfield site. Factors considered in doing so included topography, existing urban fabric, existing on-site structures, ground issues such as contamination and existing foundations, market demands and expectations, and the local authority's wider regeneration initiatives. As a result, Vision Construction claimed that it:

> ... can recognise an opportunity without having to think about what design might go on there and quite often we are quite committed to an opportunity before we go out to a competition to select an architect and that's really when a design starts. So we are quite often committed to an opportunity with no real preconceptions of what's going to go on there.

To achieve this, Vision Construction drew on in-house skills to conceptualise their initial aspirations for any development opportunity, and then commissioned external architects to make that conception a reality.

Although bespoke design was largely the province of the pioneers, the research found that some pragmatist builders had begun to recognise the potential contribution of bespoke design to the success of brownfield development. Lothian Homes, for example, a pragmatic privately owned volume builder based in Scotland, made clear that:

> ... in some ways, the good thing about a major regeneration area is you're often less constrained by surrounding buildings, because there often aren't any. So if you are building a new development right in the middle of the city centre, whatever you design there would have to fit in with all the surrounding buildings around it and that quite often kind of half designs it for you, in terms of its height, its materials, its colour, its access, everything else. Whereas if you are doing something major in a big area then there's a bit more flexibility for setting a new sort of design criteria for that area.

Pragmatists, however, tended to reserve bespoke design solutions for brownfield sites in prime or prominent locations, typically in city centres. As Arden West Scotland, a pragmatic volume plc, explained: '...we tend to use bespoke only on 'prime' city centre sites ... The choice of using bespoke is not a result of the land, it's more the location of the site.'

Speculative housebuilders almost always approached bespoke design by commissioning externally based skills. These typically included architects for design, and construction companies contracted to build the development. Edzell North West, a sceptical volume plc, stressed that importance of the external skills to bespoke developments: 'With bespoke, everything is externally designed. There is no direct involvement – it's a contractual relationship between the architect and subcontractor.'

By definition, bespoke developments required housebuilders to think afresh about the key design challenges of each site such as density, storey height and requirements for open space, rather than merely apply what has seemingly worked elsewhere. Caledonian Homes, a sceptical Scottish-based private volume builder, highlighted the implications of these challenges:

> [They] …gave us build problems in coordinating design and construction. It needs fairly close project management skills to make sure that everything is coordinated whereas with our standard house types, we know we can deliver them in X number of weeks. Bespoke are a lot longer and more complicated – we don't know if we will be doing any more of them.

Edzell North West explained how difficult it was to make bespoke development work at first '…in terms of its financial efficiency and viability' in comparison with standardised approaches. As the company commented: 'Bespoke developments are challenging, as everything is different. We're a volume producer and we've had the difficulty of getting it right first time and being as efficient.'

Table 10.2 summarises the distinction between standard and bespoke design in speculative housebuilding. As this section has shown, most speculative housebuilders have successfully transposed their conventional competencies of product standardisation onto brownfield sites. They have sought to adjust their standard designs to the individual demands of brownfield sites through changing the facade rather than developing a bespoke unit. With the exception of regeneration specialists, bespoke design solutions have generally proved too challenging for an industry culturally used to the delivery of standardised solutions. The failure of speculative housebuilders to fully embrace bespoke design solutions on brownfield land is reflective of their heavy reliance on tried-and-tested methods of residential design, and raises important policy questions to which we turn in the final section of this chapter.

Conclusion

The research presented in this chapter is consistent with the CABE audits suggesting that the well-publicised award-winning residential developments of recent years, while very welcome, are not representative of the new homes

Table 10.2   Comparing standard and bespoke design in speculative housebuilding.

	Standard design	Bespoke design
Advantages To Developer	• Standard products for standard locations, achieving blanket building regulation approval • Standard layouts and construction methods ensuring bulk purchasing of materials and greater certainty in build cost • Construction does not require highly skilled labour • Delivers house types known to have sold well in the past • Facilitates competitive land bids and selling prices	• Developmental kudos and positive marketing • Opportunity to learn new design skills for future use • Enables broader range of sites to be considered for acquisition
Advantages To Society	• Helps fulfil purchaser's desire of suburban dream home • Creates resalable products that can be readily valued for loan purposes	• New development can be better suited to its place context • Broader range of new development types available to purchase
Disadvantages to Developer	• Creates reputation for poorer quality insensitive design	• Can be very costly and therefore risky • Can involve unknown contacts, materials, and markets • Resource intensive, requiring greater management input and often more highly skilled labour
Disadvantages to Society	• Produces monotonous repetitive development that pays no regard to place context	• Potentially makes new housing more expensive

Source: Authors' own analysis.

constructed by speculative UK housebuilders during the first decade of the 21st century. Indeed, apart from a small minority of pioneer developers and pioneering schemes, the embedded culture of standardisation remains prevalent within the industry, and moreover appears to have been successfully transferred from greenfield to brownfield locations. Government policy may well have succeeded in encouraging a brownfield building boom of high-density apartments but the evidence from this study and elsewhere suggests that design quality has not generally been enhanced, and indeed, may well have suffered as an unfortunate side-effect of the building boom, to the long-term detriment of urban sustainability.

When faced with an apparent reduction in their opportunity space developers turned to skilled designers only on a temporary basis to provide them with the necessary, but initially more complex, standardised apartments that subsequently could be reproduced from location to location with limited further design input. In this sense, tighter regulation caused most housebuilders to invest in design capacity only to the extent that it enabled them to broaden their standardised products. This strategy then enabled these housebuilders to 'reclaim' any opportunity space that might have been permanently ceded to designers if bespoke development had become more commonplace at brownfield locations.

In many areas, the strategy has resulted in mundane and disconnected brownfield residential developments which contribute quantitatively to government housing and brownfield targets but, qualitatively, do remarkably little to create sustainable communities. Only in city centres does bespoke architect-designed development appear to be common. Elsewhere, despite the superficial impression of innovation, the depressingly familiar speculative housing *process* remains largely unchanged, even though it may temporarily be masked by what may seem, from external appearances, to be new housing *products*.

Does this reflect a general failure of policy instruments that have sought to achieve better-quality residential design through shaping and regulating developer behaviour more effectively? Despite particular achievements, there is no sense from our research or from the CABE findings that any fundamental change towards design has occurred in the embedded culture of the industry. It would, however, be simplistic to write shaping and regulating instruments off without further examination. Two points are relevant here. First, fundamental changes in policy directions may take several years to have any serious impact, especially if the business environment they seek to influence is as strongly path dependent as the speculative housebuilding industry. Design achievements, such as those recounted by Hall (2007) at Chelmsford (see Chapter 4), where strong development pressure and a determined local planning authority forced speculative housebuilders to make a step change in design quality, may need to be widely replicated before having any lasting impact on embedded cultures among housebuilders. It is thus too early to judge the success of the policy shift towards better quality residential design, especially at the end of a long boom. The design quality in speculative development that eventually emerges from the recession might be a fairer long-term test of policy success.

Second, the evident policy desire for better-designed housing was not necessarily consistent with other policy objectives pursued simultaneously, namely to shift the balance of new housing development strongly towards brownfield locations and, after the Barker Review (2004), to significantly increase the total number of new dwellings built each year. Both appeared to prioritise quantity over quality – on the one hand by bringing forward marginal and often poorly located brownfield sites for housing that would probably better have been developed for other purposes or greened up and, on the other hand, by stretching the capacity of the housebuilding industry to deliver increased output at a time when skilled construction labour (both professionally and manually) was in short supply. Our argument here is for, first, the integration of design policy with other relevant built environment policies and, second, for those who advocate stronger design regulation to be as concerned about its implementation as about formulation. Thus in answer to the first of our research questions posed earlier, there is certainly potential in design policy that seeks to shape and regulate developer behaviour (as witnessed by the exemplary schemes evident in our research and by the award-winning CABE developments), but how far that potential is realised depends on the extent to which design policy is consistently integrated within an overall policy regime.

One disturbing aspect of this story, however, concerns the extent to which design regulators may have believed in their own success at the same time as those whose activities are subject to regulation made determined efforts to evade the full force of that regulation. In the case studies, what may have seemed to planners to be bespoke apartment developments, specifically designed for their own locality, were merely clones of the company's standardised product that had previously been built in the next door locality, albeit with the trappings of a slightly different facade. This raises the important concern of whether a regulatory approach can ever be fully effective in encouraging creativity and individual flair. Here, we turn to answer the second research question posed earlier. Although there is much still to be achieved by the Building-for-Life initiative, its emphasis on developing capacity for better design within the industry, and indeed among regulators as well, may well have a more fundamental impact in the long term than its mere reliance on market regulation and shaping. In fact, all three may need to work together if embedded cultures within the housebuilding industry towards design are ever to be transformed but the message from this research is that capacity building needs to be regarded as of equal, if not greater importance in design policy as shaping and regulation.

Notes

1. While this may not be the most effective business strategy during the current recession, it does explain how housebuilders have conventionally made a large proportion of their historic profits.
2. For reasons of confidentiality, we use pseudonyms rather than real company names to report data from the interviews.

11

Physical-Financial Modelling as an Aid to Developers' Decision-Making

John Henneberry, Eckart Lange, Sarah Moore, Ed Morgan and Ning Zhao

Introduction

This chapter considers means to support the more effective integration of the development and design processes. Financial viability and design quality are two fundamental characteristics of development. Each influences and is influenced by the other. They should affect and ultimately determine the form of development through recursion. However, project design and financial appraisal are often treated as separate, specialist tasks. Achieving a closer, more flexible and responsive relationship between them has proved difficult. We describe the development and application of a physical-financial modelling system that may help to overcome this problem. For simplicity, a limited notion of design is adopted. This focuses on site morphology: the overall use, form, massing and density of development. However, we also note how the model may be used to explore more detailed, subtle facets of design.

Design quality and development viability

Theory, Analysis and Policy

> Urban design objectives [...] can only have any impact if they are translated into fact through the development process (Syms 2002: 235).

Urban Design in the Real Estate Development Process, First Edition. Edited by Steve Tiesdell and David Adams.
© 2011 Blackwell Publishing Ltd. Published 2011 by Blackwell Publishing Ltd.

There is a substantial literature on the development process that considers it from various methodological and theoretical standpoints (see, for example, the reviews of Healey 1991; Gore & Nicholson 1991; Ball 1998; Guy & Henneberry 2002b). The developer is '... *the key coordinator and catalyst for development.*' (Healey 1991: 224). Yet, despite their important influence on development, developers have received limited attention. Other actors, such as investors (Coakley 1994; Pryke & Lee 1995) or landowners (Goodchild & Munton 1985; Adams *et al.* 1994), have been the subjects of special study. In contrast, in a survey of the field, Parris (2010) could only identify two UK studies (by Guy *et al.* 2002; Ball 2002) and two overseas studies (Coiacetto 2006; Charney 2007) that have explored developers' character and actions in any detail.

Otherwise, the way that developers behave must be imputed from normative texts on property development (for a recent review, see Crosby *et al.* 2008). Such texts are set within the mainstream economics paradigm. They assume that developers aim to take utility-maximising decisions that are as informed and rational as possible. Utility is invariably expressed in terms of financial return, relative to risk. Consequently, development decisions turn on financial appraisals and the latter technique and its application is at the centre of all texts. In these circumstances, it is not surprising that one of the main arguments made by policymakers and other protagonists seeking to promote better design is that '... good urban design adds value by increasing the economic viability of development.' (Carmona *et al.* 2001: 8). However, this position is easier to maintain at the general than at the specific level. What matters is whether the quality of a scheme's design will enhance its financial viability to the developer, not whether it will make the wider balance of economic costs and benefits more positive. It is from this more precisely defined perspective that the evidence for a link between design quality and development viability must be assessed.

This evidence falls into two broad levels and types. Taking aggregate quantitative analyses first, hedonic analyses of the determinants of property prices are legion. Many include measures of urban design quality and their price effects. For example, Eppli & Tu (1999a; 1999b) demonstrate that, for the USA, New Urbanist design principles increase the price of single family houses by 10–15 per cent; Vandell & Lane (1989) found that offices rated highly for design achieved rents 22 per cent higher than those of poor design quality; views of, and/or proximity to, parks and stretches of water increase house prices by 6–11 per cent (Luttik 2000); hotel rooms that offer attractive views generate considerably higher income (Lange & Schaeffer 2001); and good landscaping aesthetics have a strong, positive effect on office rents (Laverne & Winson-Geideman 2003).

Such studies are frequently cited in support of the case for higher standards of design (such as in CABE publications). However, as Savills (2003) points out, hedonic analyses are based predominantly on existing rather than newly developed properties. In addition, their main strength – the substantial, general evidence base – is also, with regard to their applicability to the development context, a significant weakness. The variables in hedonic analyses are applied consistently across many varied cases. They must therefore be clearly defined and describe basic measurable characteristics. Consequently, the results of hedonic analyses are simply not refined enough to be related meaningfully to the idiosyncrasies of particular development proposals on individual sites.

It is for these reasons that much attention has been paid to more qualitative, case study research. But this methodology achieves empirical richness at the cost of a restricted evidence base. For example, some of the most quoted studies in the UK are Carmona *et al.* (2001: three pairs of case studies (6)), Savills (2003: four pairs of case studies (8)), Savills (2007: three trinities of case studies (9)) and Amion *et al.* (2007: seven single, outline case studies). In addition, the definition of the value arising from good design is drawn very widely. It includes economic, social and environmental value accruing to a wide range of actors – such as developers, investors, occupiers and the local resident and business communities – over the short, medium and longer term. However, for reasons of market structure, most of these various streams of value are not captured by the developer (Savills 2003). The developer is primarily interested in exchange value – that is, prices or rents/yields achieved on disposal (Macmillan 2006; Amion *et al.* 2007) – and, only secondarily, in the reputational value arising from corporate association with well-designed schemes.

If the relation between design and value arising from a particular aspect of the development is examined in more detail, the picture is even less clear. One of the main ways that '… good urban design can add value to development [is] through using land highly efficiently.' (Roger Evans Associates, 2007: 110); that is, by increasing the density of development. Figure 11.1 describes the argument (Fraser 1993; Evans 2004; Wyatt 2007; Ball *et al.* 2008). For a site of a fixed size, development density is represented by the amount of floor space built on it. At low densities, the marginal cost (MC) of an extra unit of floor space falls. Consider building two storeys instead of one: the cost of the foundations varies little, but the roof covers (almost) twice as much (usable) floor space. However, after a certain point, marginal costs begin and continue to rise because of the need for stronger foundations, more services such as lifts and so on.

Conversely, marginal revenue (MR) declines as development density increases. Occupiers derive less utility from property on the site as local environmental quality dwindles – because of less open space, more noise and pollution and so on – and the accessibility of the upper floors in higher buildings decreases. The optimum development density is X, where MR

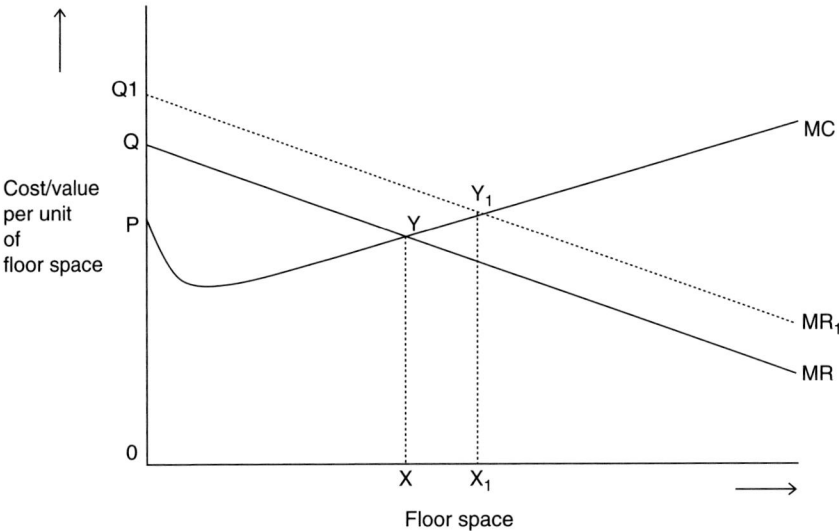

Figure 11.1   Optimum development density of a site. Reproduced by permission of Palgrave Macmillan. *Source:* Fraser (1993), reproduced in Wyatt (2007), Figure 6.2, Page 309.

equals MC, giving a site value of PQY. However, by '... creating value through the appropriate densities (sic), public space, uses and distribution of buildings' (Roger Evans Associates 2007: 110), good urban design can shift the marginal revenue curve upwards (to MR_1), allowing higher density development (to X_1) that is financially viable and increasing the site value to PQ_1Y_1.

Every element of this argument is open to question. Little is known of the positions or slopes of the MC and MR curves, or of the point of inflection of the former. Flanagan & Norman (1978) suggest that the marginal cost starts to increase at six storeys, whereas Picken & Ilozor (2003) suggest that the turning point is at 35 stories. Chau *et al.* (2007) found that for flats with views, marginal revenue *increased* exponentially with an increase in floor level and that the optimal building height was higher for a site with a 'better' external environment. Eppli & Tu (1999a; 1999b) found that house prices were higher in higher density, New Urbanist schemes than in conventional suburban developments, although this was in a very low-density environment. In contrast, Song & Knaap (2003) and Wassmer & Baass (2006) show that residents pay less for houses in denser, more central neighbourhoods.

These circumstances provide a strong justification for undertaking more qualitative, case study research, despite the very limited empirical evidence base that it provides. The reasons are reinforced by the notion that density

Table 11.1 Development and design processes.

The development process (Syms 2002)	The design process (Tunstall 2006)
0. Market appraisal	
1. Project inception	1. Inception (receiving client's brief)
	2. Feasibility (formulating design brief)
2. Site acquisition and assembly	
3. Site assessment	3. Outline proposals
4. Risk analysis	
5. Detailed design	4. Scheme design (for approvals)
6. Feasibility study	
7. Planning approval	
8. Land and development finance	5. Detailed design
	6. Construction information
	7. Measurement (bills of quantity)
9. Tendering	8. Tendering arrangements
	9. Pre-contract planning
10. Construction	10. Construction on site
	11. Completion
	12. Feedback
11. Sales and marketing	

'… is a product of design, not a determinant of it.' (Llewelyn-Davies 2000: 46). Building type and height, block size, the positions of buildings relative to one another and the distribution and quality of open space will all affect perceptions of density. Such perceptions, in turn, affect the demand for and value of development.

The development and design processes

How might the relationship between development viability and design quality – through the medium of development density and site morphology – be optimised? There is very little literature on this point, other than that relating to masterplanning/design coding (for example, DCLG 2006b) which is a second-order design process (George 1997). Recourse must instead be had to practice texts. All those reviewed by Crosby *et al.* (2008) treat the development process, whether implicitly or explicitly, as a sequence of events – as stages in the process of producing a completed, occupied scheme (see Table 11.1). Event-sequence models may vary in their levels of detail and complexity but they are essentially task and project focused (Healey 1991; Gore & Nicholson 1991). Little is said about the motivations and resources of the various actors involved in property development (who are assumed to be rational utility-maximisers) or about the wider environment within which they operate (which is assumed to approximate an imperfect market with some state regulation).

The design process is portrayed in a similar way (see Table 11.1). Being one aspect of the wider development process, it is nested within the latter. The development project and its design are conceived and then continuously developed and refined as more information becomes available. The developer faces a fundamental dilemma in this regard. In the early stages of the development process the room for manoeuvre is considerable because the developer has made limited financial or legal commitments to the project. However, the quantity and quality of information is also limited, severely restricting the reliability and accuracy of any assessments of financial viability or marketability. As the project proceeds better information becomes available but this is at the price of increased 'lock-in'. The developer knows more about the scheme but has less scope to react to that knowledge by withdrawing from or altering it without incurring substantial costs.

For the developer, the key design-related part of the development process is the transition from principles and possibilities to the position where the main physical parameters (development density, site morphology and use) are fixed. That is, the move from project inception, where '... a few simple sketches [are compared with] 'back of an envelope' calculations.' (Syms 2002: 6), to the detailed scheme design and feasibility study. The latter stage will include drawings of sufficient detail to obtain planning permission and a full financial appraisal, incorporating sensitivity and cashflow analyses. However, it is not clear how one progresses from the one position to the other. Most texts refer to a process of constant review so that '... each time the design is refined, viability is reassessed' (Adams 1994: 50). Computer packages are used by developers to assess the financial implications of change (Byrne 1996; Syms 2002; Havard 2008), and by architects to develop designs and to discuss changes with the client (Tunstall 2006). However, there is no significant integration of financial appraisal and CAD software.

All the development texts reviewed by Crosby *et al.* (2008) take a single, fixed design as the starting point of the development appraisal. Sensitivity analysis – the assessment of the impact of specified changes upon project viability – considers market variables (such as rents, yields, prices, interest rates and building costs) but not design change. This is reflected in the structure of development appraisal software. Havard (2008) illustrates the application of industry-leading software to development appraisal. Complex, sophisticated financial analyses are supported. However, the user must enter all the physical and financial details of each part of the subject scheme (Havard 2008: 238–239). These include the use, gross floor space, net/gross ratio, construction costs and rents/yields or selling prices for each building type. Consequently, if the design is changed, most of these input variables – especially those relating to floor space, use and number of floors – have to be altered manually. While this may offer a time-consuming and awkward link between design and finance, no such link is made within CAD software. Tunstall (2006) lists 14 advantages of CAD but none relate to using it to explore the relation between design form and financial structure. Techniques that provide a more effective link between design and finance therefore address an important shortcoming in the current set of analytical tools available to developers, designers and others with an interest in promoting schemes with higher design quality. It is to the development of such techniques that we now turn.

Visualisation and financial appraisal

Visualisation techniques

The physical form of the built and natural environment has long been represented in visualisations. Before the digital era, traditional analogue techniques such as plans, sections, sketches, perspective drawings, photomontages and physical models were used to portray existing environments and proposed changes to them. A key figure in the development of visualisation techniques was the English landscape architect Humphry Repton (1752–1818). In his famous Red Books, produced for most projects that he worked on (stately homes and large estates), he pioneered perspective techniques, by showing the existing situation as well as the proposed changes in the landscape by using a movable flap to unveil the underlying proposal.

Later developments in visualisation include the immensely popular panoramas of the early 19th century, the equivalent of today's IMAX cinemas. In the 20th century, physical models (for example of new housing schemes) became popular in planning and design. They were also used to simulate virtual journeys through urban landscapes (Markelin & Fahle 1979) using microscopic cameras to record on video tape. While scaled models are normally used in practice, on occasion even a 1:1 representation – that is, a real world model – is produced. The degree of abstraction or realism of the latter can range from, for example, a simple pole structure, required in Switzerland to show the volume of a proposed building, to a deceiving realism that can be achieved by full-colour printing on plastic sheets to simulate a whole building with its facades (to depict, for example, the proposed reconstruction of a palace in Berlin that was destroyed during World War II).

Advances in computer technology have supported the development of visualisation techniques for use in the design and planning process. While computing power was limited, approaches such as electronic artistic impressions (Al-Kodmany 1999) and photomontage (Lange 1994) were used. Another common visualisation technique is the production of three-dimensional models that can be rendered as still images or as pre-recorded 'flythrough' or 'walk-through' animations. This technique has no real time dependence. Images and videos can be rendered in a photorealistic style, although this may take many hours to achieve. With speed increases in computers, more sophisticated techniques have been developed which allow for interactive visualisation of three-dimensional models within the design and planning process for landscape (Lange 2001; Bishop 2005), for example to plan the position of wind turbines (Lange & Hehl-Lange 2005). Advances in dedicated 3D processing hardware have made real-time visualisation possible, especially through the use of computer game engines to provide interactive eye-level walkthroughs for 3D visualisations (Herwig & Paar 2002).

However, there are still challenges to overcome to create real-time visualisation tools (Bishop 2005). One is to provide a sufficient level of detail in the visualisation to convince the viewer to accept the visualisation as representative of the modelled area (Lange 2001; Appleton & Lovett 2003). Another is the production cost of creating such visualisations that are tied to the complexity of the model (An 2005; Lange 2001). Geographic information system (GIS) data sets can be used to help in the production of 3D models (Hoinkes & Lange 1995) and the use of this data can speed up the model development time considerably. These challenges were addressed in part of a research project examining sustainable development in urban river corridors.[1]

Developing visualisation techniques and links to financial appraisals

In this research, 3D models of areas of the River Don corridor (and selected tributaries) in and around Sheffield are being developed so that, *inter alia*, proposed physical changes or 'interventions' may be visualised and then used as part of a sustainability assessment process. These models need to be viewable in real time either as eye-level walkthroughs or as birds-eye overviews and to be sufficiently representative of the actual areas and the interventions to allow stakeholders to assess the latter. The visualisation system uses Simmetry 3d software, a design and visualisation solution based on the technologies used in the computer game industry. Simmetry 3d is PC based and can also be connected to the Rave studio, a University of Sheffield virtual reality facility that supports stereoscopic three-dimensional viewing.

Models of the existing areas of Sheffield's river corridors were constructed from various data sets, and the steps in which they were combined were as follows:

(1) A baseline terrain model was created, combining a digital elevation model (OS Land-form profile) and aerial photography (Cities Revealed).
(2) Existing landform features were created from GIS vector data (OS Mastermap) by importing these data into Simmetry 3d and applying its tools to them.

(3) Existing buildings were created from the GIS data (OS Mastermap) and photographic survey data was used to add facade textures.
(4) Interventions were introduced into the existing model either by editing the GIS vector data or by creating new models and importing them into the correct location in the existing model.

The models were linked to a financial appraisal system so that the financial implications of interventions could be assessed. The financial appraisal system already had a clearly defined data interface which required the areas of different land/building use categories to be assigned to it in order for it to compute its results (discussed in more detail in the next section). In order to implement the link it was necessary to identify the requirements of the whole system and the workflow proposed for its use. Investigation revealed that such a system should be able to:

- design a new site-layout to the correct size and scale;
- categorise design elements for financial appraisal;
- view the design in 3D and in real time;
- analyse the design in terms of the areas of its constituent parts and communicate these on to a spreadsheet for financial appraisal;
- easily allow alterations to site layout, building heights and floor space uses so that the financial implications of such design changes may be calculated;
- be compatible with the real-time visualisation system.

Analysis showed that these requirements could be met through the use of a generic 3D CAD system, with the addition of a bespoke 'plug-in' to transfer the data produced by the analysis to the financial appraisal spreadsheet. Plug-ins are small subroutines of software that may be written to work with a larger software application and, as such, can provide tailored functionality to more generic software applications. By adopting this approach, modelling of a site could be done in isolation as a pre-process to the more detailed and labour-intensive visualisation work, providing a useful resource for the creation of more detailed real-time models of the new site within the larger scale visualisation model.

   There are many 3D CAD systems available that could be used in the ways described in this chapter. However, any such system had to be compatible with Simmetry 3d, the system used for the real-time visualisations, in terms of the format of models that could be imported. This restricted the choice of CAD system. SketchUp was identified as the most suitable because it could achieve the requirements already outlined, was perceived to be easy to learn and to use, and was compatible with the visualisation system.

The categorisation of the design elements was achieved through SketchUp's 'layering' system. Layers were added that corresponded to the categories required by the financial appraisal spreadsheet. These categories were: site, hard landscaping, soft landscaping, roads and footpaths, car parking, building floor and use (for example, retail, offices and so on). Practically, this means that each design element – for example, a part of a site or a floor of a building – is assigned to the layer that best describes its use, such as soft landscaping or apartments.

The link between SketchUp and the spreadsheet package required a plug-in to be written that analysed the 3D model based on layer categorisation. This analysis computed the land use area (square metres) of the design according to the pre-defined categories. These layer categories correlated to categories in the targeted spreadsheet that computed the financial implications of the design. The user may run the plug-in whenever a financial appraisal is required. This may occur, for example, when a design has been successfully input and categorised, or when changes to the design or categorisations are made.

Preparation of a design in SketchUp typically involves the following steps:

(1) The creation of a 2D site plan.
(2) The categorisation of areas within the site plan.
(3) The extrusion of 2D building areas into massing models (that require each floor of the building to be included too).
(4) The categorisation of the floor space within the extruded buildings.

Creation of the site plan was most easily and accurately achieved by using (importing) GIS land-use data (OS MasterMap dataset) that covered the whole site and accurately defined the site area. Existing detail within the site could easily be removed and re-modelled using the tools available within SketchUp. As already indicated, models constructed in this way could be imported into a larger scale, more detailed visualisation model for real-time visualisation. This step involved fitting the site model to its actual location within the larger model, and then, if required, increasing the level of detail of the site model; for example, by adding vegetation or through the application of more realistic surface textures. An example of this is shown in Figure 11.2.[2]

The approach adopted for linking the visualisation model and the financial appraisal system has several advantages. First, linking to site design models produced early in the overall visualisation process (in SketchUp), means that experimentation with site layout and land and building use can be undertaken without the need for the more time-consuming detailed visualisation steps. Second, by creating models that are compatible with the real-time visualisation software, site designs can be incorporated easily into the more detailed visualisation model to allow for real-time walkthrough

Figure 11.2 Visualisation of the 'Streets' redevelopment option in Simmetry3d (Urban form designed by Laurence Pattacini).

visualisation. Ongoing research is looking at how the modelling and categorisation can be achieved within the visualisation system. This should provide a faster step from experimentation with site layout and categorisation to real-time walkthrough within the more detailed model. Finally, financial appraisal of the initial designs (produced in SketchUp) is almost instantaneous and informs the selection of those options to be subject to more detailed visualisation. With the development of the faster linkage between Simmetry 3d, SketchUp and the appraisal spreadsheet, similarly speedy analysis of the financial implications of detailed design changes will be possible.

The financial analysis of design changes

The financial analysis of a development proposal and of changes in its design is undertaken on a spreadsheet. The residual valuation technique is adopted, and both profit and land value residuals may be estimated. The developer's profit is derived by assessing the end value of the scheme and then deducting the costs of producing it, including land costs, construction and finance costs and professional fees. The land value is derived by substituting a minimum developer's profit for the land cost and then subtracting the costs associated with land acquisition, such as legal fees.

The structure of the spreadsheet mirrors that of the residual valuation method. There are separate sheets for land costs (based both on development value and on existing use value), construction costs (for site works and build-ings) and the value of the scheme (covering both space for sale and rent, using unit price and rent/yield comparables, respectively, and applying spec-ified net/gross ratios). The gross development value and the land and con-struction costs are then incorporated into an appraisal sheet that estimates the various finance costs and fees before calculating the developer's profit (absolute and proportionate [percentage of total costs]).

The traditional residual approach thus described has many shortcom-ings. The final result is dependent on the estimation of many variables that, because of site idiosyncrasies, requires the extensive exercise of expert judgement. Because of gearing, minor adjustments to key input var-iables can result in large changes to the residual. In order to mitigate these issues, data must be gathered and treated with caution. In addition, the traditional residual is, essentially, a cross-sectional approach. It does not deal with time. This causes some significant problems: finance costs can only be approximated; no indication can be given of the financial position during the development period; and the method cannot deal with phased developments or with changes in variables during development (Isaac 1996; Havard 2008). Finally, the treatment of interest charges as development costs raises the question of how the developer's profit should be interpreted (Crosby *et al.* 2008).

For these reasons, the spreadsheet incorporates a cashflow residual. This allows selection of the unit period and the definition of cashflow patterns for the costs and/or incomes associated with each element of the scheme (site works, [parts of] buildings and fees). Period-by-period, net terminal value and discounted cashflow calculations are performed. The internal rate of return (IRR) and the net present value (NPV) are the measures of return that are generated. There is also a facility for undertaking sensitivity analysis of the input scheme.

However, the novel aspect of the appraisal spreadsheet is its linkage to SketchUp – and, therefore, to Simmetry 3d and the Rave studio – that allows the relation between design quality and development viability to be analysed.[3] The physical dimensions of the design are transferred from SketchUp into the first sheet of the spreadsheet. The gross floor space is calculated for each building or part building by use and each type of site treatment. From this data we generate various summary measures, such as site area (using the defi-nition specified in PPS3 Housing), site coverage (per cent), development den-sity (m^2/ha) and floor area ratio (FAR) or plot ratio. Automated manipulation of this data allows it to be input into the land cost, construction cost and valuation sheets, as appropriate.

Cost and value information is automatically generated through the crea-tion of a VBA script that cross-references the SketchUp assigned site treat-ments and buildings/floors/uses to underlying databases. The latter's contents are determined by data availability and cost and by the research or application context. Currently, for example, unit building costs are derived from the BCIS cost database (Q4, 2009, adjusted for Yorkshire and the Humber) and landscaping costs from SPON, while secondary data on residential and commercial prices, rents and yields has been obtained from the Nationwide Building Society, CB Richard Ellis and IPD. This data has been augmented by analyses of local comparables and consultations with Sheffield City Council, local quantity surveyors and a panel of Sheffield property agents. There is also the potential to use probabilistic modelling to generate ranges of costs and values.

The financial analysis of the design is undertaken in three stages. First, a basic representation of the scheme is developed in SketchUp. This covers built form: building use, massing and positioning and amounts and treatment of open space. Next, SketchUp calculates the areas of the various elements (as described above) and transfers them to the spreadsheet via the plug-in. Then the spreadsheet undertakes the financial appraisal and provides an analysis of the financial structure of the development, including three measures of return (developers profit as a percentage of cost, IRR and NPV) or the development value of the site.

Once it is set up in this way, the financial implications of significant changes to the design can be assessed quickly and easily. Using facilities in SketchUp, building footprints, heights and positions, and open space areas and treatments may be altered. New financial appraisals are generated almost instantaneously. The extent of the design changes that may be analysed is inversely related to the level of detail to which the scheme is rendered in SketchUp. When changes become too substantial to model with the required accuracy, a new representation that incorporates such changes must be developed for financial analysis.

Application of physical-financial modelling

To illustrate the application of physical-financial modelling to the analysis of design quality and development viability, the case of The Wicker/Nursery Street in Sheffield is considered. The area lies immediately to the north of the River Don which here defines the northern edge of the city centre. It was badly affected by the floods of June 2007. Two alternative approaches to redevelopment have been designed by the URSULA project. 'Streets' is a relatively conservative development that proposes building alignments and massing that replicate the existing street pattern and maximise the ameliorative effect of the River Don on the scheme's microclimate (see Figure 11.3, which may be compared with its more detailed representation in Simmetry 3d in Figure 11.2). The financial structure of 'Streets' is presented in Figure 11.5. The height of the column is the gross development value. From

Figure 11.3   Visualization of 'Streets' in SketchUp (Urban form designed by Laurence Pattacini).

this are subtracted the various development costs: construction costs, professional fees, finance costs and land costs. Where, as here, total costs exceed development value, the column extends below the *x*-axis (which crosses the *y*-axis at 0) and a negative developer's profit results.[4] Given the current economic climate, it is not surprising that the scheme is not viable.

'Park' is a more radical scheme that differs substantially from 'Streets' and for which a separate representation was prepared (see Figure 11.4). A significant area of open space is incorporated into the scheme to mitigate the impact of flooding. This involves the demolition of an additional block of existing properties (at the upper-middle-right of the site; see Figures 11.3 and 11.4) as well as a large reduction in site coverage (see, for example, the area covered by the lower right-hand block in Figure 11.3). Consequently, more new floor space is built at much higher densities on some of the developed parts of the site. The financial structure of 'Park' differs markedly from that of 'Streets' for these reasons (see Figure 11.5) and the former is much less viable than the latter.

Once the representation of a scheme has been produced, it is relatively easy to assess the financial implications of design changes. Alterations in building heights, floor-plates and uses undertaken in SketchUp are immediately read off into the spreadsheet to produce a new appraisal. For example, changing the use of one of the tower blocks in 'Park' from offices to apartments increases viability (in the sense that it reduces the loss, see Figure 11.5).

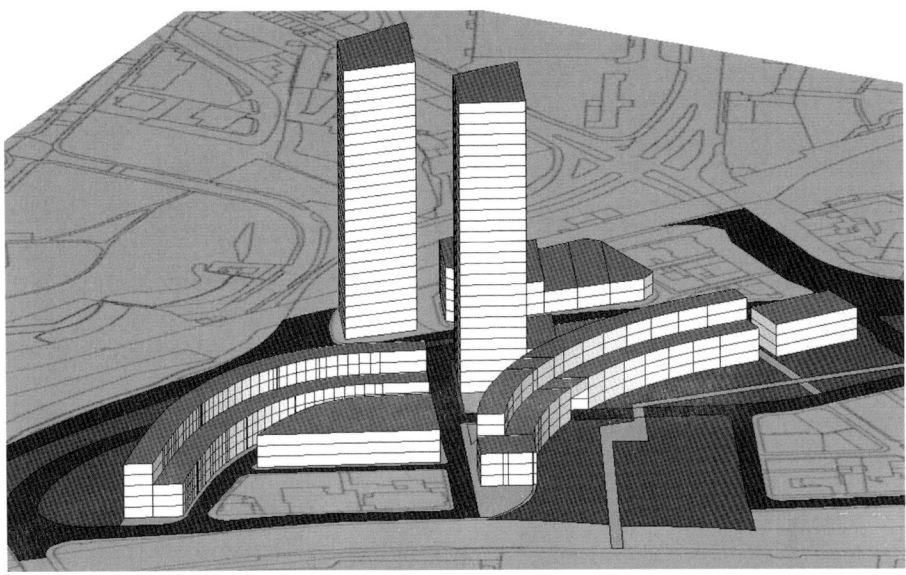

Figure 11.4 Visualisation of 'Park' in SketchUp (Urban form designed by Laurence Pattacini).

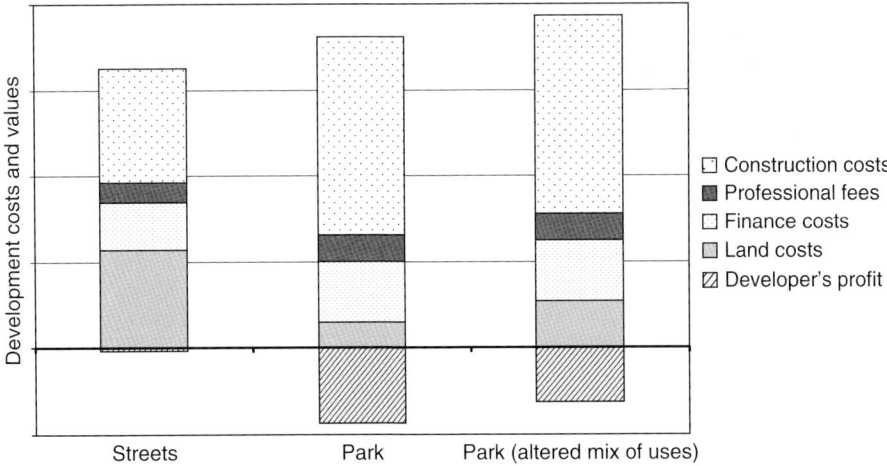

Figure 11.5 Financial structure of redevelopment options.

Conclusion

One of the key decisions that must be made by a developer relates to the strategic approach to the development of a site. This involves the identification of the broad characteristics of the scheme to be pursued, such as land-use mix, development density and built form. These characteristics have a fundamental influence on the project's financial viability, its environmental performance and the chance of it obtaining planning permission. The tools available to developers to explore development strategies are limited. Time and cost constraints often result in a combination of sketch schemes and outline (or even 'back of the envelope') appraisals being used to explore the relation between design and viability. Consequently, relatively few alternatives are considered in relatively little detail. In this chapter we have described the development and application of physical-financial modelling techniques that address this problem and offer the potential substantially to increase developers' capacity to consider alternative approaches to site development.

Clearly, the rapid representation of alternative designs and their corresponding financial structures requires simplification. Design sensitivity and financial specificity suffer as a result. The detailed distribution of land uses – such as retail units – to create active frontages around key spaces and routes may simultaneously enhance social interaction, liveliness and movement and property values. Similarly, design decisions may enhance or exploit positive externalities (for example, by increasing the number of dwellings with a waterfront view) or reduce negative externalities (for example, by reducing the number of dwellings facing onto busy roads), thereby altering property values. The modelling system can take such factors into account through a combination of detailed revisions to the basic imported designs in Simmetry 3d, followed by their return to SketchUp and their appraisal using a spreadsheet edited to incorporate the different values and costs. Currently, this is a time-consuming process but we are working both on faster exchanges between Simmetry 3d and SketchUp and on further developments of the spreadsheet to include more varied, detailed cost and value data in the appraisal.

Quite apart from this, the model also offers a new way to assess the wider relations between development viability and design quality. Methodological choice is not limited to the breadth–depth trade-off between aggregate quantitative and qualitative case study approaches. Modelling techniques allow analytical generalisation. Thus the wider implications of the replication of various sets of site-specific relations may be explored from the bottom up. Different types of development project display different links between design and value. There is not one but a series of optimum development densities, the determination of which depend on sites' characteristics and contexts. Consequently, the impact that good urban design may have on the financial structure of development will be similarly varied.

Acknowledgements

This chapter is based on work undertaken as part of the URSULA project funded by the Engineering and Physical Sciences Research Council (grant number EP/F007388/1). The authors are grateful for EPSRC's support. The views presented in the chapter are those of the authors, and cannot be taken as indicative in any way of the position of URSULA colleagues or partners or of EPSRC. All errors are those of the authors alone.

Notes

1. URSULA, funded by EPSRC (see Acknowledgement for details).
2. In order to allow easier interpretation of the transition from SketchUp to Simmetry3d, the basic representation of the proposed development is presented here.
3. At the time of writing (early March 2010), we are aware of only one other attempt to explore this link: the StrateGis Urban Developer software package (for information, see: http://www.strategis.nl). This is based on SketchUp and provides financial and other analyses of project performance, although it is not linked to more sophisticated visualisation systems. However, we have not yet been able to undertake a detailed technical comparison of the two approaches.
4. Obviously, if development costs are less than development value, then a positive developer's profit would result and that part of the column would sit immediately above the x-axis.

12

Design Champions – Fostering a Place-Making Culture and Capacity

Steve Tiesdell

Introduction

In the UK, the first decade of the 21st century has seen organisations created and individuals appointed to act as express design champions. Examples of the former include the Commission for Architecture and the Built Environment (CABE) (www.cabe.org.uk) in England, and Architecture + Design Scotland (www.ads.org.uk), created out of the former Royal Fine Arts Commissions for England and Scotland, with each becoming express proactive champions of better design, with strong educational and advocacy roles. Examples of the latter include local authorities, public bodies and some private companies appointing individuals as design advisors and champions. According to CABE, in 2006 there were design champions in England and Wales in 65 per cent of local authorities, 78 per cent of primary care trusts, 67 per cent of local education authorities, 83 per cent of police authorities, and a growing number of volume housebuilders – though each of these types of organisations is likely to interpret 'design' differently. Design champions also exist for specific projects. This chapter will focus on local authority design champions, including a specific case study of Edinburgh.

Appointing a design champion is a capacity-building instrument, representing 'investment' in strategic capacity and typically involving organisational culture change (see Schein 1992). Conceptions of the local authority 'design champion' role exist along a spectrum from a more limited role as a

Urban Design in the Real Estate Development Process, First Edition. Edited by Steve Tiesdell and David Adams.
© 2011 Blackwell Publishing Ltd. Published 2011 by Blackwell Publishing Ltd.

Table 12.1 Spectrum of archetypal design champion roles.

	Design advisor	Change agent/design champion
Role	• More limited • Design support – to increase design capacity/skill level, and to provide design support for mainstream development management/control planners	• More expansive • Change agent – to provoke, enable and lead organisational culture change
Focus	• Operational, detail • Engagement with planning as a reactive development control/management activity • Architectural and urban architectural design (first-order design)	• Strategic, broad brush • Engagement with planning as a proactive city-making/place-shaping activity • Urban design and place-making (second-order design)
Timespan	• Continuous – permanent salaried position	• Temporary – time-limited appointment
Activity	• Direct (hands-on) involvement with projects, planning applications, design review, pre-application negotiations, design/development briefs	• Involvement with visions and organisation cultural change at the strategic level
Profile	• Less public, less high profile role • Limited engagement with local media	• More public, more high profile role • Significant engagement with local media

Source: Authors' own analysis.

'design advisor' to a more expansive role as a 'change agent' or 'change leader' (see Table 12.1).[1] The lack of design skills within local planning authorities in the UK has long been a concern for designers, developers and policymakers, with audits of existing skills and training needs of practising planners also highlighting this deficit (Oxford Brookes University 2004; RTPI 2005). Appointing a design advisor (and other design staff) is thus a means to address this skills deficit. In its narrowest form, the design advisor operates within, and adds capacity to, the statutory planning system and is primarily development-control-oriented, supporting 'mainstream' planning officers during pre-application discussions on development projects and thereafter on negotiations and report writing on formal applications. More proactively, the design advisor may also help shape design policies in development plans, development/design briefs and area strategies/frameworks and masterplans.

This chapter focuses on the more ambitious vision of local authority design champions as change agents. This is a strategic and political role, in which the change agent develops a vision of positive change and leads a project to transform an organisation by getting people – politicians, local authority officers, the local design and development communities, amenity groups and the general public – to think differently about place-making; to alter every-day working practices; and ultimately to achieve better outcomes on the ground. Because local authorities have a significant role in the city, cultural change of this nature has the potential to enhance place-making in the city as a whole, not least by establishing the general and specific regulatory/ planning framework for real estate development. Some cities and municipalities do not need this type of design champion because a place-making culture is already well embedded, but in other locations, appointing a design champion is a necessary part of a larger project of organisational and cultural change.[2]

The chapter is in three main parts. The first provides a sketch of the local government context in the UK. The second examines different aspects of the design champion as change agent role. The third locates these issues in the context of the Edinburgh Design Champion Initiative.

The UK local government context

The emergence of local authority design champions must be contextualised by a brief overview of the changing context for local government in the UK. Since the mid-1970s, UK local government has lost significant powers and functions. Sometimes, this has happened through privatisation to the private and voluntary sectors (e.g. in local transport, social housing, etc), even though such services often remain funded and regulated by various central government bodies. More often, however, responsibilities have been transferred to other parts of the public sector, including through reassignment to new central government agencies (e.g. economic development, urban regeneration, further education etc). These changes have been described as a 'hollowing-out' of the local state, leading to reduced powers for elected local politicians. As a result of institutional fragmentation, the number of governmental 'actors' in cities has increased. Such organisational and operational changes have also been accompanied by financial constraints, with authorities increasingly operating in a climate of fiscal austerity and spending restrictions. A reduced proportion of income comes directly from local taxation (i.e. rates/council tax), while business rates, although still collected locally, have been centralised and are reallocated on the basis of need. As a result, local authorities often have an increased need to raise revenue through rents and charges, and especially through asset sales, such as that of development land.

The overall consequence of such changes has been to further constrain, and otherwise hinder, the capacity of local authorities to shape the future of their own cities (Davies 2009: 3), and also to highlight an increasing need for effective local leadership. The dominant model of the 1960s and 1970s – the self-sufficient local authority – has thus been superseded by an 'enabling' or 'community leadership' model (Borraz & John 2004). Alongside the more traditional focus on managing the political group and overseeing service delivery, the role of council leader has been transformed to include a much greater focus on building and maintaining a governing coalition/regime and on keeping private sector and other partners and stakeholders on board (Leach *et al.* 2003). Sweeting (2002: 3) observed that:

Leadership in local government [had become] a more expansive activity, requiring leaders to interact with other stakeholders ... to address matters of concern, whether or not they are directly within the realm of local government's service responsibilities.

This emphasis on leadership has been reinforced by changes in the institutional context. For more than a century the local political system had remained entrenched in a legal framework where parties and the leadership were invisible and informal, but from the late 1990s onwards local authorities in England and Scotland have been encouraged – and indeed required – to embrace new local political management structures. Although a range of options was put forward, including that of directly elected mayors in England, by far the most common was the creation of a leader and cabinet of 'front bench' councillors, with the remainder of councillors assuming a 'backbench' scrutiny role. Significantly, however, as Borraz & John (2004) note, while institutional structures were reformed, no new powers or additional resources were granted.

Some local political leaders have begun to appreciate the role of place-making, and often of design, within the wider city-making project. Into this situation came the emergence of the national urban design agenda (see Punter 2010: 13–21) and the appointment of local authority design champions explicitly tasked with providing design leadership. Design leadership involves cultivating the conditions under which place-making rises up the urban agenda, enabling better outcomes on the ground. Some political leaders, frequently city mayors, are credited with appreciating place quality and providing design leadership – Mayor Pasqual Maragall in Barcelona (see Marshall 2004), Richard Daley in Chicago and John Norquist in Minneapolis being prominent examples. In the UK, Ken Livingstone, former Mayor of London, and councillors such as Daniel Moylan in the London Borough of Kensington and Chelsea are also credited with having made a significant difference to place-making within their cities. There is also evidence of leadership by city hall officials – Manchester's Sir Howard Bernstein, for example, is regarded as showing what a chief executive with the will to lead and drive change can achieve (see Hebbert 2009).[3]

The design champion as change agent

A body of theory and research about change agents/leaders in organisations exists in the management literature. This highlights, for example, how, through 'charismatic' and 'transformational' leadership, visionary figures and 'corporate entrepreneurs' articulate new strategic visions and transform moribund organisations (Caldwell 2003), and it provides a theoretical background for the consideration of design champions as change agents.

The change process

While change agents are seen as key actors who catalyse and lead change projects, change happens over time, and typically involves a sequence of stages. Brenner (undated) suggests six typical stages:

(1) The 'status quo' – the initial state of a system, typically characterised by comfort, familiarity, established power configurations, relationships and routines.
(2) Some form of 'crisis' emerges that challenges or interferes with the system's present operation.
(3) Once this crisis is recognised and accepted, the system is compelled (pushed) or encouraged (pulled) to abandon the status quo.
(4) A transformative effect emerges or happens, which causes or enables people to work out how to operate effectively within the changing system.
(5) People begin interacting with the new reality, but need support and encouragement to sustain the change.
(6) A new status quo is attained as people establish new patterns, relationships and routines.

A common observation is that organisational change is disruptive and organisations do not change smoothly: false starts and backtracking happen as things that seemed 'nailed down' early on come loose later (Brenner undated).

Structure-agency

Change involves a structure-agent dynamic, with change projects seeking to change both institutional structures and procedures and the 'hearts and minds' of key personnel. A chicken-and-egg situation might appear to exist – whether to reform the institutional arrangements to provoke change in the people, or to transform the people and trust that the institutional arrangements will also change. The reality is that these go hand in hand.

This structure-agency dynamic also applies to how design champions operate, since their success and effectiveness depend on a range of factors – their personality and personal skills, the team around them and the organisational structure and culture within which they work. A design champion's effectiveness also reflects the role or task envisaged (i.e. the amount of opportunity space deriving from their institutional status/position – structure) and their perception and understanding of that role (i.e. the amount of opportunity space they appropriate through their personal skills and abilities – agency).[4] The precise array and balance of skills and attributes needed by a design champion is thus deeply situational, since it depends on the organisation and its corporate culture, and also the change project's strategic relevance, acceptability, time frame, available resources etc.

Whether a design champion is an internal or an external appointment affects both what they are expected to do and how they are able to perform their role. The internal design champion might be a politician or an officer, though in many cases it is a politician and an officer working in tandem (see CABE/NLGN 2004). To be effective, design champions must have sufficient seniority within the internal hierarchy, with a 'place at the table' in key decision-making forums. They must be able to bring various departments, organisations and individuals together and, when necessary, 'knock heads together'. The internal officer design champion is typically the head of a design team. Alternatively, however, they may have a less prescribed, more 'roving' role with licence to intervene and contribute on all place-making matters. The internal design champion is salaried and has a position within the line management hierarchy, often reporting to the head of the development/ planning department and sometimes (often more usefully) to the chief executive or council leader. The hierarchical structure might appear to frustrate and often obstruct the design champion's role as a change agent, but, equally, any change that does occur is likely to prove more enduring.

The external design champion is not salaried – though typically receives an honorarium and expenses. Such a design champion must have well-established 'status' to command respect. Their status also enables them to be an 'objective outsider' and a 'critical friend' (of the city as much as the local authority/city council). Being neither salaried nor subject to line management empowers the design champion to 'speak truth to power'. There is also potential power in the threat of a high-profile resignation. Conversely, external design champions are often closely associated with particular politicians and/or a particular administration, and thus often share their rise and fall.

Regardless of whether the position is internal or external, what matters are the powers and resources available, and the broader support for the change initiative. Change and the personification of that change in a change agent/leader can be met with suspicion. To be effective, a design champion needs a support coalition within and outwith the organisation. Without this, the design champion is likely to be a 'voice in the wilderness', supported by some politicians but largely imposed on other politicians, chief officers and rank-and-file officers, and thus less than wholly effective. With a robust support coalition, the design champion becomes the public voice and face of a wider constituency for change. If the support coalition does not already exist, then the design champion has to create it by securing buy-in from the key constituencies.

Resistance to change

Since change projects challenge existing organisational culture and values, such efforts can be expected to encounter opposition and resistance. Change is resisted for many reasons – not only due to the comfort of the familiar and the fear of the unknown, but also because successes and power bases are rooted in the past and present, and are not necessarily expectant of the future (Paton & McCalman 2000: 47). Change is thus threatening to those with a significant stake in the prevailing configuration of organisational power.

   Change not only challenges established ideas and working practices, it also confronts and challenges apathy:

> A great many employees grow apathetic in their approach to working life. Careers falter, positions of apparent security and ease are achieved, competencies are developed, and the employee becomes apathetic to their working environment. ... Change may have the audacity to wake them up from their slumbers! (Paton & McCalman 2000: 48)

Many may not accept, or admit, any need for change on the basis of it 'not being broke, so don't fix it'. Yet, despite '... resistance to the loss of the Old Status Quo' (Brenner undated), addressing that resistance positively may result in better outcomes. Indeed, not all resistance to change is negative, so the challenge is how best to cope with it, anticipating where it will come from and what can be done to turn it to advantage.

Changing people

Change agents may advocate and lead change projects, but ultimately individuals make change happen. Lasting organisational change comes from, and is owned by, the people within the organisation. Change projects must therefore challenge and change what is in people's minds – their ideas about processes, and how they relate to these and to each other. Changing the people might, on occasion, involve easing them out and hiring someone else, but, more realistically, it involves changing their behaviour, attitudes, values etc. Effective change agents thus develop a vision of a changed state that people can believe in and which is beneficial to them. Arguing that a 'vision' is a '... desired future that can work if people can be persuaded that it can and will come true', Hopkins (2001: 38) contends that it operates by challenging and perhaps changing cultural perspectives and mindsets about how the world works and about the likelihood of success. Cultural perspectives or mindsets establish how 'things' are perceived, interpreted and appraised. Mindshifts, by contrast, are '...the process whereby the way one thinks of one's position, function and core ideas is dramatically reassessed and changed.' (Landry 2000: 52)

For design champions, the key mindshifts concern the nature of design – thinking about design as place-making rather than merely as aesthetics – and its instrumental value as a problem-solving process that enlarges the stock of ideas and possibilities. As Landry (2000: 165) argues, design thinking, and its products – drawings, concepts, metaphors etc – give decision makers '... an ideas bank with which to work and out of which innovations can emerge.'[5]

It is also necessary to stimulate the demand for, and receptiveness to, such ideas – they must connect and resonate with the audience. Design champions engage with several distinct audiences. The internal audience consists primarily of the municipality – the politicians and the 'bureaucracy'. The former may start with the planning committee, but, seen more broadly, includes all local politicians. The bureaucracy includes chief officers and rank-and-file staff, and ranges from the narrower planning department or unit to encompass development, regeneration, transport/highways, property and facilities management, and the wider range of local authority duties, roles and functions. External audiences include local and national public agencies active in and around the city; the local design community; the development community; amenity and community groups; the media (especially the local media); and, more generally, the city's population as a whole.

The change agent

So, in the context of urban design, what does the change agent bring to the process of place-making? The specific identity of design champions is critical because they personify and represent the intended change. As a prerequisite, a design champion requires a passion for place-making and a track record of achievement, the latter providing reputational capital. Design champions also need certain personal attributes (leadership, commitment, determination, etc), inter-personal skills, communication skills and a range of 'political' skills – building support and alliances, negotiating and persuading, knowing when to stand and fight and when to leave the field etc. But skills in managing change itself – in understanding how organisations operate and how change projects can be implemented – are equally important. Kanter (1983) identifies a set of core change skills, which can be considered relevant to design champions:

- able to question the past and to challenge existing assumptions and beliefs;
- able to relate to, and switch easily between, operational and strategic levels;

- able to think creatively and to avoid becoming bogged down in the 'how-to';
- able to identify, manipulate and exploit key 'triggers-for-change'.

The issues discussed so far in this chapter can be explored further by grounding them in the experience and outcome of a particular design champion initiative. Accordingly, the next section explores Edinburgh's Design Champion Initiative focusing on five issues: how the change project came about; how it was designed; how the design champion led it; the limits to change; and the success of the project in terms of embedding change.

Edinburgh's design champion initiative

Edinburgh's land form and townscape are its most famous and valuable assets. Blessed with a panoramic setting between the Firth of Forth and the Pentland Hills, and sitting astride several extinct volcanoes, the city centre has been a UNESCO World Heritage Site since 1995. The whole city centre and immediate surroundings, including the medieval Old Town and the Georgian New Town, as well as districts in the suburbs, are a series of conservation areas, protected both by the city council and by a series of powerful and vigilant conservation lobbies. The city is also a major cultural centre – its 3.5 million visitors per year make it the UK's second most popular tourist destination. For much of the early 21st century, the city has had one of the strongest economies of any UK city outside London and it is one of the fastest-growing city regions in Europe, though it performs less well when compared with cities at the European scale (see Docherty & McKiernan 2008).

Initiating change

The context for what became the Design Champion Initiative was the dawning reality that the city's population and economic growth, combined with its newly regained capital city status, needed to be addressed by a new era of city making. Major developments in western Edinburgh (well beyond the World Heritage Site) – including a new corporate headquarters for the Royal Bank of Scotland, a major shopping mall and housing developments at The Gyle, and a new business park (Edinburgh Park) close to the city's airport – collectively dwarfed the New Town in terms of scale, while, to the north, the city's waterfront was emerging as a major development opportunity. The city centre also had large areas of decay, with many significant development proposals emerging.

Yet, the central city, in particular, reflected the sense that the city was resting on its laurels. Combined with a fear of, and opposition to, change, the prevalent attitude was one of 'don't spoil it', a backward-looking view seeking to minimise or disguise change. A vicious spiral had developed because opponents of change were – often rightly – afraid of getting more poor-quality development and thus increasingly opposed to any development. As Farrell (2008: 3) observed, the local authority's planning role had been '… reduced to simple defensiveness (i.e. vigilant development control), encouraged by an active conservation lobby.'

By the early 21st century, there was nascent recognition of the need for a step-change in the city's approach to planning and development, for new thinking and for civic leadership to address the future. A key proponent of change was an energetic new councillor, Trevor Davies. Elected at a by-election in October 2001, and immediately joining the planning committee, Davies (2008: 45) was puzzled why members of the committee often found themselves 'approving developments' that many knew were 'really not good enough'. He diagnosed this as a symptom of a larger problem, whereby short-term exigencies of service provision and of regulation commanded councillors' attention, crowding out proactive city-making.

Preparing for change

Preparing for change often involves creating new operational arrangements and new actors. To provoke and cajole the city – and the various interest groups within it – to 'up their game', Davies initiated an Urban Design Working Group, comprising politicians, planners, architects and others from the public and private sectors. Reporting to the city's Planning Committee in February 2003, it identified two routes for action – first, through civic leadership (articulating a vision and raising awareness) and second, through the planning process (identifying quality and encouraging higher standards) (CEC 2003).

The Group produced 25 recommendations for action, many of which were subsequently implemented. The Design Champion Initiative was thus part of wider changes within the council, including the following:

- *Design personnel and leadership* – the key actions here were Davies becoming planning committee convener in May 2003, the appointment of Sir Terry Farrell as City Design Champion in February 2004, initially for three years, and a new internal City Design Leader (Riccardo Marini) being appointed in April 2004 (becoming a permanent member of the City Council's staff in January 2007).
- *The policy framework* – the key actions here included developing the *Edinburgh Standards for Urban Design* approved as supplementary planning guidance in 2003, which translated design principles from a variety of sources into an Edinburgh context; the first ever city-wide Local Plan,

which included clearer and more specific urban design policies; and the preparation of other supplementary planning guidance in the form of design briefs, conservation area appraisals, and public realm initiatives. These were complemented by a number of capacity building events including a 'City Design Champion Lecture Series', design seminars promoting new urban design standards, and design workshops on waterfront development, tram proposals, the city skyline and other topics.

- *Design within development control and management* – the key actions here included applicants being required to produce design statements for all sites of significance; the appointment of dedicated design officers (either architect-planners or trained urban designers) in the Planning Department to advise and support 'mainstream' development management/control case officers, and an internal Design Forum established to review cases/applications.[6]

These organisational and operational changes signalled the Council's intent, but the larger challenge was to change the mindsets of key actors within the city, especially as the Design Champion Initiative was met with circumspection and suspicion in many quarters. As Davies (2008) records, not everyone wanted to play, particularly 'less-than-good architects', the council's traffic engineers and large-scale housebuilders. A pivotal moment that demonstrated the Council's resolve was the Planning Committee's victory at appeal over its decision to refuse – on design grounds and against officer advice – a volume housebuilder's proposed development at Shrub Place:

> … having a designer around was critical to getting the result we did, providing the intellectual framework to think about the surrounding city, the lives people lived, the way Wimpey's proposal ought to enhance both, but didn't, and the way in which, with ease, it could be done so much better (Davies 2008: 45)[7].

Leading change

Despite a miniscule budget, Davies (2008: 45) considers the Initiative had a 'mammoth asset' – the Design Champion, Sir Terry Farrell: 'For me and for others, with gentle and simple language, Terry sketched out … what design meant and what it could achieve.' For Davies (2008: 45), Farrell's position – 'an insider for the City but an outsider to the Council' – was crucial:

> He has no salary, no one is his line manager and no one other than he can decide what he will say, what advice or warning he will give, and when. It was beautiful, on occasion, to watch senior officials suddenly become more open to a previously resisted point of view if they thought Terry might speak publicly in its favour.[8]

The roles of the Design Champion and the Design Leader were set out in broad terms, leaving scope for interpretation by the appointees. Rather than seeking to improve poor development proposals at the eleventh hour, their aim was to focus on the 'Bigger Picture', to be proactive and to affect decisions upstream. In short, both Farrell and Marini sought to embed a culture of place-making within the local authority and the city as a whole. As Farrell (2008: 3) explains:

> I decided that I would not be involved in development control and would not advise on planning applications or be involved in any individual building issues. Instead, planning in Edinburgh needed a complete change of mindset … [a] shift from planning being driven by reactive development control to proactive and creative city making.[9]

In Marini's (2008: 46) words, 'Let's stop putting lipstick on the monkey!' The analogy is not a precise one, but the sense is that neither the monkey's attractiveness nor its nature is materially improved by lipstick.

Farrell and Marini's first task was educational – conveying their conception of design as more than architectural aesthetics or a simple battle between contemporary and traditional styles. To promote the importance of place-making, a programme of public lectures, symposiums, summits, charettes and workshops was organised, involving politicians, assorted professionals and interested citizens. Although focused on 'engagement' rather than 'consultation' – 'True city making needs enthusiasm, engagement and excitement, not passive response.' (Farrell 2008: 4) – the events were predominantly attended by the already – and the willing-to-be – converted. The unwilling-to-risk-being-converted were largely absent.

As a focus for discussion and action, Marini, along with colleague, Duncan Whatmore, developed the notion of overlapping 'City Tiles'. Substantially based on the proposed tram routes (see below), City Tiles were a reaction to the 'red line' approach of putting hard conceptual boundaries around development sites, and were a means of focusing on the integration of various place-making issues (see Figure 12.1 for an example).

The City Tiles and the output of the workshops were eventually articulated as a set of twelve challenges for the city presented to the City Council in May 2008, exhibited from May to September and published in the June 2008 issue of *Prospect* (see Table 12.2).

Limits to change

During Farrell's term, two 'Big Ticket' projects were happening in the city – the northern waterfront and the tram. These projects serve to illustrate both the potential of, and the limits to, the Design Champion Initiative.

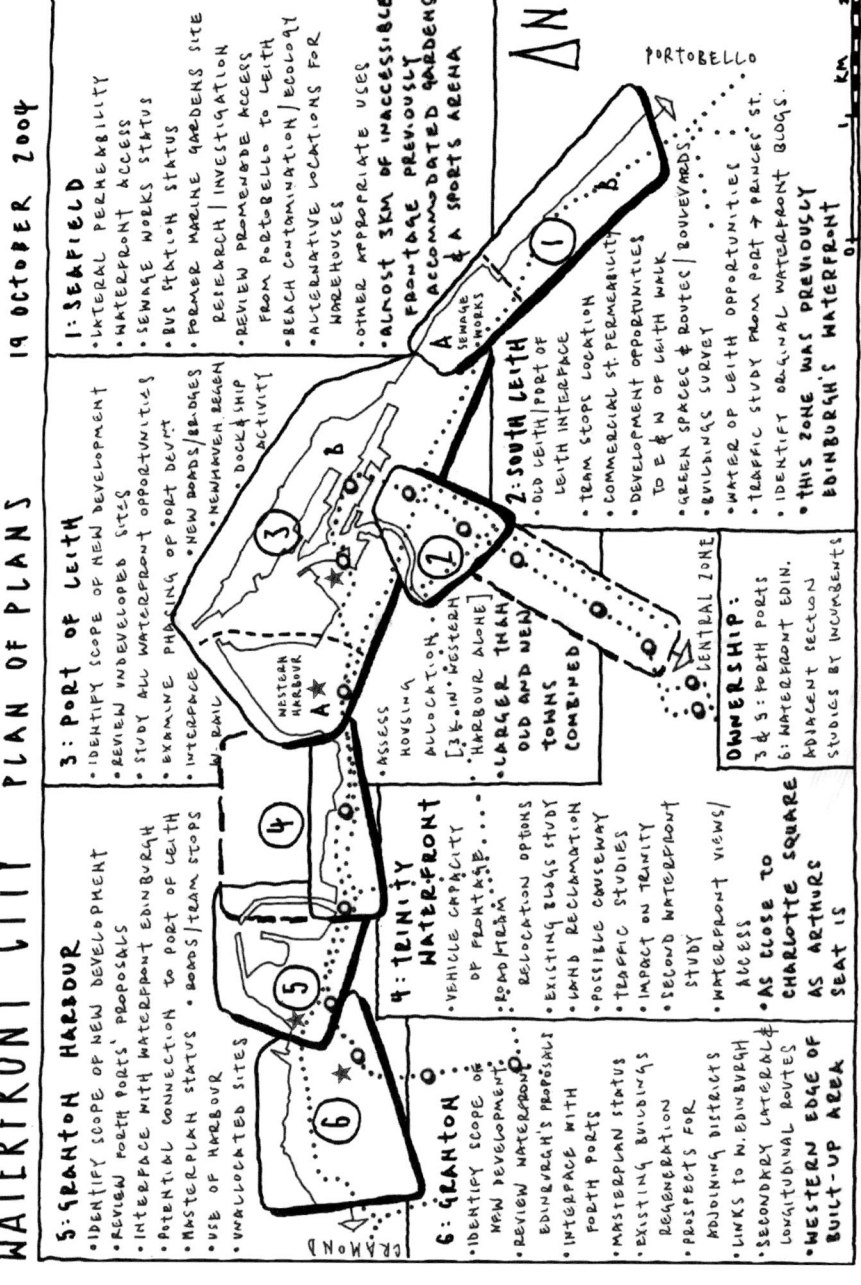

WATERFRONT CITY   PLAN OF PLANS   19 OCTOBER 2004

5: GRANTON HARBOUR
- IDENTIFY SCOPE OF NEW DEVELOPMENT
- REVIEW FORTH PORTS' PROPOSALS
- INTERFACE WITH WATERFRONT EDINBURGH
- POTENTIAL CONNECTION TO PORT OF LEITH
- MASTERPLAN STATUS • ROADS/TRAM STOPS
- USE OF HARBOUR
- UNALLOCATED SITES

3: PORT OF LEITH
- IDENTIFY SCOPE OF NEW DEVELOPMENT
- REVIEW UNDEVELOPED SITES
- STUDY ALL WATERFRONT OPPORTUNITIES
- EXAMINE PHASING OF PORT DEVT
- INTERFACE • NEW ROADS/BRIDGES
- NEWHAVEN BEACH
- DOCK & SHIP ACTIVITY

1: SEAFIELD
- LATERAL PERMEABILITY
- WATERFRONT ACCESS
- SEWAGE WORKS STATUS
- BUS STATION STATUS
- FORMER MARINE GARDENS SITE RESEARCH/INVESTIGATION
- REVIEW PROMENADE ACCESS FROM PORTOBELLO TO LEITH
- BEACH CONTAMINATION/ECOLOGY
- ALTERNATIVE LOCATIONS FOR WAREHOUSES
- OTHER APPROPRIATE USES
- ALMOST 3KM OF INACCESSIBLE FRONTAGE PREVIOUSLY ACCOMMODATED GARDENS & A SPORTS ARENA

PORTOBELLO

2: SOUTH LEITH
- OLD LEITH/PORT OF LEITH INTERFACE
- TRAM STOPS LOCATION
- COMMERCIAL ST PERMEABILITY
- DEVELOPMENT OPPORTUNITIES TO E & N OF LEITH WALK
- GREEN SPACES & ROUTES/BOULEVARDS
- BUILDINGS SURVEY
- WATER OF LEITH OPPORTUNITIES
- TRAFFIC STUDY FROM PORT → PRINCES ST.
- IDENTIFY ORIGINAL WATERFRONT BLDGS.
- THIS ZONE WAS PREVIOUSLY EDINBURGH'S WATERFRONT

CENTRAL ZONE

OWNERSHIP:
3 & 5: FORTH PORTS
6: WATERFRONT EDIN.
ADJACENT SECTION STUDIES BY INCUMBENTS

- ASSESS HOUSING ALLOCATION [36.IN 'WESTERN HARBOUR ALONE]
- LARGER THAN OLD AND NEW TOWNS COMBINED

WESTERN HARBOUR A

△N

0 | 1 Km 2

4: TRINITY WATERFRONT
- VEHICLE CAPACITY OF FRONTAGE....
- ROAD/TRAM.....?
- RELOCATION OPTIONS
- EXISTING BLDGS STUDY
- LAND RECLAMATION
- POSSIBLE CAUSEWAY
- TRAFFIC STUDIES
- IMPACT ON TRINITY
- SECOND WATERFRONT STUDY
- WATERFRONT VIEWS/ ACCESS
- AS CLOSE TO CHARLOTTE SQUARE AS ARTHURS SEAT IS

6: GRANTON
- IDENTIFY SCOPE OF NEW DEVELOPMENT
- REVIEW WATERFRONT EDINBURGH'S PROPOSALS
- INTERFACE WITH FORTH PORTS
- MASTERPLAN STATUS
- EXISTING BUILDINGS
- REGENERATION PROSPECTS FOR ADJOINING DISTRICTS
- LINKS TO N. EDINBURGH
- SECONDARY LATERAL & LONGITUDINAL ROUTES
- WESTERN EDGE OF BUILT-UP AREA

CRAMOND

Figure 12.1 The Waterfront City is divided into six 'city tile elements'. Although some elements such as Leith Docks (tile number three) have had many different masterplans, the aim of the exercise was to create an overall cohesiveness and a single vision – one Waterfront City. Reproduced by permission of the City of Edinburgh Council Design Initiative.

Table 12.2   Edinburgh Design Champion's twelve challenges.

---

1   ***The Waterfront***: A string of separately planned development sites … or Edinburgh's New New Town?

2   ***Princes Street***: Just a shopping street, or much, much more?

3   ***Haymarket:*** A complete new city district is emerging: does the city want this to be 'ad hoc' or proactively planned?

4   ***Picardy Place***: How do you make a roundabout a 'Place' again?

5   ***Waverley***: Why won't the city deliver a committed long-term plan for its key transport hub?

6   ***Lothian Road***: How, through urban redesign, can run-down key city streets become fine places?

7   ***Festival Theatre***: Exemplar private/public proactive urban design initiatives: how do you make them happen?

8   ***Outer Edinburgh***: How do you balance intensifying the core against growth and outward expansion?

9   ***The Tram***: Which is it, a larger transport engineering project or a place-making regenerator?

10   ***Governance***: A radical rethink of the approach to future city-making is needed: where are the resources, tools and new structures?

11   ***A Centre for Urbanism***: All great cities have one – why doesn't the 'European City of the Year'?

12   ***Edinburgh and Glasgow***: Are they inevitably rivals or does their future lie in closer collaboration?

Source: Farrell & Marini (2008).

The waterfront

Located in an arc close to the city centre, enjoying picturesque views of mountains and with little industrial brownfield degradation, Edinburgh's waterfront offered great potential for strategic transformation and became a key focus for demonstrating and implementing the philosophy of design champion leadership.

The northern waterfront had initially been developing through incremental, largely infill development of smaller sites in Leith. Several very large sites then became available in Granton, and a series of independent, privately commissioned masterplan-led developments for major land holdings started to come forward. Significantly, these offered no overarching vision or framework addressing the nature of the overall place being created.

Calling for 'a much higher aspiration', Farrell (2008: 6) argued for a set of 'connected regeneration projects' amounting to a 'new kind of waterfront city', which would equal the impact on the city of the New Town two centuries earlier, and urged all participants to see it '… as a linked project with a spatial framework and strong city leadership at its core.'

In June 2004, a Waterfront City Design Symposium was held, at which, for the first time, a composite map of all the waterfront masterplans/developments was produced. The composite map showed, *inter alia*, that planned roads between two land holdings did not align. The Symposium was followed by three further events designed both to raise awareness and expose critical issues. Further workshops explored the implications of the proposed tram route.

In August 2005, following considerable lobbying by the Design Champion, the City Council set up a Waterfront Development Partnership Board – a significant step in providing a more strategic and responsive to the reality of place-making. Unfortunately, Farrell was not asked to join the board as had been planned and, apart from those created at the early workshops, no over-arching urban framework masterplan for the waterfront emerged in the period of the Design Champion Initiative. One modest victory was a land reservation for a continuous promenade from the Almond to the Esk, along the full length of the waterfront.

The Design Champion Initiative came late to the waterfront, and there were major issues relating to land ownership, including the reluctance of the major landowners (with the exception of the City itself) to coordinate their developments and to focus on place-making rather than simply on development. Despite the positive achievement of wider public debate, the question was whether it was too late. The Initiative thus served to highlight what might have been achieved if the City Council had realised the water-front's potential earlier and had acted to shape its development as a coherent set of places for the wider benefit of the city. In due course, the various land holdings began to be coordinated in terms of cross connections, although not through synchronised phasing of development.

The tram
The second project was the installation of a new tram system (actually a light rail system), which, during the Design Champion's period, received funding and consent from the Scottish Government. For Farrell (2008: 28) the integration of the tram was one '... of the most challenging urban design and planning projects in the city for 100 years or more ...'.

The Initiative again came to the project late, with a fundamental problem being that the tram had been conceived and, as importantly, funded as a 'trans-port' project rather than as a city-making project. Trams have been sensitively integrated into the centres of many historic cities and into the wider life and activity of cities elsewhere in Europe and throughout much of the world. In the UK, however, funding and engineering considerations dominate, with the public realm being something to be addressed later (Farrell 2008). Farrell (2008: 28) was concerned that the sheer enormity of the engineering endeavour involved in creating Edinburgh's new trams would swamp all other matters, arguing that, without an integrated approach to pedestrian movement, what was proposed would '...not solve the core problems of how transport relates to the urban realm.' A further difficulty was that the tram was funded by Transport Scotland rather than by the City Council, but only from kerb-to-kerb (i.e. for the immediate carriageway of the tram and its platforms) rather than from 'façade à façade' (i.e. the wider public realm) as elsewhere in Europe. The City was also unable (or unwilling) to supplement the funding.[10]

The Initiative sought to cultivate a more holistic design approach to the tram routes by holding a series of workshops and charettes. However, because of earlier decisions, key aspects of the tram were effectively faits accomplis. Decisions regarding the size and speed of the trams – 43 m-long trams in two carriages travelling at 30–50 mph – impacted on the tram's physical presence, dictating the nature and size of the platform, the differential level between it and the surrounding pavements, and its general integration into the city. In addition, with no additional limitation on car movement – especially since a proposal for congestion charging had been rejected in a city-wide referendum (see McQuaid & Grieco 2005) – and the pre-existing level of bus availability continuing, the city's streets would have to cope with car, bus and other movements, as well as the tram. The geometry of all intersections was also affected by a decision to have a 'no wheel squeal' radius, which made the corner-turning radius much larger. Furthermore, stops were located for convenience of installation (including only a single stop on Princes Street) rather than being sensitive to pedestrian movement and to the qualities of the historic spaces.

Three tram workshops took place during spring–summer 2006, focusing on four key nodal points – the Haymarket, Rutland Place, Picardy Place and the foot of Leith Walk – and on the 'great streets and squares' – Princes Street, St Andrews Square and Leith Walk – '… the majestic urban backdrop for the tram route.' (Farrell 2008: 28). The workshops appraised the impact of the tram, exploring issues that had not previously been considered – building lines, pedestrian movement and the overall sense and quality of place-making. After much struggle, positive 'city-making' changes occurred at St Andrew Square, Picardy Place and, to a more limited degree, at the foot of Leith Walk.

Farrell (2008: 28) concluded that while the Initiative had been 'tenacious' and had managed to effect some changes '… many of the original decisions could not be altered due to the way the Parliamentary procedures had fixed many parameters and … to the degree of engineering momentum.' The Initiative's engagement with the tram project was thus ultimately reduced to '… trying to stop … the creation of dysfunctional spaces as a result of tram/traffic-management issues.' (Farrell 2008: 28): exemplifying Marini's analogy of putting lipstick on the monkey.[11]

Embedding change

Farrell's tenure at Edinburgh was extended to a fourth year to straddle an election period. With a subsequent change of political administration from Labour to a Liberal Democrat–SNP coalition (and, *inter alia*, Trevor Davies losing his seat), it was extended by a further year but not continued after that. Farrell thus finished as Design Champion in September 2009, and was not replaced in that role. Farrell (2008: 5) himself argued that the Design

Champion role could not *'stand in'* for the 'absence of a proper city making resource in the city', and suggested that if this was established then the role ought to be rethought, possibly as '... a set of sector or mini-champions for big aspirations such as, say, Waterfront City; planning all the city centre; the Haymarket; and re-planning all social housing.'

In retrospect, the Design Champion Initiative in Edinburgh was an ambitious project and its achievements were less significant than had been hoped. There were, however, some tangible achievements and developments. First, a proposal to continue the notion of City Tiles in the form of Area Development Frameworks (ADFs) was agreed by the City Council in early 2010, with the first two frameworks intended for completion by the autumn of that year. These were expected to help generate city visions to inform the subsequent iteration of the City Plan. Second, in May 2010, the City Council's Planning Committee agreed to set up a 'City Planning and Development Board', loosely based on Farrell's notion of a 'City-Making Board', as a mechanism to bring together the City's political leaders and senior officials to put place-making at the heart of the city's governance. Third, an Urban Room, based in the Council's own headquarters, was opened in June 2010 to provide a dedicated and permanent space accommodating up to 40 people for lectures, exhibitions, meetings and discussions about development, architecture and design in Edinburgh. While these three steps suggest that Farrell's legacy continues, more radical thinking will be needed if the scale of his ambitions for the City is ever to be realised. The challenges involved in securing a more deep-seated legacy from his period as Design Champion are now addressed in the conclusions to the chapter.

Conclusion

This chapter has explored the extent to which the appointment of design champions can help build the capacity of public agencies, and especially of local authorities, to achieve higher quality design and so transform the places for which they are responsible. Drawing on structure-agency theory and insights from the management literature, the chapter cast design champions in the role of change agents, while recognising that their capacity to influence and lead that change was deeply situational. In this context, the particular organisational structure and culture within which design champions work must be seen as equally important as their own skills, personality and immediate support team.

What then can be learnt from the Edinburgh experience about the potential effectiveness of design champions? While Sir Terry Farrell's presence in Edinburgh certainly generated a much higher profile for design in debates about the future of the city, the Design Champion Initiative did not achieve all that had been hoped for. To understand why, it is important first to con-sider how far the initiative was embedded within decision-making struc-tures in Edinburgh, second to evaluate the extent of resistance to Farrell's agenda, and finally to reflect on the timescale needed to achieve such an ambitious transformation in civic attitudes towards urban design repre-sented by Farrell's twelve challenges.

Independence versus embeddedness

In Edinburgh, Farrell deliberately positioned himself at a distance from day-to-day design-making and stood somewhat aloof from the political machina-tions of the City Council. He was not asked to participate in the Waterfront Development Partnership Board and his proposals for a City-Making Board did not come to fruition until later. In short, the Edinburgh experience pro-vides evidence of both the strengths and limitations of seeking to build design capacity beyond existing institutional structures in the hope that the driving personality and ambitious agenda of an external appointee will flood through to transform the thinking of those who have lived and struggled with those same issues often for many years.

True enough, Edinburgh's Design Champion Initiative was a well-inten-tioned and highly ambitious project to change both the City Council's design and place-making culture, and more broadly that within the city. Such ambi-tion, however, renders it open to criticism (Fraser 2008; Wilson 2009). The Initiative's actions and endeavours were also easily, but erroneously, associ-ated with, and thus conflated with, those of the City Council itself. The consequence was that the Initiative generally – and Farrell and Marini spe-cifically – unfairly became scapegoats for matters beyond their control. In this context, a statement by a local architect, rejected by those involved in the Design Initiative, is revealing at a number of levels:

> … Glasgow has got it right. Gerry Grams is stitched-into the Planning Department, with a sleeves-up design and 'fixer' role that enables and unblocks development. In contrast, Terry Farrell in Edinburgh has accepted a role with no connection to Planning and no power. It seems naive, but I can only assume that he believed that he would sketch-out his exemplar masterplans and Edinburgh's planners, traffic engineers, site owners, devel-opers and architects would see the greater public good shining out of them and change their plans to suit. As this doesn't happen in the real world the result has been a sort-of displacement activity, absorbing the energy of Edinburgh's creative architects into a game of fantasy-masterplanning while the corporates get on with business-as-usual (Fraser 2008).[12]

This comment suggests Farrell's deliberate independence and highly con-ceptual approach to raising design quality, while initially attractive, could also be seen as having inherent weaknesses. More broadly for those thinking of building capacity through the appointment of a design champion, it highlights the need to balance the advantages of novel thinking and high profile with those of close embeddedness within, or at least connectivity to, existing institutional structures.

Realism about resistance

Design champions are a means to develop strategic capacity. Appointing a design champion is a positive action, but organisational change takes time to become deep rooted. It needs buy-in at the highest levels from chief executives and from chief officers, who themselves may be suspicious of the ambitions design champions articulate. Resistance can also come from people across council bureaucracies who follow their own self-interest or professional culture rather than prioritise the well-being of the city as a whole. As Landry (2000: 40) has observed, bureaucratic mentalities and professional disciplines stifle change: 'In cities, formulaic responses thoughtlessly repeat what has gone before. Issues are approached from narrow perspectives and fail to capture reality. Solutions are driven by manageable financial calculation with no room for insight and potential.'

In Edinburgh, the Design Champion Initiative had limited success in changing the Council's bureaucracy. Reporting and reflecting on his five-year experience as Design Champion, Farrell (2009: 3) admitted to still being 'dumbfounded' by 'the apparent disconnect' between the political will and the bureaucracy charged with running the city, and expressed his frustration at being unable to get more buy-in from the bureaucracy:

> ... the impact I hoped for in terms of 'governance' issues and the expected change to the way that the council runs its affairs has been negligible. It is like making a planet change its course. I use this metaphor as opposed to the usual oil tanker because there seem to be a lack of sentient direction that you would expect in a vessel. It is there as its preordained celestial path which cannot be deviated from. This path is leading to the erosion of the wonderful assets this city has been endowed with by its past assured and proud city fathers.[13]

The battle was not with the whole bureaucracy: the Planning Department, for example, embraced it wholeheartedly and did as much as resources allowed – but the Director of City Development, Chief Executive and other directors were much less supportive. Similarly, while the planning committee was solidly supportive, beyond this it was more difficult to get much enthusiastic political buy-in. The Liberal Democrat–SNP coalition, which took power in 2007, though enthusiastic, lacked the political courage (or imagination) to go against the advice of their officers and appoint a successor to Farrell.

Farrell also expressed his frustration at the parochialism of some interest groups within the city and their failure to consider the bigger picture. Characterising planning in Edinburgh as close to a 'blood sport', he observed both its frequent descent into 'a farcical bun fight over minutia' (Farrell 2009: 2) and how those in the city seemed '... intent on... tribal warfare at a local level, taking pot-shots at each other.' (Farrell 2009: 4). While he had sought to concentrate on the bigger picture, some elements of '... the heritage lobby remained oblivious', being '... too busy navel gazing in a reactive way at the planning applications that are put before them.'

Navel gazing was not universal, however, and some 'heritage lobby' groups did buy into the Design Champion Initiative. One of the Initiative's key achievements was with the Edinburgh World Heritage, who absorbed the idea of place, and accepted the legitimacy of contemporary design in the World Heritage Site, provided that it was respectful and considered. However, although planning specialists on community councils were largely supported of Farrell's ideas, many citizens' groups could not be persuaded to think broadly about place-making issues, which in a sense reflected a failure of the Initiative to communicate its ambition for the City widely enough.

Conversely, Farrell received much more support from the development community than might have been expected. After the Shrub Place decision, developers came on side – not least because they liked Farrell's leadership and his drive for higher quality. There was also a substantial benefit to the City's better architectural practices, who received a higher share of work as quality, place and design rose up the agenda.

The Design Champion Initiative represented a powerful challenge to Edinburgh's well-established practice of limiting design interventions to development control/management decisions intended to make individual projects more beautiful. A more expansive agenda was bound to meet resistance, both within and beyond the Council. Edinburgh's experience would suggest that deliberate breaks with well-understood processes and outcomes require design champions to pay as much attention to the tactics necessary to counter potential resistance as to the articulation of ambitious design strategies.

Ambition, resources and timescale

The scale of ambition implied by Edinburgh's Design Champion Initiative should not be underestimated since it challenged both the outcomes that were, or would otherwise have been, produced at some of the most high-profile locations in the City, and the decision-making processes by which City Council had fallen in the habit of permitting developments which even its own councillors considered below acceptable design standards. Turning round an embedded culture of settling for second or even third best requires sustained commitment and progress over a lengthy timescale. Sir Terry

Farrell's appointment as Edinburgh's Design Champion carried the potential to kick start the process of organisational change but those who expected far-reaching and immediate results from his period in office had probably over-estimated his capacity to act as the agent of change in overturning well-established institutional processes and structures.

The Edinburgh experience thus highlights the need for a better appreciation of the extent to which place-making can effectively be championed by particular individuals, high profile as they might be, and suggests the need to look more closely at the extent to which individuals invited to play the design champion role are embedded within the organisation they serve, irrespective of whether their appointment is deemed external or internal. Well-developed design and place-making skills and cultures, and the resources to enable and support them, are needed across local authorities. High-profile external expertise can reinforce such expertise, but is not a substitute for it. A more realistic view of design champions might thus regard them as important figureheads in the sense that they can provide essential vision and direction to motivate organisational change, while remembering that a figurehead that becomes detached or even semidetached is no longer even a figurehead.

Acting as a change agent in moving place-making up the civic agenda requires effective engagement in challenging and transforming organisational structures and thinking. This is inevitably a much longer process than was possible during Farrell's relatively brief tenure at Edinburgh. In this sense, the scale of ambition that Farrell articulated for Edinburgh's future now needs to be matched by the commitment of the City Council as a whole to reform its entire approach to place-making. It could thus be argued that the true 'Edinburgh project', as far as urban quality is concerned, would involve radically changed mindsets within the Councils' corridors of power (and in the bureaucracies serving those in power) as a prerequisite to achieving radically changed places beyond the Council's offices. Whether Sir Terry Farrell's period as Edinburgh's Design Champion comes eventually to be seen as a provocative but short-term interruption to the normal ways of 'doing design business' in the city or as the forward-thinking pioneer of such long-term organisational change will no doubt become apparent in due course.

Notes

1. 'Advisor' and 'champion' are used here as analytic types and may (or may not) correspond to the job title and functions of actual design champions and design advisors. The framework presented here was developed following discussions with Gerry Grams, Riccardo Marini, Trevor Davies and others. While abstracted from the experiences of Glasgow and Edinburgh, it is not intended to correspond to either city. Glasgow has generally followed the design advisor approach, while Edinburgh has followed the design champion approach.

2. More generally, culture change in planning has been encouraged throughout the UK as a means to better embrace 'spatial planning' and its aspiration to create better places (Audit Commission 2006; Shaw 2006; Shaw & Lord 2007).
3. CABE/NLGN (2004) also highlight inspirational examples of local design leadership for better public places, with Chelmsford (see Chapter 4 of this book) constituting a prominent example.
4. See Chapter 1 for a discussion of the concept of 'opportunity space'.
5. See Matthews & Satsangi (2007) for a discussion of power in the redevelopment of the Edinburgh waterfront.
6. The range and scope of this set of 'new' actions suggest that Edinburgh was starting from a very low base compared to other UK cities. For a review of practices in Edinburgh, see Dawson & Higgins (2009: 107–108). A design review panel was established in 2009 – though this has been interpreted as a sop for not extending Sir Terry's tenure as Design Champion.
7. Reproduced by permission of Carnyx Group Ltd.
8. Reproduced by permission of Carnyx Group Ltd.
9. Reproduced by permission of Carnyx Group Ltd.
10. The city's perceived affluence and prosperity is a problem here as government tends to take money away – so 'city-making' relies less on public investment as such, and more on what could be squeezed from the private sector out of the development process.
11. The tram project in Edinburgh warrants extended discussion in its own right. The technical problems/challenges of cost control and project management, of minimising disruption during implementation and of ensuring the integration of the tram into the public realm of a fine, historic city became entangled with a political battle about who pays for it, and whether it was a 'national' or a 'city' project. Scottish Government funding had been voted through by the opposition parties against the wishes of the minority Scottish Nationalist government. The executive was, however, able to cap its financial contribution, with the effect that the City became responsible for any cost overrun. Stoked further by the national and local media, this has all been played out in front of an audience that is both uncertain of the tram's benefits and highly aware of its various costs. For a flavour of the situation see Hjul (2009) and Wade (2009).
12. Reproduced by permission of Carnyx Group Ltd.
13. Reproduced by permission of Carnyx Group Ltd.

13

Value Creation Through Urban Design

Gary Hack and Lynne B. Sagalyn

Introduction

Urban design is often portrayed as shaping cities through bold visions of the future. In truth, it is largely devoted to the practical task of acquiring public or collective goods through the process of building cities. The individual goods being sought can be quite varied and may include parks, plazas and open spaces, walkable and interesting streets, facilities for arts and culture, waterfront promenades, access to buildings and housing by people of all incomes, and even memorable skylines. The main objective is creating better places by ensuring that individual projects contribute to some larger sense of the city.

Collective benefits typically can only be obtained if sufficient resources are generated by development to pay for them, or if public bodies agree to invest funds – often resources that will be repaid out of future revenues from development projects. One of the central tasks of an urban designer is ensuring that the collective goods being sought are in balance with the resources that flow from the project.

The idea of harnessing the value created by development for public goods has assumed increasing importance over the past several decades as governments have faced declining resources to make direct capital investments or pay for the services that their citizens desire. Devolution of responsibilities to local governments, without corresponding resources,

Urban Design in the Real Estate Development Process, First Edition. Edited by Steve Tiesdell and David Adams.
© 2011 Blackwell Publishing Ltd. Published 2011 by Blackwell Publishing Ltd.

has forced them to look for other ways of funding infrastructure, paying for the ongoing maintenance of parks and acquiring public facilities. Onerous requirements for public procurement and difficulties of getting bonds approved by voters and local councils have also made off-budget acquisition of public goods increasingly desirable (Sagalyn 1990; Nijkamp *et al.* 2002).

There is a long history to the idea that well designed development projects can deliver public amenities while enhancing the economic value of privately held lands. Most London squares were predicated on the realisation that open spaces would make surrounding lands more marketable – and attract the right people. Russell Square was created by the Earls and Dukes of Bedford on the gardens of their estate in 1806, as a way of enticing upper middle class residents to locate on the streets they laid out surrounding it. Across the Atlantic, in 1830, the Boston architect Charles Bullfinch persuaded the Proprietors of Mt Vernon Street that greater value would be obtained by creating Louisburg Square on Beacon Hill as the centrepiece of new town houses, than would be lost in developable property. Even earlier, as new settlements were planned in America, parks and squares were viewed as features creating a special identity for residential districts. Charles Oglethorpe's 1733 plan for Savannah, Georgia, laid out closely spaced squares so that almost every house fronted on an open space, and the area today retains its value. In Philadelphia, William Penn's surveyor, Thomas Holme, platted a gridiron plan in 1690 spanning between the Delaware and Schuylkill Rivers, with four quadrants, each graced by a square at its heart; three centuries later these remain the identity-giving elements of Center City.

The 19th century redevelopment of Paris under Baron Haussmann took a somewhat different tack, demonstrating that not only squares, but grand boulevards lined by ordered facades, sites for cultural institutions, monuments and other adornments of the city can be obtained – and paid for – out of the revenues of well planned development. Bonds financed the acquisition of large swathes of central Paris and the public components of their redevelopment, and these were repaid by the sale of private development sites. Today, tax increment financing projects (TIFs) follow a similar strategy of borrowing against future revenues to construct facilities that will enhance value and provide increased revenues that typically will be directed to repay with the bonds.

The notion that the value of private properties can be enhanced through public goods remains the dominant theme of urban designers. This is a joint endeavour of those working for the public sector, structuring incentives for development, and their counterparts planning private developments. The guiding notion is the search for *reciprocity and mutuality,* where public and private interests intersect.

Design and development projects

It matters whether the development project is being driven by a private, public or public–private entity, since the mechanism of creating value is likely to differ. In the simplest case, a private individual or group owns the land to be developed, without tight prescriptive regulations that determine what and how things may be built. But other sites are owned by public entities, and still others may be held in a mixture of public and private hands, where public resources may be needed to make a project economically feasible. The actors will differ in each of the situations, as will the intersection between economics and public benefits. But the objective remains the same: finding an urban design plan that meets the political test of adequate public benefits while projecting an adequate return on private capital to justify the investment risks.

Private development

Where the site is privately owned, the urban designer will conceive a plan that has a distinct identity, taking advantage of its natural features (water bodies, historic structures, special wooded areas, sensitive lands such as dunes or steep slopes), the traditions of building in the area and the pattern of access to the site (transit or automobiles). Amenities such as parks, open spaces, schools, playgrounds, bicycle trails and gathering places will be sited with an eye to the marketability of the site, adding value to the development parcels that surround them and differentiating the project from others in the marketplace. Public bodies may require that a portion of the site be donated or sold to them at low cost (school sites, for example), while the developer may need to improve other elements (playgrounds or parks) before turning them over to a homes association or public body for long-term maintenance. All of these will be factored into the financial equation for the site: the amount of development will reflect the site acquisition and development costs, the public improvements that the developer decides (or is coerced) to make, and an adequate return on investment.

Rarely, if ever, will the public side be voiceless in the decisions about the site, since some form of public approval is ultimately necessary for most projects, large or small. Public entities may have created urban design plans for the site in advance, setting down the essential attributes they are seeking. But these are typically done with only a general understanding of the financial aspects of development, and often need to be revisited when a real developer arrives on the scene, having committed to a real price for the land. Most often, the final plans are arrived at through negotiation, with the public side pressing for a variety of public goods (not uncommonly embodied in detailed aspects of the design), for a desired mix of uses (or in the case of housing, mix of types and prices) and a development process that ensures that the site is completed expeditiously. Other interested parties, such as neighbourhood and special-interest groups, may bring other 'demands' to the table, such as mitigating traffic impacts, allowing access to facilities on the development site and taking care of surface runoff generated by the development. In turn, the developer may press public bodies for financial and other concessions – greater densities or heights than are normally allowed, in order to offset the cost of the public goods being sought, or tax and other financial concessions to directly offset costs. Brinksmanship is not uncommon, yet both sides generally have an incentive to reach an accommodation that will allow the development to proceed. If public bodies or special interest groups are too aggressive in their demands, the private developer will simply walk away, forfeiting the investment made in the site and the effort expended in the process, while public officials run the risk of alienating growth constituencies and losing taxes and other revenues.

Many American projects exemplify the dynamic of privately led, publicly sanctioned large-scale development projects. At Prudential Center in Boston, the owner of the 26-acre site (Prudential Insurance Company) wished to improve a long-dysfunctional 1960s project that included a hotel, the city's tallest office building, several residential towers and retail space. Large windswept open spaces dominated the site. To capitalise on the site's true locational value, the owners sought to change the site's image by adding at least one major office building, higher-value shopping and additional housing. Located on the seam between three city neighbourhoods, at least 19 organised interest groups (neighbourhood and business associations, the architectural society and tenants of the housing on the site) insisted on weighing in on the redevelopment plan and managed to stop Prudential's initial scheme, which they considered far too dense. The city government effectively controlled the development through its zoning and prior development agreements but its interests were conflicting: it wished to satisfy the neighbours but also wanted to harvest the additional tax revenues that the redevelopment project would generate for city coffers.

To reach an agreement, the developer and its urban designers created a participatory planning process that ultimately convened over 200 meetings where each element of the plan was discussed and debated, alternatives were considered and consensus was slowly but surely built. The dialogue was detailed. It began with determining the appropriate scale of buildings facing the surrounding streets, then moved on to the amount of retail spaces and proportion that would serve community needs, the amount of parking to be accommodated and traffic impacts, the character of pedestrian routes through the site, the open space and the full range of public benefits that would make the plan acceptable. Each step along the way, the financial pro

Figure 13.1   Prudential Center, Boston. The new office tower and housing were scaled to fit their surroundings, and adjacent neighbourhoods received large economic benefits from the project. *Source:* Gary Hack.

forma of the project was adjusted to reflect the decisions made, so the developer and designers knew how expansive they could be in their promises to the city and interest groups. Ultimately, the process produced a formula for reciprocity: interest groups endorsed and the city government approved a development with 3.6 million additional sq ft of shopping, office, hotel and entertainment spaces, centred on a network of generous arcades, and street-level commercial spaces connecting with surrounding neighbourhoods (see Figure 13.1).

The public benefits from Prudential Center were considerable. The package included a new supermarket (with subsidised rent) to serve the surrounding neighbourhoods, street improvements as far away as one mile (to smooth traffic flows), new transit station connections (to encourage ridership), subsidised transit passes for all who live and work on the site (to discourage auto usage), payments into a fund for affordable housing (to offset any rise in prices due to gentrification effects), childcare centres for employees and neighbours, job training funds, open spaces available to the neighbouring public and 24-hour-accessible arcades to allow easy passage through the site, among others. The cost of these off-site benefits added up to about $30 million. Ten years later, the redevelopment project is complete. Prudential Center has become the new centrepiece of the Back Bay, and its pedestrian arcades are packed with pedestrians strolling and shopping.

Because the scale of development at the edges of the site took its cues from surrounding streets, it now merges seamlessly with the bordering neighbourhoods, greatly enhancing the fabric of the city. After the completion of about half of the allowable development, Prudential sold its interests in the site, including the development entitlements, for a gain of over $1 billion (Hack 1994).

Each project has its own unique story, but those that get built share the common themes: engaging interest groups in the design of the site, finding an agreeable combination of public goods and private gains, and seizing an opportunity for agreement when all parties believe they must move forward – often in the midst of a recession when development is seen as benefitting all. This was the case for Riverside South in Manhattan, Canary Wharf in London, Atlanta's Atlantic Station project and Mission Bay in San Francisco. Public agencies may smooth the process by setting down urban design guidelines for large sites in advance, but inevitably these need to be open to negotiation as a developer with capital and real tenants arrives on the scene, and as those impacted by the development make their wishes known. Urban designers working for private developers drive the process, but they also need to find solutions that create reciprocity as they work through their design approach.

Public development

Where projects are publicly initiated, a different dynamic prevails. If a site is in public ownership, a definitive urban design plan may be created by or for a public entity. Alternatively, the public land owner may formally call for planning and financial proposals from private parties who are willing to serve as master developers. Under either arrangement, the public body will have considerable control over the use, density and form of private uses, enforced through the disposition process (land sales or leaseholds), which usually mandates some form of design review of proposed structures. Public ownership does not obviate the need to keep an eye on the balance of revenues and costs for public goods since the project needs to be attractive to developers and the private individuals who will buy or lease the completed space.

Public bodies face a range of choices about how much responsibility they assume in bringing added value to a site. At one end of the spectrum, they may create the plan for a site's development, adopt detailed building design guidelines, install all common infrastructure and create open spaces, then sell or lease parcels to developers who agree to follow the rules they set down in disposition documents. This was the process followed at Battery Park City (BPC) in New York, a 92-acre site in lower Manhattan, developed by the Battery Park City Authority from 1970 through 2010. It has planned

Figure 13.2   Battery Park City, New York. Innovative public spaces and infrastructure were installed by the public development corporation in advance of development, setting the tone for the development. *Source:* Gary Hack.

and built exemplary public spaces, commissioned public art, installed streets and infrastructure and promoted the site, commonly referenced as 'the beach' during the early years when it was all sand dredged from the bay, as a family-friendly place to live and work (see Figure 13.2). With the public components in place in advance of development, developers are able to market their space and units within a complete environment, building on the enhanced value of development sites created by the public entity.

To finance the infrastructure for this new city neighbourhood, capital was raised through tax-exempt bonds collateralised by the future stream of land lease revenues. Battery Park City, like many public entities in the USA, has the added advantage of being exempt from local property taxation, negotiating instead 'payments in lieu of taxes' (known as PILOTs), which further enhanced the resources that could be used for constructing high-quality public amenities and creating affordable housing. The string of open spaces along the waterfront of BPC serves residents of adjacent areas as well as the 9000 new residents and 40,000 people working there. The project has created three new elementary and middle schools, a dynamic new home for New York's highest-achieving public high school, and facilities for three new museums. This bundle of public goods and the many awards that the project has garnered is a testimony to the success of the urban design and development prowess of the authority (Gordon 1997).

Figure 13.3 Main Street, Hammarby-Sjostad, Sweden. Light rail systems and infrastructure provided by Stockholm City Government and other public agencies prior to private development established the quality of life for the neighbourhood. *Source:* Gary Hack.

Public development projects such as BPC are common in European cities, particularly Scandinavia, where there are long traditions of leasehold development on public land and where local governments have cultivated the skill and capacity to carry out complex infrastructure projects and oversee multi-phased developments. At Hammarby-Sjostad in Stockholm, in a 250-ha former shipyard and industrial zone, a detailed urban design guided the transition to a mixed-use residential neighbourhood, beginning in 1990. The Tvarbanan light rail line was extended to the site in advance of most development (see Figure 13.3), and an innovative system of advanced and ecologically attuned infrastructure was installed to support the development. The area has a district heating system, fuelled in part by wastes, a vacuum garbage collection system, solar energy installations, overland storm drainage where runoff is reused for irrigation and purified before reaching the sea. A host of smaller innovations advance the state of the art of sustainable community building. The goal was to reduce carbon emissions by 50 per cent; and although this has not entirely been met, the site is a model for closed-circuit ecological systems. The achievements of the Hammarby site reflect the work of more than 30 private developers, each designing, constructing and marketing their own units or space within the envelopes prescribed in the urban design plan.

In publicly initiated developments, the tendency is to invest in higher-quality infrastructure or greater public benefits, limited only by project revenues. Off-budget accounting and mixing of resources from several sources often obfuscates the issue of whether the public entity has been adequately compensated for its land ownership or risk. This is more than just an accounting problem; it is difficult to benchmark projects since most are unique ventures on unique sites and without obvious precedents. A careful study of the redevelopment of the Faneuil Hall-Quincy Market area in Boston estimated that the inflation-adjusted return to the public was about 6 per cent, taking account of direct investments and foregone property taxes (Sagalyn 1989). Knowing this, the more difficult question is what is a reasonable return to the public, particularly for large-risk, pioneering projects aimed at transforming a district while making development feasible for private investment?

One way of offloading some of the public risks and providing greater financial accountability is to lease a site to a master developer who assumes the cost and financial risks of planning and installing common facilities and infrastructure, as well as normal development and marketing risks. The lease amounts directly reflect the value created by public actions in assembling, planning and approving the entitlements for a site. An example of this is the disposition of the four key development sites in New York's Times Square–42nd Street Redevelopment Project. In exchange for obtaining the development rights to the sites, the developer (Prudential Insurance Company and Park Tower Realty) provided a cash payment to the 42nd Street Development Project which covered the costs of acquiring several of the street's mid-block historic theatres, obligated itself to take the financial risk of rising land acquisition costs through eminent domain, and agreed to contribute to the costs of reconstructing the major subway interchange at the nexus of the project. Shifting these financial risks to the developer made the project possible at a time of great fiscal severity for the city. Reciprocity in this case meant insulating public bodies from the uncertain financial and political risks of land acquisition and complex infrastructure improvements (Sagalyn 2001).

Public–private development

In complex urban development projects, public and private interests are often so entwined that it is difficult to parcel risks and returns neatly. A true joint venture may be necessary to accomplish what is desired. Urban design in such a situation needs to be done collaboratively to ensure that both private and public imperatives are met, and the powers and resources of several public and private entities may need to be pooled to accomplish the task. The public–private relationship can take a variety of forms: turnkey projects

Figure 13.4 Montage Development, Beverly Hills, California. Public-private development allowed sites to be combined, and a layered mixed use development to be created. *Source:* Athens Group.

where the city contracts to have specific facilities built for public use as part of a larger project, and pays for them; projects where the public entity takes the lead in building public components then passes the project off to private developers; joint ventures where a new public–private entity is created to build and maintain the project; and joint-stock corporations where interests are pooled and outside investors join in to carry out the project. Even the simplest of these arrangements requires skill on both the public and private side, and a great deal of goodwill and patience in working through the risks and rewards.

There are many examples of successful public–private projects in California. A particularly notable one is in Beverly Hills, where the city's parking authority owned six parcels of land on a block at the intersection of the city's most fashionable streets (Canon and Beverly Drives and Wilshire Boulevard), alongside eight parcels that were owned by a private developer. There were great advantages to developing these sites in a coordinated manner. The city conceived of a project that involved aggregating the public and private lands and creating a mixed-use development with a luxury hotel, condominiums, a health spa and high-end retail uses (see Figure 13.4). To make the development palatable, it also included a 1100-space parking garage open to the public, and a large public open space as the focal point for the larger surrounding district. Thus there was reciprocity, which would ultimately be tested in a referendum forced by opponents of the project: the city benefited through tax revenues, realising the value of its sites, and a fine new open space; the landowner gained value from a larger site in a choice location, with the synergy of mixing uses; and the broad public gained through access to parking and an enhanced public realm. The city enabled the project by rezoning the site, greatly increasing its value and by closing the alleyway that bisected the site, allowing it to be developed as a single parcel. The private developer, the Athens Group, brought to the table the capital needed, as well as the skills of planning, designing, managing construction, marketing and managing the project. It took the lead in creating both the public and private elements of the project, with the city retaining the right of approving their design. On completion, the below-grade parking (along with its property rights) and the public garden were transferred back to the city. The Montage Hotel is the city's finest, and the project has been quite profitable for the developer.

A far more complex public–private project, the 87-acre Yerba Buena Center in San Francisco, shows just how large the benefits can be in joint development. In contrast with the previous example, this project was led by a public entity, the San Francisco Redevelopment Authority. Its origins were in the much-criticised 1960s urban renewal project at the edge of the downtown area, which displaced thousands of people and businesses and languished for many years without clear ideas about its reuse. The centrepiece of the project is now a massive convention centre (the Moscone Center), largely below ground so that its roof can provide open space for the Yerba Buena Gardens and sites for several facilities and events. The centre created an immediate demand for hotels and visitor attractions, which the project's planners anticipated by providing several additional sites for office, retail, commercial entertainment and cultural uses. San Francisco's severe restraints on development elsewhere made these sites highly attractive (Sagalyn 1997).

The genius in the Yerba Buena plan was in harvesting the value created by the sites to acquire a collection of cultural and recreational resources serving a wide cross-section of the city's residents, including a large passive park, rimmed by cafes and places to lounge, a museum of modern art, a second museum for experimental visual projects, a performance centre, a children's centre and carousel, an interactive playground, an indoor skating rink and bowling centre, a technology centre for children and youth and a modern Jewish Museum – all paid for in whole or part by proceeds from the private development. Three hotels now stand in the ring surrounding the cultural facilities, along with several housing complexes – for a range of incomes, from luxury to single room occupancy (SROs) – offices, retail shops and a commercial entertainment complex (see Figure 13.5). It is unlikely that this rich array of cultural facilities, and the quality of the open spaces, could have

Figure 13.5   Yerba Buena Center, San Francisco. The site value from private development was harvested to create a collection of cultural facilities and open spaces at the heart of the site. *Source:* Gary Hack.

been created without the direct allocation of resources from the commercial development sites and the persistence of a skilled public agency. To be sure, other resources were required, and each institution is faced with having to provide for ongoing programming and maintenance. Had the project revenues flowed instead to the city's general fund, there undoubtedly would have been many other claims on the resources, and it is unlikely that they would have been devoted to the attractions that make Yerba Buena a success.

Each public project needs to create its own logic for using public goods to stimulate private actions and for tapping the private revenues to achieve them. In the Netherlands, public–private projects have involved pooling of public and private lands for commercial development (as in the Beurspassage project in Central Rotterdam), joint brownfield cleanup and redevelopment projects (as at Eemskwartier in Amersfoort) and rail- or transit-oriented joint development projects (as at Amsterdam Zuidas). In most cases, funding was blended from a variety of sources (public investments, pension funds, private investments) and urban design plans had to meet the test of providing a reasonable return on funds invested (Nijkamp *et al.* 2002). In Japan, privatised railway companies such as JR East have undertaken ambitious station area developments, cooperating with national governments (who own the underlying lands) and local prefectures. At Kyoto Station, the result has been a remarkable public realm within and adjacent to the station.

Perhaps the most ambitious public–private project to date is the reconstruction of central Beirut, undertaken by Solidaire, a unique joint-stock corporation that acts with many of the powers of a governmental entity. Created by the late prime minister, Rafic Harari, when Beirut was in total ruins, Solidaire assembled all the rights for the land (public and private, ownership and leases) apportioning shares in the corporation proportional to their value. A second class of shares was offered for public subscription, to provide resources for reconstructing infrastructure and carrying out the development. This system of rights pooling allowed a new urban design plan to be prepared for the collective reconstruction of the area and to be carried out, providing a public realm far superior to Beirut's pre-war city centre. Private development is taking place within the design framework of the plan, and is carefully controlled, while Solidaire has effectively put in place a well designed network of streets, parks, waterfront promenades and marinas, markets and other public places, repaying the costs from the proceeds of land value sales and leases.

Strategies for enhancing value

We have seen a variety of projects predicated on the idea that well designed urban projects can create the resources for public goods that help to make them a success. Many of the ideas about value creation have long been incorporated into the urban designer's toolkit, and public policies have been designed to create the incentives necessary to induce developers to deliver public goods (see Chapter 1). It seems like second nature to assume that public spaces and amenities will yield returns to developers, but the field is curiously lacking in direct evidence about how much is contributed by various moves. The difficulty lies in making head-to-head comparisons of unique situations with widely varying attributes. Nonetheless, from project experience and research studies, a picture is beginning to emerge from at least six strategies about the dimensions of value creation.

Urban design

Urban design plans that offer policy stability can enhance the value of sites. Uncertainty forces developers to discount site value to reflect the risk of reaching an agreement with local authorities. A lengthy approvals process can affect the timing of development and can cause developers to miss favourable periods on the economic cycle, increasing the costs of holding sites. The prospect that future development might block views or access

Figure 13.6 Coal Harbor residential area, Vancouver. Design guidelines require the bases of all high-rise residential buildings in the downtown to be either ground oriented housing (shown) or commercial spaces, to ensure there is activity on the street. *Source:* Gary Hack.

to a site, or take away market advantage by flooding the market with competitive uses will also be reflected in what developers are willing to pay for a site. They dislike uncertainty even more than costs that are substantial but certain.

Cities can insist upon projects meeting onerous urban design standards, provided these are clear in advance, the market is robust enough to accept what is being sought and enough development is permitted on a site to make the economic equation feasible. In Vancouver, Canada, where strong urban design guidelines have been in place for nearly 15 years, downtown housing developments must place all parking below ground, street faces must be lined with housing or commercial spaces (see Figure 13.6), developers must contribute 2.75 acres of public open space per 1000 residents (or pay for its creation elsewhere), and tall residential towers can be no more than 90 ft wide in their widest dimension (diagonally) and must be spaced to allow views to distant mountains. The costs of meeting these design requirements are factored into the value that developers pay for land. Since these requirements are applied consistently on all sites, developers benefit from the public goods created – interesting and lively streets, views to the surrounding mountains from every tall building, generous open space and plenty of sunlight at street

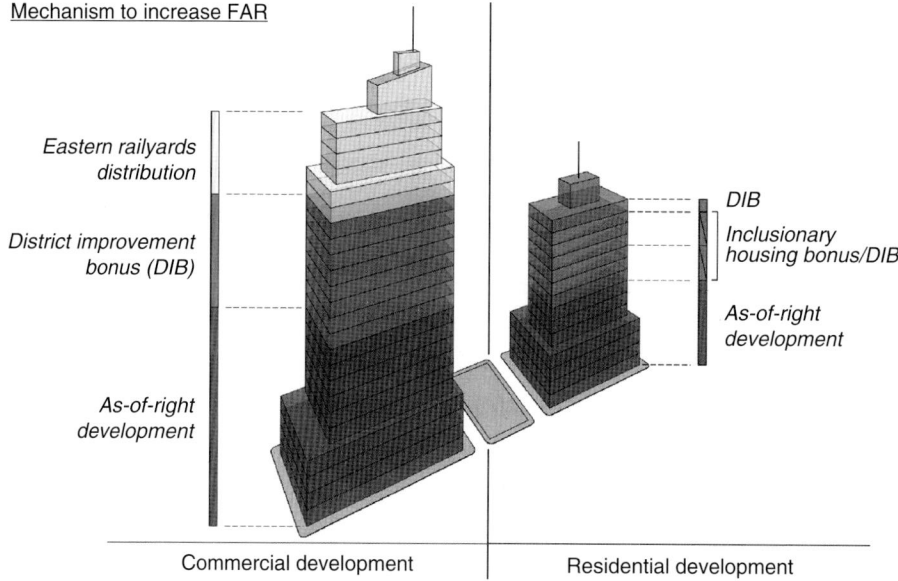

Mechanism to increase FAR

Eastern railyards
distribution

District improvement
bonus (DIB)

As-of-right
development

DIB

Inclusionary
housing bonus/DIB

As-of-right
development

Commercial development   Residential development

Figure 13.7   Hudson Yards incentive zoning, New York. Densities in this planned development area may be more than doubled by making contributions to a district improvement fund, including affordable housing, or transferring development rights from areas designated for parks or lower density. *Source:* New York Department of City Planning.

level. The requirements may be more demanding than in other cities, but values of residential property in downtown Vancouver are very high, at least in part because of the high level of design controls.

Density

Increasing the amount of building allowed on a site is the surest way to create value that can be tapped to offset the cost of public goods. In New York City, and many other American cities, incentive zoning offers the opportunity to increase the allowable floor area ratio (FAR) in exchange for specific public purposes – improving a subway station, creating a public open space, incorporating affordable housing, preserving a historic structure, preserving or creating a legitimate theatre or other cultural venue, among others. In the best of such schemes, the amount of additional development allowed takes account of the costs of the public goods and provides an additional incentive for the developer to elect the bonus (Kayden 1978).

Zoning recently passed for the Hudson Yards District of midtown Manhattan introduced a sophisticated system of incentives aimed at accomplishing the urban design plan adopted by the city (see Figure 13.7). On the most intense sites, developers can increase their allowable FAR from the base level of 10 to as much as 33 by purchasing additional development rights (a 'District Improvement Bonus') at $113 per sq ft of additional buildable space – funds that go directly into the creation of open spaces, a grand boulevard, infrastructure and transit facilities in the area – and by purchasing and transferring development rights from other parts of the area that are by design scheduled for lower-density development. Bonuses are also offered for inclusionary housing, and developers may also transfer rights from other lower-density areas to increase their development from a base FAR of 6.5 to as much as 12. Through this system of transfers and purchases of development rights, the built form, infrastructure and amenities needed to make Hudson Yards a viable and lively district of the city will largely be self-financed.

Using density as the instrument to create funds for public goods may be more limited in districts smaller than Hudson Yards and density-based incentives are only relevant in places where development rules significantly constrain development. Where conditions are favourable, development rights may be augmented through a statutory system (such as zoning in New York), through an official planning review process (as in the UK) or a discretionary review process (as in Boston).

Building heights and views

Even if the intensity of development is strictly regulated, allowing buildings to be taller can have a powerful impact on the value of a site. Our review of office leasing prices in US cities suggests that values increase in direct proportion to heights, above the average heights of adjacent structures that block views. In midtown New York, a rule-of-thumb is that office rents rise $.50 per sq ft per floor, increasing from about $45 at the base of a 60-story building to $75 at the top, an increment of 68 per cent. Iconic views can command even greater rents: a view of Central Park can push rents to $100, a 122 per cent increment. In other American cities, height similarly increases office value: 20–45 per cent in Chicago, 20–50 per cent in Boston: 20–30 per cent in San Francisco – in all cases, the value gain depends upon the type of views and the height of surrounding buildings.

The experience in other countries is similar, and applies to housing as well as offices. In Hong Kong, the sales value of residential units with distant views was found to be only 3 per cent higher than units with no views, but units facing mountains directly behind the development were discounted by 6 per cent (Jim & Chen 2009). In the Netherlands, a house with scenic views of water could attract a price 10–12 per cent above those without (Luttik 2000). In the old town of Guangzhou, China, houses with a river view were priced 6 per cent higher than those without. And in Bellingham, Washington, single-family houses with full ocean view were priced almost 60 per cent higher than comparable houses without the view (Benson *et al.* 1998).

Many cities have established view corridors to maintain important prospects, or limit the heights of development along water edges so that views from more distant properties are not blocked. In Vancouver, 27 view cones have been established by the local government, mainly to preserve views to distant mountains from roads leading to the downtown peninsula. Although based on the flimsiest of surveys of what residents value (only 3 per cent of those surveyed identified these views as important) the corridors impact development in the downtown area in important ways. By one analysis, there are only three sites available between the view cones where very tall buildings may be built (Henriquez 2009). The rules have forced the city into case-by-case negotiations over heights on other development sites, bending its rules to allow taller buildings when other important public purposes are achieved.

Open spaces

There is plenty of both anecdotal and empirical evidence on the value of open spaces as an amenity. Housing in the blocks facing Central Park in New York commands a significantly higher value than that even one block distant – perhaps 10–20 per cent more. Units facing the park typically are valued at least 20 per cent more than units in the same building without park views. Researchers abroad found that in Turkey, the price of a house was increased by 20–33 per cent by the presence of 7–14 m^2 of green space per capita on a housing site (Altunkasa & Uslu, 2004), a figure comparable to what many cities call for in their regulations. Finnish studies pegged the incremental value lower, with apartments adjacent to open spaces selling for about 7 per cent more than units 500 m away, although this may reflect the generous amount of open space surrounding the city studied (Tyrvainen 1997; Tyrvainen & Miettinen 2000). Where the adjacent open space is a golf course, a California study found that it added 7.6 per cent to property values on average (Do & Grudnitski 1995). Earlier studies of the value of undeveloped land in Philadelphia and Boulder, Colorado, suggested that its value could be as much as 10 times higher if adjacent to an open space with a stream, and that values decline with every foot away from the amenity (Correll *et al.* 1978).

Even small open spaces can make a very large difference. We have noted the increased value of houses surrounding Louisburg Square in Boston, roughly an acre in size, which persists almost two centuries after they were built. Houses that face the park sell for as much as 60 per cent more per sq ft than the average on Beacon Hill. At Battery Park City, in New York, fingers of open space such as Rector Park and Teardrop Park, which connect to the more extensive waterfront esplanade, allow units to be marketed 'facing the park' rather than streets. Substantial boulevards, such as Commonwealth Avenue in Boston or Park Avenue in New York confer the same advantages.

Figure 13.8 Woodwards Development, Vancouver. A complex mixed use development was made possible in part by allowing greater heights and densities than are normally permitted. Reproduced by permission of Henriquez Partners Architects.

Mixed uses

In theory, allowing or encouraging mixed uses is favourable to developers, offering flexibility in what they build and allowing them to spread their risks across several markets for space. On large projects, it may also allow the developer to create an internal market for other uses – housing that generates retail demands and offices that create the opportunity for restaurants and shops. Mixing uses is also considered a public good, reducing the need for travel, generating life on streets through more of the day and night, and, where housing is included, helping create a sense of community.

Where the objective is to mix occupancy of a site, or add non-market uses into the mix, the key may be, as we have noted, using density incentives. In New York City, several new theatres have been built by developers in exchange for added rights to build additional office or residential space above. The Woodward's Project in downtown Vancouver, a complex 1.1 million sq ft project of mixed uses, includes space for a university school for contemporary arts, 200 affordable housing units, a supermarket, office space for non-profit organisations, office space for federal and city agencies, and a childcare centre, as well as 536 market-rate condominiums (see Figure 13.8). The project was made possible by granting the developer the right to build more space on the site, exceeding the site's prior height restrictions, and permitting enhanced development rights on another site that the developer owns elsewhere in the downtown.

A similar strategy has been adopted in the West Chelsea area of New York, where the High Line Park threads its way through a jumble of old warehouses and new designer chic buildings. The city allowed transfer of development rights from the elevated park to adjacent sites and, in line with newly enacted special district zoning, sold enhanced development rights to cover a large portion of the costs of constructing the High Line Park. The award-winning park has become a magnet for development, helping West Chelsea evolve into a unique mixed-use district anchored by galleries, restaurants, shops, offices and housing.

In reality, mixing uses may or may not add to the value of a site; it depends upon the circumstances. The requirement that the ground floor of structures be occupied by retail uses may not match market demands. In downtown Boston, where this is a requirement, it is sometimes necessary to subsidise retail spaces to attract tenants, thereby diminishing the value of sites. Mixing uses vertically can also be more costly, requiring dual elevator systems (when housing is located over offices), transfer of plumbing risers, redundant mechanical systems and other expenditures that may or may not be offset by denser use of the land. A more important issue may be the rigidity of financing sources. In the USA, housing finance is often provided by different institutions than commercial mortgages, and housing lenders may cap the amount of non-residential space they finance at 20–25 per cent of the total project. The inability to conform to this may force developers into residential mortgages with significantly higher interest rates. Mixed-use projects, which are often developed on a larger scale than single-use projects, are more complex to finance and can accumulate additional costs because developers must consider exit flexibility – that is, the ultimate sale of the individual parts: retail, office and housing condominiums. As a result, in large-scale projects such as the Time Warner Center at Columbus Circle in New York, each use will typically be financed separately, a more complex and often more costly set of transactions.

As with all issues where design and finance intersect, the devil is in the details. Mixing uses remains a valid public good, and in many instances it is the key to adding value to a site. But the mix must be carried out with a detailed understanding of markets and sources of financing.

District identity

A central purpose of urban design is often to create neighbourhoods or districts with a unique and memorable character. A single building cannot do this; creating identity requires consistency among many buildings in an area.

It may be achieved through the form of streets, open spaces and buildings, through consistency of materials and details, and through the uses that are attracted to the area. Sometimes the rules may be mandated in local develop-ment codes or standards, while in other instances they are negotiated through discretionary review processes. A land developer may go beyond local require-ments and adopt a pattern book for any sites he sells to homebuilders.

Districts with distinct identity can have greater economic value than faceless or confused areas. A Turkish study found that harmony between the building facades and colours was the most effective factor in promoting high land values, and that consistent and interesting architectural features ranked just behind this (Topcu & Kubat 2009).

Identity is the central theme of New Urbanist communities, which are governed by prescriptions that range from the form of streets to architec-tural details. A study of the value of this bundle of character-giving features has found that buyers are willing to pay a premium of about 11 per cent for single family homes in such communities (Eppli & Tu 1999a). While the study did not disaggregate the contributions to this premium, it is fair to assume that overall identity plays a role. Of course, New Urbanist commu-nities are not for everyone: market studies have found that about one third of US households are prepared to trade off the size of lot and adopt the form of housing that predominates in such communities (Hirschhorn & Souza 2001; Bohl 2002).

Forging a unique identity through urban design can often provide market-ing advantages. The Times Square/42nd Street area of New York, by the 1980s, had declined to the point that it was avoided by all but the hardiest of souls, the result of pornography, prostitution, poor retail outlets, deterio-rated buildings and streets, and the poor condition of its subway stations. One of the city's objectives was to move office development into the area, while reviving the theatre and night life traditionally identified with 42nd Street. Through a series of moves, it tapped the office developers on key sites for funds to renovate the major subway hub below the square. Among the incentives the city provided was the right – indeed the requirement – that the lower 60 ft of buildings be covered with illuminated signs, restoring the traditional identity of the district (see Figure 13.9). The sign requirement became so lucrative to existing property owners that they erected Potemkin structures, with few if any uses behind the bright facades. There is, of course, much more to the story of Times Square's revival, but today it is the top tourist attraction in New York City; ground-floor shops and offices com-mand premium rents, and the theatre industry has been substantially revived. The signs and bright lights played a critical role in this transforma-tion (Sagalyn 2001).

In Shanghai, where new look-alike high-rise towers dominate the land-scape of new residences, Xintiendi, a restored district of traditional

Figure 13.9 Times Square, New York. Required signage establishes a powerful character for the area, and was key to its revitalization. *Source:* Gary Hack.

houses and shops, adapted to serve young Shanghaiese and tourists looking for a place to dine, shop and be seen in sidewalk cafes, is among the most attractive destinations. The painstaking restoration, undertaken by a Hong Kong developer, was a calculated investment to create a special identity and a marketing advantage for his large office, housing and retail project located adjacent to Xintiendi (see Figure 13.10). The same approach is evident in dozens of examples around the world, where the transfer of unused development rights from historic structures has enabled their preservation.

Coupling urban design and development

The strategy of acquiring public goods through development projects is not without its critics. One line of attack is the assertion that public goods acquired privately are never truly public goods. The often-cited example is pedestrian areas in shopping malls, which courts in the USA have held are indisputably private space, subject to rules set by the owners. Making the leap to other types of privately owned or managed space, critics have argued

Figure 13.10 Xintiendi Development, Shanghai. Adaptive reuse of historic French Quarter houses created an identity that was exploited for surrounding office development. © Shui On Group.

that undesirable people or behaviours will be excluded if they are not in the commercial interests of the owners. (Sorkin 1992; Kohn 2004)

Studies of New York City's public spaces created in exchange for allowing increased amounts of development catalogue a variety of abuses of the 'publicness' of such spaces, including the absence of any signs indicating that the public can use them, restricted hours of availability, appropriations of the spaces for commercial purposes and a general lack of maintenance (Kayden 2000). However, careful observational studies of Bryant Park in New York and Copley Square in Boston – both parks that were improved, and are now managed, by public–private business improvement districts – found that the rules of use and management practices conformed to commonsense norms and were not unduly burdensome (Kim 1997). A recent study of privately created public spaces in Dutch cities reached similar conclusions, noting in the case of the Statenplein in Dordrecht, '... in principle anything may happen there that falls within the range of what is permitted under the local ordinance. The investors have no influence on that ...' At the Beursplein in Rotterdam, a privately redeveloped shopping street in the central commercial district, users were not even aware of the boundaries of public and private space, and privatisation had no discernable effect on pedestrian behaviour (van Melik *et al.* 2009). The conclusion we take from these studies is that much depends upon the rules that are negotiated between public bodies and private developers, and that urban designers protecting the public interest must be vigilant in anticipating private responses.

A second more serious criticism of obtaining public goods through private development projects is that there is no free lunch. Simply put, the public will ultimately pay for what is received – through direct grants, lower land prices when it sells land to developers (as in the Netherlands), property tax concessions (as in the USA) or future costs that the public assumes because of density increases, including congestion and increased public maintenance costs. Moreover, unless offset by clear and significant efficiencies in production, facilities may be more costly, even if the real costs are hidden from view, since private developers will wish to be paid for their risk and the developer's cost of borrowing is generally higher than that of public bodies. Hence, some critics have argued that public agencies ought to collect what is due, and finance the balance of what is needed, and then control the process and form of what they seek to achieve.

Such an approach underestimates the role that public bodies can have in shaping private development to their purposes, as the Vancouver and New York examples we cite illustrate. In both cities, public bodies maintain final approval power over what is built, even if the results are negotiated rather than prescribed. There may be many reasons why public bodies do not want to assume the risks of development: they may lack the staff to properly manage such projects, may not have easy access to capital to construct them, cannot make multi-year commitments in a changeable political climate, may not wish to carry projects on their balance sheets or, perhaps more notably, want to avoid the risk of exposing failure or front-page headlines about cost overruns. If they are to be effective partners, clearly, public agencies need to have access to urban designers and financial analysts equally skilled as their private counterparts, and they need to memorialise expectations in tightly drawn legal agreements. The fact that so many public bodies have opted for having private developers construct the bulk of cities is evidence that they see advantage in such arrangements.

Urban designers will need to adapt to these new circumstances if they hope to play a leading role in shaping the form of cities. New skills are essential: understanding markets and financial models, acquiring knowledge of legal arrangements for parcelling rights to land and facilities, learning about innovative precedents for complex public–private arrangements, and mastering the skills of negotiation to reach successful agreements. Applying their three-dimensional creativity to the task, urban designers are especially skilled to serve as the intermediaries for urban development projects. Their visions about better cities and visualisation skills remain essential, but need to be grounded in the practical knowledge of how to make these a reality. Mastering both the visioning and the practicalities of carrying out projects can make urban designers true city builders.

14

Connecting Urban Design to Real Estate Development

Steve Tiesdell and David Adams

Introduction

This book has reported diverse international experience, drawn from academia and practice, on the relationship between urban design and real estate development. Rather than applying architectural aesthetics across a large urban canvas, urban design has been interpreted as a place-making activity. This perspective presumes that those keen to see far better places created than typically produced by real estate development are inspired to foster a culture of place-making, which can then be deployed to challenge narrow thinking among those responsible for much of today's urban environment. Although this challenge is sometimes confined to those working within real estate development, it is – or should be – a matter of public debate. Indeed, at times it is one of intense public controversy.

This explains why the book has examined in some detail how public policy can help locate urban design and place-making more centrally within real estate development. Indeed, by seeing urban design as an activity that has broader, but indirect, influence on the thinking of those who produce the built environment, as well as one with immediate and direct impact on the quality of particular projects, we can apply George's (1997) distinction between second- and first-order design. While the book has highlighted exemplars of urban design as a first-order activity across the USA, Canada, Europe and the UK, it has done so in the context of looking at how urban

Urban Design in the Real Estate Development Process, First Edition. Edited by Steve Tiesdell and David Adams.
© 2011 Blackwell Publishing Ltd. Published 2011 by Blackwell Publishing Ltd.

design, as a second-order activity, can create a 'decision environment' that makes developers, financiers, designers and other actors in the development process take place-making much more seriously. Urban design, in this sense, acts as an integrative problem-solving activity, which transcends and connects what might otherwise be the detached thinking of each different development actor or profession (Brain 2005), while, at the same time, making places more sustainable by joining up key elements such as infrastructure and development (as Falk shows in Chapter 2). Thinking about urban design as a second-order activity thus explains why the overarching research question in the book has been: How successful are particular public policy instruments in framing (and reframing) the relationship between designers and developers to the advantage of urban design (place) quality?

The purpose of this concluding chapter is to synthesise what we, as editors, consider can be drawn from individual chapters in response to this research question. We approach this task by concentrating on four main themes. We look *first*, in the next section, at the potential impact of urban design on the economics of real estate development by considering the extent to which better design enhances, rather than detracts from, development value. This sets the context for our *second* theme, which explores relations between designers and developers. Here, we review how attitudes towards place-making can vary greatly between different types of developer. We then reinterpret our earlier thinking about 'opportunity space' in the light of evidence presented by various contributors to the book. As a *third* theme, we focus on policy design comparing the effectiveness of the different policy tools we presented in the first chapter in helping to achieve higher quality development and better places. This leads to our *final* theme, which highlights key research implications of some of the main conclusions of this book.

Urban design and development economics

Does better urban design pay? This apparently simple question disguises more complex ones. First, we may wish to investigate what 'pay' means in this context for, as we indicated in Table 1.4, developers are concerned with risk, timing and other crucial factors, as well as immediate costs and revenues. Secondly, we may need to ask 'For whom does better urban design pay?', since, as we again indicated in Chapter 1, numerous actors participate in the real estate development process, some on the demand side and some on the supply side, as a result of which place quality can be undermined by producer–consumers gaps. Thirdly, we should bear in mind that if better urban design was deemed to 'pay' in the same way as adding more floorspace to a development, then this book might not be necessary. In this case, rather than simply forcing developers to adopt higher design standards, policy might seek to establish the benefits of better urban design (financial and otherwise) to developers themselves, and make these widely known in the hope that this will reorientate developer thinking in a more 'rational' direction. Hence, discussion of the relationship between urban design and development economics is fundamental to subsequent policy choices.

Two of the later chapters in this book review evidence on whether better design adds value to private real estate. Hack and Sagalyn (Chapter 13) approach this from a historical perspective, arguing that investment in the public realm has long brought financial benefits to neighbouring properties. Henneberry *et al.* (Chapter 11) add a more contemporary perspective, reporting the results of a series of recent studies across the real estate literature that calculate specific increases in property values that have been attributed to particular design elements. They remain concerned, however, about whether the results of such general hedonic analysis can be applied to specific developments. As a result, they react cautiously to the claim that '... good urban design adds value by increasing the economic viability of development' made by Carmona *et al.* (2001: 8) and, indeed, in similar terms by others. Hack and Sagalyn's response is more direct, arguing frequently from North American experience that urban designers who set out to create value can do so to the benefit of both the developer and the intrinsic quality of the development. Significantly, for this win-win result to be achievable, Hack and Sagalyn (p. 280) call for urban designers to be become skilled in

> ... understanding markets and financial models, acquiring knowledge of legal arrangements for parcelling rights to land and facilities, learning about innovative precedents for complex public–private arrangements, and mastering the skills of negotiation to reach successful agreements.

In other words, better urban design more than pays for itself, even in a narrow sense, but only because urban designers make determined attempts to make sure it does.

In a broader sense, several contributors to the book make the point that better regulation of design quality, and indeed better design standards more generally, reduce development risk and often enable development to happen more quickly. If correct, both these claims would make developments more economically viable, since uncertainty and delay are well known causes of upward pressure on development costs. Hall (Chapter 4), for example, puts forward a strong case in favour of clear design policies, arguing that it saves developers time and trouble to know well in advance exactly what will be required on particular sites, even to the extent that this can then be factored into land prices. Tolson (Chapter 8) takes a similar view in relation to design competitions, suggesting that competition briefs lacking clarity and prescription may actually deter developer interest since each competitor will have to invest their own resources in working up potentially abortive designs. In this context, Hack and Sagalyn argue that the master developer, when working alongside a public agency, has the potential to achieve both creative design and risk reduction for the public sector, through the arrangements that are struck with individual plot/parcel developers. Carmona (Chapter 3) sees design codes as offering developers a helpful balance between certainty and flexibility, which allow the financial implications of different design choices to be evaluated with some confidence early in the development process. This chimes with Punter's discussion of design review (Chapter 9), which suggests that the earlier in the development process such reviews take place, the more effective they are. More broadly, Falk (Chapter 2) emphasises the role of urban design in maximising urban property values through effective coordination of social and physical infrastructure with development, while Carmona sees the coordination potential of design codes as a mechanism to bring together multiple teams and development phases to achieve a coherent design vision across a large site.

All this seems sensible enough until Henneberry *et al.* interrupt with the cautionary note that the current structure of real estate markets means that most of the value streams generated by better design are not captured by the developer. By highlighting such producer–consumer gaps, we are prompted to ask for whom better urban design pays and perhaps, who pays for it. In the latter context, Hack and Sagalyn's response is clear – pointing to Canadian experience, they argue that strong urban design guidelines in Vancouver worked precisely because they were well known, consistently operated and thus factored in the value that developers pay for land. Yet what Henneberry *et al.* allude to is the reluctance of trader developers to invest in better design if they consider that potential purchasers are unlikely to repay their efforts for doing so. While recognising that this dilemma reflects the power relations of development, Henneberry *et al.* concentrate on finding a technical solution by linking a simplified form of CAD through to viability analysis to enable the financial implications of successive design iterations to be instantly tested. This may well shift the relationship between developer and designer in Bentley's (1999) terms from that of a battlefield to more of a master–servant relationship, in which 'value from design' is determined in an instrumental rather than creative way. In practice, much will depend on the attitude and nature of the developer. We thus return to these issues later in this chapter.

It cannot be presumed that most developers would readily invest in better design, even if the financial benefits of doing so were abundantly evident. In this context, Hall's experience of Chelmsford persuaded him that national developers were reluctant to depart from their tried-and-tested (but dismal) designs, primarily because of their ignorance of local market conditions, which made them slow to bring forward alternative forms of development that combined better quality design with greater financial return. Hall thus argues that tighter design regulation not only 'turned the town around' in relation to the quality of its new development but was also fundamental in forcing developers to grasp what was in their own best interests. In contrast, in the North American context, Hack and Sagalyn call for 'reciprocity' between private developers and regulatory authorities by way of allowing developments that provide collective benefits to the public realm to benefit from increased densities, greater height or other forms of regulatory flexibility. As these two very different approaches suggest, public policy choices in this arena may impact as much on the way in which developers think about the value of urban design as upon the prospects of achieving better quality design itself. We thus return to the issue of policy choice later in this chapter, having first sought to disaggregate the term 'developer' and to explore what can be learnt from the various contributions to this book about power relations between developers and designers.

Opportunity space and developer–designer relations

As Punter contends in Chapter 9 (p. 197), '... the principal determinant of design quality remains the commitment of the developer to design excellence and sustainability, and the skills of the design team retained to execute the project.' The central research question for this book thus concerned the impact of urban design policy instruments on developers' (and thence on designers') decision-making and, in particular, their impact on those factors – reward, risk, uncertainty, time etc – that would make them more likely, or less likely, to provide higher quality development and to contribute to producing better places. In this section, we seek to draw together what can be learnt from the various contributions about developer attitudes towards urban design, how this might differ between different types of developer and the state of developer–designer relations in practice.

There are some excellent examples in the book of developers who value good urban design. In Love and Crawford's account of Madinat Al Soor (Chapter 5), they highlight the developer's desire to achieve what has otherwise been lacking in the Dubai of the 21st century – street-level intimacy and scalar variability. In the USA, Hack and Sagalyn demonstrate the strong commitment of the Prudential Insurance Company in Boston to a participatory planning process that helped create a design that now merges seamlessly with the surrounding neighbourhoods and greatly enhances the fabric of the city. In the UK, Syms and Clarke (Chapter 7) recount how developers have worked hard in the historic town of Kendal to carefully integrate a mixed-use development, anchored by a food store, into the grain of the place. While all such examples are welcome, the real issue is whether they are representative of attitudes towards urban design across the development industry more widely.

A contrasting and more pessimistic view of the commitment of developers to design quality is provided by a newly appointed design officer within the planning department of the City of Edinburgh Council, who observed:

> What really shocked me coming to work here were some of the absolutely dire developments you see every day, and it is not a minority. Volume housebuilders, generic house types, pastiche, really low quality material. There is only so much a regulatory process like planning can do to raise design up the agenda, if the quality brought to the table by the private developer doesn't have an aspiration (Raeburn 2008: 68).

As Adams and Payne (Chapter 10) point out, design matters may not necessarily be high on the agenda of many private developers. They argue, for example, that UK housebuilders are primarily land-focused rather than design/place-focused and demonstrate an embedded culture of standardisation in product design. When challenged by tighter regulation, their response has primarily been to make relatively limited changes to the standard product range, but not to transform underlying design processes or development practices. What is perhaps most ironic about the well-known reluctance of many UK housebuilders to innovation is their claim, as Carmona highlights, to know the market best. Hall berates this attitude for its lack of imagination, arguing that the costs of better design are actually marginal in comparison with overall development costs and, most likely, would be more than repaid by additional revenues. To him 'developer failure' is attributable to a lack of expertise and commitment and its logic of following the path of least regulatory resistance, avoiding risk and maintaining strict cost control, needs to be countered by much stronger regulation.

What must be remembered, of course, is the desire and ability of powerful sectional interests, such as developers, to capture the regulatory processes intended to manage their activities. This is well illustrated by Marantz and Ben Joseph (Chapter 6, p. 115), who, in their account of the evolution of zoning and other forms of regulation in the USA, contend that:

> Asking how regulation affected these developers would be somewhat misleading, because they exerted great control over regulation. We therefore seek to understand why large-scale developers sought certain types of regulation, and how the results have affected the built environment.

In this context, the Edinburgh experience, reported by Tiesdell in Chapter 12, is pertinent. He recounts how Edinburgh's real estate developers warmed to Sir Terry Farrell's leadership as the city's Design Champion, not least because they liked his drive for higher quality. These two contributions suggest a more complex relationship between regulators and the development industry, in which a mutually advantageous agenda might emerge over time.

Discussion so far has not distinguished between the attitudes of different types of developers to urban design, yet several contributors highlight this as an important component of understanding any developer's likely commitment to design matters. Punter, for example, suggests that investor-developers, who have a long-term interest in the quality of the place they create, regard design review much more positively than trader-developers, whose intentions are to sell out once development is completed. However, even the latter are not necessarily a homogenous group for he notes '... the welcome emergence of a new breed of niche developers who have an interest in urban regeneration, conservation and sustainability alongside innovative architecture and urban design' (p. 197). The long-term investment of such developers may be not so much in any *particular* place but in their own reputation to create quality places more *generally*. This chimes with the distinction made by Adams and Payne between pioneers, pragmatists and sceptics among UK housebuilders, with only the first showing real interest in bespoke design. In a recent paper we sought to tease out the distinction between 'place-based' and 'non-place-based' entrepreneurs, suggesting that

> ... place-based entrepreneurs are those who actively work with the grain of a city, responding to local factors, seeing added value in design, and taking a broader view of where development potential exists. They are typified by locally, relatively small-scale, independent entrepreneurs. Non-place entrepreneurs tend to ignore, undervalue, or actively work against the grain of a city. They take a more limited view of where development potential exists and are generally risk-averse. They are typified by externally based institutional investors (Adams & Tiesdell, 2010: 199).

What this suggests is the need to take a more fine-grained look at how different types of developers approach design quality, and in setting a future research agenda at the end of this chapter, we return to the urgent need to move on from highlighting examples of different types of developer to reaching a more rigorous understanding of the variety of attitudes and approaches to design across the industry more widely. To contextualise this search, it is important to understand the varied motivation of development actors, which we set out in Table 1.1 in the opening chapter, and to seek ways in which gaps between those who produce the built environment and those who consume it can be closed.

Nevertheless, it is important not to hold developers solely responsible for place quality, without taking into account the wider socio-economic and politico-regulatory context. In the first chapter, we thus introduced opportunity space theory, which highlights how this broader context affects the agency and interaction of development actors. Such actors negotiate, manoeuvre, interact, scheme and plot to make the best use of their opportunity space, while also seeking to enlarge it so as to gain greater autonomy and freedom to achieve their own goals. Although private-sector actors strategise to achieve private goals, they might also be prepared to meet public policy goals where these coincide or align with their own private goals. This might happen voluntarily and altruistically, but they may also be coerced into doing so by the need for regulatory consents and indeed, as Hall suggests, where the regulatory constraints actually guide them towards what is actually in their own best interest (and perhaps also the community's best interest). It should thus be recognised that public-sector actors also strategise to constrain, shape or otherwise influence developers' behaviours and actions and that of their designers.

We suggested that the developer's opportunity space is constrained by various external forces – the site or physical context, the public policy context and the market. Although more or less fixed at any point in time, these forces change, often radically, over time. Such change can open up (and close down) 'windows of opportunity' at particular points in the development cycle, which adds a dynamic dimension to the concept of opportunity space.

Several contributors to this book offer insights on the application of opportunity space theory, especially to the relationship between developers and designers. Hack and Sagalyn (p. 270) demonstrate the potential of designers who '... incorporate ideas about value creation into ... their toolkit' to expand their own opportunity space in the face of demands upon their developer clients to deliver high-quality public goods as part of new development projects. Hall argues that tighter regulation in Chelmsford forced housebuilders to commission specialist external architects rather than rely on in-house design technicians, while Tiesdell notes that one consequence of Sir Terry Farrell's period as Edinburgh Design Champion was to shift design work to the city's better architectural practices, who were better able to respond to the quality, place and design agenda championed by Farrell.

However, both Carmona and Punter, commenting respectively on design codes and design review, make the important point that design expectations need to be made clear by planning authorities at an early stage in the development process, before developers have become too committed financially to any particular design. As Henneberry *et al.* make clear: 'In the early stages of the development process the room for manoeuvre is considerable because the developer has made limited financial or legal commitments to the project' (p. 224). This would suggest that the relative opportunity space between developers and designers may shift rapidly at a certain point in the development process, after which regulatory intervention that is intended to tip the balance in favour of designers may prove ineffective. Exploring how this balance changes over time, Adams and Payne argue that UK housebuilders turned to skilled designers to overcome an apparent reduction in their own opportunity space caused by increased regulation, but that this was only temporary and that they subsequently returned to limited design input as soon as the contribution of skilled designers could be standardised.

Of course, the presumption that better design outcomes come when more opportunity space is yielded to designers is open to challenge, since it relies, perhaps wrongly, on designers not misusing the opportunity space they are given. The possibility of course exists of what might be termed 'designer failure'. Commenting on criticism of new development on Edinburgh's waterfront and of the local authority for having 'allowed it to happen', one of the city's design officers (John Deffenbaugh) observed: '... those designs and those buildings originated on someone's drawing board. A qualified architect designed those buildings, but the city bears the brunt of the criticism.' (Raeburn 2008: 68)

Rather than an overarching single cause, it can be hypothesised that designer failure has several partial and interrelated causes, about which, in the absence of more systematic research, we can only speculate. An initial non-exhaustive list might include:

- the desire to satisfy the building or development sponsor without regard for the wider public or collective interest;
- an inherent lack of design ability – not all designers are actually good designers or indeed sensitive to place, in which case narrower 'architectural' (i.e. building-centric) values may trump broader 'urban' (i.e. place-centric) values;
- failures or gaps in the education of designers;
- various moral hazards – including acting in one's own self-interest by, for example, seeking the acclaim of peers, publication in journals, career progression etc;
- ideological imperatives, such as views of architecture as primarily a visual art and of architects as primary artists.

While opportunity space theory provides a conceptual framework for understanding the relationships between developers and designers, a more nuanced account could usefully reflect the varied motivations of designers and the critical importance of time, both in relation to the development cycle as a whole and in reflection of the timing of the designer's input.

Policy choices and policy design

We now turn to the implications of these issues for policy design. Here we focus on the four subsidiary research questions established at the start of the book:

- What public policy instruments are available to facilitate better quality urban development and better places?
- How do particular policy instruments impact on the decision environments or opportunity space of developers and designers?
- In what other ways do particular policy instruments impact on design quality?
- Are some types of policy instruments more effective than others in facilitating higher quality development and better places?

In this section, we explore the four types of policy instruments outlined in the first chapter to compare the potential effectiveness of market shaping, market regulation, market stimulus and capacity building in helping to achieve higher quality development and better places. However, in doing so, three notes of caution are required.

First, to allow an analytic focus on means, this book has deliberately separated ends and means, and thus implicitly assumes mechanistic means–end rationality in terms of cause and effect (i.e. that certain means will produce certain ends). The real situation is more complex and nuanced because means and ends are highly interrelated. Brain (2005: 233), for example, observes how:

> Researchers typically assume that it is possible to test the relationship between the means and end as relationship of cause and effect, remaining agnostic with respect to the value of the end and the possibly, independent value of particular means.

But, he argues, policymakers inevitably seek to '... achieve an end with means that are never neutral in themselves. In the context of the urban landscape, every design and planning decision is a value proposition, and a proposition that has to do with social and political relationships.' (Brain 2005: 233). Brain's contention, with which we agree, is that value propositions and value positions cannot be simply ignored.

The end that this book promotes is the creation of better places. It is thus based on the desirability of place-making and the promotion of place-making, rather than place-breaking, policy instruments. For analytical purposes and to focus on means rather than ends, we have put to one side the issues of what is a 'good' or 'better' place in order to focus on delivery. There are different attitudes and opinions as to what constitutes a 'good' place. There is also extensive discussion, including the development of a body of normative theory, in urban design and other academic literature, along with much assertion in policy documents, about the qualities and attributes of good places. We thus consider that, in any particular circumstances, 'higher quality' and 'better' can be defined and agreed through a deliberative process and, in turn, made the objective of public policy and of design processes.

Second, however, using public policy instruments to compel and encourage developers (and their designers) to produce better design entails, in effect, some form of state intervention to correct the market failure of 'bad places'. But this risks the fallacy of supposing that the alternative to imperfect markets is 'perfect government'. Highlighting the prevalence of government, as well as market, failure, public choice theory focuses on planning as a political activity (e.g. Poulton 1997; Pennington 2000). By emphasising how state intervention distorts prices and encourages rent-seeking behaviour, public choice theory expressly challenges welfare economics approaches. It also highlights how the costs of policy formulation, monitoring and enforcement are often neglected. Although, in principle, a mode of analysis (and apparently neutral between the costs of government and market failure), an overarching theme of public choice theory is that state intervention creates more problems than it solves and its most prominent advocates have tended to promote a vision of the 'minimal state' (Ward 2002). Public choice economists have been quick to highlight the costs of government, which are often direct, and bear on identifiable actors (such as taxpayers), but less quick to highlight the benefits, which are more diffuse, bear on the community-at-large and are more difficult to measure.

It is thus a political question which imperfect form of organisation will lead to a better outcome. For example, if you cannot regulate well (or if there are insufficient skills and aptitudes within the existing workforce to regulate well), the dilemma arises whether it is better to regulate 'poorly' or not to regulate at all. Doubting the ability of public sector planners to regulate to produce better places, many may argue (sometimes with good cause) that their actions simply worsen the situation. Equally, both wholly unregulated development and wholly regulated development can produce good places. But it remains a matter of probabilities which approach is more likely to produce better places more frequently.

Third, policy-making in any one sector does not occur in isolation but inevitably takes places within a context determined by numerous other policy demands. What therefore deserves careful consideration is the extent to which the pursuit of better quality urban design conflicts with other broader policy priorities. In the UK, for example, some would argue that design requirements should not be allowed to outbid the urgent need for more homes to be built or to be built on brownfield sites, where development costs are generally higher.

As Hall notes in Chapter 4, others have argued that stringent design policies cannot be justified in areas of economic decline, where development at any price is often at the forefront of local politicians' minds. Hall's response to this implicit moratorium on design regulation (pp. 90–91) is clear:

> Although the experience related here took place in a context of high land values, there is no reason to suppose that the type of policies applied in Chelmsford would not be equally successful where land values are low. The tragedy is that, in areas of economic decline, councils may be reluctant to press developers to produce higher standards in case they go away. However, as has been explained, good design is certainly not less, more often more profitable. Moreover, as is often pointed out elsewhere, it can add value within the process of regeneration. Reluctance on behalf of both parties to pursue higher standards is more in the mind than in the pocket.

Bearing in mind these three provisos, we now focus more closely on state–market relationships with respect to design and development processes and outcomes, and summarise what we consider the various contributions to this book tell us about how particular public policy instruments can be deployed to frame (and reframe) the relationship between designers and developers to the advantage of place quality.

Market shaping

In the opening chapter, we identified market shaping as covering those policy instruments that provide the overarching context for market actions and transactions. We drew particular attention to the importance of plans (including policy guidance and planning briefs) and emphasised the distinction between plans that are developmental (in the true sense that they set out intended public actions), regulatory and indicative.

   The strongest evidence in this book on the potential of market shaping to achieve higher quality development and better places came from Falk (Chapter 2) in his account of why many European cities manage to deliver much better places than their British competitors. He ascribes the European success to the importance of civic leadership, effective financial mechanisms and especially the way in which infrastructure provision and place-making are closely related through the appropriate uses of true development plans. Significantly, Falk (p. 38) comments that:

> ... the incentive of infrastructure means that 'design strings' can be attached. In other words, infrastructure *is* fundamental to place-shaping and to putting urbanist principles into practice. The term infrastructure, incidentally, needs to embrace not just the hard physical infrastructure of roads and utilities, but also the soft or social infrastructure of schools,

shops and meeting places that can make or break new communities. Exemplary schemes like in Freiburg or Stockholm also benefit from their connectivity to high quality infrastructure, such as municipal tram systems or district heating schemes.

As Falk suggests, in some cases, such as in the Netherlands, public land ownership was also central to making best use of available land. This linkage between ownership and development in shaping design quality is explored in more detail by Love and Crawford, who look at the importance and manner of land subdivision in achieving design quality in the USA and elsewhere. Significantly, they highlight the relationship between public officials, master developers and masterplanners as having the potential to control ultimate place character through rules established in the pre-development phase. This chimes with Carmona's view that, when well used, design codes can provide an effective framework to achieve better-designed development, with less local opposition, and in a manner that creates a level playing field for developers.

Creating better places through market shaping can achieve wider benefits beyond better quality design, for as Falk argues, in a competitive urban environment, those cities that adopt the most integrated framework for new development are best placed to succeed and most likely to move up the urban league.

Market regulation

Regulatory instruments control market actions and transactions and limit an actor's opportunity space by restricting the available choices. What becomes apparent from the various chapters in the book is the need for more sophisticated forms of design regulation, while still providing clarity to market actors. Punter, for example, highlights how design review as a capacity building instrument (see below) can be deployed to overcome what he considers some of the limitations of 'negative development control'. Love and Crawford emphasise the importance of reinforcing regulatory guidelines by a careful parcel map, which can help craft the character of successful urban districts. They berate urban governments, who they claim are often complicit in maintaining large parcels, for their failure to ensure the right balance of regulatory controls to break down mega-projects by careful use of plots, streets, blocks and other infrastructural components. However, as Hall points out, in Chelmsford, effective design regulation demands political will at local and, in the UK, at national level. It may also require re-staffing or at least retraining of the professional cadre who work for and represent local political leaders, to ensure the skills and culture necessary to transform the design thinking of those subject to regulation. Yet, it is important to note the warning from Marantz and Ben-Joseph, who argue forcibly (p. 134) from an American perspective that:

From Frederic Howe to Andrés Duany, proponents of urban change have long called for better government regulation on the built environment. And while their messages have influenced the debate, they have achieved success only to the extent that their ambitions aligned with the most powerful figures in real estate development.

Market stimulus

In the opening chapter, we contrasted market regulation and market stimulus. We suggested that while regulation often operates negatively, for example, by directing demand away from specified locations, it cannot generally attract demand (and development) to a location. In practice, regulatory instruments are often supplemented by stimulus instruments that seek to facilitate markets working better – they 'lubricate' the market by, for example, having a direct impact on financial appraisals. While regulatory instruments generally stop things from happening, stimulus actions increase the likelihood of some desired event or action taking place by making some actions more – and sometimes less – attractive to, and rewarding for, particular development actors (i.e. they change the pattern of incentives within the decision environment). In this context, Hack and Sagalyn provide some particularly instructive examples of stimulus instruments, showing how they have been used to achieve better quality development and improved public realm. These measures include consent for additional high-value development (and hence extra tax revenues) in Boston, public-sector intervention as master developer in New York, density bonuses again in New York, site assembly and infrastructure provision in Stockholm and property rights pooling in Beirut.

Experience of stimulus instruments in the UK seems quite tame in comparison. Adams and Payne consider that residential design policy has deployed the full range of policy instruments outlined in Chapter 1, apart from those involving financial stimulus. Syms and Clarke distinguish between instruments intended to stimulate more development and those meant to encourage better quality design, and suggest that only rarely do these two purposes come together. They also point out that the UK's long tradition of supporting development in regeneration areas through grant subsidy was brought to an end in 1999, when it was deemed anti-competitive by the European Union. They therefore look to a range of policy and regulatory measures to stimulate better design among developers, but it remains difficult to assess how far such measures actually persuade developers to change their behaviour to the extent of enthusiastically embracing design practices that they would otherwise have been reluctant to adopt.

In this context, Tolson calls for the public sector in the UK to learn from the European experience and to be prepared to act as place promoter. Although he points out that developer competitions, especially those organised by the public sector, can go horribly wrong, he retains faith in the potential for municipalities and other public agencies to stimulate well designed development by putting themselves in the driving seat. Specifically, Tolson (pp. 180–181) argues that:

> History has shown from Edinburgh New Town to Glasgow's Crown Street that the best solutions require the public sector to participate. Somehow, we have lost this participation and have been driven by political ideology that the market is best placed to deliver places. This does not appear to be the case in continental Europe. Sadly, to get more public participation will take time, since there is a lack of resource and development skill in the public sector. Indeed, it will take some brave politicians to make a radical shift by allowing the state to invest and actively engage in value-generating activity instead of monitoring the costs of others.

What the British experience suggests, in comparison with that from Europe, the USA and elsewhere is the need for a radical rethink of how better quality design can be stimulated by creating new policy instruments that encourage developers to want to create high quality places. This links closely to the final type of policy instrument outlined in Chapter 1 – capacity building – to which we now turn.

Capacity building

In Chapter 1, we defined capacity building instruments as those that enhance the abilities and capacity – skills, knowledge, networks, rules of operation, working practices etc – of development actors. We also commented that in developing effective capacity building measures, public agencies may need to demonstrate innovation and insight into market processes – the capacity built serves to overcome obstacles to development and to release development potential. Several contributions to the book, including Punter's account of design review and Tiesdell's discussion of design champions, address the importance of capacity building in the public sector. Both reflect on how cultural and organisational change on design issues, within and beyond local authorities, can enhance designers' relative opportunity space. Hall takes an even stronger view of what he calls the need for 'regime change' towards design within local authorities, encompassing enhanced profession skills and greater political determination to tackle poor design. Both Adams and Payne and Henneberry *et al.* explore the potential for capacity building within the private sector. The first of these contributions questions the commitment of private sector housebuilders to design innovation and quality, while the second explores the extent to which new methods of financial analysis might help developers better understand the benefits of urban design (or perhaps, less charitably, extract maximum financial benefit from limited design improvements).

Across these various contributions, two main themes emerge. The first is the importance of building design capacity, to the extent that other policy instruments could work more effectively if skills and mindsets in both the public and private sectors were more readily attuned to knowing how to create better places in a financially beneficial way. The exemplars from different parts of the Europe and America presented by different contributors to this book suggest that such an ambition is not over-optimistic. But the second main theme coming through the various chapters is that capacity building consumes time and resources and can never be seen as a quick fix. In many cases, poor design practices have become culturally embedded by the strength of path dependency, illustrated, for example, by the sustained running-down of design skills within local planning authorities and the scale of investment needed to turn this decline around. Similarly, lack of competitive behaviour among housebuilders has allowed individual companies to prosper without necessarily developing as learning or adaptive organisations. Thus, while capacity building needs to be seen as an integral part of the design policy armoury, it may not, by itself, produce immediate policy victories in the short term.

Towards a research agenda

We conclude this chapter, and indeed the book as a whole, by sketching out what we see as some of the essential components of an urban design research agenda in the years ahead. Our focus here is not on what constitutes good urban design but rather on how it can best be delivered.

From the various accounts reported in the book, we see genuine attempts made over the past decade or so to restore urban design, and more precisely place-making, to a more central position within urban and planning policies. Our first research priority concerns the extent to which this has become well embedded within the public sector. Here, we need to discover whether the achievements reported in this book and elsewhere are representative of a fundamental cultural shift across the public sector or whether they actually remain fairly isolated examples of good practice that are rarely replicated. The nature of power relations within and beyond local authorities is worthy of investigation here, for there are important concerns around how key local players, including city mayors and chief executives, see urban design (and more particularly place-making) as a crucial part of the new urban agenda in contrast to those who regard it as worthy of sacrifice when times get tough. Now that economic times are certainly getting tougher and municipalities are having to fight harder for every last resource, it becomes essential to see whether recent design progress has become well embedded in organisational culture or whether it is likely to be threatened in the new age of austerity. This concern links closely to the earlier discussions on whether better urban design is regarded as a cost or a benefit.

Second, we have argued consistently that one of the critical tests of design policy is the extent to which it shifts developer attitudes and approaches, which would include a far greater commitment to the use of skilled design expertise in development projects. Yet, as alluded to earlier, the development industry, at least in relation to design issues, remains something of a black box. We have suggested that some developers have a greater long-term commitment to design quality, either because they are likely to retain the development in their ownership for some considerable time ahead or because they might have a vested interest in building their own reputation on quality design.

Nevertheless, established and accepted categorisations of developer types hardly begin to unlock this distinction. For example, while this book has contained some highly critical comment about UK housebuilders, it is well known that certain housebuilders stand well apart from their breed in their commitment to design matters. Why is this? Similarly, one might expect investor-developers with their long-term real estate holdings to be especially interested in design quality but it would seem that, for many, this interest stops at the front door of their newly completed developments and does not even extend to the immediate public realm beyond. Again why is this? So we suggest that a second important research priority would be a thorough study of why attitudes to the value, benefits and costs of design vary between developers. This type of research needs to set design issues alongside other demands on corporate strategy, including financial considerations. It could usefully explore developers' perceptions of specific policy instruments, and their effects on developer behaviour, especially over time, to see whether they spark any long-term change in developer strategies. Such work might be complemented by ethnological studies of the social dynamics, power relations and strategising between developers and their designers, including investigation of the extent of developer commitment to, and investment in, high quality design skills.

In conclusion, we regard the rich insights produced throughout this book in answer to the research questions as but work in progress. It is indeed a measure of the maturity of urban design as a focus of academic enquiry that the various contributions to this book have been able to engage so fully with the relationship between design and development and thus with the crucial issue of delivering, rather than merely articulating, the best of intentions. But we also recognise that there is still a considerable distance to travel in this journey, and our hope in editing this book is thus to spur further debate, knowledge and action on the delivery, in practice, of higher quality development and better places.

References

A+DS (Architecture + Design Scotland) (2009) *Report on Design Review Feedback*, A+DS, Edinburgh.

Adair, A., Berry, J., Deddis, B., Hirst, S. & McGreal, S. (1998) *Accessing private finance: the availability and effectiveness of private finance in urban regeneration*, Research Report, RICS, London.

Adair, A., Berry, J., Gibb, K., Hutchison, N., McGreal, S., Poon, J. & Watkins, C. (2003) *Benchmarking Urban Regeneration*, Research Report, RICS, London.

Adair, A., Berry, J., McGreal, S., Deddis, B. & Hirst, S. (1999) 'Evaluation of investor behaviour in urban regeneration', *Urban Studies*, **36**, 2031–2045.

Adam, R. (1997) *The Consumer, The Developer, The Architect and the Planner: Whose Design is Good?*, paper given to the Good Design in Speculative Housing Seminar, Royal Fine Art Commission, London.

Adams, D. (1994) *Urban Planning and the Development Process*, UCL Press, London.

Adams, D. (2004) 'The changing regulatory environment for speculative housebuilding and the construction of core competencies for brownfield development', *Environment and Planning A*, **36**, 601–624.

Adams, D. & Tiesdell, S. (2010) 'Planners as market actors: Rethinking state–market relations in land and property' *Planning Theory & Practice*, **11**, 187–207.

Adams, D., Russell, L. & Taylor, C. (1994) *Land for Industrial Development*, E. & F. Spon, London.

Adams, D., Allmendinger, P., Dunse, N., Tiesdell, S., Turok, I. & White, M. (2003) *Assessing the Impact of ODPM Policies on Land Pricing*, Research report for the Office of the Deputy Prime Minister (ODPM), London.

Adams, D., Watkins, C. & White, M. (2005) (eds) *Planning, Public Policy and Property Markets*, Blackwell Publishing Ltd., Oxford, UK.

AIA Miami (2008). *AIA Position Paper Re: Miami 21*, American Institute of Architects, Miami Chapter, Miami, FL, available at: http://www.aiamiami.com/pdf/news/20080630_miami21-pospaper.pdf

Aldred, T. (2010) *Arrested Development: Are we building houses in the right places?* Centre for Cities, London.

Alexander, E. R. (2001) 'A transaction costs theory of land use planning and development control: Towards an institutional analysis of public planning', *Town Planning Review*, **72** (1), 45–75.

Al-Kodmany, K. (1999) 'Using visualization techniques for enhancing public participation in planning and design: process, implementation, and evaluation', *Landscape & Urban Planning*, **45** (1), 37–45.

Allied Tube & Conduit Corporation versus Indian Head (1988) 486 US 492.

Altunkasa, M. F. & Uslu, C. (2004) 'The effects of urban green spaces on house prices in the upper northwest urban development area of Adna (Turkey)', *Turkish Journal of Agriculture & Forestry*, **28**, 203–209.

Amin, A. (2003) 'The Economic Base of Contemporary Cities', in Bridges, G. & Watson, S. (2003) (eds), *A Companion to the City*, Blackwell Publishing Ltd., Oxford, UK, 115–129.

Urban Design in the Real Estate Development Process, First Edition. Edited by Steve Tiesdell and David Adams.

Amion Consulting, Taylor Young, Donaldsons and Shaw, D. (2007) *Economic Value of Urban Design*, Final Report to NWDA/RENEW Northwest, Amion Consulting, Liverpool.

An, K. (2005) *Implementation of Real-Time Landscape Visualisation for Planning Process*, Trends in Real-Time Landscape Visualisation and Participation Proceedings, Anhalt University of Applied Sciences, 184–194.

Appleton, K. & Lovett, A. (2003) 'GIS-based visualisation of rural landscapes: defining "sufficient" realism for environmental decision-making', *Landscape & Urban Planning*, **65**, 117–131.

Attorney General versus Williams (1899) 174 Mass. 476.

Audit Commission (2006) *The Planning System: Matching Expectations and Capacity*, Audit Commission, London.

Baillieu, A. (2009) 'No need to spoil the party', *Building Design* 1883, 11 September, 6–7.

Ball, M. (1983) *Housing Policy and Economic Power*, Methuen, London.

Ball, M. (1986) 'The built environment and the urban question', *Society and Space*, **4**, 447–464.

Ball, M. (1998) 'Institutions in British property research: A review', *Urban Studies*, **35** (9), 1501–1517.

Ball, M. (1999) 'Chasing a snail: innovation and housebuilding firms' strategies', *Housing Studies*, **14**, 9–22

Ball, M. (2002) 'Cultural explanation of a regional property market: A critique', *Urban Studies*, **39** (8), 1453–1469.

Ball, M., Lizieri, C. & MacGregor, B. (2008) (2nd Edition) *The Economics of Commercial Property Markets*, Routledge, London.

Barbre, E. S. (1972) 'Validity and construction of "zoning with compensation" regulation', American Law Reports, ALR 3d, Vol. 41, Thomson/West, St Paul, MN.

Barker, K. (2004) *Review of Housing Supply – Delivering Stability Securing Our Future Housing Needs (Final Report – Recommendations)*, HM Treasury, London.

Barlow, J. (1999) 'From craft production to mass customisation. Innovation requirements for the UK housebuilding industry', *Housing Studies*, **14**, 23–42.

Barlow, J. & Ball, M. (1999) 'Introduction – improving British housing supply', *Housing Studies*, **14**, 5–8.

Barlow, J. & Bhatti, M. (1997) 'Environmental performance as a competitive strategy? British speculative housebuilders in the 1990s', *Planning Practice and Research*, **12**, 33–44.

Barlow, J. & King, A. (1992) 'The state, the market and competitive strategy: the housebuilding industry in the United Kingdom, France and Sweden', *Environment & Planning A*, **24**, 381–400.

Barlow, J. & Ozaki, R. (2003) 'Achieving 'customer focus' in private house building: Current practice and lessons from other industries', *Housing Studies*, **18**, 87–101.

Barnes, Y. (2004) *'Design Codes: The Implications for Landowners and Developers'*, paper given to the HBF Annual Design Conference, HBF, London.

Barnett, J. (1974) *Urban Design as Public Policy*, Harper & Row, New York.

Barnett, J. (1982) *An Introduction to Urban Design*, Harper & Row, New York.

Barrett, S. M., Stewart, M. & Underwood, J. (1978) *The Land Market and the Development Process*, Occasional Paper 2, School for Advanced Urban Studies, University of Bristol.

Barron, D. J. (2003) 'Reclaiming home rule', *Harvard Law Review*, **116** (8), 2255–2386

Barton, S. E. & Silberman, C. J. (1994) (eds) *Common Interest Communities: Private Governments and the Public Interest*, Institute of Governmental Studies Press, Berkeley, CA.

Bassett, E. M. (1922) *Zoning*, National Municipal League, New York, NY.

Bateman, A. (1995) *'Planning in the 1990s: A Developer's Perspective'*, Report, No.1, February, 26–9.

Baxter, S. (1909) 'The German way of making better cities', *The Atlantic Monthly*, July, 72–85.

Ben-Joseph, E. (2004) 'Double standards, single goal: Private communities and design innovation', *Journal of Urban Design*, **9** (2), 131–151.

Ben-Joseph, E. (2005) *The Code of the City: Standards and the Hidden Language of Place Making*, MIT Press, Cambridge, Mass.

Ben-Joseph, E and Szold, T. S. (2005) *Regulating Place: Standards and the Shaping of Urban America*, Routledge, New York.

Bennett, E. (2005) 'Prescott: What Urban Task Force?' *Building Design*, No. 1702, 9 December, 2.

Benson, E. D., Hansen, J. L., Schwartz Jr, A. L. & Smersh, G. T. (1998) 'Pricing residential amenities: the value of a view', *Journal of Real Estate Finance & Economics*, **16**, 55–73.

Bentley, I. (1999) *Urban Transformations – Power, People and Urban Design*, Routledge, London.

Bettman, A. (1923) 'Constitutionality of zoning', *Harvard Law Review*, **37**, 834–859.

Biddulph, M., Hooper, A. & Punter, J. (2004) *Evaluating the Impact of Housing Design Awards for Housing*, RIBA Enterprises, London.

Billingham, J. & Cole, R. (2002) *The Good Place Guide*, Batsford, London.

Bishop, I. (2005) *Visualization for participation: the advantages of real time*, Trends in Real-Time Landscape Visualization and Participation, Wichmann, Berlin, 2–15.

Black, J. S. (1997) 'Quality in development, by design or process?' *Proceedings of the Town and Country Planning Summer School*, 80–82.

Blaesser, B.W. (1994) 'The Abuse of Discretionary Power', in Scheer, B. & Preiser, W. (1994) (eds) *Design Review: Challenging Urban Aesthetic Control*, Chapman & Hall, New York, 42–50.

Blaesser, B. W. (2008) *Discretionary Land Use Controls: Avoiding Invitations to Abuse of Discretion* (11th edition), West Group, St. Paul, MN.

Bo01/City of Malmö (1999) *Quality Programme – Bo01 City of Tomorrow*, Bo01/City of Malmö, Malmö – available at http://www.malmo.se/English/Sustainable-City-Development/PDF-archive/pagefiles/kvalprog_bo01_dn_eng.pdf

Bohl, C. C. (2002) *Place Making*, Urban Land Institute, Washington DC.

Borraz, O. & John, P. (2004) 'The transformation of urban political leadership in Western Europe', *International Journal of Urban & Regional Research*, **28** (1), 107–120.

Brain, D. (2005) 'From good neighbourhoods to sustainable cities: Social science and the social agenda of New Urbanism', *International Regional Science Review*, **28** (2) 217–238.

Brand, S. (1994) *How Buildings Learn: What happens after they are built*, Penguin Books, Harmondsworth.

Brenner, R. (undated) *Fifteen tips for change agents*, available at http://www.chacocanyon.com/essays/tipsforchange.shtml (accessed 12 April 2010).

Briffault, R. (2002) 'Smart growth and American land use law', *Saint Louis University Public Law Review*, **21**, 253–260.

Brooks, R. C. (1915) 'Metropolitan free cities', *Political Science Quarterly*, **30** (2), 222–234.

Burdette, J. (2004) *Form-Based Codes: A Cure for the Cancer Called Euclidean Zoning?* unpublished Masters dissertation, Virginia Polytechnic Institute, Blacksburg VA.

Byrne, P. (1996) *Risk, Uncertainty and Decision Making in Property Development*, (2nd Edition), E. & F. N. Spon, London.

CABE (2002) *Design Review*, Commission for Architecture and the Built Environment, London.

CABE (2004a) *Design Coding, Testing its Use in England*, Commission for Architecture and the Built Environment, London.

CABE (2004b) *Creating Successful Masterplans: A Guide for Clients*, Commission for Architecture and the Built Environment, London.

CABE (2004c) *Housing Audit – Assessing the Design Quality of New Homes: London, the South East and the East of England*, Commission for Architecture and the Built Environment, London.

CABE (2004d) *Design Reviewed: Masterplans*, Commission for Architecture and the Built Environment, London.

CABE (2004e) *Design Reviewed: Town Centre Retail*, Commission for Architecture and the Built Environment, London.

CABE (2004f) *Design Reviewed: Urban Housing*, Commission for Architecture and the Built Environment, London.

CABE (2005) *Housing Audit – Assessing the Design Quality of New Homes in the North East, North West and Yorkshire & Humber*, Commission for Architecture and the Built Environment, London.

CABE (2006a) *How CABE Evaluates Quality in Architecture and Urban Design*, Commission for Architecture and the Built Environment, London.

CABE (2006b) *How to do Design Review: Creating and Running a Successful Panel*, Commission for Architecture and the Built Environment, London.

CABE (2007a) *Housing Audit: Assessing the Design Quality of New Housing in the East Midlands, West Midlands and the South West*, Commission for Architecture and the Built Environment, London.

CABE (2007b) *A Sense of Place: What Residents Think of their New Homes*, Commission for Architecture and the Built Environment, London.

CABE (2007c) *CABE Schools Design Panel: Information Pack*, Commission for Architecture and the Built Environment, London.

CABE (2009) *Survey of Local and Regional Design Review Panels, their Location, Type and Impact*, Commission for Architecture and the Built Environment, London.

CABE, Landscape Institute, RTPI & RIBA (2009) *Design Review: Principles and Practice*, Commission for Architecture and the Built Environment, London.

CABE/NLGN (2004) *Local Leadership for Better Public Places: Building sustainable communities*, Commission for Architecture and the Built Environment/New Local Government Network, London – available at http://www.cabe.org.uk/publications/local-leadership-for-better-public-places

Cadell, C., Falk, N. & King, F. (2008) *Regeneration in European Cities: Making Connections*, Joseph Rowntree Foundation, York – available at http://www.jrf.org.uk/publications/regeneration-european-cities-making-connections – also available at www.urbed.co.uk

Calcutt, J. (2007) *The Calcutt Review of Housebuilding Delivery*, DCLG, London.

Caldwell, R. (2003) 'Change leaders and change managers: Different or complementary?' *Leadership & Organisation Development Journal*, **24** (5), 285–293.

Cambridgeshire Horizons (2008) *Cambridgeshire Quality Charter for Growth*, Cambridgeshire Horizons, Cambridgeshire – available at http://www.cambridgeshirehorizons.co.uk/

Carmona, M. (1998) 'Design control: Bridging the professional divide – Part 1: A new framework', *Journal of Urban Design*, **3** (2), 175–200.

Carmona, M. (2001) Housing Design Quality: Through Policy, Guidance and Review, London, E. & FN Spon.

Carmona, M. (2009) 'Design coding and the creative, market and regulatory tyrannies of practice', *Urban Studies*, **46** (12), 2643–2667.

Carmona, M. & Dann, J. (2007) (eds) 'Design codes', *Urban Design*, Issue 101, Winter, 16–35.

Carmona, M., Carmona, S. & Gallent, N. (2003) *Delivering New Homes: Processes, Planners and Providers*, Routledge, London.

Carmona, M., de Magalhaes, C., Edwards, M., Awuor, B. & Aminossehe, S. (2001) *The Value of Urban Design*, CABE and DETR, Thomas Telford, Tonbridge.

Carmona, M., Marshall, S. & Stevens, Q. (2006) 'Design codes: Their use and potential', *Progress in Planning*, **65** (4) 209–289.

Carmona, M., Tiesdell, S., Heath, T. & Oc, T. (2010) *Public Places, Urban Spaces: The dimensions of urban design* (second edition), Architectural Press, London.

CBC (1994) *Springfield Basin and Chelmer Waterside*, Chelmsford Borough Council, Chelmsford.

CBC (1996) *Land North East of Chelmsford*, Chelmsford Borough Council, Chelmsford.

CBC (1997) *Chelmsford Borough Local Plan*, Chelmsford Borough Council, Chelmsford.

CBC (2001) *Beaulieu Park Northern Area*, Chelmsford Borough Council, Chelmsford.

CBC (2002a) *Chelmer Waterside Strategy*, Chelmsford Borough Council, Chelmsford.

CBC (2002b) *Chelmer Waterside Area 4: Land North East of Canal*.

CEC (City of Edinburgh Council) (2003) *The Quality of Urban Design: Report of the Urban Design Working Group*, Report to Planning Committee 6 February, City of Edinburgh Council, Edinburgh.

Charney, I. (2007) 'Intra-metropolitan preferences of property developers in Greater Toronto's office market', *Geoforum*, **38**, 1179–1189.

Chau, K-W., Wong, S. K., Yau, Y., and Yeung, A. K. C. (2007) 'Determining optimal building height', *Urban Studies*, **44** (3), 591–608.

Chused, R. H. (2001) 'Euclid's historical imagery', *Case Western Reserve Law Review*, **51**, 597–616.

Coakley, J. (1994) 'The integration of property and financial markets', *Environment & Planning A*, **26**, 697–713.

Coiacetto, E. (2006) 'Real estate development industry structure: Consequences for urban planning and development', *Planning Practice & Research*, **21** (4), 423–441.

Colomb, C. (2007) 'Unpacking New Labour's "Urban Renaissance" Agenda: Towards a socially sustainable reurbanisation of British Cities?' *Planning Practice & Research*, **22** (1), 1–24.

Commission on Building Districts & Restrictions (1916) *Final Report*, City of New York, Board of Estimate and Apportionment, Committee on the City Plan, New York.

Committee on the District of Columbia (1910) *Hearing before the Committee on the District of Columbia on the Subject of City Planning*, Government Printing Office, Washington DC.

Congress for the New Urbanism (1996) *Charter of the New Urbanism*, available at: http://www.cnu.org/sites/files/charter_english.pdf

Congress for the New Urbanism (2004) *Codifying New Urbanism: How to Reform Municipal Land Development Regulations*, American Planning Association, Chicago, Ill.

Congress for the New Urbanism (2010) *CNU Board – Congress for the New Urbanism*, available at: http://www.cnu.org/board

Consolidated Appropriations Act, 2010 (2009) Public Law 111–117, 111th Cong., 1st sess. 2009: 123 Stat 3034, 3084–85.

Correll, M. R., Lillydahl, J. H. & Singell, L. D. (1978) 'The effects of greenbelts on residential property values: Some findings on the political economy of open space', *Land Economics*, **54** (2), 207–17.

Crosby, N., Henneberry, J. & McAllister, P. (2008) *Unconventional Conventional Wisdom: Rethinking Development Appraisal*, paper presented at the ERES Annual Conference, Krakow.

Cullen, G. (1961) *Townscape*, Architectural Press, London.

Cullingworth, B. (1999) *British Planning: 50 Years of Urban and Regional Policy*, Athlone, London.

Cuthbert, A. (2010) Review article: 'Whose Urban Design? *Journal of Urban Design*, **15** (3), 443–448.

Databuild Research and Solutions (2008) *Survey of Local and Regional Design Review Panels, their Location, Impact and Type*, Databuild, Birmingham.

Davies, T. (2008) 'Why all politicians need a designer around', *Prospect*, **130**, 45, available at http://www.urbanrealm.co.uk/features/211/A_former_Politicans_view_on_Edinburgh%27s_Urban_Design.html (accessed 11 August 2010).

Davies, T. (2009) *Effective City Leadership in the International Era*, Paper given to EURA Conference on City Futures, Madrid.

Dawson, E. & Higgins, M. (2009) 'How local authorities can improve design quality through the design review process: Lessons from Edinburgh', *Journal of Urban Design*, **14** (1), 101–114.

DCFW (2005) *Design Review in Wales: The experience of the Design Commission for Wales' Design Review Panel: 2003–2005*, DCFW, Cardiff.

DCFW (2007) *Design Review in Wales: The experience of the Design Commission for Wales' Design Review Panel: 2005–2007*, DCFW, Cardiff.

DCLG & DCMS (Department for Communities & Local Government & Department for Culture, Media & Sport) (2009), *World Class Places: the Government's Strategy for Improving Quality of Place*, DCLG, London.

DCLG (Department for Communities & Local Government) (2005) *Planning Policy Statement (PPS) 1: Delivering Sustainable Development*, DCLG, London.

DCLG (Department for Communities & Local Government) (2006a) *Preparing Design Codes: A Practice Manual*, DCLG, London.

DCLG (Department for Communities & Local Government) (2006b) *Design Coding in Practice: An Evaluation*, DCLG, London.

DCLG (Department for Communities & Local Government) (2006c) *Planning Policy Statement (PPS) 3: Housing*, DCLG, London.

DCLG (Department for Communities & Local Government) (2009) *Live Table 209 House Building: Permanent Dwellings Completed, by Tenure & Country*, DCLG, London.

DCLG (Department for Communities & Local Government) (2010) *Planning Policy Statement (PPS) 5: Planning for the Historic Environment*, DCLG, London.

De Monchaux, J. & Schuster, J. M. (1997) 'Five Things to Do', in Schuster, J. M, with De Monchaux, J. & Riley II, C. A. (1997) (eds) *Preserving the Built Heritage: Tools for Implementation*, University Press of New England, London, 3–12.

Department of Commerce (1926) *A Standard State Zoning Enabling Act (revised edition)*, Government Printing Office, Washington DC.

Department of Commerce, Advisory Committee on City Planning (1922) *A Zoning Primer*, Government Printing Office, Washington DC.

Department of Commerce, Division of Building and Housing (1928) *Survey of Zoning Laws and Ordinances in 1927*, United States Department of Commerce, Washington DC.

DETR (Department of the Environment, Transport & the Regions) (1998) *Places, Streets and Movement: A Companion Guide to Design Bulletin 32 Residential Roads and Footpaths*, DETR, London.

DETR (Department of the Environment, Transport & the Regions) (2000) *Planning Policy Guidance 3 (revised): Housing*, The Stationery Office, London.

DfT (Department for Transport) (2007) *Manual for Streets*, DfT, London – available at http://www.dft.gov.uk/pgr/sustainable/manforstreets/pdfmanforstreets.pdf

Do, A. Q. & Grudnitski, G. (1995) 'Golf courses and residential house prices: An empirical examination', *Journal of Real Estate Finance & Economics*, **10**, 261–270.

Doak, J. & Karadimitriou, N. (2007) '(Re)development, complexity and networks: A framework for research', *Urban Studies* **44** (2), 209–229.

Dobriner, W. M. (1963) *Class in Suburbia*, Prentice-Hall, Englewood Cliffs, NJ.

Docherty, I. & McKiernan, P. (2008) 'Scenario planning for the Edinburgh city region', *Environment & Planning C: Government & Policy* **26** (5), 982–99.

DoE (Department of the Environment) (1980) *Development Control: Policy and Practice*, Circular 22/80, HMSO, London.

DoE (Department of the Environment) (1996) *Household Growth: Where Shall We Live?* Cm 3471, The Stationery Office, London.

DTLR & CABE (Department of Transport, Local Government & the Regions & Commission for Architecture & the Built Environment) (2001) *By Design, Better Places to Live: A Companion Guide to PPG 3*, Thomas Telford Publishing, Kent.

Duany, A. & Plater-Zyberk, E. (1992) 'The second coming of the American small town', *Wilson Quarterly*, **16** (1), 19–50.

Duany, A. & Talen, E. (2002a) 'Making the good easy: The smart code alternative', *Fordham Urban Law Journal*, **29** (4), 1445–1469.

Duany, A. & Talen, E. (2002b) 'Transect planning', *Journal of the American Planning Association*, **68** (3), 245–266.

Duany, A., Plater-Zyberk, E. & Speck, J. (2000) *Suburban Nation, The Rise of Sprawl and the Decline of the American Dream*, North Point Press, New York.

ECC (Essex County Council) (2005) *The Essex Design Guide*. Essex County Council, Chelmsford (a reprint of Essex Planning Officers Association (1997) *A Design Guide for Residential and Mixed Use Areas*).

Ellickson, R. C. & Been, V. L. (2005) *Land Use Controls: Cases and Materials* (3rd edition), Aspen Publishers, New York.

Ellis, C. (2002) 'The New Urbanism: Critiques and rebuttals', *Journal of Urban Design*, **7** (3), 261–291.

Elmore, R. F. (1987) 'Instruments and strategy in public policy', *Policy Studies Review*, **7** (1), 174–186.

English Partnerships (2007a) *Design Codes: The English Partnerships Experience*, English Partnerships, London.

English Partnerships (2007b) *National Brown Strategy: Recommendations to Government, A Policy Submission*, English Partnerships, London.

English Partnerships (2008) Best Practice Note 27 – Contamination and Dereliction Remediation Costs, English Partnerships, London.

Eppli, M. J. & Tu, C. C. (1999a) *Valuing the New Urbanism: The impact of New Urbanism on prices of single family homes*, Urban Land Institute, Washington.

Eppli, M. & Tu, C. C. (1999b) 'Valuing New Urbanism; The case of Kentlands', *Real Estate Economics*, **27** (3).

European Commission (2007) *State of European Cities*, European Commission, Brussels – available at http://ec.europa.eu/regional_policy/sources/docgener/studies/pdf/urban/stateofcities_2007.pdf

Evans, A. (2004) *Economics and Land Use Planning*, Blackwell Publishing Ltd., Oxford, UK.

Falk, N. (2006) Towards Sustainable Suburbs, *Built Environment*, **32** (3), 225–234.

Falk, N. (2008) *Beyond Ecotowns: The Economic Issues*, URBED, London – available at http://www.prparchitects.co.uk/assets/pdf/6.pdf – also available at www.urbed.co.uk

Falk, N. (2009) Investing in the Green Recovery in Hackett, P. (2009) (editor) *Regeneration in a Downturn*, Smith Institute, London, 43–51.

Faludi, A. (1989) '*Keeping the Netherlands in shape: Introduction', Built Environment*, **15** (1), 5–10.

Farrell, T. (co-authored with Marina, R.) (2008) 'Twelve challenges for Edinburgh', *Prospect*, **130**, 2–43.

Farrell, T. (co-authored with Marina, R.) (2009) *Edinburgh's First City Design Champion: February 2004 to September 2009: Report to Full Council 17 September 2009*, City of Edinburgh Council, Edinburgh.

Fields, T. (1995) 'Federal agency brownfields initiatives.' *Environmental Law Institute's Redeveloping Brownfields Workshop*, Washington, DC.

Fischler, R. (1995) Strategy and History in Professional Practice: Planning as World Making in Liggett, H. and Perry, D. C. (1995) (eds) *Spatial Practices*, Sage London, 13–58.

Flanagan, R. & Norman, G. (1978) 'The relationship between construction price and height', *Chartered Surveyor*, **5** (4), 68–71.

Fraser, M. (2008) 'Malcolm Fraser objects to Planners', *Prospect*, **131**, available at http://www.urbanrealm.co.uk/features/215/Malcolm_Fraser_objects_to_Planners.htm (accessed 11 April 2010).

Fraser, W. (1993) *Principles of Property Investment and Pricing*, Macmillan, London.

Freund, E. (1904) *The Police Power: Public Policy and Constitutional Rights*, Callaghan & Co.

Frug, G. E. (1980) 'The city as a legal concept', *Harvard Law Review*, **93**, 1057–1154.

Fulford, C. (1998) *The Costs of Reclaiming Derelict Sites*, Town & Country Planning Association, London.

Gardiner, J. (2004) 'The codemaker', *Housing Today*, 23 January, 26–28.

Garner, B. A. (2004) (editor) *Black's Law Dictionary* (8th edition), Thomson/West, St Paul, MN.

Garreau, J. (1991) *Edge City: Life on the New Frontier*, Doubleday, London.

Gates, C. (2006) 'RIBA Warns Over Design Codes', *Building Design*, No. 1712, 10 March, 6.

George, R. V. (1997) 'A procedural explanation for contemporary urban design', *Journal of Urban Design*, **2** (2), 143–161.

Gibb, K. (1999) 'Regional differentiation and the Scottish private housebuilding sector', *Housing Studies*, **14**, 43–56.

Godfrey, H. (1910a) 'The problem of city housing: The problem abroad', *The Atlantic Monthly*, **105** (3), 403–413.

Godfrey, H. (1910b) 'The problem of city housing: The problem at home', *The Atlantic Monthly*, **105** (4), 548–558.

Goodchild, R. N. & Munton, R. (1985) *Development and the Landowner*, Allen Unwin, London.

Gordon, D. L. A. (1997) *Battery Park City: Politics and planning on the New York waterfront*, Spon Press, Abingdon.

Gore, T. & Nicholson, D. (1991) 'Models of the land development process: A critical review', *Environment & Planning A*, **23**, 705–730.

Granovetter, M. (1985) 'Economic action and social structure: The problem of embeddedness', *American Journal of Sociology*, **91.3**, 481–510.

Grebler, L. (1950) *Production of New Housing; A Research Monograph on Efficiency in Production*, Social Science Research Council, New York.

Gries, J. M. (1926) Zoning ordinances adopted during 1925, *Municipal Index 1926*, The American City Magazine, New York, 92.

Guy, S. & Henneberry, J. (2000) 'Understanding urban development processes: Integrating the economic and the social in property research', *Urban Studies*, **37** (13), 2399–2416.

Guy, S. & Henneberry, J. (2002a) 'Bridging the Divide? Complementary perspectives on property', *Urban Studies*, **39** (8), 1471–1478.

Guy, S. & Henneberry, J. (2002b) 'Approaching Development', in Guy, S. & Henneberry, J. (2002) (eds) *Development and Developers: Perspectives on Property*, Blackwell Publishing Ltd., Oxford, UK, 1–18.

Guy, S. & Henneberry J. (2004) 'Economic Structures, Urban Responses: Framing and Negotiating Urban Property Development', in Boddy, M. & Parkinson, M. (2004) (eds) *City Matters: Competitiveness, Cohesion and Urban Governance*, Policy Press, Bristol, 217–236.

Guy, S., Henneberry, J. & Rowley, S. (2002) 'Development cultures and urban regeneration', *Urban Studies*, **39** (7), 1181–1196.

Haar, C. M. (1955) 'In accordance with a comprehensive plan', *Harvard Law Review*, **68**, 1154–1175.

Habe, R. (1989) 'Public design control in American communities', *Town Planning Review*, **60** (2), 195–219.

Hack, G. (1994) 'Renewing Prudential Center', *Urban Land*, November.

Hall, T. (2007) *Turning a Town Around: A Pro-active Approach to Urban Design*, Blackwell Publishing Ltd., Oxford, UK.

Hall, T. (2008a) 'Bridging the Gap: An example of applying urban morphology to successful planning practice', *Urban Morphology*, **12** (1), 54–57.

Hall, T. (2008b) 'The form-based development plan: Bridging the gap between theory and practice in urban morphology', *Urban Morphology*, **12** (2), 77–96.

Harvey, D. (1989) *The Urban Experience*, Blackwell Publishing Ltd., Oxford, UK.

Havard, T. (2008) *Contemporary Property Development* (2nd edition), RIBA Publishing, London.

HBF & RIBA (Housebuilders' Federation and the Royal Institute of British Architects) (1990) *Good Design in Housing*, HBF, London.

Healey, P. (1991) 'Models of the Development Process: A Review', *Journal of Property Research*, **8**, 219–238.

Healey, P., McNamara, P., Elson, M. & Doak, J. (1988), *Land Use Planning and the Mediation of Urban Change*, Cambridge University Press, Cambridge.

Heath, T. (2009) 'Nottingham: A Consistent and Integrated Approach to Urban Design' in Punter, J. (2009) (editor) *Urban Design and the British Urban Renaissance*, London, Routledge, 148–164.

Hebbert, M. (2009) 'Manchester – Making it Happen', in Punter, J. (2009) (editor) *British Urban Design and the British Urban Renaissance*, Routledge, London, 51–67.

Heights of Buildings Commission (1913) *Report of the Heights of Buildings Commission to the Committee on the Height, Size and Arrangement of Buildings of the Board of Estimate and Apportionment of the City of New York*, New York: City of New York, Board of Estimate and Apportionment.

Henriquez, R. (2009) 'Downtown Vancouver Capacity Study', *Cities Program*, Simon Frazer University, October.

Heriot-Watt University, School of the Built Environment (2007) *Design at the Heart of House-Building*, The Scottish Government, Edinburgh.

Herwig, A. & Paar, P. (2002) *Game Engines: Tools for Landscape Visualization and Planning*, Trends in GIS and Virtualization in Environmental Planning and Design, 161–172.

Hinshaw, M. L. (1995) *Design Review*, Planning Advisory Group Report 454, American Planning Association, Chicago.

Hirschhorn, J. S. & Souza, P. (2001) *New Community Design to the Rescue: Fulfilling Another American Dream*, National Governor's Association, Washington, DC.

Hjul, J. (2009) 'Edinburgh tram sham is a warning to other cities', *The Sunday Times*, 3 May, available at http://www.timesonline.co.uk/tol/news/uk/scotland/article6210924.ece (accessed 11 April 2010).

HoC ODPM (House of Commons ODPM: Housing Planning Local Government and the Regions Committee) (2004a) *The Role and Effectiveness of CABE, Session 2003–4*, House of Commons HC 1117-I, London.

HoC ODPM (House of Commons ODPM: Housing Planning Local Government and the Regions Committee) (2004b) *The Role and Effectiveness of CABE, Written Evidence*, House of Commons HC 1117-II, London.

HoC ODPM (House of Commons ODPM: Housing Planning Local Government and the Regions Committee) (2005) *The Role and Effectiveness of CABE, Fifth Report of Session 2004–5*, House of Commons HC 59, London.

Hoinkes, R. & Lange, E. (1995) '3D for free: Toolkit expands visual dimensions in GIS', *GIS World*, **8** (7), 54–56.

Hood, C. (1983) *The Tools of Government*, Chatham House Publishers, Chatham.

Hood, C. (2008) 'Intellectual obsolescence and intellectual makeovers: Reflections on the tools of government after two decades', *Governance: An International Journal of Policy, Administration & Institutions*, **20** (1), 127–144.

Hood, C. & Margetts, H. Z. (2007) *The Tools of Government in the Digital Age*, Palgrave-Macmillan, Basingstoke.

Hooper, A. & Nicol, C. (1999) 'The design and planning of residential development: standard house types in the speculative housebuilding industry', *Environment & Planning B: Planning & Design*, **26**, 793–805.

Hopkins, L. D. (2001) *Urban Development: The Logic of Development Plans*, Island Press, Washington DC.

Housing Forum (2009) *Land for Homes – Creating Value through Community Leadership and Co-investment – Working Group Report*, Housing Forum, London – available at http://www.housingforum.org.uk/downloads/land-for-homes-010409.pdf

Howard, E. (1898) [2003] *To-morrow: A Peaceful Path to Real Reform* (Hall, P. G. et al., eds) Routledge, London.

Howe, F. C. (1905) *The City: The Hope of Democracy*, Charles Scribner's Sons, New York.

Howe, F. C. (1910a) 'City Building in Germany', *Scribner's Magazine*, 47(5), 601–614.

Howe, F. C. (1910b) 'A Way Toward the Model City', *The World's Work*, Dec, 13794–13801.

Howe, F. C. (1910c) 'Düsseldorf: A City of To-morrow', *Hampton's Magazine*, 25(6), 697–709.

Howe, F. C. (1911a) 'The German and the American City', *Scribner's Magazine*, 49(4), 485–492.

Howe, F. C. (1911b) 'The Municipal Real Estate Policies of German Cities', in *Proceedings of the Third National Conference on City Planning*. Third National Conference on City Planning, University Press, Philadelphia, Penn, 14–26.

Howe, F. C. (1911c) 'The America of To-morrow'. *Hampton's Magazine*, 24(5), 573–584.

Howe, F. C. (1912) 'In Defence of the American City', *Scribner's Magazine*, 51(4), 484–490.

Howe, F. C. (1913a) *European Cities at Work*, Charles Scribner's Sons, New York.

Howe, F. C. (1913b) 'The Remaking of the American City', *Harper's Magazine*, July, 186–197.

Howlett, M. (1991) 'Policy instruments, policy styles, and policy implementation: National approaches to theories of instrument choice', *Policy Studies Journal*, **19** (2), 1–21.

HUD News Release 09–130 (2009) *Shelly Poticha Appointed as HUD Senior Advisor for Sustainable Housing and Communities*, available at: http://www.hud.gov/news/release.cfm?content=pr09–130.cfm&CFID=26033498&CFTOKEN=65467235

Imrie, R. & Street, E. (2006) 'The attitudes of architects towards planning regulation and control', Project Paper 3 in *'The Codification and Regulation of Architects' Practices'*, Kings College London, London.

International Code Council (2010) *About ICC*, available at: http://www.iccsafe.org/AboutICC/Pages/default.aspx

Isaac, D. (1996) *Property Development: Appraisal and Finance*, Macmillan, London.

Jackson, K. T. (1987) *Crabgrass Frontier: The Suburbanisation of the United States*, Oxford University Press, New York.

Jacobs, J. (1961) *The Death and Life of Great American Cities*, Vintage Books, New York.

Jim, C. Y. & Chen, W. Y. (2009) 'Value of scenic views: Hedonic assessment of private housing in Hong Kong', *Landscape & Urban Planning*, **91**, 226–234.

Kanter, R. M. (1983) *The Change Masters: Corporate Entrepreneurs at Work*, Thomson, New York.

Kayden, J. S. (1978), *Incentive Zoning in New York City: A Cost-Benefit Analysis*, Lincoln Institute of Land Policy, Cambridge.

Kayden, J. S. (2000) *Privately Owned Public Space: The New York City Experience*, John Wiley & Sons, New York.

Kim, J. (1997) *Privatization of Public Open Spaces: Public Process and Private Influence*, unpublished PhD dissertation, Massachusetts Institute of Technology.

Knack, R., Meck, S. & Stollman, I. (1996) 'The real story behind the standard Planning and Zoning Acts of the 1920s', *Land Use Law & Zoning Digest*, **48** (2), 3–9.

Kohn, M. (2004) *Brave New Neighborhoods: The Privatisation of Public Space*, Routledge, New York.

Koolhaas (1972) *City of the Captive Globe* (artwork) See: http://www.moma.org/collection/browse_results.php?criteria=O%3AAD%3AE%3A6956&page_number=1&template_id=1&sort_order=1

Ladd, B. (1990) *Urban Planning and Civic Order in Germany, 1860–1914*, Harvard University Press, Cambridge, Mass.

Lai, R. (1988) *The Invisible Web: Law in Urban Design and Planning*, New York, Van Nostrand Reinhold, New York.

Lakoff, G. (2006) *Don't Think of an Elephant! Know your values and frame the debate*, Chelsea Green Publishing, White River Junction, Vermont.

Landry, C. (2000) *The Creative City: A Toolkit for Urban Innovators*, Earthscan, London.

Lang, J. (2005) *Urban Design: A Typology of Procedures and Products*, Architectural Press, Oxford.

Lange, E. (1994) 'Integration of computerized visual simulation and visual assessment in environmental planning', *Landscape & Urban Planning*, **30** (1–2), 99–112.

Lange, E. (2001) 'The limits of realism: Perceptions of virtual landscapes', *Landscape & Urban Planning*, **54** (1–4), 163–182.

Lange, E. & Hehl-Lange, S. (2005) 'Combining a participatory planning approach with a virtual landscape model for the siting of wind turbines', *Journal of Environmental Planning & Management*, **48** (6), 833–852.

Lange, E. & Schaeffer, P. V. (2001) 'A comment on the market value of a room with a view', *Landscape & Urban Planning*, **55**, 113–120.

Laverne, R. & Winson-Geideman, K. (2003) 'The influence of trees and landscaping on rental rates at office buildings', *Journal of Arboriculture*, **29** (5), 281–290.

Leach, D., Lowndes, V. & Wilson, D. (2003) '*Comparing Leadership Approaches in English Local Government: A Research Agenda*', paper to Annual Conference of the Political Studies Association, University of Leicester.

Leinberger, C. B. (2005) 'The need for alternatives to the nineteen standard real estate product types', *Places* **17** (2), 24–29.

Leinberger, C. B. (2008) *The Option of Urbanism: Investing in a New American Dream*, Island Press, Washington D. C.

Lich, N. & Darin-Drabkin, D. (1980) *Land Policy in Planning*, George Allen & Unwin, London

Llewelyn-Davies (2000 [reissued 2007]), *Urban Design Compendium*, English Partnerships and the Housing Corporation, London.

Logan, T. H. (1976) 'The Americanization of German zoning', *Journal of the American Institute of Planners*, **42** (4), 377–385.

Lorzing, H. (2006) 'Reinventing suburbia in the Netherlands', *Built Environment*, **32** (3), 298–310.

Lowndes, V. (2002) 'Between rhetoric and reality: Does the 2001 White Paper reverse the centralising trend in Britain?' *Local Government Studies*, **28** (3), 135–147.

Lubove, R. (1962) *The Progressives and the Slums: Tenement House Reform in New York City, 1890–1917*, University of Pittsburgh Press, Pittsburgh, Penn.

Luttik, J. (2000) 'The value of trees, water and open space as reflected by house prices in the Netherlands', *Landscape & Urban Planning*, **48** (3–4), 161–167.

Macmillan, S. (2006) 'Added value of good design', *Building Research & Information*, **34** (3).

Mantownhuman (2008) *Manifesto: Towards a New Humanism in Architecture*, www.mantownhuman.org

Marini, R. (2008) 'Project Edinburgh: Let's stop putting lipstick on the monkey!' *Prospect*, **130**, 46–49, available at http://www.urbanrealm.co.uk/features/192/The_urban_challenge_faced_by_edinburgh_by_Riccardo_Marini.html

Markelin, A. & Fahle, B. (1979) *Umweltsimulation. Sensorische Simulation im Städtebau*, Schriftenr. 11, Städtebaul. Inst. Universität Stuttgart. Krämer, Stuttgart.

Marsh, B. C. (1909) *An Introduction to City Planning: Democracy's Challenge to the American City*, privately printed, New York.

Marsh, B. C. (1911) *Taxation of Land Values in American Cities*, privately printed, New York.

Marshall, T. (2004) (editor) *Transforming Barcelona*, Routledge, London.

Matthews, P. & Satsangi, M. (2007) 'Planners, developers and power: A critical discourse analysis of the redevelopment of Leith Docks, Scotland', *Planning Practice & Research*, **22** (4), 495–511.

Mayer, M. (1978) *The Builders: Houses, People, Neighborhoods, Governments, Money* (1st edn), Norton, New York.

McGlynn S. (1993) 'Reviewing the Rhetoric', in *Making Better Places: Urban Design Now*, Hayward, R. & McGlynn, S. (1993) (eds), Architectural Press, Oxford, 3–9.

McKenzie, E. (1994) *Privatopia: Homeowner Associations and the Rise of Residential Private Government*, Yale University Press, New Haven.

McQuaid, R. & Grieco, M. (2005) 'Edinburgh and the politics of congestion charging: negotiating road user charging with affected publics', *Transport Policy*, **12**, 475–476

McQuillin, E. (2009) *McQuillin's Law of Municipal Corporations*, Thomson/West, St Paul, MN

Meikle, J. (2009) *Notes on the Demand for, and the Costs and Benefits of, Design Review*, unpublished research paper, Commission for Architecture and the Built Environment, London.

Miami 21 Code, 2009. Available at: http://www.miami21.org/PDFs/FinalDocuments/FULLDOCUMENT.pdf

Mintrom, M. (1997) 'Policy entrepreneurs and the diffusion of innovation', *American Journal of Political Science*, **41** (3), 738–770.

Musibay, O. P. (2009) 'Miami 21 implementation delayed', *South Florida Business Journal*, December 18.

NAHB Land Development Services Department (2007) *LEED ND FACT SHEET*, National Association of Home Builders, accessed 26 February 2010 from: http://www.nahb.org/fileUpload_details.aspx?contentID=116358

Nasar, J. L. & Grannis, P. (1999) 'Design review reviewed: administrative vs discretionary methods', *Journal of the American Planning Association*, **65** (4) 424–433.

Needham, B. (1989) 'Strategic planning and the shape of the Netherlands through foreign eyes: but do appearances deceive?' *Built Environment*, **15** (1), 11–15.

Nichols, J. C. (1914) Housing and the real estate problem. *Annals of the American Academy of Political and Social Science*, **51**, 132–139.

Nijkamp, P, van der Burch, M. & Vindigni, G. (2002) 'A comparative institutional evaluation of public–private partnerships in Dutch urban land-use and revitalisation projects', *Urban Studies*, **39** (10), 1865–1880.

ODPM (Office of the Deputy Prime Minister) (2003) *Sustainable Communities: Building for the Future*, DCLG, London – available at http://www.communities.gov.uk/communities/sustainablecommunities/sustainablecommunities/

ODPM (Office for the Deputy Prime Minister) (2005) *The Future for Design Codes: Further Information to Support Stakeholders Reading Draft PPS3*, ODPM, London.

Oxford Brookes University (2004) *Skills Base in the Planning System: Survey Results*, Local Government Association, London.

Panerai, P., Castex, J., Depaule, J. C. & Samuels, I. (2004) *Urban Forms: The Death and Life of the Urban Block*, Architectural Press, Oxford.

Parolek, D., Parolek, K. & Crawford, P. (2008) *Form-Based Codes: A Guide for Planners, Urban Designers, Municiplities, and Developers*, John Wiley & Sons, Hoboken, New Jersey.

Parris, S. (2010) *Institutional Ecologies of Commercial Property Development*, unpublished PhD Thesis, Department of Town & Regional Planning, University of Sheffield.

Paton, R. A. & McCalman, J. (2000) *Change Management: A guide to effective implementation* (2nd edn), Sage Publications, London.

Payne, S. L. (2009) *The Institutional Capacity of the UK Speculative Housebuilding Industry*, unpublished PhD Thesis, Department of Urban Studies, University of Glasgow – available at http://theses.gla.ac.uk/853/

Pennington, M. (2000) *Planning and the Political Market: Public Choice and the Politics of Government Failure*, Athlone, London.

Peterson, J. A. (2003) *The Birth of City Planning in the United States, 1840–1917*, John Hopkins University Press, Baltimore.

Peterson, J. A (2009) 'The birth of organized city planning in the United States, 1909–1910', *Journal of the American Planning Association*, **75** (2), 123–133.

Picken, D. H. & Ilozor, B. D. (2003) 'Height and construction cost of buildings in Hong Kong', *Construction Management & Economics*, **21**, 107–111.

PlaceMakers (2010) *SmartCode Complete*, available at: http://www.smartcodecomplete.com/learn/links.html

Polikov, S. (2008) 'The new economics of place', *Chamber Executive*, **35** (4), 7–18.

Poole, S. (1987) 'Architectural appearance, review regulations and the first amendment: the good, the bad and the consensus ugly', *Urban Lawyer* **18**, 287–344.

Popular Housing Forum (1998) *Kerb Appeal: The External Appearance and Site Appeal of New Houses*, Popular Housing Forum, Winchester.

POS, HBF and the DETR (Planning Officers' Society, House Builders' Federation and the Department for Environment, Transport and the Regions) (1998) *Housing Layouts – Lifting the Quality*, HBF, London.

Poulton, M. C. (1997), 'Externalities, transaction costs, public choice and the appeal of zoning', *Town Planning Review*, **68**, 81–92.

PRP, URBED & Design for Homes (2009) *Beyond Ecotowns: Applying the Lessons from Europe*, PRP/URBED/Design for Homes, London – available at http://www.prparchitects.co.uk/research-development/research-publications/2008/beyond-eco-towns.html – also available at www.urbed.co.uk.

Pryce, G. & Levin, E. (2008) Beyond reason, *RICS Residential Property Journal*, September/October 2008, RICS, London.

Pryke, M. & Lee, R. (1995) 'Place your bets: Towards an understanding of globalisation, socio-financial engineering and competition within a financial centre', *Urban Studies*, **32**, 329–344.

Punter, J. (2007) 'Developing urban design as public policy: Best practice principles for design review and development management', *Journal of Urban Design*, **12** (2) 167–202.

Punter, J. (2009) (editor) *Urban Design and the British Urban Renaissance*, Routledge, London.

Putnam, R. D. (2000) *Bowling Alone: The Collapse and Revival of American Community*, Simon and Schuster, London.

Pyatok, M. (2000) 'Comment on Charles C. Bohl's "New Urbanism and the City: Potential applications and implications for distressed inner-city neighborhoods" – The politics of design: The New Urbanists versus the Grass Roots', *Housing Policy Debate*, **11** (4), 803–814.

Rabin, C. (2009) 'Surprising vote kills Miami 21 zoning overhaul', *The Miami Herald*, 7 August

Raeburn, S. (2008) 'Roundtable', *Prospect*, **130,** 68–69, available at http://www.urbanrealm.co.uk/features/193/Planners_discuss_Edinburgh_design.html

Rand, A. (1993) *The Fountainhead*, Signet, New York.

Rasmussen, S. (1937) *London: Unique City*, MIT Press, Cambridge, Mass.

Reade, E. (1987) *British Town and Country Planning*, Open University Press, Milton Keynes.

RIBA (Royal Institute of British Architects) (2005) *RIBA Practice Bulletin: Design Codes Risk Pattern Book Housing*, 2nd March, RIBA, London.

Rodgers, D. T. (1998) *Atlantic Crossings: Social Politics in a Progressive Age*, Harvard University Press, Cambridge, Mass.

Roger Evans Associates (2007) *Urban Design Compendium 2: Delivering Quality Places*, English Partnerships & the Housing Corporation, London.

Rombouts, J. (1999) 'Aesthetic Control management in the Flanders region of Belgium,' *Urban Design International*, **4** (1&2), 25–29.

Rowland, I. D. & Howe, T. N. (1999) (eds) *Vitruvius: Ten Books on Architecture*. Cambridge University Press, Cambridge.

Rowley, A. (1998) 'Private-property decision makers and the quality of urban design', *Journal of Urban Design*, **3** (2), 151–173.

RTPI (Royal Town Planning Institute) (2005) *A Survey of Discipline Knowledge and Generic Skills of RTPI Corporate Members*, RTPI, London.

Rudlin, D. & Falk, N. (2009) *Sustainable Urban Neighbourhoods: Building the 21st century home* (2nd edn), Architectural Press, London.

'S. 1619 2009, HR 4690' (2010) *Livable Communities Act of 2009*, United States Congress

Sagalyn, L. B. (1989) 'Measuring financial returns when the city acts as an investor: Boston and Faneuil Hall Marketplace', *Real Estate Issues*, **14** (Fall/Winter), 7–15

Sagalyn, L. B. (1990) 'Explaining the improbable: Local redevelopment in the face of federal cutbacks', *Journal of the American Planning Association*, **56,** (4), 429–441.

Sagalyn, L. B. (1997) 'Negotiating for public benefits: The Bargaining calculus of public–private development', *Urban Studies*, **34** (12), 1955–1970.

Sagalyn, L. B. (2001) *Times Square Roulette: Remaking the city icon*, MIT Press, Cambridge, Mass.

Salamon, L. (2002) *The Tools of Government*, Oxford University Press, Oxford.

Savage, R. (2001) *Planning for Acceptable Housing Development*, unpublished MPhil Thesis, University College London, London.

Savills (2003) *The Value of Housing Design and Layout*, CABE and ODPM with Design for Homes, Thomas Telford, Tonbridge.

Savills (2007) *Valuing Sustainable Urbanism*, The Prince's Foundation and English Partnerships, London.

Schaller, C. (1999) 'Aesthetic control management in the German planning process', *Urban Design International* **4** (1&2), 39–45.

Scheer, B. C. (1994) 'Introduction' in Scheer, B & Preiser, W. (1994) (editors) *Design Review: Challenging Urban Aesthetic Control*, Chapman & Hall, New York, 1–10.

Scheer, B. C. & Preiser, W. (1994) *Design Review: Challenging Urban Aesthetic Control*, Chapman & Hall, New York.

Schein, E. H. (1992) *Organisational Culture and Leadership*, (2nd edn), Jossey Bass, San Francisco.

Schuster, M. (2005) 'Substituting Information for Regulation: In search of an alternative approach to shaping urban design', in Ben-Joseph, E. & Szold, T. (2005) (eds), *Regulating Place: Standards and the Shaping of Urban America*, Routledge, London, 333–358.

Scottish Executive (2003) *Planning Advice Note 67: Housing Quality*, Scottish Executive, Edinburgh.

Scottish Government (2010) *Designing Streets: A policy statement for Scotland*, Scottish Government, Edinburgh – available at: http://openscotland.net/Resource/Doc/307126/0096540.pdf

Seidel, S. R. (1978) *Housing Costs & Government Regulations: Confronting the Regulatory Maze*, Center for Urban Policy Research, New Brunswick, NJ.

Shapiro, R. M. (1969) 'The zoning variance power – Constructive in theory, destructive in practice', *Maryland Law Review*, **29** (1), 3–23.

Shaw, D. & Lord, A. (2007) 'The cultural turn? Culture change and what it means for spatial planning in England', *Planning Practice & Research*, **22** (1), 63–78.

Shaw, D. (2006) *Culture Change and Spatial Planning*, DCLG, London.

Shirvani, H. (1990) *Beyond Public Architecture: Strategies for Design Evaluation*, Van Nostrand Reinhold, New York.

Smead, E. E. (1935) 'Sic Utere Tuo Ut Alienum Non Laedas: A basis of the State police power', *Cornell Law Quarterly*, **21**, 276–292.

Smith, K. B. (2002) 'Typologies, taxonomies and the benefits of policy classification', *Policy Studies Journal*, **30** (1), 379–395.

Song, Y. & Knaap, G. J. (2003) 'New Urbanism and housing values: a disaggregate assessment', *Journal of Urban Economics*, **54**, 218–238.

Sorkin, M. (1992) (ed) *Variations on a Theme Park: The New American City and the End of Public Space*, Noonday Press, New York.

Southworth, M. & Ben Joseph, E. (1996) *Streets and the Shaping of Towns and Cities*. McGraw-Hill, New York.

Stamps, A. & Nasar J. (1997) 'Design review and public preferences: effects of geographical location, public consensus, sensation seeking and architectural styles', *Journal of Environmental Psychology*, **17**, 11–32.

Stille, K. (2007) 'The B-plan in Germany', *Urban Design*, **101** (Winter 2007), 24–26.

Street, E. (2007) 'The codification and regulation of architects' practices, Project Paper 5 in '*The Codification and Regulation of Architects' Practices*', Kings College London, London.

Sutcliffe, A. (1981) *Towards the Planned City: Germany, Britain, the United States, and France, 1780–1914*, St Martin's Press, New York.

Sweeting, D. (2002) 'Leadership in urban governance: The Mayor of London', *Local Government Studies*, **28** (1), 3–20.

Syms, P. (1994) 'The Funding of Developments on Derelict and Contaminated Sites', in Ball, R. & Pratt, A. C. (1994) (eds) *Industrial Property: Policy and Economic Development*, Routledge, London, 63–82.

Syms, P. (2002) *Land, Development and Design*, Blackwell Publishing Ltd., Oxford, UK.

Syms, P. (2010) *Land, Development and Design*, (2nd edn), Blackwell Publishing Ltd., Oxford, UK.

Teaford, J. C. (1984) *The Unheralded Triumph, City Government in America, 1870–1900*, Johns Hopkins University Press, Baltimore, MD.

Thaler, R. H. & Sunstein, C. R. (2008) *Nudge*, Penguin Books, London.

Tiesdell, S. & Adams, D. (2004) 'Design matters: Major house builders and the design challenge of brownfield development contexts', *Journal of Urban Design*, **9** (1), 23–45.

Tiesdell, S. & Allmendinger, P. (2005) 'Planning Tools and Markets: Towards an Extended Conceptualisation', in Adams, D., Watkins, C. & White, M. (2005) (eds) *Planning, Public Policy and Property Markets*, Blackwell Publishing Ltd., Oxford, UK, 56–76.

Toll, S. I. (1969) *Zoned American*, Grossman Publishers, New York, NY.

Topcu, M. & Kubat, A. S. (2009) '*The Analysis of Urban Features that Affect Land Values in Residential Areas*', in Koch, K., Lars, M. & Steen, J. (2009) (eds), Proceedings of the 7th International Space Syntax Symposium, KTH, Stockholm, **26** (1), 26:9.

Tunstall, G. (2006) *Managing the Building Design Process* (2nd edn), Elsevier, Oxford.

Tversky, A. & Kahneman D. (1981) 'The framing of decisions and the psychology of choice', *Science*, **211** (4481), 453–458.

Tyrvainen, L. (1997) 'The amenity value of the urban forest: an application of the hedonic pricing method', *Landscape & Urban Planning*, **37**, 211–222.

Tyrvainen, L. & Miettinen, A. (2000) 'Property prices and urban forest amenities', *Journal of Environmental Economics and Management*, **39**, 205–223.

Tyrwhitt, R. P. (1826) *The Reports of Sir Edward Coke, Knt.*, J. Butterworth & Son.

Unsworth, R. (2007) 'City living' and sustainable development: the experience of a UK regional city, *Town Planning Review*, **78** (6), 725–747.

Urban Task Force (1999) *Towards An Urban Renaissance*, E. & F. N. Spon, London.

Urban Task Force (2005) *Towards a Strong Urban Renaissance*, available at http://www.urban-taskforce.org

US Census Bureau (1993) *United States, 1790 to 1990, Population*, US Census Bureau, Washington DC, available at: http://www.census.gov/population/www/censusdata/files/table-4.pdf

US Census Bureau (1999) *Nativity of the Population for the 50 Largest Urban Places: 1870 to 1990*, US Census Bureau, Washington DC, available at: http://www.census.gov/population/www/documentation/twps0029/tab19.html

US Department of Housing & Urban Development (2010) Director Shelley Poticha/US Department of Housing & Urban Development (HUD), available at: http://portal.hud.gov/portal/page/portal/HUD/program_offices/sustainable_housing_communities/director_shelley_poticha

US Green Building Council (2007) Pilot Version, LEED for Neighborhood Development Rating System.

US Green Building Council (2010a) USGBC: LEED for Neighborhood Development, available at: http://www.usgbc.org/DisplayPage.aspx?CMSPageID=148 (accessed 26 February 2010).

US Green Building Council, 2010b. USGBC: Member Directory. Available at: http://www.usgbc.org/myUSGBC/Members/MembersDirectory.aspx?CMSPageID=140.

US Green Building Council (undated), *Fact Sheet: LEED® for Neighborhood Development*, available at: http://www.usgbc.org/ShowFile.aspx?DocumentID=6423.

Vandell, K. & Lane, J. (1989) 'The economics of architecture and urban design: Some preliminary findings', *Real Estate Economics*, **17** (2), 235–260.

van Doren, P. (2005) 'The Political Economy of Urban Design Standards', in Ben-Joseph, E. & Szold, T. (eds) *Regulating Place, Standards and the Shaping of Urban America*, Routledge, London, 45–66.

van Melik, R., van Aalst, I. & van Weesep, J. (2009) 'The private sector and public space in Dutch city centres', *Cities*, **26**, 202–209.

van Weert, C. J. W. (1999) 'Aesthetic control management in the Netherlands', *Urban Design International* **4** (1 & 2) 15–20.

Vedung, E. (2007) 'Policy Instruments: Typologies and Theories' in Bemelmans-Videc, M-L, Rist, R. C. & Vedung, E. (2007) (eds) *Carrots, Sticks and Sermons: Policy instruments and their evaluation*, Transaction Publishers, London, 21–58.

Ventre, FT (1973) *Social control of technological innovations: the regulation of building construction*, unpublished PhD thesis, Massachusetts Institute of Technology, Cambridge, Mass.

Vigar, G., Healey, P., Hull, A. & Davoudi, S. (2000), *Planning, Governance and Spatial Strategy in Britain: An Institutional Analysis*, Macmillan, Basingstoke.

Village of Euclid versus Ambler Realty Co (1926) 272 US 365.

Wachs, M. & Dill, J. (1999) 'Regionalism in Transportation and Air Quality: History, Interpretation, and Insights for Regional Governance', in Altshuler, A. A. *et al* (1999) (eds) *Governance and Opportunity in Metropolitan America*, National Academy Press, Washington DC.

Wade, M. (2009) 'SNP inertia over Edinburgh trams fiasco', *The Times*, 21 March – available at http://www.timesonline.co.uk/tol/news/uk/scotland/article5946990.ece (accessed 11 April 2010).

Walters D. (2007) *Designing Community, Charrettes, Masterplans and Form-based Codes*, Architectural Press, Oxford.

Ward, H. (2002) 'Rational Choice', in Marsh, A. & Stoker, G. (2002) (Editors), *Theory and Methods in Political Science*, Macmillan, Basingstoke, 65–89.

Wassmer, R. W. & Baass, M. C. (2006) 'Does a more centralized urban form raise housing prices?' *Journal of Policy Analysis & Management*, **25** (2), 439 – 462.

Weaver, C. L. & Babcock, R. F. (1979) *City Zoning*, Planners Press, American Planning Association, Chicago IL.

Weiss, M. A. (1987) *The Rise of the Community Builders: The American Real Estate Industry and Urban Land Planning*, Columbia University Press, New York.

Wellings F. (2006) *British Housebuilders, History & Analysis*, Blackwell Publishing Ltd., Oxford, UK.

Wellings, F. (2001) *Private Housebuilding Annual 2001*, Credit Lyonnais Securities Europe, London.

Wickersham, J. (2001) 'Jane Jacobs's critique of zoning: From Euclid to Portland and beyond', *Boston College Environmental Affairs Law Review*, **28** (Summer), 547–563.

Wikipedia (2010) Design by Committee, available at: http://en.wikipedia.org/wiki/Design_by_ committee (accessed 7 September 2010).

Wilkinson, R. & Pickett, K. (2010) *The Spirit Level: Why equality is better for everyone*, Penguin, London.

Williams versus Parker (1903) 188 US 491.

Williams, F. B. (1913a) 'Germany can aid New York in skyscraper problem', *New York Times*, 21 September, SM5.

Williams, F. B. (1913b) 'Zone system advocated to end city congestion', *New York Times*, 21 December, SM14.

Williams, N. & Taylor, J. M. (2003) *American Land Planning Law*, Thomson/West, St Paul, Minn.

Wilson, P. (2009) 'Wilson's wrap: Less than commanding performance', *Urban Realm*, 25 May 2009.

Worley, W. S. (1990) *J. C. Nichols and the Shaping of Kansas City: Innovation in Planned Residential Communities*, University of Missouri Press, Columbia, MO.

Worpole, K. & Knox K. (2007) *The Social Value of Public Spaces*, Joseph Rowntree Foundation, York.

Wyatt, P. (2007) *Property Valuation in an Economic Context*, Blackwell Publishing Ltd., Oxford, UK.

Index

Urban Design in the Real Estate Development Process, First Edition. Edited by Steve Tiesdell
and David Adams.
© 2011 Blackwell Publishing Ltd. Published 2011 by Blackwell Publishing Ltd.